THE PEDESTRIAN AND THE CITY

The Pedestrian and the City provides an overview of and insight into the development and politics of, and policies on, walking and pedestrians: it covers the evolution of pedestrian-friendly housing estates and the attempts to create independent pedestrian footpaths from the nineteenth century up to the present day. Key issues addressed are the fight against urban motorways, the destruction of walkable neighborhoods through road building, the struggle of pedestrianization, and the popularity of traffic calming as a powerful policy for reducing pedestrian accidents.

Hass-Klau also embraces past and present practical research in walking, where US contributions continue to be important. The book provides detailed insights from 26 cities, of which 16 are from North America, and the rest from Germany, Norway, Denmark and Britain, as well as references to other European countries and cities. Each city includes general transport information and more specific walking issues, such as pedestrianization and other forms of car-restraining policies.

Each of the cities was visited and discussions with local officials took place, and information was critically assessed through numerous site visits and photographs.

As the pedestrian environment becomes ever more crucial for the future of our cities, the book will be invaluable to students and practicing planners, geographers, transport engineers and local government officers.

Carmen Hass-Klau was born in Germany and studied Urban and Regional Planning in Berlin, followed by postgraduate degrees in Britain. She still has her own consultancy, Environmental and Transport Planning, has published numerous books and articles, and was Professor of European Public Transport at Wuppertal University, Germany. She is an academic advisor at Stavanger University, Norway.

THE PEDESTRIAN AND THE CITY

Carmen Hass-Klau

Routledge
Taylor & Francis Group

NEW YORK AND LONDON

First published 2015
by Routledge
711 Third Avenue, New York, NY 10017

and by Routledge
2 Park Square, Milton Park, Abingdon, Oxon OX14 4RN

Routledge is an imprint of the Taylor & Francis Group, an informa business

Library of Congress Cataloging in Publication Data
   Hass-Klau, Carmen.
   The pedestrian and the city / Carmen Hass-Klau.
   pages cm
   Includes bibliographical references and index.
   1. Pedestrians. 2. Pedestrian traffic flow—Planning. 3. Pedestrian areas—
   Planning. 4. Streets—Planning. 5. City traffic—Planning. I. Title.
   HE336.P43H373 2014
   388.4'1—dc23
   2014018275

ISBN: 978–0-415–81439–3 (hbk)
ISBN: 978–0-415–81440–9 (pbk)
ISBN: 978–0-203–06739–0 (ebk)

Typeset in Corbel
by Florence Production Ltd, Stoodleigh, Devon

MIX
Paper from
responsible sources
FSC® C013056
www.fsc.org

Printed and bound in Great Britain by
TJ International Ltd, Padstow, Cornwall

*To the Pennsylvanian half of my family and
to my unknown South Italian relatives*

CONTENTS

FIGURES

TABLES

FOREWORD

Carmen Hass-Klau's first book, with Sir Peter Hall, was *Can Rail Save the City* (1985), and in 1986 she was the first user in English of the phrase 'traffic calming', her translation of the German *Verkehrsberuhigung*, in a letter to *The Times*. She was sole author of her second book *Pedestrian and City Traffic* (1990), which was described by Sir Colin Buchanan as a 'public service' for its history of the development of ideas for the safeguarding of pedestrians. Her influential technical manual on traffic calming, *Civilised Streets* (1992), had sales all over the world, and I have seen unofficial photocopies, stiff with highlighting, in local authority offices. I was pleased to publish her important paper, 'Impact of pedestrianisation and traffic calming on retailing' (1993), in the very first issue of the journal *Transport Policy*. Her papers and reports on pedestrianization, public transport, especially light rail, and their impacts have been an important part of the library of transport planning.

So this is a book with a provenance, experience, an international scope, a recognition of political context and a multi-disciplinary expertise. The word 'pedestrian' in English has had an alternative meaning of prosaic, hence boring or unoriginal, since the 18th century, and it is alas true that academic studies and public plans about walking as a mode of transport are thought of, by many governments and academics, as worthy but peripheral. Carmen Hass-Klau has always challenged this stereotype. Not only is she one of the longest-established and most influential thinkers on pedestrians and traffic, but she has also built that position by an altogether unique personal style, in writing and speech. There are perhaps a dozen scholars in the world who could have made a good fist at writing an authoritative book with a rather similar title to this, but none of them, I am certain, would or could have written this book.

Part of this uniqueness is no doubt connected with her cosmopolitan personal trajectory – a child in the devastated city of Nuremberg (later to become an international icon of pedestrianization) in the early post-war years, a degree in engineering in the Technical University of Berlin, a rare German government scholarship to do a Masters and PhD in planning at Reading University, then employment as a local government planner, the Principal of the consultancy she founded, a university professor, and a background of family and homes in six countries (Germany, USA, UK, Spain, France, Croatia). Outspoken in discussion, she has described the UK style of traffic calming as 'it doesn't matter how expensive it is, as long as it looks cheap', slated the type of traffic calming which is composed of little more than 'humping anything that moves', and speculated why some of the best conference speeches are by people whose own transport achievements are appalling.

Some of that outspokenness simmers in the case study visits she reports here. One of the principles of evidence Carmen has developed is that she never permits herself to generalize about countries or cities she hasn't visited, and has no great respect for others who do. By 'visit' she means primarily on foot, walking the streets and judging their quality and design as an experience, not as a theoretical exercise, seeking advice from the local planners in charge, but never taking their word for it without seeing for herself. It is only after decades of doing so that one can make personal judgements that have the authority of experience and knowledge, and this is given context by her taste for digging into the historical background of plans over a long period. Together, the experiential and historical method produces pen pictures of the pioneering cities of street style, and their followers, which are full of insight and rediscovered elements. (The Inner London council housing estate where I spent five years of my childhood turns out to have an importance in the design of residential space in the history of planning in the 1920s of which I was completely unaware, for example.)

The word 'provenance' is not used once in this volume, but it imbues everything in the book: the importance of provenance in ideas, the provenance of urban streetscapes, the lasting traces of now-forgotten history and plans. I have considered myself tolerably well read in the history of transport ideas, but the account given here gives an unfamiliar picture, and one that has never really been told. 'History' here includes not just the sequence of government recommendations, but also the global development of ideologies and social systems – American capitalism, a network of mostly socialist architects, the influence of some enlightened commercial companies in providing living conditions for their employees, Nazi Germany, Soviet Communism and its influence on post-war East Germany. One of the thought-provoking themes is the way in which she shows that remarkably closely related developments in Europe and the USA were justified by their supporters in terms of quite different ideologies, aesthetic movements, and welfare motivations, but nevertheless converged in form. This means that when she walks a street in post-unification East Berlin, for example, what she sees and explains is informed by a different intellectual tradition than is contained in the conventional training of traffic engineers and transport planners. One result, for example, is a quite new understanding of the role of Le Corbusier in transport planning and one which contained pernicious elements under the rhetoric.

Her overall assessment is quite a critical one, especially the story she tells of declining trends in walking even in countries and cities that seek to reverse them (and have in some cases had great successes in reversing both the increase in car traffic and the decline in public transport). The final chapter is, however, not a pessimistic one, but full of good entirely practical advice on how to improve the conditions for walking and the lot of the pedestrian. Where there have been improvements, she does not dwell on the influence of her own work, but it does deserve a share in the credit. That's a chapter that the next author in this field should try to write, the role of Carmen Hass-Klau herself in influencing the developments she reports. Meanwhile you won't read a book like this by anybody else.

Phil Goodwin
Emeritus Professor of Transport Policy
University College London and the University of the West of England
May 2014

PREFACE

In recent years, walking as a mode of transport and as an essential human activity has become recognized – in principle – as the source of great benefits. These include:

- physical health and mental well-being
- walking instead of using the car (and to some extent public transport) reduces CO_2 output
- a high level of walking in neighborhoods creates social benefits and improves the perception of security
- a walking-friendly environment increases the pleasure of enjoying urban life and historic areas
- investment in walking has economic advantages, for instance increase in house prices, turnover and tourism
- being nearly universally accessible, but with no start-up cost, and no training beyond the essential learning process in the first years of life
- provision of infrastructure and facilities are an order of magnitude cheaper than provision of roads, rail and vehicles for car and public transport travel.

So why has walking been the poor relation in all strategic transport policy and government programs, and of little interest to industry – so much so that policies on walking are usually subsumed under the general heading of 'walking and cycling' – two utterly unlike modes of transport? And why at a personal level has walking been in long-term decline with only a minority of cities converting into practice the benefits which are so apparent in principle?

One explanation lies in that last bullet point – the huge advantage of low cost has the disadvantage of fewer opportunities for profit and headlines and spectacle – there are fewer mayors or ministers of transport present for the opening of a new traffic-calmed area, and fewer opportunities for rhetoric about long-term infrastructure, and fewer vested interests lobbying behind the scenes for large commercial contracts. This is one reason why in some cases it is easier to win support for a 'big' pedestrianization scheme than for smaller local improvements.

Another often-cited reason is that the quality of evidence and proof seems to be weaker, because surveys routinely only include a few walking trips, consultants' models often ignore it entirely, and the theories of travel choice focus more on easy-to-measure quantities like time and cost, and the simpler claims of economic advantage, and ignore motivations like health, pleasure, convenience, very local activities, and the indirect economic advantage of more pleasant urban environments. However, that is a rather spurious argument since there is now so much evidence on the success of walking improvements – the problem is more that the evidence is ignored or swiftly forgotten.

Motivation

The conception of this book started as a second edition of the book I researched in the late 1980s and published in 1990. That focused on a comparison of West Germany and the UK, and the idea was to extend the case studies to a wider range of countries with more up-to-date data, addressing the question of what has happened since 1990. In total I evaluated 30 cities in six countries (the United States, the UK, Germany, Denmark and Norway, and one case study from Canada). I walked around in the city centers of all of them, some of the inner cities, and a few suburban areas and had very helpful discussions with local politicians, officials and activists.

In the progress of the research, however, it became clear that what was required was a new book, not a revision of the old one. It was not only a question of updating data and judging progress but it also became a question of re-appraising the historical background, the political pressures, the influence of ideologies and social systems, and the practical constraints.

For this reason the first chapter starts with North America, which had previously been of little interest to the more advanced European development, but actually became a source of great insight into the way in which grand road building for the 'motor-car economy' wrecked conditions for pedestrians and the life of many cities. This was seen in even more intense form during Hitler's Germany, and in watered-down form in the UK. The story of the Third Reich continued indirectly to the events and the philosophy of urban transport and pedestrian planning that occurred in post-war West Germany, and was mirrored by the effect of Soviet thinking on what happened in post-war East Germany – creating tensions following reunification.

The book is divided into two parts; in Part I, I study the historical dimensions and in Part II, I get involved in the more practical questions and experience of promoting walking. I am of the opinion that one cannot understand Part II if one does not know the background discussed in Part I (a gap in the knowledge of many pedestrian campaigners and planners). It is not the history of a specific city – although I am convinced that this is important too – but the broad background which I tried to deliver.

But this is also a book about my love affair with the city. I can remember when I was struggling to find a Ph.D. topic. I had just come back from England and walked for the first time more consciously through pedestrianized streets in a historic city center which had previously been full of cars. It was such a joy and I felt so blissfully happy that I could not understand why every city on this earth did not introduce the same policy and frankly even today I still cannot understand it. My happiness was connected with the ability that I could walk around freely and see for the first time the beauty and diversity of the urban environment. It is the interaction between walking and seeing that is so fantastic and near to impossible in urban spaces full of cars. It is the discovery of beautiful buildings, unknown spaces, views, good or bad street designs, shops, restaurants, cafes and activities other people are involved in, and much more; that is urban walking for me and that is what I judge when I walk around in old and new cities. The story about the pedestrian and the city is also about a kind of interdependency on each other. What city would we have if there were no pedestrians anymore? It would certainly not be a city as known and loved.

This great feeling I still have when I see exciting spaces, this kind of wow effect is not even possible when cycling and certainly not when driving a car.

Consequently, this book is also a declaration of commitment to the historic city centers, the traditional neighborhoods, not only the 19th-century ones but also those suburbs which for some were dreams of a better life. The destruction which has been inflicted on the urban structure is for me sometimes difficult to bear.

Critics will say I am not a realist. I do not mind the criticism because I think we have had too much unreal 'realism' and we need more protectors, more people who are on the side of the weaker participants and that no doubt includes the pedestrian who has very little influence and power to fight against inhuman changes. But that has to be done on a genuine evidence base, honest analysis of weakness as well as strength, serious thought, the best possible professional expertise, and an acceptance of the cultural and historical world.

ACKNOWLEDGMENTS

The research on this book is based on my experience in working in the wide field of traffic calming, pedestrianization and public transport in my consultancy and as a professor at the University of Wuppertal. But the contents are also based on the many trips I did during the last years in the United States, Canada and Europe. This book would have been impossible if a large number of professionals had not kindly provided the information and the time for discussions and walks around their city. I am most grateful for their help and support. Altogether I counted more than 60 people who supported my work. Unfortunately I cannot mention all of them here.

My greatest thanks has to be addressed to my husband Dr. Graham Crampton; without his help this book would have taken one year longer and would not be what it is today. The second person I am very much indebted to is Professor Phil Goodwin who read all my chapters and made very useful critical comments. I also would like to express my thanks to Randy Wade from the City of New York. She was absolutely wonderful in showing me her city and read some of my US chapters. Oliver Gajda from San Francisco made me understand better how his remarkable city works. Mike Weiner's discussions in Savannah and later in Munich helped me write something useful about his city. Tracy Newsome from Charlotte very patiently answered my many questions despite my rather critical views of the city. I also would like to mention Lucia Gonzalez who was very helpful. Suzanne Lennard supported me in getting more contacts in Portland and this was very valuable. In Denver I have to mention Cynthia Patton for her backing and Douglas M. Grenzer for his map of Denver which was sent to all the other US cities as a model. Overall I am grateful to Steven M. Castongia in Charlotte, Chris David in Washington, Carmen Piekarski in Portland, Charlie Ream in San Francisco, Philip Overcash in Charleston and many more for the time it took to produce the maps for this book. In Vancouver, Steve Brown had to answer many of my queries and he did it very efficiently, I would like to acknowledge him and other members in his office who helped me as well, and Starla Talbot should be mentioned here.

I was very delighted that Lars Gemzøe was happy to read my chapter on Denmark and my appreciation also goes to the consultancy of Jan Gehl that provided maps of Copenhagen and Odense (Michael Nielsen and Camilla van Deurs) for me. In Germany I am grateful to Dr. M. Klamt for reading my Munich chapter and offering some additional data. B. Gutzmer from Freiburg must be credited for his time and endurance to answer all my questions. Without the help of several professionals in the Ministry of Transport in Oslo I could not have written the chapter about Norway. I especially would like to express my gratitude to Guro Berge. My chapter about London would have been impossible to fill with facts without the help of Ian Simmons (City of London), Louise McBride (Borough of Camden) and Jeanette Baatman (TfL).

I am obliged for the support and help I received from my two secretaries, Diana Kent and Sylvia Wiethaup. Last but not least I am in debt to my Ph.D. student Helge Hillnhütter who did the drawings of several maps and made some critical and useful remarks on my chapters I gave him to read. Even so, I am glad I did not give him all the chapters because I may very likely not have wanted to send the book to the publisher at all.

Needless to say, despite all these efforts the author alone bears responsibility for any error or omissions.

DEFINITIONS

ACS American Community Survey.

AMPTA American Public Transit Association.

BRT Bus Rapid Transit – buses use a busway and it is impossible for cars to move into such a lane or park there. However, in the United States they are often simply only bus lanes.

Busway This is a right of way operated with modern, often articulated buses. The right of way is separated from car traffic – it is not only a bus lane – and may be designed like a tramway with high-quality bus stops. The right of way is well integrated into the urban environment and the design standards are high. Some of the best examples are the busway (Line 4) in Nantes, the TEOR lines in Rouen and the Trans Val-de-Marne busway in the Ile-de-France (Department 94).

Das Neue Bauen A style of new architecture developed after the First World War (1919). Its founder was the architect Walter Gropius who opened the first school in Weimar in 1919; it moved later to Dessau. It became especially important for large-scale construction of functional but good tenement housing.

High visibility crossings These have more or less the same function as zebra crossings but whether cars have to stop when the pedestrian is standing on the side of the sidewalk or when the pedestrian has a foot on the crossing depends on the state in the United States.

Laubenganghäuser These were developed at the end of the 1920s, for instance in Hamburg or Dessau. This type of housing block allowed the open entrances to be toward the noisy street but the living quarters overlooked the quieter parts of the estate. They were cheaply built housing blocks – mostly four to six floors.

Light rail or tram A tram may have to share its own right of way with other traffic although large sections of the lines could also have their own right of way. At junctions they will have to mix with other traffic. Modern tram vehicles have low-level floors (40–100%) with easy access for people with disabilities. The average speed is relatively low at 18–20km/h. Normally passenger capacity is lower (about 175–230 passengers) for trams than for light rail vehicles (350 passengers) but with the new 45m long trams that is no longer an issue.

Light rail in contrast may have most of its corridors separated from other traffic, but it may also be running partly on street level and partly in tunnels. If it is separated from other traffic it will have an automatic signaling system. One has to remember that the light rail vehicle was originally a mode filling the gap between an underground railway and a traditional (old-fashioned) tram. In the past there was a clearer distinction between tram and light rail, but nowadays that is increasingly difficult to define, as modern trams have changed so much in comparison to the old-fashioned version. In recent years most cities have opted for trams whereas light rail was a more common mode of the 1970s and 1980s in Europe.

Garden City   The concept was developed by Ebenezer Howard in his book *Garden Cities of Tomorrow*. It was first published in England in 1898. It became a relatively influential social movement and two garden cities and one garden suburb were actually built in England. It had a great impact in many other European countries before the First World War but in Europe only small-scale garden suburbs were built. Nevertheless the idea stayed very influential.

Green modes   Cycling, walking and transit – although some experts would argue that public transport is not really very environmentally friendly, I would partly agree to that but I still have included it. There is also car sharing but I have not discussed that in this book,

Inner city area   This does not mean city centre but mostly 19th-century housing areas built close to the city centre.

Motorways   Called Interstates in North America

Public transportation   Transit.

TOD   Transit Orientated Development means high density mostly housing development around rail, light rail or tram stops

Tram   Streetcar in the American chapters, the characteristic is slightly different to the European tram.

Verkehrsverbund   This is a public transportation organization where all public transportation modes (bus, tram, train, boat) have a coordinated timetable and the same price structure. With one ticket all the different modes can be used. In Germany a Verkehrsverbund area can be very large. The largest covers the City of Berlin and the State of Brandenburg. Mostly they are not as large but still substantial. Nearly all of Germany is covered by the Verkehrsverbünde.

Part I

HISTORY

FROM INNOVATIVE STREET LAYOUTS TO THE FIGHT AGAINST URBAN MOTORWAYS IN THE UNITED STATES

The quality and design of streets have always been important issues for walking and more details on this are provided in the final chapter. Some specific street layouts are more popular with pedestrians than others. Narrow medieval streets, crooked lanes and numerous irregular squares made walking interesting and easy when only a few vehicles could access them because the streets were too narrow. However, historically these streets were mostly filthy and rich people hardly used them. This changed during the 19th century when main drains were constructed and most street areas could be converted into cleaner space.

The renaissance and baroque street layouts that developed during the 15th and 16th centuries changed all this. The streets became wide and straight and the squares large and more geometrical. But it was only in the 18th and even more so in the 19th century when the number of coaches and carriages increased and crossing a road as a pedestrian became more difficult and often dangerous that sidewalks were built to safeguard pedestrians and also to keep them away from busy carriageways. Unfortunately, relatively little is known about when the first sidewalks were built.[1]

The avenues of earlier centuries which were often used for marching changed largely into boulevards during the 19th century. These were streets for pleasurable walking on a scale previously unknown. Normally the wide central reservations of such streets were bordered by trees and used by pedestrians for strolling and mutual admiration. The central walkway also offered the best view of the newly constructed public and private buildings. Furthermore, boulevards had generous sidewalks with even more rows of trees. There was space for everybody from the students and workers on foot to the aristocrats on horseback and the ladies in carriages. In short, this mixing of the different classes had been unknown in previous centuries. Many boulevards were modeled on Paris; the new plan developed by Napoléon III and put into practice by the new prefect *Georges-Eugéne Haussmann*.[2] The *Haussmann Plan* of Paris started in 1849[3] and was completed in 1898 (Carmona 2002, p. 149). It was the desired street layout for many cities, not only in Europe but also in the New World, in particular for capital cities such as Berlin and Vienna. Although the Haussmann Plan destroyed most of the previous city, it left the historic monuments intact. It was urban renewal on a scale and with a brutality only known following the large fires that plagued many cities. In a sense, the demolition matched the destruction that occurred during urban motorway building a century later, but maybe that is a lame comparison because the biggest assets of this plan were the creation of numerous boulevards, parks and gardens. What the effect was on walking and healthier living we do not really know but it did create the space for more wheeled traffic and later on for cars.

The majority of North American towns still had nothing like that. Residential and public buildings were constructed along a grid street layout. This was easy, cheap and did not involve sophisticated planning but not all North American cities were happy with this type of street plan and it is here where our story starts.

Innovative Street Layouts

Who actually had control over streets and alignments in most US cities was by no means clear. To facilitate improvement, street commissioners were appointed at the beginning of the 19th century, at least in the large east coast cities. However, they were often powerless if private owners subdivided land and designed streets to their own liking. Even by the turn of the 20th century, it was only *Pennsylvania* that had passed legislation requiring every municipality to have an overall plan for its streets and alleys. Its major city *Philadelphia* had already developed a tradition of regulated urban expansion and street planning since its foundation in 1682 (Reps 1965, pp. 161, 169). Altogether Philadelphia had a very sophisticated street network consisting of different street widths, with some of the streets being very narrow and paved with cobblestones. The *Intra City Business Property Atlas* by *Franklin* (1939) shows how varied the street widths were (and still are).

Boston (Massachusetts) also had a European street pattern, even more so than Philadelphia. Boston's street network even as late as 1929 was reminiscent of a medieval city, except for *Boston Common* and the *Public Garden* (the parks close to the city center) (Capan map of Boston 1929). Jacobs (1995) describes how the street layout changed over a relatively short time period, mostly because of public redevelopment and road projects (pp. 264–265).

Figure 1.1
Street map of Boston

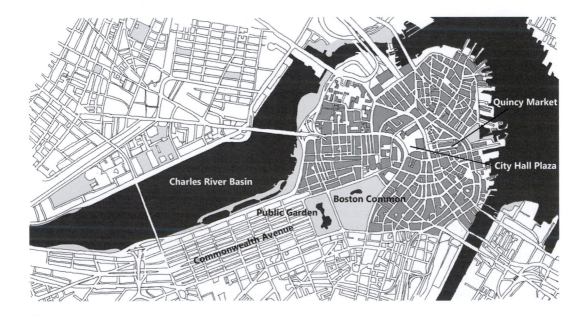

Possibly the most interesting street plan in North America was developed by *J. E. Oglethorpe* for Savannah. The settlement was founded in 1733, about 60 years later than Charleston (1670). Oglethorpe and his colonists settled about 16 miles inland from the coast, on the Savannah River (Wilson 2012, pp. 101–102). Although the street layout is a grid, the high number of squares changes the street appearance and these squares form their own wider 'green' grid. It made walking from square to square an enjoyment in nearly all seasons (for more details see 'Savannah' in Chapter 14).[4]

Another street plan, which was quite widely imitated, was that of *Washington, DC*. *Pierre Charles L'Enfant*, a self-made engineer, designed the city at the end of the 18th century (1791). The main avenues were extremely wide and bordered with trees (160–400ft/52.5–131m) and they had plenty of space for walking (Reps 1965, pp. 250–251). L'Enfant was of French origin and his ideas were influenced by the designs of Paris and Versailles, though he had also studied street plans of other European cities (ibid, p. 247). Several other towns, for instance *Buffalo, Detroit, Indianapolis, Madison* (ibid, p. 325), were strongly influenced by Washington's street plan (see Figure 13.12: map of Washington DC).

Daniel H. Burnham and *Edward H. Bennett* introduced a *Plan of Chicago* to the public in 1909; again it showed some similarities to the Haussmann Plan of Paris. It consisted primarily of wide boulevards, diagonal roads, and large squares and parks (Hines 1974, pp. 328–329). A remarkable street hierarchy was suggested and it already included elements of traffic division. Through traffic was to be separated from residential traffic. The boulevards, the widest being 572ft (188m),[5] had been designed by *Frederick Law Olmsted*'s firm[6] (Condit 1973, pp. 32, 73). The Chicago Plan stimulated similar improvements in other cities, for example *Minneapolis* (Heckscher and Robinson 1977, p. 22).

From the middle of the 19th century, a new movement had derived largely from English landscape gardening. The main characteristic in terms of street design was the heavily curved street, which was in total contrast to the conventional street block. Such designs were first applied for walkways through cemeteries and later parks. Frederick Law Olmsted and *Calvert Vaux* became well known for the design of *Central Park* in *New York* (1858). Olmsted had visited *Birkenhead Park* near *Liverpool* after the first people's park had opened to the public in 1847. Olmsted (1852) admitted that nothing like that was known in the United States (pp. 78–79). It has been argued that Olmsted had copied Birkenhead Park with its separate footpaths and a carriageway drive when designing Central Park in New York, but the footpaths and street design in Central Park are not really comparable with Birkenhead.

He also influenced street planning in some suburban housing developments. One of the best known is *Riverside*, Illinois, near *Chicago* (1869). The street layout of Riverside includes some large green areas and a variety of street widths (Reps 1965, pp. 344–345).

Another of his plans was for a workers' town commissioned by the *Apollo Iron and Steel Company* of Pennsylvania. It was named *Vandergrift* and is located about 30 miles northeast of Pittsburgh. Vandergrift was the second 'New Town' for workers around a factory in the United States.[7] The first plots for sale were available in the town in 1896 (Vandergrift Centennial Committee 1996, p. 25).

Vandergrift was built in the large bend of the river *Kiskiminetas*. Olmsted's town plan fitted beautifully into this bend. As the river so is the street network; all the

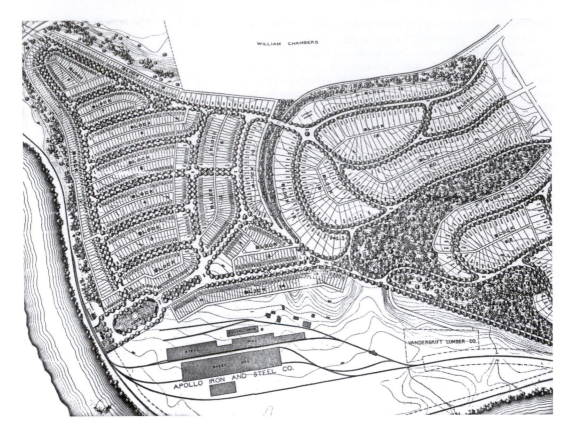

Figure 1.2
Olmsted's original plan of
Vandergrift

streets are curved. Vandergrift's streets were paved with yellow bricks, all had sidewalks and trees were planted along most streets. It had tree-lined greens and its own park (today called Kennedy Park). In addition, a green belt went through the town and although it was not a garden city, it came close to it.

Even so, it was not really a town for the working class, only the skilled and well-paid workers and the business owners could afford the prices for both the plot and the construction of a house (ibid, p. 25). The unskilled and low-paid laborers lived near Vandergrift, for example in *Vandergrift Heights*, which had developed at about the same time as Vandergrift. But Vandergrift Heights was not a workers' paradise, there was no street plan and the streets were unpaved; sidewalks, if they existed at all, were made out of boards, all the luxuries of Vandergrift were missing and the plots and houses were small and without bathrooms (ibid, p. 43).

The son of Frederick Law Olmsted was even more prolific than his father. He designed *Forest Hills Gardens* located in New York (Borough of Queens). The construction started in 1910. The street layout consists of curved streets, a mini roundabout, small squares and two very short cul-de-sacs that feel so intimate that one hardly dares to enter.[8] The street design looks like a mixture of German and English garden suburbs, especially *Hampstead Garden Suburb* in London[9] but most houses have North American features. The station square is a particularly close replica of different continental styles. This street design discourages through traffic and reduces car speeds. In fact, Forest Hills Gardens

Figure 1.3
Ivy Close, Forest Hills
Gardens

is an interesting example of a (very likely) unintentional traffic calming scheme developed in the early 20th century. Unsurprisingly, this small area today includes some of the most expensive and desirable streets in New York. Without any clear borders, the historic part of Forest Hills Gardens is continued with the traditional grid blocks and there the car speeds were much higher.

There were a number of other housing developments designed by Olmsted (Sr., Jr. or their firm). Hegemann (1925) mentioned *Roland Park* (1891), Baltimore, which used the division of roads and footpaths and the grouping of housing in the form of cul-de-sacs as part of their design (pp. 119–124). The idea of separating roads from footpaths was taken up again and developed further about three decades later.

Housing for a Better World

During the late 19th and the early 20th century, the United States failed to rival a number of European countries in the principles and powers of urban planning, but at the beginning of the 1920s the concept of regional planning gained momentum. It was largely caused by the desire to improve overcrowded and congested cities and the need for controlled urban growth but it also included ideas and concepts about traffic and transportation. Regional planning agencies were created in several parts of the United States, of which the *Regional Plan Association of New York and its Environs* (RPA), formed in 1921, was the earliest. It included most of the important planners of the time. Several other regional planning agencies were also set up (Scott 1969, pp. 192–221).

As a kind of opposition to the RPA, the *Regional Planning Association of America* (RPAA) was formed in 1923. It included, among others, *Lewis Mumford, Clarence Stein, Henry Wright,*[10] *Frederick Lee Ackerman, Edith Elmer Wood, Catherine Bauer, Alexander Bing* (ibid, p. 223). About half of them were architects (Sussman 1976,

p. 20). They believed in garden city principles, and they were of the opinion that these should become the main settlement form for regional plans in America. Many members had studied British and very likely German planning examples, especially the garden cities and garden suburbs.[11]

One of the first practical achievements of the RPAA was the formation of the *City Housing Corporation* in 1924. The main purpose of this organization was to build garden cities (Stein 1958, p. 19). The Corporation started to develop a derelict industrial site – called *Sunnyside Gardens* – for housing in the Borough of Queens in New York City. Its main objective was to provide low-cost but well-designed flats and houses. The major disadvantage of the site was that local government officials had already planned the typical grid blocks. This implied that a major through road had to remain unchanged, despite the danger of increased accidents and the separation of the community into two parts (Wright 1935, p. 37). Although Wright could prove that housing developments based on a grid layout were needlessly expensive, they could not overcome the existing street regulations (Churchill 1983, p. 212).

In Sunnyside Gardens, because of the rigid street layout, only a few cul-de-sacs could be built (Stein 1958, p. 24). During the four years of constructing Sunnyside, different forms of housing blocks emerged. Apart from private garden space, the characteristic Sunnyside block also included a communal green in its center. A network of footpaths, which connected the different family units within a housing block, accessed this green space. Although footpath connections

Figure 1.4
Open space inside the Sunnyside housing block

between different blocks existed, one still had to cross roads used by motorized traffic. By 1928, the corporation had constructed houses for 1,202 families on about 77 acres of land (ibid, p. 21). This was nearly the same design but the density was higher in the housing blocks in Europe, for instance in Berlin. The *Riehmer Hofgarten* in Berlin *Kreuzberg* was built between 1881 and 1892 (Baedeker 1986, p. 305). The whole block consisted of 20 different connected housing units constructed at high standards. The block had the size of about 87,500sqm (21.6 acres). The yard was left open and contained gardens and narrow residential streets, which joined several major streets (ibid, p. 305; Wedepohl 1970, p. 116). The *Ideal Passage* in Berlin Rixdorf (between *Fulda-* and *Weichselstraße*) included 121 tenement flats, which were built by a housing association in 1907/8. It had several large inside garden yards, which were connected by pedestrian footpaths (ibid, p. 124). The Ideal Passage was seen at the time as a model of social housing (Baedeker 1986, p. 326). At nearly exactly the same time as Sunnyside Gardens was built, the *Larkhall Estate* in southwest London was started (1926). It consists of 16 blocks of flats linked by five courtyards connected with arches and pedestrian footpaths.[12] Although the green spaces behind the houses in Sunnyside Gardens are much larger, the design idea is the same as in the continental examples.

Today Sunnyside Gardens is still a remarkable place although it is difficult to find the original housing blocks since much has been changed over the years. What did strike me was that they were not as massive as the German examples (or Larkhall in England) but more like the first housing blocks built in Eisenhüttenstadt during the 1950s, one of the new towns in East Germany. The design of the houses was very creative. One can feel how the architects and the planners tried to find the best options in terms of housing style, green space and footpath design. The houses were designed so that the living rooms in Sunnyside are still facing the road (although even today the traffic along there is minimal). Some German architects, for instance J. F. Haeuselmann, had already changed the location of the living rooms so as to overlook the 'quiet inside yards' and not the traffic road (Haeuselmann 1916, p. 54). A very good example can be found in Berlin-*Charlottenburg* in the *Haeuselmannstraße*.

Gurlitt (1929)[13] pointed out that the president of the City Housing Corporation (*A. M. Bing*) mentioned that Sunnyside Gardens was modeled on a German settlement (p. 27) though he did not say which community he had in mind. Visiting Sunnyside Gardens, I could not really see any similarity with German building styles.[14] There is no proof in the literature I studied that this was actually the case.

Sunnyside Gardens was a financial success, and the City Housing Corporation wanted to build a garden city and chose a site only 16 miles from New York in *Fair Lawn*, New Jersey. They soon had to abandon the idea of a *Green Belt* and also could not attract any industry in or near to the site (Stein 1958, p. 39). It was planned to build three neighborhoods for about 25,000 people (Bamberg 2011, p. 45). Each of them was to have its own school and shopping center (Christensen 1986, p. 58). Since the construction of Sunnyside Gardens, the members of the Corporation had developed their ideas further.

Radburn, a small neighborhood within Fair Lawn, contained an uncommon street layout. The street hierarchy consisted of:

- a separate network of over eight miles of pedestrian and bicycle paths
- service roads for direct access to the houses
- collector roads around the housing blocks
- distributor roads.

Over- or underpasses were constructed to enable pedestrians to cross roads safely (Schaffer 1982, p. 7). All housing blocks were grouped together around large greens and parkland.

As Stein (1958) had pointed out, none of the ideas were specifically original. The separation of different transportation modes in the form of independent roads or paths with over- and underpasses could already be seen in Central Park in New York (p. 44) or in Roland Park in Baltimore (also designed by Olmsted). There is no proof of whether the idea of functional division of roads was a copy of Olmsted's street layouts, or was borrowed from Britain or Germany. In Germany, functional division of streets was common at that time, and it had already been well established in the British garden cities and garden suburbs. Several authors and Stein himself suggested that Parker and Unwin's street layouts were in a sense the parent of Sunnyside Gardens and Radburn (Jackson 1985, p. 152). Wright (1935) wrote that the cul-de-sacs used in Radburn were derived both from the current English practice and from their own experiment in Sunnyside Gardens (p. 42). According to Bamberg (2011), the cul-de-sacs were loosely based on Unwin's Hampstead Garden Suburb (p. 47).

Like Sunnyside Gardens, Radburn showed many similar features to German street layouts, particularly the ones used by *Hermann Jansen.* It is interesting to note that in the 1925 version of the Radburn plan, the garages were grouped together, something commonly used during the late 1920s and 1930s in Germany. But later in Radburn the garages were built adjacent to the houses. In the later housing developments, such as *Chatham Village* and *Baldwin Hills Village* (see below), they were grouped together as originally had been planned for Radburn.

There is evidence that a detailed design for Radburn was already shown to a wide audience of British and German planners during the *International Town, City and Regional Planning and Garden City Congress* in New York in 1925. Gurlitt (1929) wrote about Radburn that it was built like a European village with the design standards that had been common in Germany before the First World War. He continued that by German standards it was far too old-fashioned and it would not be admitted at any international or national planning competition. He was wondering why in a country as technically advanced as the United States, Radburn was seen as an expression of modern times and as an example of urban culture (p. 30).

Although Gurlitt was not impressed by Radburn's housing design – neither was Stübben[15] – he was certainly interested in the new street layout. In the United States it had become evident that although modern technology can create miracles, it also potentially creates many negative effects, such as the high number of accidents, especially involving children. He praised the equal treatment of all transportation modes and concluded that Radburn was an escape into old times, the period when there was still peace in the streets. He hoped that the Radburn layout would also have some influence on German settlement planning.

Sadly, Radburn was not an immediate economic success. From the start its house prices had been much higher than in Sunnyside Gardens (Schaffer 1982, p. 150). When in 1929 the *Wall Street Stock Market* crashed, the City Housing Corporation was financially ruined. Only two superblocks were built (Stein 1958, p. 37), and about 400 families moved in (Lubove 1963, p. 62).

Despite the partial development, Radburn today is still very popular as a residential area although it was never expanded. When Stein went back after 20 years, only two fatal accidents had been reported to him, and both were on the main highways (Stein 1958, p. 51).

Garvin (2002) described Radburn 'today' and mentioned that there is a world of difference between Radburn and the neighboring residential areas. Some 47% of Radburn's residents walked to the shops but only 8% did so outside of Radburn. Equally impressive was the cycle use – 25% of Radburn's residents used bikes, whereas outside only 8% cycled (p. 330).[16]

Figure 1.5
Chatham Village Tower

Chatham Village is located in the center of Pittsburgh (south of the *Monongahela* River). The first 131 houses were designed and built by Stein and Wright and completed in 1932 (Bamberg 2011, p. 71). They were originally planned as low-income homes but they materialized as rental housing for the middle classes and were an immediate success (ibid, p. 53).

It has a very similar road design to that used in Radburn (Stein 1958, p. 76). Chatham Village had also a miniature green belt of 29 acres on three sides (Bamberg 2011, p. 74). It included about 2 miles (about 3km) of pedestrian trail (Stein 1958, pp. 76–77). All houses are two storeys and single-family dwellings built in rows and all have individual features (ibid, pp. 78–79).

Originally, the Village had four shop units located on the corners nearest to the city center of Pittsburgh (Bamberg 2011, p. 78). Although built in the 1930s, it still has features of early central European garden cities or suburbs, such as towers, walls and narrow openings. Next to the garages and within the housing estate, the walls especially are reminiscent of a medieval town wall.

The second phase was built between 1935 and 1936, which increased the total number of houses to 197 (ibid, p. 90). The conversion to a corporation occurred in 1959 under the *National Housing Act* (ibid, p. 124). In addition to Chatham Village, three more small housing settlements were built in the 1930s and at about the same time the federal government picked up similar ideas (see below):

- *Phipps Garden Apartments* (Queens, New York) built in 1931 by Stein and Wright
- *Hillside Homes* (Bronx, New York) in 1935 also designed and built by Stein and Wright
- *Colonial Village* (Alexandria, Virginia) built in 1935, which became the model for many Garden Apartments later on (Chase, Horak and Keylon 2012, p. 14).

The Greenbelt Towns

In 1935, the federal government set up a home construction program and created the *Resettlement Administration* (Christensen 1986, p. 72). The *Greenbelt New Town Program* was directed by *Tugwell*. He was concerned about urban and rural poverty and he developed the idea of satellite towns as an alternative to slum clearance and as new homes for poverty-stricken farmers (Myhra 1983, pp. 232–236).

President *Franklin D. Roosevelt*, who was influenced by RPAA's members, proposed the building of *Greenbelt Towns*. These were modeled on garden cities, though this notion was not mentioned at the beginning of the program (Christensen 1986, p. 77). A *Green Belt Towns* publication looked at public housing in Europe (UK, Netherlands, Belgium, Germany and Switzerland) and members of the *Division of Urban Settlement* went to Frankfurt, Berlin, Amsterdam, Rotterdam and The Hague for inspiration.

Members of the RPAA were employed to assist in the Program. The initially planned 50 communities were later reduced to only four: *Greenbelt, Greendale, Greenhills* and *Greenbrook*. According to Stein (1958) the Greenbelt Towns included three principles:

- the separation between footpaths and roads for cars (Radburn principle)
- the neighborhood concept
- the garden city objectives (p. 225).

Greenbelt was planned for 2,000 housing units but only 892 dwellings were built. The construction of three of the Greenbelt Towns began in 1935. Greenbelt in Maryland was only 10 miles (16km) away from Washington (Arnold 1983, p. 198). The total settlement was designed in the form of a crescent. Possibly the *Crescent* in *Bath* (England) was in the back of the minds of the chief architects (*Ellington and Wadsworth*) (Stein 1958, p. 119).

As with previous developments, Greenbelt did not attract industries of any significance (ibid, p. 130). The Radburn principle had been applied more fully than in any of the earlier settlements, for example the community center had completely separated networks for motor vehicles and pedestrians. In most cases direct access by car to the rear of the houses was not possible because garages were grouped together to form a kind of barrier as applied already in Chatham Village. The housing settlement was encircled by a ring road, again as in Chatham Village. The main feature of Greenbelt was its lengthy footpath network and underpasses were built to cross major roads.

In 1941, 7,000 people lived in Greenbelt although only a very small part of the whole site had been developed by then (see above). The land of the town was in public ownership and was sold to a private co-operative housing association in 1953/54 (Arnold 1983, p. 200). By 1984, it accommodated 18,000 people (ibid, pp. 198–199).

Greendale in Wisconsin (near Milwaukee) was developed from 1936 to 1938. It was planned for 1,200 housing units but only 740 dwellings were built. It also contained a separate pedestrian network but without over and underpasses because of funding restrictions (www.thegreendalehistoricalsociety.org, accessed 21.12.12).

Greenhills in Ohio (near Cincinnati) also included a separation of footpaths and roads but not as comprehensively as in Greenbelt. It was planned for 1,000 housing units and 730 dwellings were built (www.greenhillsohio.us).

Greenbrook was supposed to become the largest town and industrial areas were included in the plan (Christensen 1986). But Greenbrook, designed by H. Wright in 1935, was not even started (pp. 75, 84).

By the end of 1936 the mood of the country had changed, and the Congress was reshuffled. The political environment had become unfriendly to planned communities and in December of 1936 the whole program was axed and the Resettlement Administration was dismantled. During the 1940s, several Greenbelt Towns were extended but none was designed with a Radburn-type street network (Myhra 1983, pp. 233, 246).

Garden Apartments

Despite the change of mood and political will, garden apartments were still built. One small settlement in Los Angeles, *Baldwin Hills Village*, opened in 1941. Stein was employed as a consultant and some of the original elements of earlier housing developments re-appeared (Stein 1958, p. 189). Baldwin Hills Village

Figure 1.6
Baldwin Hills Village
Green

was probably the most comprehensively developed housing estate without direct access by car. The access streets had been replaced by garage courts. There were no streets within the 68 acres (275,000sqm) of the village. In total 627 units were built,[17] and about 2,000 people lived there in 2012. The village changed from rental apartments into condominiums between 1973 and 1978 (internet information and email from Steven Keylon, Los Angeles, November 2012).

About one-quarter of the area is covered by green space, which consists of an inner park and garden courts. It forms the rectangular center of the housing settlement. The Village, as it is called today, is one of the jewels of Los Angeles.[18] It is like a world of its own and it makes one wonder how such a peaceful settlement can exist among the many multi-lane roads and the vast amount of traffic.

Part of the development was also an elementary school designed by *Robert E. Alexander*, in collaboration with the landscape architect *Garrett Eckbo*. The school is now separated from the Village by a six-lane road but it was already a busy road at the time when Baldwin Hills Village was built. Although an extension of the Village was considered, doubling the size of the housing area, one is amazed how one could have built a school on such a busy road. Shops, restaurants and a movie theater along *La Brea*, between *Rodeo* and *Coliseum*, helped the residents to cater for their daily and cultural needs; even a church was built just south of Coliseum (information from S. Keylon, LA 2012).

The 'garden apartments' period was between 1937 and 1955 (Chase, Horak and Keylon 2012, p. 3). Some of them did not separate pedestrians from car traffic but all of them used the 'superblock' concept and turned the house entrances toward the gardens. This type of settlement was very popular in Los Angeles because of its climate. In total 38 garden apartment developments are known (including Baldwin Hills Village) (ibid, p. 6). Most of them were small, between 1,200 to 4,000 units.

Congested Cities and the Motorway Revolt

At the beginning of this chapter I pointed out that apart from a few special street designs, most cities had simple grid blocks as their street layout. Smith (2006) mentioned that since 1785, the Federal Land Ordinance had dictated the rectangular street grid in many cities (p. 5). This did little to protect residents or pedestrians at first from wheeled traffic and later from motor vehicles. Whereas the European medieval streets would shield residents from such traffic to some extent because of their large number of alleys, lanes and narrow streets, the grid had the opposite effect. Traffic could pour in and spread easily, even into purely residential areas. Heckscher and Robinson (1977) talked about the deformation of these plans by the automobile (p. 24). Yet there were significant differences in the quality of conventional grid blocks. The grid in New York was inadequate even by early 19th-century standards because streets intersected too frequently and apart from *Broadway* other north–south arteries were then missing (Reps 1965, p. 299).

Traffic of all kinds fought for space in the city centers. With growing motorization, the combination of streetcars and motor vehicles became a dangerous mix. There was a lack of sufficient car parking spaces, traffic management and traffic signals (Unwin 1923, p. 11). It was therefore not surprising to find traffic restrictions or the closure of streets in the city center of some North American cities. They appeared to have been quite common and were frequently mentioned in the literature from 1900 onwards and these restrictions continued during the 1920s (Burnham 1906, p. 182; Condit 1973, p. 37; Robinson 1916, p. 35; Stein 1958, p. 69). Unfortunately, we know little about the real reasons or the scale of these road closures.

The dramatic increase in car ownership[19] was hardly paralleled by new road construction. The choked city streets generated discussions and plans about street widening, extensions and motorways during the late 1920s but it took until the end of the Second World War when petrol rationing ended in the United States before a massive road building program was started.

Serious concern about road safety also became an issue during the 1920s and 1930s. Approximately 24,000 people were killed annually and 600,000 injured by motor vehicles in 1925 (Scott 1969, p. 187). Starr (2009) gives a statistic for Los Angeles County quoting that in 1939, 962 people were killed and 23,898 were injured in one year (p. 247). As a result of this high number of road accidents, several initiatives were set up; for instance the *Policyholders' Service Bureau of the Metropolitan Life Insurance Company* that undertook a traffic survey to demonstrate the best traffic control measures for reducing deaths and injuries.

One of the arguments for the rapid expansion of motorways after 1945 was that it was believed motorway construction would reduce the number of road accidents. Already the Federal Highway Act of 1944 had paved the way to build more roads. This was followed by the Federal-Aid Highways Act of 1956 (also known as the National Interstate and Defense Highways Act), which provided generous funding. The federal government paid 90% of all motorway construction costs with the rest coming from the states. It was planned that by 1972, 41,000 miles (59,800km) of *Interstate Highways*[20] would be built (ibid, pp. 247–248).

At the beginning, the road construction agencies had little to fear from any opposition. However, some residents did realize the destruction that motorways would impose in their neighborhoods. A number of influential authors criticized the alienating effects mass car ownership, modern housing and office development had on the urban environment, for example, *Lewis Mumford, Shirley Hayes, Raymond S. Rubinow* and *Jane Jacobs*.[21]

Mumford (1964) was particularly outspoken about the negative impact of the private car. In his final chapter of his book *The Highway and the City* he wrote:

> Perhaps the only thing that could bring Americans to their senses would be the clear demonstration of the fact that their highway program will, eventually, wipe out the very area of freedom that the private motor car promised to retain for them.
>
> (p. 176)

Unfortunately, even if one had demonstrated this fact to the American people, they would not have believed it. All nations have so far been obsessed about the freedom the car promises. All over the world one can observe that countries are not really able to learn from the transportation mistakes other countries have made. Mumford demanded that the inner city should be re-planned for pedestrians and that public mass transportation had to be rebuilt and extended. He continued in writing that

> every urban transportation plan should, accordingly, put the pedestrian at the center of all its proposals.
>
> (p. 186)

Jacobs (1961) went on to formulate ideas and concepts for more livable streets in urban areas. Her influence started to change the then existing ideology of urban renewal. Fishman (2007) analyzed how the beginning of the opposition to a proposed urban motorway in one neighborhood in New York had created criticism in many more neighborhoods and in other cities. Often the fight took many years, such as the fight against the *Manhattan Expressway*, proposed after the Second World War by *Robert Moses* (the city-wide *Commissioner of Parks* in New York); it was finally stopped in 1969 (p. 127). Moses (1970) was of the opinion that the Interstate Highways

> must go right through the cities and not around them.
>
> (p. 293)

and he was not alone in this belief.

Urban-based resistance also started in California, for instance in *San Diego, Long Beach, Beverly Hills* and *San Francisco*. The citizens of San Francisco were very effective in their revolt against urban motorways. The plan put forward in San Francisco in 1949 was so outrageous that resistance quickly formed. The most controversial project was the double-decker elevated *Embarcadero Freeway*, which was to run from the *Bay Bridge* along the waterfront and link further to the *Golden Gate Bridge*. There were other controversial urban freeways.[22] The Embarcadero Freeway was opened in 1957 but was never completed and connected to the Golden Gate Bridge. In 1961 the city voted against most of the proposed freeways and by 1968 none of the freeways which were supposed to cross the city had been built (Starr 2009, pp. 258–259). However, some freeways were built even in San Francisco.[23] The 1989 earthquake helped to solve the problem with the Embarcadero Freeway; it simply collapsed, as did some parts of the elevated 101 route. The 101 was later routed along one of the existing roads.

New York and San Francisco are two good examples of opposition against motorways and the fight to keep a more pedestrian-friendly environment. There were countless other examples in the United States, some of which I have mentioned in other chapters. Even so, the majority of the population was grateful for the convenience the car brought them; any damage to the urban environment was either not understood or not acknowledged.

A great admirer of what was achieved in the United States in terms of new road construction and pushing motorization forward was Adolf Hitler. His ideas about cars and motorways are discussed in the next chapter.

Notes

1 The first known sidewalks were built in Roman times. The medieval streets had no sidewalks as they were mostly too narrow. I would speculate that the first sidewalks appeared in the second half of the 17th century, in London from 1666 onwards and in Paris during Napoleonic times but the heyday of sidewalk construction was the 19th century.

2 Born in 1809.

3 New street planning and building had already taken place under his predecessor *Charles de Rambuteau* (Carmona 2002, pp. 124, 149).

4 Oglethorpe wanted to create an equitable society hence there would be no rich or poor sections in the city, and slavery was not allowed. When reading about the philosophy of Oglethorpe, one can only conclude that he was one of the forefathers of the garden city movement. The main question that comes to mind is what was the origin of his unusual street plan? John Reps speculated that the template of Savannah was the design of the *Piazza della Carlina Carlo Emanuele* in *Turin* (quoted from Wilson 2012, p. 42). Studying the map of Turin, I think his speculation is far-fetched. Lane (1994) showed two town plans, the *Pietro di Giacomo Cateneo*'s plan of the ideal city published in 1567 and another by *Robert Montgomery* in 1717; both look very much like Oglethorpe's street layout (pp. 36–37). In the two models, the squares are of different sizes. As Oglethorpe wanted an equal society, it was logical for him to make all squares the same size; hence he left out the large square in Cateneo's plan. Strangely enough it was hardly copied anywhere else in the United States apart from the neighboring Georgia settlements of *New Ebenezer, Frederica* and *Darien* (Wilson 2012, p. 153).

5 By comparison the *Champs Elysées* in Paris is 70m wide and *Unter den Linden* in Berlin is only 60m wide.

6 The design was very likely carried out by Frederick Law Olmsted's firm or Frederick Law Olmsted (Jr.) as Frederick Law Olmsted (Sr.) had died in 1903.

7 Pullman in Illinois was the first planned factory 'town' in the United States. It is located about 12 miles south of the city center of Chicago and was more a suburb than a free-standing town. The town was completed in 1881 and was built to a very high standard

with running water, gas and indoor toilets (Miller 1997, p. 225). In total 1,700 residential units were built; it had more than 10,000 inhabitants in 1890 (Beberdick 1998, p. 39). But in 1894 workers went on strike because their wages but not their rents were reduced. (In 2013 it was a very disappointing settlement to visit; the communal buildings were badly deteriorated.) Other well-known European industrial workers' settlements at the time, such as *Saltaire*, 1851 (T. Salt), *Port Sunlight*, 1888 (Lever), *Bournville* (Cadbury) or *Margarethenhöhe* in Essen (Krupp), were villages or suburbs. Apart from Saltaire and Port Sunlight, Bournville was built at about the same time as Vandergrift, and Margarethenhöhe later in 1912.

8   All streets are private and belong to the community.

9   It is interesting to note that both developments were built around the same time. The building of Forest Hills Gardens started in 1908 and the Hampstead Garden Suburb Trust was founded in 1906, with building probably starting two years later.

10 Henry Wright was a landscape architect and he certainly was familiar with Olmsted's practice of street divisions.

11 It was not only the RPAA that believed in garden cities, *John Nolen* who studied landscape architecture and city planning was also interested in the same ideas. He designed 27 new towns, including the well-known *Mariemont* in Ohio (1921–1925). Mariemont was another American version of a continental garden suburb (Collins 2009, pp. 178–179).

12 The estate was designed by *Grey Wornum* and *Louis Soissons*. Soissons had designed *Welwyn Garden City* in 1920. The first three courtyards were finished in 1929 and the last two were built between 1929 and 1931 (www.britishlistedbuildings.co.uk, accessed 13.2.2014).

13 Gurlitt was an architect and professor at the University of Dresden.

14 Maybe it was a kind of arrogance from Gurlitt, remembering that he was a German professor.

15 Hermann Joseph Stübben wrote the widely read book the *Städtebau* (urban buildings) in 1890 and had been responsible for the planning of Cologne (Hass-Klau 1990a, p. 29).

16 According to Lee and Stabin-Nesmith (2001), the area of Radburn in 1990 contained 674 families and a population of about 2,900 who lived on 149 acres of land; this was about 10% of the total population of Fair Lawn (pp. 155–156). The authors were able to compare the conventional suburban development of Fair Lawn with Radburn using 1990 Census data. The statistical areas (which did not exactly fit the original Radburn blocks) that were occupied by Radburn residents were divided into blocks from A to D. Group A had the highest and D the lowest proportion of Radburn residents.

According to the Travel to Work Census, 67% of the Radburn's residents (average of block A–D) drove to work by car alone compared to 75% of all inhabitants of Fair Lawn (ibid, p. 168). The high public transport use of 19% and 20% of the Radburn residents in Block A and C compared to 10% in all of Fair Lawn seems to be more related to the lower income in these two Radburn groups than reflecting the Radburn design itself, as pointed out by the authors (ibid, pp. 169–170). However, cycling which was nearly three times as high in groups A and B than in Fair Lawn, and was at least in group B not related to lower income, supports the evidence from Garvin (2002). The authors discovered a higher price premium for Radburn houses – apart from the fact that they were still particularly popular with large families. The research period stretched from 1951 to 1995. The highest price premium was 33% from 1951 to 1955 at the height of suburban development along the east coast but in the following years it was still between 14 and 25% (ibid, p. 177), which confirms that in property market terms, pedestrian-friendly developments pay off.

17 In 2014 there were 629, because the original clubhouse was converted into two large flats.

18 Another is the main Los Angeles Union Station.

19 From 1.2 million in 1914 to over 23 million by 1930 (Hass-Klau 1990a, p. 95).

20 Interstate highways are motorways.

21 Shirley Hayes and Raymond S. Rubinow managed to close one of the first streets in New York in Washington Square Park to car traffic in 1958 – see Fishman 2007, p. 127.

22   •   The Park Presidio Freeway that was to run from the Golden Gate Bridge through the Presidio Park – today the Golden Gate Recreation area.
     •   Junipero Serra Freeway was to go through the Golden Gate Park (south of the Presidio Park) and run to San Jose
     •   Panhandle Freeway was supposed to run also through the Golden Gate Park and connect with the Central Freeway
     •   The Central Freeway was to connect with the Mission Freeway and the Southern Freeway.

23   Examples are the *John F. Foran* Freeway (I-280), which runs from Mission Bay south through the city to Daly City, the I-80, which runs from Oakland again into the city and finally Route 101, although officially not a freeway, but still a massive road with freeway character.

2

MOTORIZATION AND FOOTPATH PLANNING DURING THE THIRD REICH

Adolf Hitler and the Promotion of Motorization

Fest (1974) stressed that Hitler was ideologically a man of the 19th century but he was also regarded by many of his contemporaries as modern and forward looking (p. 757). In terms of transportation, he was particularly interested in pushing forward two developments (apart from aeroplanes): the construction of motorways and the design of a small car. There is no doubt that the promotion of the *motorway program* was the responsibility of Adolf Hitler himself. However, plans to build motorways had already been developed during the 1920s. Hitler saw representatives of the HAFRABA[1] as early as April 1933 after he had announced the building of a motorway network two months earlier (Petsch 1976, p. 142). Already in 1932, HAFRABA had suggested a 5,000–6,000km motorway network. Despite opposition from the Ministry of Transport, German Rail and the Ministry of Defense, Hitler insisted on the HAFRABA plan (Minuth 1983, p. 307). He extended the motorway length slightly to 6,500km (about 4000 miles). The first stretch of motorway was opened between Frankfurt and Darmstadt in May 1935 (Frenz 1986, p. 21). It was Hitler's plan to build 1,000km of motorways every year, until the planned 6,500km were completed (Minuth 1983, p. 743). 3,000 km of motorway had already been built by the end of 1938 (Huber and Müller 1964, p. 179). However, the problem with German motorways was that hardly any cars used them, as motor vehicle ownership was so low (Table 2.1).

There was tremendous rivalry among German car manufacturers and it was the disagreements between them which led Hitler to decide to have a small car built by *Ferdinand Porsche*. According to Nelson (1970), this car was never intended to be used for military purposes – even the factory itself was not planned to be safe from air raids (ibid, p. 73). Hitler believed that the promotion of cars would weaken the existing class structure (Minuth 1983, p. 464). What he meant by this becomes clearer from an interview he gave to an American journalist in 1933: 'That little car of his [referring to Ford's standardized car production] has done more than anything else to destroy class differences' (Baynes 1942, p. 867). It was his vision to make the car 'The people's mode of transport' (Hitler 1938 in Baynes 1942, p. 974). Clearly this slogan had a positive psychological effect, and so had the construction of motorways. He even talked about the psychological effect himself and its value in raising the morale of the German people (ibid, p. 742). He thought that the car industry was to become the most important and most successful industry of the future (Minuth 1983, p. 513), and German cars had to become the fastest and the best in the world. At least he was right with that.

The promotion of motorization was one of Hitler's first priorities when he came to power in 1933. He dropped the existing car and motorcycle tax for new

Table 2.1 Motor vehicles per 1,000 inhabitants

Country	1922	1938
USA	100	250
Great Britain	11	53
Denmark	8	38
France	6	50
Switzerland	5	–
Belgium	4	27
Germany	3	23

Sources: Ehlgötz 1925, p. 45; Verkehrstechnik 1939, p. 199 (recalculated)

registrations (existing cars also got some tax reductions) (Napp-Zinn 1933, p. 84). He also made it easier to get a driving license and changed some stringent traffic laws, including the abolition of speed limits,[2] with some exceptions (Nelson 1970, p. 24).

The building of the car factory was begun in 1938 (Huber and Müller 1964, p. 179) but the first car did not leave the factory until 1940 (Nelson 1970, p. 70). By then the Second World War had already started and the cars that were produced were used only for military purposes.

Ideal Communities

Apart from motorization, the promotion of new communities was one of the most important tasks of the new government. Obviously the speed of housing construction declined with the beginning of the war and stopped altogether by 1942/43 (Schneider 1979, p. 26). Yet the amount of new housing built during the Third Reich period was nearly as much as during the Weimar Republic (1919–1932: 2,036,453; 1933–1939: 1,983,964 (Teut 1967, pp. 252–253).

The newly built housing estates were copies of traditional garden suburbs and they also included the idea of neighborhoods, which had already been applied during the 1920s. The garden city philosophy was intrinsically a socialist movement, but the National–Socialist ideology used many of the socialist paradigms, such as the dislike for large cities or the concept of grouping houses around village greens. In fact, the settlements developed during the Nazi period were much more a replica of Parker and Unwin's ideal housing communities than some of the existing German garden suburbs. Both the garden city idea and the neighborhood concept needed only some slight ideological adjustment to fit extremely well into the propaganda of the Third Reich.

Impressions of the ideal settlement and its preferred street layout were first stated in two simultaneous exhibitions called *The Street* and *German Settlement* in Munich in 1934. A model village was built for the exhibition. It was located in *Ramersdorf*, which is within the City of Munich. It contained 192 houses of 34 different house types, which varied between 60 and 120sqm floor space (Säume 1934, pp. 552, 555). The houses were supposed to be owner occupied and all had gardens. The model village consisted of several large green spaces. The main green area in the center had the shape of a ribbon of about 450m width, which acted as a connecting green belt between the gardens of two rows of houses. The streets in the heart of the settlement were narrow and two were cul-de-sacs. There were footpath connections mostly between the green spaces. No garages were built or planned. This part of Ramersdorf also had a good public transportation connection, a newly extended tramline. The criticism at the time was that the footpath connections between the green open spaces were not good enough, the streets were still too wide and one street was totally unnecessary (ibid, pp. 552–553).

The main characteristics of this settlement were the steeply roofed houses, a low density, the extensive use of green spaces and many footpaths. This model was in the following years repeatedly planned and built all over Germany. The village green became the physical and social center of a community. The movement of pedestrians was most important and the car had to play a subordinate role (Schneider 1979, p. 123).

In 2014 the 'Nazi Siedlung', as the locals call it, is still very popular. Some women I chatted with told me that it was impossible to buy one of these houses. They never came on the market; they were already gone long before. Its popularity stems from the green open spaces, which make it like an island in the midst of much more densely built urban surroundings. In addition, the relatively large plots have given the owners many possibilities for extensions, including the construction of a garage and the narrow streets allow only careful driving at low speeds.

Probably the most impressive settlement built during 1936–1938 is located in Hamburg-North, in close proximity to the S-Bahn station *Kornweg*. Klein-Borstel was built by the Frank brothers, though the architect was *Paul A. R. Frank*, who had gained a reputation during the 1920s for developing a particularly cheap social housing form in Hamburg (Laubenganghäuser – see definition) (Marg and Fleher 1983, p. 95). The Frank brothers had established their own housing corporation and the plan for the 'Franksche' settlement included terrace housing for 547 families. Each house had its own garden of about 200sqm (Pook 1982, p. 5).

The area the Frank brothers required was one already interspersed with a few houses, and some streets. The most remarkable aspect of the planned settlement was its street layout. Frank himself wrote in 1934 that terrace housing did not need wide streets. Access can be given by one main road and from that several smaller roads including children's playgrounds can open up the community (Frank 1934, p. 8). This was built in Klein-Borstel. Two access roads ended up in squares and the rest of the settlement has very narrow residential streets between 3.50 and 4m. None of the houses have direct access to any street. In fact, the main 'street' network consists only of footpaths.

The narrowness of the residential roads is strengthened by high hedges. One of the most impressive parts is the entrance to the settlement, reminding the visitor of a medieval gate. A similar design can be seen at Chatham Village near Pittsburgh in the United States, built at about the same time (Chapter 1) or later in Eisenhüttenstadt in the GDR built in the 1950s (Chapter 5). A main wide footpath leads to an impressively designed row of houses. This neighborhood has a unique quality which has been acknowledged, and it is now a conservation area. Today this community appears to be one of the best 'natural' traffic calmed areas in Hamburg. Some of the narrow streets are designed as shared space and car drivers have very little choice other than to drive at low speed.

Figure 2.1
Plan of Ganghofer settlement, Regensburg

Figure 2.2
Typical pedestrian footpath
and mini-square

Regensburg, a city of 154,000 inhabitants in 2013, is located on the Danube. Two settlements were built both at about the same time. One, the *Ganghofer* neighborhood, contained 1,100 housing units and was built for workers of the *Messerschmidt* aeroplane factory. This community was constructed from 1937 to 1943. It included a mixture of about 100 owner-occupied houses and rented terrace houses containing six flats. The gardens were large and half of their area was used for the cultivation of vegetables and fruit (Stadt Regensburg 2008, pp. 258–259). This area is nearly unchanged because it has not been in private ownership.[3] Most of the houses have been modernized but the original streets and footpaths have not been changed. The settlement certainly has the feel of a garden suburb. The streets are slightly curved and several were planned as and still are cul-de-sacs. There are two types of streets (widths 5m and 7m) and two types of footpaths (widths 2.50m and 3.50m). Trees were planted along the wider footpaths. When a footpath meets a street, the continuation of the footpath is not straight but staggered as was used in the first German Garden City, *Hellerau* near *Dresden* in 1909 (Hass-Klau 1990a, pp. 62, 67). Several footpaths contain tiny squares. As in all these settlements, a green open space was built in one section.

Most, possibly all, of the planned housing settlements built during the Nazi period contained completely separate pedestrian footways though today many have disappeared because of legal problems – it was publicly owned land – and also because times changed. Separate footways were seen as an important part of town planning during the Third Reich but they were also used to reduce costs. Reichow (1941) wanted to implement them in cities throughout Germany and in the new German East[4] (p. 336). Heinrich Himmler's *Guidelines for Planning and Design of the Cities in the East* (Himmler 1942, pp. 347–357, Allgemeine Anordnung No 13/11) included separate footpath and bicycle networks.

In addition to new communities, two new towns were built. The most important one was clumsily called *Town of the Strength through Joy Car*, today known as *Wolfsburg*, and the second was the *New Town of the Hermann Göring Industries*, today called *Salzgitter*.

Pedestrian Planning in Hitler's New Town: Wolfsburg

The first new town was the result of special circumstances and had little to do with deliberate town planning. If the German car industry had not been so inflexible, Hitler would probably not have decided to build his own plant (Nelson 1970, p. 42). To build a town in addition was the idea of *Bodo Lafferentz*, an adviser to *Robert Ley*. Ley became the main organizer of the Volkswagen production. Lafferentz argued that it was difficult to find qualified workers and in order to attract them, the offer of new housing was a powerful incentive, especially because the German housing stock was still in such poor condition (Schneider 1979, p. 30).

After several suggestions, the private land of *Count Werner von der Schulenburg* was chosen, near the small town of *Fallersleben* and not far from *Braunschweig* (Nelson 1970, p. 55). *Albert Speer* had the main planning responsibility for the town. He appointed the young unknown architect *Peter Koller* to design the town plan. Koller, who had refused to work with Albert Speer on Hitler's Berlin plan (Schneider 1979, p. 31), was unhappy about the assignment, but as he later said, was too young to say no.[5] His different design attempts for the main street layout resulted in a close copy of Speer's Berlin street plan (ibid, pp. 34–35).[6]

Still, the basic design of Wolfsburg was a garden city with wide and numerous main streets. This stood not in direct contrast to the architectural and planning ideas of Adolf Hitler and Albert Speer. One obvious explanation was that Hitler and Speer were interested in monumental buildings and wide streets but hardly ever in the design or planning of new neighborhoods.

Koller's main problem with the assignment of Wolfsburg was how to 'combine the world of gardens, flowers and vegetables with the world of cars' (Koller 1987). Koller designed a footpath network, which would allow school children not to cross any traffic streets. He had already designed a similar plan for *Zagreb* in 1931. Even the main ring road was planned to be in a cutting in order to lead the pedestrian footpaths over it (Schneider 1979, p. 74). Many of Hermann Jansen's plans from the 1920s made sure that school children did not have to cross roads. The GDR[7] used the same design for their new towns.

Hitler had accepted Koller's plan of Wolfsburg in 1938. The town center – the *Stadtkrone* – was located on hilly terrain.[8] It was surrounded by a 60 to 100m (198–330ft) wide ring road. The width of the street was designed in order to cope with the predicted peak-hour traffic although it was assumed that workers would not use their cars for commuting trips. Such lack of logic was quite common during the Third Reich.

Offices and some large flats were planned to be located along the ring road. The first ring road was only a semi-circle and the straight boundary was transformed into a wide shopping and business street. A second ring road followed the first one at a radius of 600–900m, and a third ring road was planned, partly overlapping the second one. Its function was to combine the upper, hillier part of the town with the lower part of Wolfsburg (Kautt 1983, p. 37).

The two main green corridors were to access on one end the town center and on the other the forest.[9] They were complemented by a system of smaller open spaces and pedestrian footpaths. The pedestrian street network was to be kept largely independent from the main streets because, as Koller (1939) argued, the

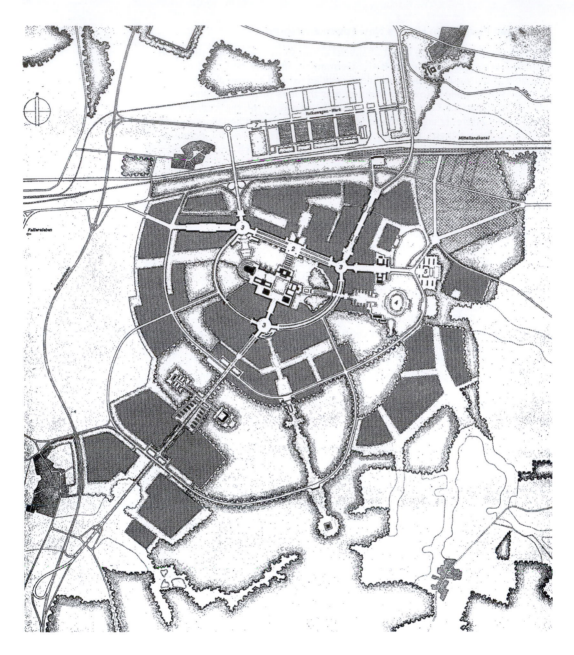

Figure 2.3
Plan of Wolfsburg

streets of Wolfsburg were to be used much more than in other towns by cars. Housing was grouped together around open green spaces (p. 158).

The construction of the Volkswagen factory and the town were started simultaneously in May 1938 (Koller 1940, p. 662). The first housing community – *Steimkerberg* – was built between 1938 and 1939. It contained 438 housing units, which were built partly as single, semi-detached and terraced housing. It was a settlement for the better-off families. Steimkerberg was surrounded completely by forest. Only one traffic street led to this community. The streets inside the community were smaller. A pedestrian network complemented these streets and gave access to the forest and to other parts of the town. The center was an open green space, like a village common, which was connected to the rear with U-shaped shopping facilities, which could be reached from the front by service vehicles and from the back by pedestrians (the same design was used by Jansen in the 1920s).

Today Steimkerberg is still one of the most popular housing areas in Wolfsburg. Being in private ownership, the appearance of the houses has changed. It gives the feeling of an enchanted area, somewhat removed from the realities and certainly the cruelty of the time in which it was built. At the beginning of the 1980s, Steimkerberg had become a conservation area.

A New Approach for City Centers

Several main city center issues were discussed during the 1930s and 1940s. All of them were interrelated and connected with street planning. The most important question was what type of traffic should and should not enter a town center.

Pedestrianization

There were planners who wanted to restrict motor vehicle use in the city center. The first articles on pedestrianization were published. Strangely enough this movement seemed to become stronger as the years went by (Güldenpfennig 1935 (quoted as Niederndodeleben); Abel 1942). A number of cases became known in which actual road closures had taken place, for instance in *Rendsburg 1937*, *Kassel 1935*, Lübeck (data not known) (Monheim 1975, p. 207; Landesamt für Denkmalpflege Hessen 1984, p. 22).

Güldenpfennig suggested new plans for the area around the cathedral in Cologne, which included a large square for the use of pedestrians only[10] (Niederndodeleben 1935, p. 708). *Adolf Abel* was a strong advocate for pedestrianization. His plan for the town center of *Wuppertal* (1938) included several large pedestrian axes. The article *The Return of Traffic Space to the Pedestrians* (1942) was another example of intensifying the discussion about town center pedestrianization. He talked about the importance of this subject in modern urban planning. A plan for *Baden-Baden* was included, which showed a large pedestrian network for the historic spa town (pp. 221–229). Abel (1950) demanded the strict separation between pedestrians and motor traffic and elucidated that the separation of transportation modes was the only way to ensure the survival of our cities. He used Venice as an example and pointed out that the secret of its success was the physical separation of transportation modes.

The work of Adolf Abel became better known after the Second World War. He was not particularly popular with the Nazis after Hitler had openly disapproved of Abel's reconstruction plan of the famous *Glaspalast* in Munich (Bayerische Akademie der Schönen Künste 1985, p. 154).

Similar thoughts, although not as radical, were also expressed by the *Deutsche Gemeindetag* (German Association of Local Authorities) (1941), which wrote about town center streets. If streets were not wide enough, they should either receive arcades, be changed into one-way streets or be closed to wheeled traffic during the main shopping hours (p. 10).

No Through Traffic

The question of what to do with through traffic in city centers was already being discussed during the Weimar Republic. In many cities the city center streets were simply widened but this was not a real solution. During the Nazi period, the main intention was to keep through traffic out despite opposition. A typical example was Nuremberg where the plan was to take through traffic out and direct it into a ring road around the historic city wall. However, this plan originated from Hermann Jansen, who suggested it in 1923 (Liedke 1995, p. 126, www.stadtatlas-muenchen.de/stadtatlas-nuernberg, accessed 18.12.13). All through traffic was finally taken out in 1972.

More Road Constructions and Street Widening

There were also traffic engineers and planners who wanted to sacrifice parts of the city center to the needs of motorization. Hitler's vigorous promotion of the car supported this policy (Egloffstein 1935). There were many articles demanding street widening, one-way streets, and new road construction in urban areas and city centers. In order to make space for the motor vehicle, it was suggested to abolish front gardens, cut street trees, abandon sidewalks (or to narrow them), and/or take out trams (Beblo 1935). Many of these discussions continued and the demands for street widening and more roads were fulfilled after the Second World War, but not during the Nazi period.

Often transportation planners who were in favor of street widening in the city center were for a strict street division of modes in residential areas in order to avoid accidents (Müller 1935, p. 403).

A New Vision for the City Center

This approach was most dangerous for the historic city centers. It was put forward by powerful members (Gauleiter) of the Nazis. They knew little about urban planning and cared even less about the historic heritage of German cities (Speer 1970, pp. 314–315). Most party members modeled their newly designed town centers on Hitler's plan for Berlin (ibid, p. 142). Though Hitler himself had some respect for historic buildings, in his passion for creating a capital of the 'first' German People's Reich (Baynes 1972, p. 600) he was quite willing to destroy large historic parts (Speer 1970, p. 77). He had a similar approach for Munich, but in Nuremberg the historic town center remained untouched (Petsch 1976, p. 92).

Hitler's original intention was to reconstruct five cities (Berlin, Munich, Nuremberg, Hamburg and Linz) into monumental cities, later another 27 cities were added (Speer 1944, p. 13). The radical redevelopment of cities was based on the 'Reichsgesetz über die Neugestaltung deutscher Städte' (The Law to Redesign German Towns) from October 1937. All of Hitler's city plans were based on similar design principles, consisting of two main street crossing axes on which the major public buildings were located.

In the plan for Berlin and Munich, a great hall dominated the design. In addition, four wide ring roads were planned for Berlin in order to take some of the traffic out of the city center. Green axes were to lead from the outskirts to the city centers (ibid, p. 11).

The square in front of the hall in Berlin was to be kept car free, which gave Speer some problems with the north–south traffic flows (ibid, p. 77). As all the town designs were very similar, one can assume that the feature of a traffic-free main square was copied in all the other plans. But these squares had little to do with pedestrianization. Their main intention was to emphasize architecturally the great hall or some other monumental buildings of the Third Reich. The similarity to the urban planning features of the city centers in the GDR is striking. It is strange that nobody picked that up and the ones who did, did not dare to speak out about it (Chapter 5).

There was no clear party line on any of these approaches and obviously it did not include a clear answer to the traffic problems in city centers. It meant little if a planner daydreamed about car-free streets but the traffic engineer of the same town could politically push through some street widening projects. Despite these ideas, very little changed in most towns and the big alterations came after most cities were destroyed during the final stages of the Second World War, but this is another story which is discussed in the next chapter.

Notes

1 The most influential organization was the *HAFRABA* (*Verein zur Vorbereitung der Autostraße Hansestädte – Frankfurt – Basel* = Organization for Preparing a Motor Road from Bremen via Hamburg, Frankfurt and Basel), which was formed in 1926. It was a private organization including members from banks, harbors, construction firms and even local authorities which had managed to build the first stretch of motorway between Cologne and Bonn during the last years of the Weimar Republic (Petsch 1976, p. 142). The predecessor of HAFRABA, the *National Automobile Society* and the *Benzolvereinigung* had built in Berlin a 9km (8.5 miles) long motorway used as a racetrack, the AVUS (Automobil- Verkehrs- und Übungsstraße), in 1921 (Frenz 1986, p. 18).

2 The street regulations of 1934 (Reichsverkehrsstraßenordnung, 28.5.1934) more or less abolished speed limits; only on some streets a speed limit of 40kph was laid down. The relaxation of the speed limit continued until 1939. The speed limits agreed in the 1939 regulations were 60kph in built-up areas and 100kph outside, but these were reduced five months later to 40kph and 80kph (25mph and 50mph) respectively. Lorries and buses had to drive at lower speeds, in 1923 at 25kph or 30kph according to their weight, and from 1939 onwards at 40kph in built-up areas (Horadam 1983, p. 21).

3 It belonged to a housing association of Bavaria (Bayerische Heimstätte für Wohnungs- und Kleinsiedlungswesen).

4 The area of occupation in the East of Europe, mainly Poland.

5 This quote was given by Koller in 1945 during an interview with a British reporter.

6 Koller, who had studied in Vienna and Berlin, was significantly influenced by *Hermann Jansen*. His urban planning concepts and his street layouts were derived from Jansen's work. He was also a student of *Heinrich Tessenow*, who had partly planned and built the German Garden City, Hellerau. Koller wrote that Tessenow influenced his architectural design standards (Koller 1987).

7 GDR = German Democratic Republic = East Germany which was ruled by a communist party from 1949 to 1989.

8 The concept of Stadtkrone was developed by Taut in 1919. Taut had also designed the garden suburb '*Falkenberg*', in Berlin in 1913.

9 One was about 3km (2.4 miles) long.

10 This was built after the Second World War.

3

THE ROLE OF THE PEDESTRIAN AFTER THE SECOND WORLD WAR IN WEST GERMANY

The Early Years

Political Background

After the Second World War, the Allies (Soviet Union, United States, France and Great Britain) divided Germany into four occupation zones: the French, the British, the American and the Russian. The Red Army had conquered Berlin but with the agreement of the Western Allies the city was divided into four zones as well in July 1945.

In June 1948, a currency reform – the creation of the Deutschmark – took place in the three German parts controlled by the Western Allies and in West Berlin but not in East Germany or East Berlin. In May 1949, a new German constitution was agreed and the Federal Republic of Germany was formed in the western part of Germany. In the same year, in October 1949, the German Democratic Republic (GDR) was created in East Germany. East Berlin was regarded as the capital, although strictly speaking that was illegal since in principle Berlin was controlled by the four Allies.

There were two major transportation and planning impacts on post-war West Germany – one was the rapid growth in car ownership and the other was the ideas of the *Charter of Athens*, which would be influential not so much in the post-war period but much more so during the late 1960s and 1970s in East and West Germany. Let us have a closer look at what were the circumstances and the contents of this famous charter.

The Charter of Athens

The first congress of the CIAM (Congrès International d'Architecture Moderne) took place in a small village in Switzerland in *La Sarraz* in 1928 and the declaration was signed by 24 experts from eight countries (there was nobody present from outside Europe or from the UK, Sweden, Denmark, Norway, Portugal or Russia).[1] These meetings continued irregularly in different locations throughout Europe until 1959 (there was no conference between 1938 and 1946).

The Swiss architect *Le Corbusier* was one of the most well-known representatives of this movement. The *Charter of Athens* agreed in 1933 was formally written and published by Le Corbusier ten years later (Hilpert 1988, p. 13). However, unknown to most, the Charter had already been published in French and Greek in 1933 and one year later in the Swiss journal '*Weiterbauen*' (Heft 1–2). There were some significant changes between the original version (below the Swiss version) and Le Corbusier's publication. His version of 1943 has used (some would say abused) the collective basis of the original for his own personal reinterpretation.

The 'functional city', which was the original title of the 1933 conference on a boat to Athens, was widely discussed in Germany during the 1930s. It occupied the minds of both the urban planners who stayed and worked in Germany and those who had left the country during the Nazi period. One has to remember that many of the principles manifested in the Charter had already been used in practice mainly in Germany and the Netherlands during the 1920s and even earlier.

The conclusions and demands of the Charter were based on the study of 33 cities, a remarkable achievement, including:[2]

* Berlin, Köln, Dessau, Frankfurt
* Amsterdam, Den Haag, Rotterdam, Utrecht
* Roma, Verona, Como, Genoa, Littoria (now known as Latina)
* Baltimore, Detroit, Los Angeles
* Genf, Zurich
* Madrid, Barcelona
* Brussels, Charleroi
* Oslo, Stockholm
* Budapest, Prag, Zagreb
* London
* Paris
* Athens
* Warsaw
* Dalat
* Bandoeng.

The analysis of different elements relating to the study cities, and the exact and unified rules for all these cities, had been agreed during meetings in Berlin and Barcelona in 1931 and 1932 (ibid, p. 200). It is not clear whether British or American experts were represented, but considering that London and several American cities were part of the study, this could be assumed, although there are no details.

The international architects of the CIAM were 'modern' and criticized any imitation of historic buildings and styles (ibid, p. 23). They rejected the historic city, especially the 19th-century, high density, overcrowded one, and wanted new functional urban areas, characterized in terms of urban planning by three functions: living, working and recreation. Urban planning had to guard the fulfillment of these functions.

The division of functions had already been mentioned in the declaration of La Sarraz in July 1928 (ibid, p. 96). The first author I am aware of who mentioned the division of functions was *Bruno Taut* (1919) in his book 'Stadtkrone' which he wrote during the First World War. He talked of the separation between housing and industry by green verges. He wanted a green belt around the city and one large green axis starting in the center (Stadtkrone) and becoming wider toward the west of the city. It would include different types of parks and the university. The industry is located in the east and along the railway line (Taut 1919, pp. 63, 64, 71).

Taut's ideas were well known in professional circles hence the division of urban functions was not a new concept at the time when the Charter of Athens was discussed.

Le Corbusier's Charter consisted of three sections (95 paragraphs) (major changes between the original and Le Corbusier's version are added in italics):

- The city and the region (§1–8)
- The present condition of cities – criticism and improvements (§9–70)
- Conclusions (§71–95).

The first part was concerned with the role of the city and its regions (§1). It also included a number of different determining aspects from the principles of psychological and physiological order to the economic, social and political impacts and the historical influences within cities (§2–8). This part is really the philosophical background of the Charter. It is woolly and strange and not at all convincing. The earlier Swiss version is in contrast clearer and more precise.

Most important was the second part and some of the conclusions. The second part was divided into five sections:

- Housing
- Recreation
- Work
- Transport
- Historic heritage of cities.

Under housing it was concluded that:

- The population density was too high for the existing buildings and this resulted in all kinds of negative impacts, for example lack of sunlight (§9).
- The growth of cities ate up more and more green space (§11).
- Roads and junctions have negative effects in terms of noise, dust and pollution (§16) on buildings constructed along them.
- Quite often there was not enough sunlight within flats because houses were built along traffic routes (§17).
- Schools were frequently located on traffic streets and were too far away from the residential areas (§19, ibid, pp. 114–129).
- *Suburbs were built without plans and without regular connections with the city. Suburbs were a symbol of decline but at the same time an option for experimentation. They were a kind of 'scum' that surrounds the city. During the 19th and 20th centuries the scum had become a flood. The suburbs were the source of revolts, and trying to produce garden cities was an illusory paradise and an irrational solution. Suburbs were urban mistakes* (§20, ibid, p. 130). (The original version does not include any of this. It only concludes that 'the suburbs were part of the city' (ibid, p. 60).)

In the Charter it was demanded that it should *not* be permitted to build housing along transportation roads and that the division between the pedestrian and car traffic was paramount. Housing had to be located away from motorized traffic and *pedestrians needed to have their own network*. So far nothing of this was put into practice in contemporary cities (§27, ibid, p. 134).

It was pointed out in the Charter in the section recreation that there was not enough green open space in cities (§30). It insisted that:

- Cities had to become green cities. In contrast to garden cities where the green space was private, in future the green space should be public (§35).
- Unhealthy housing blocks had to be demolished and the space created had to be used as green open land (§36).
- Within the new green spaces schools, kindergartens, youth centers or any other general buildings should be built and these buildings ought to be only short distances away from the living areas (§37; this was the typical design by Hermann Jansen in the 1920s, the settlements in the Third Reich and later in Eisenhüttenstadt and Halle-Neustadt in East Germany).

It came to the conclusion with reference to work that the trips were too long between the working places and living areas (§42) *and that traffic congestion was a problem at peak hours* (§43). The original version only mentioned that 'there were peak hours'.

It demanded that:

- The distance between working and living areas had to be reduced (§46).
- The industrial parts of a city had to be located independently from the housing areas and they should be separated by green axes (§47).
- Industries must be built along railroads, canals and rural streets (§48).
- The shops of tradesmen were closely connected with city life and they had to be in the city center (§49).
- The 'business city', whether private or public, had to have good traffic connections with the housing areas but also with industries and the shops of tradesmen (§50).

The following opinion with reference to traffic was expressed:

- The origin of the existing road network was historic (§51).
- The streets were built for pedestrians and carriages but today they were inadequate for motor vehicles (§52).
- *The dimensions of the streets were no longer appropriate and conflicted with the full exploitation of the new speeds of motor vehicles and the orderly development of the city* (§53). This paragraph was not in the original version but instead another paragraph was included which was not in Le Corbusier's version of 1943. It emphasized that high speeds were dangerous for road users and the example of Berlin was mentioned (600 people killed and 12,000 injured — I assume that this is an annual figure but the year is not given) (ibid, p. 208).
- It was thought that the widths of the streets were not sufficient. The attempts to widen streets were quite often a difficult and mostly ineffective undertaking (§55).
- The street network was with reference to mechanical speeds (of motor vehicles) irrational because it lacked exactness, adaptability, differentiation and usefulness (and as a result was inefficient) (§56).
- Streets that were used for 'representation' could be a hindrance to traffic (§57).

It was requested within the Charter that:

- Statistics and analysis of traffic flows in cities had to be carried out regularly (§59).
- Streets should be classified according to their functions and should be built according to the vehicles and the driven speed (§60).
- At busy junctions through traffic should be at a different physical level in order not to be held up (§61).
- The traffic streets should be classified according to their character and had to be built according to the vehicles and their speeds. *The pedestrians had to use other routes than vehicles (§62). This demand was as important as the demand that housing should have sufficient sunlight* (which meant no north-facing locations for houses).
- Streets should be differentiated according to their function: living streets for residential use, *streets for walking*, streets for through traffic and main traffic streets (§63).
- The streets with large traffic flows were to be isolated with green verges (§64; ibid, pp. 145–151).

Under the section on the historic inheritance of cities it was agreed that:

- The historical values had to be retained which meant the preservation of single buildings or *urban ensembles* (§65). The original version included the notion of 'neighborhoods', instead of urban ensembles (ibid, p. 210).
- Historic buildings would be kept if they were the expression of former culture and if they were of general interest (a very weak phrase) (§66; ibid, pp. 151–152).
- The demolition of slums around historical monuments would give the opportunity to create green spaces (§69). It could well be that the demolition *of unhealthy houses and slums around historic monuments would destroy century-old neighborhoods; this was a pity but inevitable* (ibid, p. 153). The original did not have this strong demand for pulling down whole historic neighborhoods. It mentioned that by demolishing dilapidated housing, green spaces can be created (ibid, p. 210).

The conclusion consisted of general and more specific propositions. It emphasized that the key tasks of urban planning were within the four functions (living, working, recreation and the useful movement between these functions). It established that urban planning had so far only tackled transportation (§77).

There were three major points where the agreed Charter of Athens of 1933 differed from Le Corbusier's published version of 1943:

1. Le Corbusier's disgust with suburbs was not shared by his colleagues.
2. The issue of road safety, which was already a real problem in large cities, was not mentioned at all by Le Corbusier.
3. Le Corbusier was far more radical in demolishing historic neighborhoods than was agreed in the 1933 Charter.

One of Le Corbusier's opinions was especially interesting. He commented that the human race was condemned to spend many tiring hours in vehicles of all kinds and increasingly forgot one activity that was more healthy and natural than any other: walking (§80, ibid, p. 159). Altogether Le Corbusier was mostly pedestrian friendly. In his publication of the *Ville Radieuse* (1930), he wrote that the pedestrians should have their own network so that they will never have to meet a vehicle. The ground level belongs entirely to the pedestrian (Houghton-Evans 1975, p. 73). But in an earlier publication *Toward New Architecture* (1925) that was not the case (ibid, p. 61). The reason for his pro-pedestrian attitude may have had more to do with the desire that motor vehicle circulation could move unhindered without any pedestrians around.

It was also stressed that high-rise buildings will improve traffic and recreation because more space would be available (§82). Finally, Le Corbusier believed that 'private interests will in future be subordinate to the interests of society' (§95; Hilpert 1988, p. 166). This statement was not published in the original version but in the draft (ibid, p. 213).

Although most of the ideas of the Charter had been known and some were practiced by the most forward-thinking planners before the Second World War, it had a stronger effect after Le Corbusier's publication in 1943, possibly because many believed there was a real chance of rebuilding cities according to these principles. The 1943 version of the Charter provided the justification for huge road building programs and the destruction of the historic parts of the city, as was happening in most US cities. That it did not take off in the same way in Europe had many reasons, but the basic strategies of the Charter were followed and the demand for road building had no limits; many historic quarters were damaged or completely destroyed as a result.

The Missed Chance of Reconstruction

At the end of the Second World War there was hunger, destruction and confusion in Germany. Most German cities, particularly the large ones, were not only badly damaged but some parts had been totally flattened during the bombing raids. The period up to 1950 could be classified as the time of improvisation. It was most important to repair and patch up. People organized food production and went slowly back to their work places, if they still existed, or tried to find new work. Mostly women helped to clear up the ruins and rubble. Having to break completely with the political past, nothing would have been more natural than to start planning from scratch and implementing new transportation ideas.

Many German cities started to plan along those lines. There were three conflicting plans in *Berlin:* The *Collective Plan*, the *Zehlendorf Plan* and the *Hermsdorfer Plan* (see also Chapter 5). All three had already been presented in 1945 or 1946. The Collective Plan, designed by *Scharoun*, was to change major parts of Berlin into a linear city, whereas the Zehlendorf Plan by *Moest* and *Görgen* was modeled on the *Speer Plan* (see Chapter 2). The Hermsdorfer Plan had a garden city layout suggested by *Heyer* and was as unrealistic as a linear city (Werner 1976, pp. 74–83). In the end, the Zehlendorf Plan, which was the most compromised one, survived for West Berlin.

The first post-war plan of *Munich* was prepared by *Meitinger* in August 1945. His ideas were published one year later and showed that most of the city, especially the historic city center, was to be rebuilt as before the war. The plan included a few corrections to improve traffic flows for motor vehicles. He suggested arcades along some of the main city center streets and squares, for example the buildings along one side of the *Marienplatz* were to be slightly set back. He was in favor of constructing pedestrian passages, which could be created by removing ruins and buildings inside traditional overcrowded courtyards. These yards should also have shops and beer gardens (which have always been very important for Munich's social life) (Landeshauptstadt München 1946, pp. 35–36). The publication of the City of Munich in 2013 with the title *Across the City Center Through Courtyards and Passages* is an interesting ironic reference to the Meitinger Plan as these walks are suggested in order to 'unburden' the main pedestrian streets (Landeshauptstadt München, Referat für Stadtplanung und Bauordnung 2013, np).

In order to keep the parked cars out of the city center a 50–70m (165–231ft) wide ring road was planned including a ring for parked cars (Nerdinger 1984, p. 84). The ring road, which resembled Stübben's large avenues, included six car lanes. On each side there were parking facilities and a dense avenue of trees. The ring road included sidewalks of 8m (26ft) width, on each side of which 2m (7ft) were used as a cycle path (Landeshauptstadt München 1946, p. 27). Meitinger was of the opinion that everybody who came by car should park outside the city center and walk (ibid, p. 26). This way, he argued, no space would be lost inside the city center, and motor traffic could drive through it. Most of the newly planned buildings should be constructed along the city center ring road. Meitinger designed in total four ring roads and about nine radial roads, some of which were planned to be of 50m width. Yet the carriageways themselves were small, and only two lanes of motor traffic in each direction were possible. Plenty of space was provided for pedestrians and cyclists, including a wide margin for trees (13.50m on each side) (ibid, p. 38).

Adolf Abel had different ideas on how to rebuild Munich's city center (for some other details about Abel, see Chapter 2). In 1946, he provided a plan for Munich's city center. The main feature of the plan was the strict separation of motor vehicles from pedestrians. He argued that if an independent pedestrian network could be created, then the existing road space would be sufficient for motor traffic (Abel 1947 in Nerdinger 1984, pp. 86–89). The center point of his pedestrian town was to be a newly created square (*Marienhof*) behind the town hall. From there five pedestrian axes would lead through the courtyards of the town center, which had to be created. Squares, streets and arcades would complement the courtyards. The facades of shops and the entrances of houses would open toward the yards and squares and not toward the motor traffic streets. The plan was greeted with enthusiasm by the City Council but soon forgotten, and instead the main urban planner, *Leitenstorfer*, suggested a more conventional plan, which borrowed some features of the Meitinger Plan.

Needless to say the accepted plan did not solve the traffic problems, which became apparent with the growth in motorization. The first *General Transport Plan* was agreed in 1963. In this plan some kind of traffic restraint was pointed out. In the *Land Use Plan* of the same year, pedestrianization was mentioned. The argument used in favor of pedestrianization was to counteract out-migration of the population from the city center (Landeshauptstadt München 1963, p. 24).

According to Mulzer (1972), a very comprehensive new plan was designed for *Nuremberg*, which was not implemented (p. 49). We also know of new plans for *Hanover, Cologne, Stuttgart, Karlsruhe, Munster, Freiburg* and *Hamburg*. Again, most of them were too 'modern', too different to be realistic (Nerdinger 1984, p. 12). Nearly all German cities went the way of the big compromise, 'the motto was no experiments' as *Alexander Mitscherlich* (1969) one of the most famous critics of post-war Germany, emphasized (ibid, p. 62).

The lack of implementation of anything new can be largely explained by the fact that the planners and engineers who were active during the Nazi period were typically still working, the unwillingness to change the existing property laws, the lack of funds and also by the pressing need to build housing at a rapid rate. This became even more apparent with the waves of refugees which flooded into West Germany in the post-war period, nearly all from the East.[3]

All these various factors had the result that most war-damaged German cities were largely reconstructed as they had been before. *Hillebrecht* (1957) talked about the missed chance. Instead of clinging to traditional forms, leafy and generously spaced cities should have been built with satellite towns on the edges of the urban areas (ibid, p. 69). Many other planners were of the same opinion (Brix 1954, p. 159; Hoffmann 1961, p. 178).

Massive Road Building in Urban Areas

In the very early post-war years, the main transportation modes were the existing trams and trains, apart from walking and cycling. Especially in the big cities it was most important to repair rail transportation. Private cars hardly existed (Pirath 1948, p. 29).

The car promoted by Hitler, the *Volkswagen*, was seen by British automobile experts as being 'too ugly, bizarre, noisy and flimsy'; to consider building this car was regarded commercially as a completely uneconomic enterprise (Nelson 1970, p. 83). Even so, the *Beetle* was extremely popular with the military and already in 1945 the Volkswagen factory started to produce cars again. In 1949, 46,000 cars were manufactured, comprising 50% of all cars made in West Germany (ibid, pp. 86, 127). In 1961, the five millionth Beetle had been produced (Sachs 1984, p. 87).

In 1950 West Germany already had 598,000 private cars (2.4 million motor vehicles) (Der Bundesminister für Verkehr 1975, p. 109), which was about the level of 1933. Ten years later, about four million cars and nearly eight million motor vehicles traveled on Germany's roads. Such growth rates imply some substantial problems in the densely built up urban areas, which had largely not been rebuilt for cars. Similar to other countries, the growth rate of motorization had also been completely underestimated in West Germany, and traffic-restraint policies were not seriously considered. Criticism was expressed that not enough money was spent on road building in relation to the growth of motor traffic (Bogner 1965, p. 93; Schaechterle 1970, p. 15).

In general, the fastest adjustment to motor traffic took place in the cities located in the Ruhr area because of the industrial importance of coal and steel. The 80km (about 50 miles) long *Ruhrschnellweg*, originally built between 1925 and 1930, the most important east–west axis in the Ruhr, was already in 1954 being rebuilt to motorway standard.

But there were other cities, too, that quickly adapted their street network to the growing demands of motorization. Apart from Frankfurt, Hanover and Hamburg, Stuttgart was another example. It had already planned major new roads of 32–40m (105–132ft) widths just after the war (four in a west–east direction and three in a north–south direction) (Pirath 1948, pp. 40–41). It became even more car orientated after the motor industry (*Daimler-Benz* and *Porsche*) began to boom. The *General Traffic Plan* of Stuttgart suggested in 1962 an outer motorway ring, a middle motorway ring of 31km (19 miles) length, and an inner major ring road around the city center plus 11 radial streets at nearly motorway standard. But this was not enough, and in addition 66km of urban motorways and 24km of urban streets for fast moving traffic (nearly motorway standard) were proposed. Sixty-five junctions inside the city had to be newly built or rebuilt, of which 28 were supposed to be totally free and 37 partly free of crossing traffic. Many other streets had to be adjusted to the new traffic demands. This totally car-orientated plan was for a city of about 600,000 inhabitants (Först 1962, p. 182).

A decline of road investment occurred for the first time (in real terms) in 1976 and a substantial reduction was experienced from 1981 to 1990 (Der Bundesminister für Verkehr 1992, p. 113).

There were several ideas on motor transportation, which were shared by most road engineers, for instance that no buildings should be allowed along fast and major roads, which was one of the demands from the Charter of Athens. Transport experts were of the opinion that motor traffic had to move fast and the faster traffic was, the higher the road capacity. Moving car traffic was important for the economic health of a city. The efficiency of junctions was of crucial importance. Roundabouts were regarded as safe but they were disqualified as 'brake disks' as they slowed traffic down (Mäcke 1954, p. 129). The first traffic lights with green for motor traffic at constant speeds were first established in Frankfurt in 1952. They had originally been designed to improve road safety but were later used to increase traffic capacity (Anon 1953, pp. 47–48; see also 'Denver' in Chapter 13).

Others saw the need to separate traffic in order to improve road safety. Some accepted that some road space could be used for pedestrian streets, for example Hollatz, Hillebrecht, Körte, Tamms or Hoffmann.

Several urban planners warned about the dominance of car use. They were for severe restriction of motor vehicles not only in the city center but also in residential areas. Not surprisingly they were mainly the architects close to the Garden City Society, for example Bernoulli (1954) wrote a short article called 'Fußgängerstadt' (Pedestrian City), but there were others like Ernst May, Hans Bernhard Reichow and Friedrich Gunkel.[4]

Ernst May (1963) made no secret that he thought German transportation experts had got it all wrong. He denounced the massive road building programs and called them misguided investments and the wrong operations for the organism of a city. It was not the city that had to be changed to accommodate traffic, but traffic that had to be changed to be accommodated to the city. Motor traffic had to be restricted and large parts of the city had to be protected from it. The first step in the right direction was pedestrianization but it was important to extend these areas. He disagreed with parking facilities in the city center because they would create even more traffic. He suggested instead the promotion and modernization of public transportation. He demanded cutting tax advantages for company cars and increasing petrol taxes. The raised funds should be used to promote public transportation (pp. 183–184).

Reichow's book (1959), called misleadingly Die autogerechte Stadt (The Car Perfect City), advocated a street layout for residential areas which was similar to the Nazi settlements. That was not surprising because Reichow had been an active planner during the Nazi period. After the war he built several housing estates, which were closely modeled on previous design, for instance *Hohnerkamp* in Hamburg, 1953/54 or *Neu Vahr*, Bremen 1957–1962 etc. (p. 74). His most important achievement was the *Sennestadt* in Bielefeld, which was designed for 24,000 inhabitants (Ritter 1964, pp. 136–137).

The post-war road building euphoria was seen by him only as a large 'surgical operation', which would not solve the general traffic problem (Reichow 1959, p. 5). The town as such had to be changed. He wrote that if we do not develop different cities, 'we will become slaves of a transportation technology which disdained human dignity' (ibid, p. 16). Working and living quarters had to be planned as close together as possible in order to reduce distances. These demands appear modern to us today but they had already been discussed widely in the late 1920s and 1930s and expressed most prominently in the Charter of Athens in 1933.

His main objective was to improve road safety. This was only achieved if the different transportation modes were separated. Pedestrianization in the city center was an important part of his plan. But in the residential areas housing was to be designed in such a way that children could reach schools without crossing roads. Shopping and other infrastructure facilities were arranged on the same principle. He talked about the adverse effects of motor vehicles, the noise and pollution they created and that people had to be protected. Many ideas of modern traffic calming were already included in his book. Like most traffic planners of his time, he wanted to have moving car traffic but he pointed out that with his type of town this could be achieved and at the same time road safety could be improved considerably. But when his book was published, it had no impact and his ideas were regarded as regressive. It is not surprising that Reichow's ideas were not welcomed in the 1950s; they reminded too many of Nazi communities.

SENNESTADT IN 2013

Studying Sennestadt in more detail and even visiting this town one finds a number of interesting facts. The town, located about 10km from the center of *Bielefeld*, had 21,000 inhabitants in 2013 with a low population density (848 inhabitants per sqkm) (www.bielefeld.de, accessed 23.11.13). The first flats were ready for occupation in 1958 and the settlement was finished in the middle of the 1960s. It achieved city status in 1965 but lost it again in 1973 and is now part of Bielefeld (www.sennestadtverein.de, accessed 23.11.13).

The street layout is most remarkable as it is indeed a copy of a 1930s community. It has a large and long green park in the center and many cul-de-sac narrow streets. Access from the houses into the center park, to the shopping arcades, to the sport center and to one of the schools is possible via an independent footpath network, the pedestrian network is 27km (17miles) long. My experience of Sennestadt both wandering around and seeing how people live there was far more pleasant than the large housing estates built in the 1970s and 1980s in East and West Germany, which were all modeled on Le Corbusier's ideas and design.

Road safety was the aspect of German road transportation policy that appeared not to have received great priority although the accident statistics were horrific (Table 3.1). In 1950, 2.7 people were killed per 1,000 motor vehicles. In 1960, the figure had declined to 1.8. Ten years later the figure was down to 1.1 and in 1990 – the year of unification – it had declined to 0.2 people per 1,000 motor vehicles and in 2010 it was 0.04 (Der Bundesminister für Verkehr 1974; Bundesministerium für Verkehr, Bau und Stadtentwicklung 2012).

There were many reasons for the high number of accidents in Germany. Not only was the number of cyclists and motor cyclists very high but more importantly there was also no speed limit for some years after 1952. In addition it was easy to pass the driving test, the roads were in bad condition, traffic signaling either did not exist or was not geared to the new demands, and the careless attitude of many new car owners did not help.

In general, there was a dislike of building pedestrian islands and crossings because they were seen as reducing the speed of the moving traffic (Müller 1954, p. 149). Pedestrians were given priority at zebra crossings as late as 1964, although such crossings had existed since 1952 (Schubert 1966, p. 29).[5] Before, pedestrians had only been 'safe' at crossings with traffic signal installations. In 1958, a speed limit of 50kph was introduced in built-up areas (Horadam 1983, p. 23). There was relatively little research carried out on road safety issues. Federal research on road safety started as late as 1972 (with the formation of the Safety Research Department in the BASt).

Studying several city center plans before and after the Second World War, one can clearly see that all cities had made some adjustment to motorization. In most cases, even in the Bavarian cities, streets and junctions were widened, new junctions proposed, avenues of trees cut down and often sidewalks narrowed. New ring or radial roads were designed and existing ring roads enlarged. Many plans left through traffic in the city center, and even the ones which deliberately stated the intention to build ring roads in order to exclude through traffic, for instance in Nuremberg and Freiburg, still widened their city center streets and did nothing to restrict motor traffic.

In many city centers substantial changes in the street network were made for the first time since the medieval period. This was not only true for the large cities but also for the smaller towns, for example Ulm and Heilbronn (DAfSL 1961, pp. 217–391). The urban heritage was mercilessly made the victim of the car, the symbol of Germany's growing prosperity.

Some ideas expressed by experts appear extreme today but they were accepted wisdom in the 1950s and 1960s. The ideology of Professor *Kurt Leibbrand*[6] was typical of its time. He had written a book in 1957 called *Verkehrsingenieurwesen* (Traffic Engineering). Leibbrand's other important book, *Verkehr und Städtebau* (1964) (Transport and Urban Planning), was compulsory reading for every transportation engineer and he influenced many in favor of his ideas. He was used by many German cities as a consultant to give advice on how to cope with motor traffic.

Separation of transportation modes was positively valued but mainly because the faster vehicles could move faster if pedestrians and cyclists were excluded (Leibbrand 1964, p. 252). He thought that independent pedestrian footpaths were an exaggeration and the upkeep was far too expensive; they were only

Table 3.1 Number of motor vehicles and road casualties in West Germany: 1950–2010, in 1,000 (from 1995 onwards in united Germany)

Year	Motor vehicles	Cars and estates cars	Killed	Injured
1950	2,368	598	6.3	150.4
1956	5,897	2,136	13.4	383.1
1960	8,004	4,490	14.4	455.0
1966	13,147	10,302	16.9	456.8
1970	16,783	13,941	17.5	360.1
1974	20,424	17,341	13.8	317.6
1978	21,611	21,212	13.4	367.0
1982	28,158	24,105	10.6	348.1
1986	31,367	26,917	8.1	333.8
1990	35,554	30,685	7.1	333.0
1995	47,267	40,404	8.5	379.5
2000	51,609	42,324	7.5	504.1
2005	54,520	45.376	5.4	433.4
2010	50,902	42,301	3.6	371.2
2012	51,735	42,928	4.0	392,4

Sources: Der Bundesminister für Verkehr 1974, pp. 110–111, 117; Der Bundesminister für Verkehr 1990, pp. 126–127, 142; Bundesverkehrsministerium 1997, pp. 140, 163; Bundesministerium für Verkehr, Bau und Stadtentwicklung 2012, pp. 132–133, 157 (the accident figures are from 2011).

necessary if motor traffic was really 'disturbing', though no definition was given as to what was meant by disturbing. He pointed out that the word 'pedestrian city' was 'downright absurd' because a town cannot exist without motor traffic. The best retailing locations were the major motor traffic routes (ibid, pp. 264–265).

He and others seriously believed that car use in the city center was crucial for its economic health. No research on this topic was carried out. It was simply a question of belief not knowledge. Concern was expressed that urban areas that were difficult to reach by car would lose their value and become slums (Steiner, Guther, Leibbrand 1960, p. 50). Leibbrand was convinced that without motor traffic the death of a city was unavoidable. He gave as an example *Regensburg*,[7] whose narrow street network could not cope with motor traffic. He wrote:

> The narrow lanes of medieval Regensburg are motor traffic hostile. Large parts of the historic center already show signs of frightening decline. If it is to be saved then more traffic has to enter.
>
> (Leibbrand 1964, p. 100)

Others were openly against any kind of pedestrianization. *Reindl* (1961) wrote that:

> pedestrianization is seen by some as the panacea but in reality it implies a bankrupt declaration of existing traffic regulations. Obviously pedestrians will be in favor but one has to consider that streets have not been made for pedestrians but for wheeled traffic. In the age of motor vehicles it would be anachronistic not to allow cars on the streets . . . Pedestrian areas have also

to be denied because of psychological reasons. They educate people to behave carelessly with traffic and therefore sabotage all the efforts of road safety.

(p. 3)

It is interesting that the psychological reason quoted above is used even today not to build car-free housing estates.

Car Restrictions in City Centers

Already in the 1950s, complaints about traffic congestion and the lack of parking spaces became an even more serious problem in the city centers than it had been in the 1930s and 1940s. The majority of road transportation engineers believed that relief could be found in one-way streets, arcades, construction of bridges and tunnels for pedestrians, investment in public transportation and radical street widening and more road building.

A few transportation experts simply accepted that city centers would never be able to cope with the future demand of the motor traffic if one was not willing to sacrifice the city center to car use, for instance Hollatz, Tamms and Körte.[8]

Hollatz (1954) thought that it was crucial that through traffic was kept out of city centers. He could not imagine designing city center streets which would eliminate one-fifth of the city center housing area in order to have enough road space. Such estimates were carried out for Hamburg (but similar calculations are known for Hanover and Munich). He was strongly in favor of large-scale pedestrianization in the city center (pp. 60–62).

Körte (1958) wanted to construct a wide orbital road around the city center. The additional space needed could come from the inner-city areas, which were in need of urban improvement. Major radial roads would end at this ring road. The majority of parking spaces were to be located next to the major city center ring road (it was a very similar idea as the Meitinger Plan in Munich – see above). The city center was for him an area in which the pedestrian would have priority and pedestrian areas and quiet shopping streets would be part of it (ibid, p. 42). He was also for a strict street classification, which was very differentiated with reference to residential streets, such as residential collectors, residential streets, residential paths and cul-de-sacs (ibid, p. 45). The official road classification made by the 'Sachverständigen Kommission' in 1965 left only one classification for residential streets.

Tamms (1961) was of the opinion that cars searching for parking spaces should not even be allowed to enter the city center, and suggested park and ride, and kiss and ride systems, like in the United States (pp. 7–8). He believed that the streets could not indefinitely be improved. Nevertheless, he was in favor of constructing a large overall street network (ibid, p. 30). But he too was in favor of pedestrian areas in the city center (ibid, p. 46).

Deselaers (1955) was also critical toward motor vehicle use. He questioned the motivation for wide streets in the town centers in order that cars could drive faster than 40kph, and that the car owners have their parking spaces as close as possible to the shops. He argued that it was not necessary to narrow down sidewalks and cut down trees. He accused planning departments of valuing motor vehicle speed more highly than safety, peaceful living, walking and the gardens in front of houses. Residential and shopping streets needed to be changed into living streets by narrowing down the carriageways, and by creating play streets in residential areas (ibid, p. 510).

The beginning of small-scale pedestrianization

Despite or because of the large-scale road building investments, pedestrianization in the city centers took place from a very early stage. These schemes were also the result of ideas and concepts that had floated decades before. For instance, *Kiel* had planned in 1946 to take the motor traffic out of the city center and to implement pedestrianized streets. The plan also included a wide green belt around the city center and a pedestrian network, which would have connected the green areas outside with the shopping center (Mäcke 1977, p. 27). These ideas combined with an acute problem of road space in most city centers resulted in the introduction of pedestrianization very quickly in the postwar years.

Wilhelmshaven (100,000 inhabitants), *Lippstadt* (40,000 inhabitants) and *Bonn* (280,000 inhabitants) were the first cities that closed city center streets at least on some days during the week between 1945 and 1948 (Monheim 1975, pp. 107, 173, 238). In all three cases, the pedestrianized streets were much larger than the 300m Leibbrand had suggested. At that time, only *Kassel* built a modern pedestrian precinct in the city center. This was very much in contrast with what was happening in Britain and the United States; there the pedestrian precinct was the primary form of pedestrianization.

In 1955, 21 cities already had traffic-free streets but these early pedestrianized streets were short, on average about 400–900m (about 0.3–0.6 miles) (Monheim 1980, pp. 44–55, 70). Most cities that closed streets to car traffic were located in North Rhine-Westphalia, and some were cities from neighboring states. The reason was primarily that North Rhine-Westphalia was at that time very prosperous economically and had one of the highest car-ownership levels. Traffic separation was accepted by many transportation experts and seen as a practical solution. Cities that pedestrianized in these early years were mainly cities that had carried out relatively little street widening in the city center, except for Bochum. None of the Bavarian cities followed the examples of North Germany and the Ruhr area. The first south German city to close a street to car traffic was *Freiburg* in 1957 (Monheim 1975, p. 130) (for more about Freiburg, see Chapter 9).

Between 1960 and 1966, 63 cities had pedestrianized streets (ibid, p. 69). But most cities opted for smaller scale closures and the length of the pedestrian streets was mostly under 1,500m (less than 1 mile); exceptions were *Oldenburg*, *Göttingen* and *Essen* (Monheim 1980, p. 71).

Apart from pedestrianization, no other car restraint policies were used, except the *zone and collar system* in *Bremen*. Bremen was the first German city that successfully restricted through traffic in the city center in a different form. The city center was divided into four cells. Motor traffic could enter and leave a cell by the city center ring road. No access was provided between these cells (Hall and Hass-Klau 1985, p. 52). The experiment began before Christmas in 1960. Although the scheme worked very effectively and opposition quickly quietened down, it was not copied by any other major German city. It was first imitated abroad in *Gothenburg*, Sweden.

Uncertainty about the future transportation policies

At the beginning of the 1960s, there was a kind of helplessness about what to do with urban road traffic. What was needed for the future? More road building or the promotion of public transportation and/or the implementation of traffic restraint? Hence, the federal government passed a law in 1961 that was supposed to answer the most important transportation issues.

The Federal Law (1961) demanded the setting up of a committee of transportation experts with reference to improving the transportation conditions in local authorities; 23 experts were appointed. The work of these experts started in 1962 and the findings were published in 1965. The group of experts consisted largely of transportation professors, representatives of public transportation organizations, of an automobile organization (ADAC) and of trade and commerce. Only a few of them were known to have a more critical view towards cars in urban areas (e.g. Wehner, Hillebrecht, Hollatz and Tamms).

The federal government had set several major transportation questions, which the committee had to address and to suggest improvements, such as:

- How could one improve the road transportation conditions in local authorities?
- How could private and public transportation, pedestrians and cyclists be better coordinated in order to improve the efficiency and the economic conditions of transportation in general?
- How could parking be improved?

The main result of the report (Hollatz and Tamms 1965) was a compromise but it was clearly in favor of promoting the car. The role of public transportation was emphasized but it was made clear that:

> it cannot be considered to restrain private motor transportation; a rational design for urban traffic was needed. A sensible division of the different transportation modes was necessary, which implies traffic restraint in particular locations.
>
> (Hollatz and Tamms 1965, p. 194)

There were some critical remarks about car use, for instance the warning 'traffic space for everybody' cannot be fulfilled (ibid, p. 193). Only four pages were devoted to issues on pedestrians and cyclists (ibid, pp. 118–121). Overall, the report was written rather vaguely. Professor Gunkel (1965) commented and called it:

> tough and leaden reading in contrast to 'Traffic in Towns' which inspires readers with enthusiastic thoughts. The German report has a puritanical appearance combined with dryness.
>
> (p. 18)

Parts of a slightly more 'radical' version were available and were published by the *Deutscher Städtetag*[9] in 1962 (the author was Professor Tamms). Tamms was of the opinion that the typical American shopping center consisting of a pedestrianized core was not usable for the European city. He was for large-scale pedestrianization and accessibility of these areas by public transportation only (p. 27).

By the end of the 1960s, major public transportation investment had started and more large-scale pedestrianization was proposed. This will be discussed in the next chapter.

Notes

1 A preliminary meeting had taken place in Stuttgart one year earlier (Pfankuch 1978, pt 2, p. 35). The meeting in 1929 was in Frankfurt led by Ernst May under the title 'Housing for the existence minimum', it is quite likely that Catharine Bauer attended this (see Conclusion Part 1); 1930, in Brussels under the title 'Rational building constructions'; and 1937, in Paris under the title 'Housing and recreation' (Rowohlts deutsche Enzyklopädie 1957, Le Corbusier 'An die Studenten – Die "Charte d'Athènes"').

2 Pfankuch 1978 does not mention these cities. He pointed out that the contents of the Charter was strongly influenced by the experiences of the large settlements built during and after the First World War and in the 1920s in the Netherlands (Amsterdam, Rotterdam), Germany (Dessau, Frankfurt, Berlin, Celle) and France (Pressac).

3 There was a huge wave of German refugees from the areas that after the Second World War had become part of Poland and the Czech Republic, and East Germany.

4 Friedrich Gunkel was professor at the Technical University of Berlin.

5 This was in East Berlin where the number of cars was much lower than in the large West German cities—for more about pedestrians in East Germany, see Chapter 5.

6 Leibbrand was professor at the Technical University in Zurich, Switzerland.

7 Regensburg is a middle-sized city on the Danube in Bavaria; it was one of the few cities that had not been destroyed during the war and therefore still had its old medieval street layout (see also Chapter 2).

8 They were particularly important because the first two were later involved in a similar report for Germany as 'Traffic in Towns' was for Britain.

9 Deutsche Städtetag is an association of German cities representing their interests.

reactions of planning authorities and commercial representatives toward them. The book contained street plans of many German towns and cities and showed on maps the development of pedestrianization over time. His second book (1980) contained a comprehensive review of the literature on pedestrianization and pedestrian studies. Details on methods of pedestrian counts, attitudes to walking, pedestrian behavior and the use of transportation modes to and in the town centers were also discussed.

Three hundred and seventy pedestrianized areas existed in 1977, the majority were located in city centers.[6] A survey in Bavaria in the middle of the 1980s showed that out of 151 towns, 82 had pedestrianized or traffic calmed shopping streets and a further 47 towns were planning to implement such schemes in the near future (Monheim 1986, pp. 30–31, 1987, p. 13). Most towns with over 50,000 inhabitants have a pedestrianized area. In general, the largest cities have the longest pedestrian streets; some have networks of over 5,000m (3.1 miles) (Monheim 1986, p. 30). But there are also middle-sized towns which have a large number of pedestrian streets, such as Freiburg, Bonn, Oldenburg, Gottingen, Hameln and many more (tables in Chapter 8 give examples of the length of pedestrianized streets in 2010).

Many town center streets were not completely pedestrianized; they still allowed limited access by cars other than service vehicles but the streets were redesigned in favor of pedestrian and bicycle use, although some were later fully pedestrianized. The town center of Garmisch-Partenkirchen is a good example of that.

Strangely enough, the two largest cities in Germany, *West Berlin* and *Hamburg*, still had relatively little pedestrianization by the end of the 1970s. This was particularly true for West Berlin (1.8 million inhabitants). With reunification significant changes have occurred, but in terms of pedestrian street size Berlin is not the leading German city. Since the 1970s, Hamburg (2.2 million inhabitants) has enhanced its city center pedestrianization substantially and has also been able to combine traditional pedestrianization with the construction of modern shopping arcades. In 2010 the size of pedestrianization is large (see Chapter 8). There is also a very attractive continuous pedestrian route[7] of 11km beginning at the harbor and running along the Elbe.

Since the early 1970s, pedestrianization as a planning and transportation policy has become a well-established feature of Germany's city centers. Urban planners saw pedestrianization as an improvement of the urban environment, which encouraged people to enjoy the newly created urban space. But many traffic engineers saw pedestrianization simply as the 'exclusion zone' of a town. The majority of the town had to be served as effectively as possible by motor vehicles.

Hardly anybody expressed a critical view (except retailers – see below) about the newly created pedestrianized areas. *Dietrich Garbrecht*'s (1978) article with the provocative title 'Fußgängerbereiche – ein Alptraum?' (Pedestrian Areas – a Nightmare?) severely criticized the design of existing pedestrian areas using Hanover as an example. Garbrecht accused German planning departments of having pedestrian areas that lacked imagination and were monotonous. He missed the urban excitement which still could be found in many towns in Italy. He coined the phrase 'When you have seen one pedestrian street you have seen them all' (p. 5). Garbrecht's criticism hit the spot and an important message became apparent during the late 1970s, which was that the big success of

Figure 4.1 Before pedestrianization of the main shopping street in Garmisch-Partenkirchen

Figure 4.2 After pedestrianization

Munich's and Freiburg's pedestrianization was the result of attempts by these cities to take into account the specific character of the historic urban structure. But it was also true that even large-scale pedestrianization did not reduce the dominance of motor vehicle use in the remaining parts of the urban areas.

Garbrecht (1981) was of the opinion that little thought was given to pedestrian facilities. He wanted a pedestrian network that was as comprehensive as the street network for cars. In urban areas, wider sidewalks were needed so that benches could be provided and people had plenty of space to stand together, chat and sit down if they wished. He missed open spaces and play areas. Residential streets had to become 'living streets' again for all road participants, especially for the pedestrians and children. He concluded that urban areas would be improved considerably if they were designed in a more pedestrian-friendly manner; thus many car trips could be substituted by walking. It was important that walking in towns became a pleasure. Promoting walking would result in more 'humanity' in the areas we live in and in towns in general (pp. 208–210). His thoughts and ideas are still a major issue at the time this book is published.

The rediscovery of the pedestrian and with it the interest in environmentally improved city centers and residential areas was expressed in a number of major national and international publications, which flooded the German market by the end of the 1970s, such as *Peters'* book *Die Fußgängerstadt* (The Pedestrian City) in 1977 or *Uhlig's* book, *Die fußgängerfreundliche Stadt* (The Pedestrian Friendly City) in 1979.

It was fairly quickly established that pedestrianized areas were good not only for pedestrians, but also (and this was previously unknown) for the turnover of shops, cafés and restaurants, although it was often difficult initially to convince the traders of this. In addition, a number of other advantages became apparent, for example pedestrianized areas were good for tourism and leisure.

In 1978, the Research Institute of Trade (FfH) published its findings on the impact of pedestrianization on retailing. It compared 1,066 businesses in the pedestrianized streets of 11 towns of varying population size with streets located outside the pedestrianized areas (750 businesses). Different types of business were included:

• retailing
• restaurants
• pubs
• hotels
• handicraft businesses and other service sector firms.

Table 4.1 shows the overwhelmingly positive impact on retailing with an average increase of 83% compared with only 20% outside the pedestrianized streets. An adverse factor was the increase in rents and property prices within pedestrianized streets. Even after taking account of the growth in these costs, 47% of the businesses inside the pedestrianized area reported a rise in profits and 16% reported a decline. Outside the pedestrianized area 32% reported a boost in profits and 19% a decline.

Further research published by the German Chamber of Commerce (Industrie- and Handelskammer) in 1979 included 233 local authorities and 331 pedestrianized areas. Businesses in 141 pedestrianized streets experienced an increase in turnover, 24 said there was no change and five saw a reduction. In the streets outside, 24 observed some growth, 75 had no change and 20 experienced a drop in turnover, but rent per sqm add to costs in most of the 110 researched pedestrianized streets, 30 streets faced no change and two a decline (Hass-Klau 1993, pp. 22–28).

Surveys ten years later in three middle-sized towns (Hamelin, Gottingen and Freiburg) revealed similar results. There were 71% of the traders who thought pedestrianization had a positive effect on retailing and in Freiburg there were 85% of this opinion. Only 5% in Freiburg believed pedestrianization was bad for trade and in Gottingen and Hamelin 10% of the retailers assumed that (ibid, p. 24). These results had an impact on the legal situation within pedestrianized streets. An important court decision was made as early as 1976 that concluded that pedestrianization created economic advantages for the owners, and because of this, the owners had to contribute to the cost of its implementation.

Table 4.1 Effect of pedestrianization on turnover in percent

Type of business	Increase	Decline	No change
Within ped. streets			
Retailing	83	3	14
Hotels	28	8	64
Restaurants	63	1	36
Outside ped. streets			
Retailing	20	17	63
Hotels	20	2	78
Restaurants	25	5	70

Source: Hass-Klau 1993, pp. 21–31

Traffic Calming: Ideas and Practice

Around the same time when many city centers had been pedestrianized on a larger scale, local resident associations of various political colors were formed in many towns to fight against new road proposals and to demand the reduction of cars in 'their' residential streets. In order to fight seriously against new road proposals, resident associations had to get advice or to employ transportation experts. The more radical and forward-thinking urban planners and traffic engineers would support such groups and call for a radical change of the existing planning and transportation policies. They pointed out that even large-scale pedestrianization and newly built public transportation systems had not stopped the deterioration of the urban environment as a whole, and that pedestrianization was only the sweetener for the fully motorized city most traditional transportation planners were aiming for.

The environmental argument to reduce road building and motor vehicle use was strengthened by the oil crises of the mid-1970s. Yet none of the established political parties showed any great interest in environmental issues, thus a new party, the Greens, emerged in 1977 (Kiper 1983, p. 164).[8]

The request for a major rethink in the urban areas was also supported by research and statistics. It clarified the way in which substantial socio-economic change had taken place in the majority of German cities. There was primarily the issue of out-migration of residents, which had started approximately from the middle of the 1960s, and somewhat later the out-migration of jobs from the densely built-up urban areas not only into the suburbs but also, much more worrying for the local authorities, into the region. This has had an effect on the income of local authorities, which mainly comes from business taxes.

Apel's research (1971) on the adverse effects of car traffic on the environmental quality of urban streets highlighted that substantial motor traffic was one of the reasons why many residents moved out of housing areas. This was broadly interpreted as *unfavorable housing and living conditions* by the Federal Ministry of Regional Planning, Housing and Urban Development (BMBau) in various reports.[9] Some civil servants who were involved in urban regeneration in the BMBau increasingly showed an interest in road transportation and car issues. However, road transportation was under the supervision of the Federal Ministry of Transport, and this gave rise to potential conflicts.

The improvement of residential streets became part of the whole process of regeneration and it was increasingly seen as important to create *livable* streets (*Wohnstraßen*) – instead of *'motor vehicle'* streets. Such streets would give equal rights to pedestrians, children and cyclists. The adverse effects of car use, specifically with reference to densely built-up urban areas, were stressed and classified into several major nuisances: noise, pollution, high speed, severance and an increased number of accidents.

The BMBau publication *Verkehrsberuhigung: Ein Beitrag zur Stadterneuerung* (Traffic Calming: a Contribution to Urban Development) opened the discussions about a newly created phrase *traffic calming* (BMBau 1979). It was not known where it came from, who used it first and no official definition existed. The importance of the publication lay in the fact that what had been researched and discussed by many planners before, now received an official acknowledgment. It repeated the main message, which was that urban regeneration consisted of more than modernizing and improving the housing stock. The quality of life was dependent on its surroundings, and that included among other things the quality of streets. It continued to point out that urban streets had lost their original character, their social function and their role in providing facilities for the weaker road participants. The main function left for these streets was to cater for motor vehicles.

The report included articles on several major urban transportation issues, such as the need for a general new orientation of road transportation, stronger promotion of public transportation, significant improvements of road safety with new street layouts, and, particularly important, the legal framework for their implementation. The whole range of these questions was then subsumed under the heading of traffic calming.

The publication by *Pfundt* et al (1975), *Verkehrssicherheit neuer Wohngebiete* (Road Safety in new Housing Areas), became important. The authors had studied road safety in newly built housing areas and came to the conclusion that the separation of transportation modes (pedestrian, cyclist and motor traffic) was crucial to improve road safety. They established that a clear street hierarchy was needed, containing short cul-de-sacs. Motor traffic should be concentrated into major roads and public transportation stops should be accessible from a pedestrian network. As a whole, their findings were not something outstandingly new; they had been written about and believed in by many traffic engineers and planners for decades, but for the first time there had been statistical evidence that street design influenced road safety.

The German concern about pedestrian safety was also expressed by the opening of a new research department on road safety in the Federal Research Institute (BASt) of the Federal Ministry of Transport in 1972.

Even in the early 1980s, 'traffic calming' remained a vague concept. Some experts included a whole range of alternative urban transportation policies; others saw it as a new design form or simply as engineering measures to reduce motor vehicle speeds in residential streets. A more theoretical justification for traffic calming came from Britain. The concept of *Buchanan's environmental areas* was used in academic and political arguments for applying traffic calming. The practical experience of how these livable streets could be designed came from the Netherlands, where since the end of the 1960s a new street layout, called *Woonerven*, had been practiced.

The first articles and discussions about the Dutch *Woonerven* and their applicability appeared in the German planning and transportation journals by the end of the 1970s, though several transportation planners had studied Woonerven in the Netherlands before (Kahmann 1979). In 1976, two German planners and a traffic engineer (*Eichenauer, von Winning* and *Streichert* (1978)) received a contract from a small suburb of Munich (*Unterhaching*) to improve the existing street layout. They travelled to Delft and were convinced that the Dutch Woonerven could be applied in German towns. A research grant[10] helped them to carry out surveys on the effects such *Wohnstraßen* (living streets) would have in Unterhaching on a whole range of aspects, such as road user behavior, accidents and changes of noise and speed level of motor traffic. Over 9,000sqm of road surface were rebuilt (p. 3).

The major research questions were:

- Are the risks for road participants greater when roads are rebuilt to mixed use?
- What effect does mixed use have on motor noise?
- How do road users behave in these redesigned streets?

The results were surprising, and they were not what skeptical traffic engineers had forecast. The redesigned roads had less through traffic but far more pedestrians on the streets, they stayed there longer and more communication took place. All road participants felt more secure and they took more notice of each other. Accidents did not, as predicted, increase; they actually declined, although the number of road conflicts stayed the same, no dangerous behavior by car drivers was noticed. The reduction of the average speed varied according to the change of the road surface, and motor noise had declined because of the lower speeds.

At the end of 1976, a large-scale traffic calming project in residential areas was launched in *North Rhine-Westphalia*. The objective was to improve traffic conditions in local authorities by modifying physical road design (Woonerven and related measures) with newly developed traffic signs which, combined together, were supposed to be able to improve the living quality in residential areas. The specific aims were to:

- improve road safety
- reduce through traffic
- achieve slower speeds
- create more open spaces and
- provide more trees, shrubs and flower beds for the areas.

The chosen streets were not to exceed more than 500 motor vehicles hourly, during peak hours (Der Minister für Wirtschaft, Mittelstand und Verkehr des Landes Nordrhein-Westfalen 1979, p. 14). *Before and after* studies were carried out. Thirty residential areas were selected of which 13 were intensively redesigned, others partially. Funds were provided by the ministry and the local authorities themselves. The criteria chosen in the 'before and after' survey were:

- traffic volumes
- motor vehicle speed
- behavior of motor drivers, pedestrians and children
- quality of the urban environment, which included changes in the safety level (number of accidents, severity of accidents), accessibility, noise, and acceptance by the residents.

The measures ranged from cul-de-sacs, one-way streets, loops, totally re-designed streets (mixed use), partial change of street character in the form of road humps, raised road junctions, bottlenecking, sharp bends in the form of car parking spaces at a right angle to the right of way, experimental traffic signs, new layout of parking spaces, planting of trees, etc. In most cases a combination of different measures was applied.

The results were extremely encouraging. The decline in the number of accidents by 20% was important but the decline in the number of severe accidents by more than 50% was crucial (ibid, p. 37). Through traffic was discouraged if a number of combined measures were used, but loops and barriers were not seen as ideal because they increased the length of car journeys. There was also a notable decline both in the noise level (ibid, p. 45) and in traffic speed, though there were differences according to the measures applied (ibid, p. 32).

A third research project took place in *Berlin Charlottenburg*.[11] The results of North Rhine-Westphalia, Unterhaching and Berlin-Charlottenburg turned traffic calming overnight into an acceptable transportation policy and 1979 can be regarded as the year in which traffic calming really came into vogue. By 1979 already 96 traffic calmed areas were recorded, about 67 were implemented in high-density housing areas built at the turn of the 19th century (Glotz 1979, p. 45). One of the important learning processes of these early years was that traffic calming in one street would push unwanted traffic into parallel streets. It was thought that the problem could be overcome by an area-wide approach to traffic calming. By 1980 the pressure for traffic calming had become so strong that a new traffic sign (Z *325/326 StVO*) was implemented.

In 1980 an *area-wide traffic calming project* was launched in cooperation with four ministerial departments.[12] The research included 'before and after' studies with control areas, where no measures were implemented. Substantial financial and practical commitment was asked for by the local authorities but financial help was also given by the Federal Ministry of Regional Planning, Housing and Urban Development (BMBau). Five towns and cities of different size and structure and one village were selected. The areas to be treated by traffic calming measures were much larger than in North Rhine-Westphalia and they included major roads and shopping areas.

The following places were selected:

- *West Berlin* (2.5 million): a high-density housing area – *Moabit* built around 1900, containing 30,000 people.
- *Mainz* (190,000 inhabitants) located in Rhineland Palatinate, it included an area of 15,000 people and consisted of a mixture of an old village and modern housing of 610 hectares.
- *Esslingen* (90,000 inhabitants) located in Baden-Württemberg, in a housing area near the city center with 11,000 inhabitants.
- *Buxtehude* in Lower Saxony (33,000 inhabitants) wanted to implement traffic calming in about one-third of the town, involving 10,000 inhabitants.
- The city center of the Bavarian city of *Ingolstadt* (91,000 inhabitants).
- The small historic village of *Borgentreich* with 2,300 inhabitants in North Rhine-Westphalia (BfLR, BASt, UBA 1983).

The 'before' research was mostly carried out over 1982–1983, though there were some delays in a few towns. The 'after' research took place between 1987 and

1988. The South German towns (Mainz, Ingolstadt and Esslingen) delayed the program, some because of political rows and others because of financial bottlenecks, or both.

The first results were published in 1985 and 1988 for the Northern German towns and in 1990 for the South German towns. Similar results were achieved in both parts of the country (BfLR, BASt, UBA 1985, 1988). They showed, for instance in Buxtehude, a substantial reduction in the number of severe injuries. The assumed accident costs declined from about €3 million to €1.9 million (Fiebig and Horn 1988, p. 103). As in previous studies, the main outcome was that traffic calming had positive effects on reducing noise, pollution and speed levels of motor traffic and it was supported by the residents.

A survey instigated by the DIFU (German Institute for Urban Affairs) remarked that out of 127 towns, 98 had implemented traffic calming in 1988. The DIFU report concluded that most of the existing traffic calming measures were still isolated, covering only a few streets, but in 26 towns area-wide traffic calming had been implemented. Another important survey carried out by the Deutsche Städtetag (Organization of German Cities) concluded in 1985 that increasingly a high interest in improving not only residential but also major urban roads was expressed. The 63 towns out of 137 that participated in the survey had already started to plan changes to major roads. Apart from increasing road safety, the second most important objective was improvement of the urban quality in these streets (BMBau 1986, p. 9; 1988).

Conflicts about 30kph (20mph) Speed Limits and other Disagreements

From the beginning of the 1980s, active discussions took place about the costs these traffic calmed streets imposed on local authorities and the time period it would take to cover most streets with such measures. One of the major objectives in implementing traffic calming – to improve the pedestrian environment – was mostly forgotten. Therefore many local authorities abandoned designing Woonerf-type streets and experimented with selected measures, which would reduce motor vehicle traffic speed but not automatically reduce traffic volumes. This form of street design would still come under the newly implemented traffic sign (Z325/326 StVO) dating from 1980. However, other local authorities had not carried out any changes on the road surface at all but simply put up 30kph speed limit signs in residential areas. *Hamburg* and *Buxtehude* had started to implement such speed limit signs in 1983. By 1987, 557 speed limit areas could already be counted in Hamburg covering over 1,000km of streets (Runge 1984; Morlock 1987).

Soon many other towns followed the Hamburg example, often simply because it was cheap to put up a traffic sign and the residents could not accuse the local transportation departments of failing to act. In March 1985 the federal government gave the 30kph traffic sign a trial period up to December 1989. The regulation was made permanent in 1990. Many professional discussions focused from 1985 onwards on the issue of whether the 30kph traffic sign alone was effective enough in reducing motor speeds. Most transportation experts agreed that this was not the case and it had to be supported by physical traffic calming measures or be strictly controlled by the police. The Deutsche Städtetag carried out a survey on local authorities in 1986, asking whether they had implemented 30kph speed limits. The result was that the small local authorities especially had done so to a large extent but, apart from Hamburg, the larger cities showed considerable reluctance to implement only speed limit signs (Morlock 1987, p. 593).

The most fundamental attacks on traffic calming were launched by the *retailing* organizations. They argued that it hindered businesses because driving had become more difficult. Not only would customers stay away but also delivery would be more difficult. The BMBau started to research the 'difficulties' the retailing trade had with traffic calmed streets and it was concluded that traffic calming had no directly adverse effects on retailing. There were problems but they could be overcome with cooperation from both sides (BMBau 1988).

Research on this issue was also carried out in the demonstration projects of area-wide traffic calming financed by various ministries (see above), which started in 1980 and was finally concluded in 1992. In most of the towns businesses in traffic calmed areas did slightly better than those in control areas without traffic calming but this positive effect was related to how intensively the area had been traffic calmed (Hass-Klau 1993, pp. 26–27).

Very early on, political differences over the concept of traffic calming developed. There were the more radical planners and academics, such as *Heiner and Rolf Monheim, Rudolf Menke, Peter Müller, Dieter Apel, Hartmut Topp, Reinhold Baier, Dietrich Garbrecht* and many more who saw traffic calming as an *overall concept* which included different but related policies. In their opinion, traffic calming implied a reduction of the amount of motor vehicle journeys and a reduction of road space provided for motor vehicles in urban areas, and area-wide traffic calming included the major traffic roads. However, it was agreed that different policies and traffic calming measures had to be used according to the characteristics of the built-up area, the type of street and the traffic volume. That meant, for example, that in major roads a reduction in the width and/or number of carriageway lanes, wider sidewalks, new bicycle paths and trees could be implemented in order to make the traffic situation bearable and give more space to pedestrians and cyclists.

Yet there were others who saw traffic calming as a selective road traffic engineering policy. This included directing all through traffic into major roads, thus relieving residential quarters from unnecessary motor traffic. They argued that the capacity of the existing road network was very limited, and as a result of traffic calming, further roads had to be built or the existing ones had to be widened (Lindemann and Schnittger 1976, p. 353). The opposition reacted strongly to such suggestions and verbal and written arguments were fought (Müller 1979). Other urban planners and traffic engineers were caught between the two sides and tried to pursue a more moderate position.

From 1979 onwards, the active campaigning of the more radical traffic calming group was successful.[13] The new federal government recommendations included all the various elements of traffic calming in different types of streets. When traffic calming had started, no clear regulations or rules on what were the most effective measures in achieving the desired effects were known. A substantial level of experimentation with different design elements was part of this approach. Assistance was given by several BMBau publications, for instance on design variations and costing. Most controversial became the BMBau publication (1982) *Planungsfibel zur Verkehrsberuhigung* (Planning Design of Traffic Calming). The publication was strongly criticized not only by the Federal Ministry of Transport, which felt that this time the BMBau had really gone overboard, but also by other organizations, mainly because, as they argued, some of the technical aspects of street rebuilding, which had been quite controversial, were stated as facts. *Stadtverkehr im Wandel (Change in Urban Traffic)* was even more controversial; it was produced with great style understandable by everybody (BMBau 1986).[14] A storm of protest arose after its publication and this time several heads in the BMBau rolled and the progressive movement inside this Federal Ministry came to a halt.

Apart from the controversy, which went on at a ministerial level, disagreement also took place in many towns. The first row over street design blew up in *Berlin* between the historians and the planners. New forms of traffic calming had to be implemented in Berlin, keeping the historic character of the streets. Yet there were others who also argued against the massive rebuilding of streets, for instance *Müller* and *Topp* (1986) who asked whether traffic calming was a new form of urban destruction. Their main argument was that traffic calming should start in the heads of car drivers and could only be successful if it was fully supported by governments at all levels (federal, states and local authorities). Physical traffic calming should be applied only as a supporting measure.

By the end of the 1980s, the skepticism of the traditional traffic engineers about traffic calming had still not completely disappeared and many did not want to implement traffic calming measures but the pressure from residents to apply them was forcing more and more local authorities to change their streets. Overall the political climate had by then become frostier and traffic calming was often seen more as an isolated transportation policy and not, as originally intended, as a policy to improve the urban environment and give equal rights to all road users. Because of the strong pressure from the residents many local authorities had little option other than to continue their traffic calming efforts. As an official from the Federal Ministry of Transport had pointed out at the end of the 1990s, nobody talks about traffic calming, but everybody is doing it.

Notes

1 *Traffic Problems of Local Authorities in the Federal Republic of Germany* – for more details see Chapter 3.
2 Only Berlin and Hamburg had constructed underground networks before the Second World War.
3 Opening of the first S-Bahn line.
4 By the middle of the 1980s and at the beginning of 2000, three more S-Bahn systems had been added (Nuremberg 1987, Cologne 1991, Rhein-Neckar 2003, excluding Berlin which had invented the S-Bahn slogan and system in 1924 (Schreck et al 1979, p. 179; Falko Schmitz, informal information 2010)). Today a number of large and some smaller cities have, if no real S-Bahn networks, several S-Bahn lines most of which were existing old suburban railway lines, such as Hanover, Dresden, Chemnitz, Magdeburg, Halle-Leipzig, Freiburg, Bremen and Rostock.
5 A good example is Karlsruhe that has started to put its tramlines underground.
6 Since 1977 no complete survey on the scale and characteristics of German pedestrianization has been carried out.
7 In the US this would be classified as a Greenway.
8 The Greens entered nearly all Land Parliaments in the early 1980s and the Federal Parliament in the 1983 election with 5.9% (Statistisches Bundesamt 1988). They gained further support in the 1987 election where they reached 8.3%, which made them the third most important political party. Their political objectives included the promotion of alternative transport modes to car use and a more 'human' urban environment.

The State of Baden-Württemberg had been ruled by members of the Conservative Party since 1952. This changed to a member of the Green Party in 2011 as a result
of a coalition between Social Democrats and the Green Party. However, they did
rather poorly in the 2013 German election where they lost about 3% after getting 11%
in 2009.

9   It was included in the Federal Planning Report (*Raumordnungsbericht* 1972)
     (BMBau 1973, p. 25, p. 63) and again in the *Städtebaubericht* (Urban Report) 1974
     (BMBau 1975).

10   From the Federal Research Institute of Road Transport (BASt).

11   Another important research project was financed by the Federal Ministry of Transport
     and the motoring club ADAC. They commissioned research on pedestrian safety and
     the results were used to make recommendations for local authorities. The main part
     of the report consisted of describing experiences and suggestions on traffic calming
     in residential streets (Der Bundesminister für Verkehr, Allgemeiner Deutscher
     Automobil Club 1977). It justified traffic calming on the following grounds, which are
     still applicable today. Traffic calming reduced:

     • the number of accidents and their severity
     • average motor speed driven
     • noise and pollution
     • communication deficiencies of residents
     • parking problems
     • rat runs.

     The report included ten German towns that had introduced traffic calming measures
     (ibid, p. 44).

12   These were: the Research Department of the Federal Ministry of Regional Planning,
     Housing and Urban Development (BMBau); the Bundesforschungsanstalt für
     Landeskunde and Raumordnung (BfLR); the Bundesanstalt für Straßenwesen (BASt);
     and the Federal Research Department of the Environment (UBA).

13   The existing *RAST-E, Richtlinie für die Anlage von Stadtstraßen, Teil: Erschließung
     (Federal Recommendations for the Design of Urban Roads)* which had been in practice
     since 1971, and had been recommended by the Forschungsgesellschaft für das
     Straßenwesen (Research Society of Roads) was renewed in 1985. The *EAE 85 –
     Empfehlungen für die Anlage von Erschließungsstraßen (Recommendations for Design
     of Residential Urban Streets)* – had this time been worked out by both traffic engineers
     and urban planners of the federal government. This work had started in 1979 (BMBau
     1985, p. 3).

14   It was to succeed a similar publication, *Wohnstraßen der Zukunft (Living Streets for
     the Future)* (BMBau 1980) which had been published in more than one million copies
     in 1980.

5

THE 'BETTER GERMANY'? URBAN PLANNING, TRANSPORT AND PEDESTRIAN-FRIENDLY DEVICES IN EAST GERMANY

Political Background

At the end of the Second World War, East Germany was under the control of the Soviet Union. Under its domination a communist government, the German Democratic Republic (GDR), was formed in 1949. The changes made were drastic. The farmers were brutally forced into collective farming. Production in East Germany was mainly geared toward promoting industrial output and not consumer goods that were urgently needed. Hence living conditions in the East were grim compared to West Germany.

There were administrative 'reforms'. Instead of the traditional States, East Germany was changed into 14 Districts (Knopp et al 2003, p. 47). East Germany had 621 cities of which only East Berlin, Leipzig and Dresden had more than 500,000 inhabitants.

With the death of Stalin in 1953, the new Soviet government forced the East German government to alter its political course, and hope rose within East Germany that there would be a positive change. The political uprising of 1953 started as a simple demand by the construction workers in Berlin to reduce their workload. The protests that followed very quickly changed into a political demand for the resignation of the leader *Walter Ulbricht* and the unification of Germany. The uprising was crushed and the SED[1] stayed in power. In order to appease the population, wages, salaries and pensions rose and the prices of key consumer goods and public transportation tickets were reduced (Schroeder 1998, p. 246). A policy of high subsidies for rents, food and many other goods and services would continue until the end of the GDR. Even so, the continuous exodus of mostly educated and highly skilled people from East Germany to the West continued.

By 1961, it was clear that the end of its State was in sight because of the number of people leaving East Germany daily. In order to stop the population exodus, the East German army constructed a wall up to 3.6m high within Berlin and around West Berlin (168km/105 miles). They also significantly strengthened the borders between East and West Germany.

With a change in power to *Erich Honecker*, a short period of economic growth and an increase in the availability of consumer goods took place. However, this was largely based on an increase in 'foreign' debt (credits were easily obtained from West Germany) and the higher participation rate of women. Table 5.1 shows

Figure 5.1
Berlin Wall

Table 5.1 Number of cars: comparison between West and East Germany

Year	Number of cars in East Germany	Number of cars in West Germany	Cars per 1,000 pop in East Germany	Cars per 1,000 pop in West Germany
1950	75,710	598,000	4	12
1960	298,575	4,490,000	17	81
1970	1,159,778	12,905,000	68	213
1980	2,677,703	23,192,000	112	377
1988	3,743,554	28,878,000	225	470
1991•	5,630,000	31,322,000	356	486

Sources: Saitz 1977, p. 44; Der Bundesminister für Verkehr 1978, pp. 120–121; Der Bundesminister für Verkehr 1980, pp. 105, 122–123; Der Bundesminister für Verkehr 1992, pp. 132–133; destatis.de, accessed 24.2.11

*Since 1990 Germany has been unified.

the level of car ownership in both countries and per 1,000 population. The dominance of West German car ownership compared to East Germany is overwhelming.

By the middle of the 1980s, *Mikhail Gorbachev* started his reforms within the Soviet Union and he wanted similar reforms in those countries it politically dominated. On 9 November 1989, the four border checkpoints between East and West Berlin opened. It is significant that the final breakdown of the East German government took place in Berlin, the city where the GDR State was first announced exactly 40 years previously. In 1990, the East German parliament decided unanimously to become part of the Federal Republic of Germany. A currency reform took place in July 1990 (Funken 2008, p. 229).

What happened to pedestrians and cities under communist rule in East Germany?

'National in Style but Democratic in Content': The First Housing Projects and their Pedestrian Streets

After the horrors of the Second World War, a vision of a new type of city was in the heads of many planners and architects in the newly formed German Democratic Republic (GDR). The first reconstruction plan – the *Kollektivplan* – of the undivided City of Berlin by *Hans Scharoun* (1893–1972) in 1946/47 included the total demolition of the remaining housing stock and the complete reconstruction of major parts of Berlin. It was in fact a linear city and such city design was the most favored in Russia during the late 1920s.[2]

In 1931, Joseph Stalin (1879–1953) changed town planning to a different direction. It is not clear why Stalin influenced town planning so late as he had already become the unchallenged leader by 1928. Modern architecture was seen as being bourgeois and 'traditional' architecture became the basis of the Soviet Union construction style. Although the physical architecture was affected by the change in ideology, the planning principles of Western architects were not really touched. This was the same under Adolf Hitler (see Chapter 2). Many ideas first put into practice by Ernst May, for example the neighborhood facilities within a housing block and some of the ideas by Miljutin or Le Corbusier, were used in the Moscow Plan of 1935.

A mixture of a 'new' architectural style and well-established 'Western' concepts was the ideological framework that confronted the East Germans. According to Keim and Hain (1995), the *Kollektivplan* of Berlin was heavily criticized in Moscow, especially the suggested transportation provisions. It was seen as being too sterile and mainly concerned with (car) traffic and nothing else. It was described as denying Berlin's own history, and the existing urban mixture of the city center was lost because of the provision for the car. The planners of Moscow were of the opinion that the center should not be designed for the car but for people and for demonstrations (ibid, p. 93).

Overall city plans were great for intellectuals but housing people was more urgent. Hence the first housing blocks, built along the destroyed Frankfurter Straße (*Friedrichshain*) in East Berlin (see below), were *Laubenganghäuser*, also planned by *Scharoun* and built in 1949/1950 (see definition). They were strongly disapproved by Ulbricht (the most powerful communist of the GDR) as not being adequate for a socialist city because they were not impressive enough. The 16 Principles of urban planning,[3] which became the basis of urban planning in East Germany (1950), gave some 'clear' indications of what a future socialistic city (and housing blocks) should look like.

One of the first housing projects built according to these 'principles' was also in the former *Frankfurter Straße*, which was renamed Stalinallee on the 70th birthday of Stalin in 1949; this name was changed again in 1961 to Karl-Marx-Allee. The style of the housing blocks built had to be 'democratic in its content but national in style'. They were supposed to be based on the style of *Schinkel*'s buildings (see below) but were in reality mostly straight copies of the new building blocks in Moscow (Durth 1999, pp. 77–78). The architect *Hermann Henselmann* (1905–1995) built the first housing block (five floors high), which included one high-rise building of nine floors, very close to the Stalinallee (*Weberwiese*). The three-room flats were 96sqm in area and had built-in kitchens. In just under eight months (April 1952), 123 flats were completed. Even today

Figure 5.2
Housing block at Weberwiese

the houses are very impressive but it is difficult to imagine what they meant in 1952 when nearly the entire city center of Berlin was still in ruins. Such luxury was known neither in the West nor in East Germany. If that was what socialism had in store, who would not support it?

Stimmann quoted an article from the GDR with the title: 'Rented Barracks under Capitalism and Palaces under Socialism'. It included the following:

Imagine the picture – of the Stalinallee – a thousand times over

Imagine a thousand times the generous dimension of this street, the technical comfort of the flats, the attractive shops, the quality of the social services, the restaurants and pubs, and you will have an approximate image of the fortunate life in a socialist residential neighborhood of the future.

(Riecke 1954)

An even more impressive housing project followed along the Stalinallee; building started in February 1952 and lasted until 1958. It became the biggest and most important housing project of the GDR during the 1950s (Topfstedt 1999, p. 470).

Several architects, for example Henselmann, *Richard Paulick* (1903–1979), were responsible for the 2.3km (1.4 mile) redesign of the Stalinallee. In total 2,200 flats were planned (exhibition in Berlin 2011). At both ends representative squares (*Strausberger Platz* and *Am Frankfurter Tor*) marked the beginning and end of this section of the street. The buildings actually continued until *Niederbarnim Straße*. The square at the Frankfurter Tor was never built, most probably because a tramline crossed the Stalinallee.

The first 1,000 flats were finished in December 1952. As with Weberwiese, the flats were again large, 93sqm for three rooms, and had all the comfort of the time. They were the most popular flats ever built in the GDR. Similar housing blocks were erected in Leipzig, Magdeburg and Dresden (ibid, pp. 470–473).

The back of these housing blocks was a different world; they were tranquil and contained large green spaces with trees, areas for children and footpaths. These led to passages between the housing blocks and to other streets. This design of housing blocks was not uncommon in Germany and was used by several architects from around 1900 onwards (see Chapter 1).

Figure 5.3
Strausberger Platz

Thought was also given to the pedestrian space in front of the housing blocks. The width of the former Frankfurter Allee had changed from 39m (129ft) to 84m (277ft) (including sidewalks) at its widest. The street runs more or less in an east–west direction. The northern side of the sidewalk is much wider than the southern side. Near the Strausberger Platz the sidewalk at the northern side of the Karl-Marx-Allee – the sunniest side – is about 40m (132ft) whereas at the southern side the sidewalk is about 14m (46ft). The sunnier side includes a tree-lined boulevard *within* the wide sidewalk area. This would allow the workers to enjoy the evening sun.

Although the sidewalk width on both sides varies, the ratio stays about the same. In comparison to the original width of the Frankfurter Allee, the sidewalks were much narrower, about 4m (13ft), including today a bicycle track on the northern side and 4.4m (15ft) on the southern side.

If one compares the width of the Karl-Marx-Allee with Hitler's east–west axis in Berlin, the carriageway alone was 50m wide and the total width of the northeast axis was to be 90–100m (297–330ft) (Petsch 1976, p. 105), then the Karl-Marx-Allee appears rather narrow but Hitler was difficult to beat on most issues.

These houses were renovated in the early 1990s and are today as impressive and popular to live in as they were in 1952.

Figure 5.4
Model of Karl-Marx-Allee, the north side of the sidewalk is much wider

New Towns: Eisenhüttenstadt, Halle-Neustadt and Schwedt

In the Soviet Union the connection between industry and the development of a city was strong and this started as early as the post-revolutionary period. This sentiment was picked up in the GDR in Paragraph 3 of the urban planning principles. It was used to justify the construction of new towns. This was in contrast to West Germany where new towns were not part of a post-war planning concept. The connection between a specific industry and a new town was the model for the GDR.[4] The dominant industry in *Eisenhüttenstadt* was iron and steel processing, in *Hoyerswerda* it was the construction industry, in *Halle-Neustadt* the chemical industry and in *Schwedt* the petro-chemical industry. Functionally, they were quite often satellite towns attached to existing urban settlements but they had independent city status.

The first new planned town was called *Stalinstadt,* later after Stalin's disgrace renamed Eisenhüttenstadt. It was supposed to be a city of no more than 30,000 inhabitants (Topfstedt 1988, p. 26) but in reality it grew much faster and by 1968 it had over 42,000 inhabitants.

It is located next to the small historic town of *Fürstenberg* and construction started in 1951. It was the first socialist city for factory workers. It was designed in grid form and was built according to the 16 paragraphs of Urban Planning Principles (May 1999, p. 141). Through a system of footpaths and green axes it was possible for pedestrians to commute quickly from the housing quarters. Each of the three very wide pedestrian streets (*Erich-Weinert-Allee, Pawlow Allee, Heinrich Heine-Allee*) led to a school, a hospital and a large restaurant (ibid, p. 13), just as demanded by the Charter of Athens (paragraph 37). None of the pedestrian routes had over- or underpasses, hence roads still had to be crossed but with so little car traffic that did not pose a problem.

According to Topfstedt (1988), it was not admitted openly that the original design of Stalinstadt was a mixture of the experiences of German garden suburbs and the housing settlements for the workers of the 1920s and even more so of the 1930s (p. 478).

The center of the town contained a large square and the plan was to connect the square via a wide boulevard with the main gate of the factory. This gate was to be designed in a similar way to the entrance of a palace, which would have been an interesting idea in the true communist tradition. Unfortunately it was never built.

In 1964, the town center was still not completed although a number of buildings had been constructed, such as the town hall, a theater, shopping arcades, a department store and three high-rise buildings (ibid, p. 31 and informal information Stadtplanungsamt, Frau *Haubold*, May 2011). The main town center street (*Leninallee*, today *Lindenallee*) was 55m (182ft) wide and, again as in East Berlin, the sidewalk on one side of the road was much wider, here the eastern side. The east side was particularly used at the weekends and the western side at the end of a working day (Haubold). In later years, there were complaints of too much car traffic in the Leninallee and it was said that 'car traffic disturbs the functions of the society and the relationships between people' (Klement 1978, n.p.).

Figure 5.7
Main pedestrian precinct in
Halle-Neustadt

Figure 5.7
Main pedestrian precinct in
Halle-Neustadt

car parking spaces are now close to the housing blocks and many footpaths
have disappeared and new ones have been built. In a few parts the original
street plan can still be seen. The living rooms look out onto large green and
wooded spaces and the narrow roads give access to the back. The major roads
have pedestrian underpasses. The original main pedestrian precinct is also still
there in the center of Halle-Neustadt on two floors. Indeed it looks very similar
to the town center design of the first and second generations of English new
towns. The lower tier shopping centers have wide pedestrianized streets with
ground floor shops. In 2011, the existing shops catered for lower income groups,
only a post-1990 shopping center offers higher quality goods.

Some of the existing housing blocks were empty and awaiting new buyers,
others have been destroyed. A major road was built during the 1960s and went
from the main railway station of Halle straight to Halle-New Town, mostly
elevated with no account taken of the effect it had on the historic buildings in

the city center of Halle, but knowing the GDR ideology most of them would have been demolished anyhow.

The Town of *Schwedt*, a small town on the river Oder about 100km from Berlin, was nearly completely destroyed at the end of the Second World War. It became the petrochemical center of the GDR. A new housing estate originally planned for 17,000–20,000 inhabitants increased in size to 52,500 in 1989[5] (Führ 2010, p. 62; www.schwedt.eu/sixcms, accessed 17.04.11).

The design for this housing estate by *Selman Selmanagic* accepted in 1960 was, according to Führ (2010), influenced by the three Greenbelt towns built in the United States between 1935 and 1938. He wrote that part of this design was a clear physical separation between pedestrian and car traffic. The new center contained also a wide and long pedestrianized street (pp. 68–69, 83–84). The SED leaders did not notice the US copy because this type of design was not uncommon in Germany (see Chapter 2). In fact, it was the other way round. When the Greenbelt towns were planned in the United States, they were partly modeled on English and German settlements (see Chapter 1).

The Housing Problem

The housing problem in East and West Germany was different. East Germany had not suffered as much destruction as the West. The percentage of housing built *before* 1945 was still roughly two-thirds of the existing housing stock and was nearly twice as high as in West Germany in 1971 (Melzer 1983, pp. 14, 132). But this type of housing was of little interest to the new East German State.

Even in 1971 only 23% of the population lived in owner-occupied housing and 62% of all flats were still privately owned. This was reduced to 54% ten years later and reduced further during the late 1980s but private housing was, despite communism, still an important part of the housing market (ibid, pp. 190, 165). The rent levels were kept very low and normally accounted for about 3–4% of the net income of East Germans. Although price levels rose over the years, rents were too low to create enough income to improve private houses and flats.

It was believed that real progress within a society could only be achieved if the means of production were in the hands of the State, and the construction industry became an important focus of this objective. Between 1963 and 1968 nearly all construction firms were nationalized (Urban 2007, p. 150).

With the increase of housing standardization, the construction of new housing estates changed from locations within the city to the outskirts, as it was cheaper and much more convenient to build there. A total of 80% of all new housing was built on the edge of cities (Schöller 1986, p. 25). The housing design of the 1950s also changed and the large green inner yards with their pedestrian paths disappeared with the new industrial construction techniques (Topfstedt 1999, p. 493).

Yet the number of flats that could be built was reduced because of the high costs generated by expensive public buildings being constructed in town centers. This created anger within the population who were still waiting to move into new flats (as the existing ones were deteriorating). The public pressure became so powerful that the construction of these public buildings, even the half-constructed ones in the city center, was stopped (Andrä 1996, p. 150).

Another big wave of large housing estate construction came after 1970 and these estates were even bigger than the previous ones.[6] But building bigger and bigger housing estates created a growing financial problem. The installation of services and the construction of roads increased the total cost per newly built unit to such a high level that they could not be compensated by the industrialization of the housing blocks themselves. The more newly built flats were completed, the more flats stayed empty in the historic urban areas. The decline of the historic parts of the city became a real political issue (ibid, p. 156). But these large housing estates were not only built in the large cities; they also influenced the smaller towns. For instance, the City of Bautzen had 52,053 inhabitants in 1989 of which more than a third lived in the new housing estate *Gesundbrunnen* (Kosbar 2002, pp. 95–96).

During the 40 years of the GDR's existence, the State could not build sufficient housing for its inhabitants despite the constant construction of new housing and advanced building technology; the existing housing stock continued to deteriorate and people simply moved from the old flats into the new ones. With every two new flats built, roughly one flat of the existing stock was lost between 1971 and 1981 (Schöller 1986, p. 17).

A further difficulty with the new housing estates was that with the increase in car ownership the road connections between the historic city and the estates were not widened or improved, hence despite the lower number of cars compared to West Germany, traffic congestion in the rush hours was extremely severe (interview with Jäschke, Verkehrsbetriebe Jena, March 2010). Some 66% of all local authority roads were classified as either unusable or heavily damaged and through traffic was still using the traditional city center shopping streets in nearly half of all 'county' towns (Kreisstädte) just before unification in 1989 (Pfau 1990, pp. 2, 14).

Table 5.2 shows how little was actually built; whereas in West Germany 6,418km of motorways were built since 1955, the GDR constructed only 481km, even fewer kilometers of A-roads (major through roads) were built in the GDR.

A substantial number of cars ran with a mix of diesel and oil, which increased the air pollution to unhealthy levels. Although public transportation was improved, the East Germans were even keener to drive their cars than the West Germans because cars were very expensive and the waiting time for a new car was on average between 12 and 17 years (www.mdr.de/damals, accessed 6.4.11). Second-hand cars were up to three times more expensive than a new car because there was no waiting period.

Table: 5.2 Length of major roads in km

Years	East Germany		West Germany	
	Motorways	A-roads	Motorways	A-roads
1955	1,374	11,224	2,200	24,400
1960	1,378	10,957	2,500	24,400
1970	1,413	11,003	4,100	32,200
1980	1,687	11,419	7,292	32,300
1988	1,855	11,326	8,618	31,200

Sources: Staatliche Zentralverwaltung für Statistik 1956, 1981, 1989; Der Bundesminister für Verkehr 1975, 1990.

Reconstruction of Destroyed and Neglected City Centers and Urban Areas

The destroyed city centers in the large cities urgently required reconstruction after the Second World War. But large numbers of small and medium-sized cities that had not been destroyed were in need of renovation. Only a few cities were able to renew their historic town centers, such as *Görlitz* and *Stralsund*. The general rule of the State was to neglect historic buildings and eventually replace them with new construction.

A reconstruction law (*Aufbaugesetz*) to rebuild and improve cities was passed in 1950. It included nine cities (Berlin, Dresden, Leipzig, Chemnitz, Magdeburg, Dessau, Rostock, Wismar and Nordhausen). One year later the number increased to 53 and in 1958 the number was reduced again to 11, though even this was not achieved (Topfstedt 1999, pp. 465–466).

According to Paragraph 6 of the Urban Planning Principles, the design of town centers was the expression of a socialist society and they were to serve the development of a socialist community life. That meant they had to be built for political and cultural activities as well as for educational, recreational and material objectives. One of the main functions of the town center was to provide adequate space for demonstrations, parades and cultural activities.

It was not acknowledged what social function these squares and wide streets would have when there were none of these activities. It was also clear that new housing had to be part of the city center, an important objective in the West German cities too but there it was far more difficult to put into practice. In contrast to the West, where land use functions in the city centers were largely taken over by retailing and offices, in East Germany this was not an issue and planning could be done according to the agreed principles of the Party.

After the ambitious plans for city center reconstruction at the beginning of the GDR had mostly failed, a new phase of city center plans started at the end of the 1950s with plans for East Berlin, Leipzig, Karl-Marx-Stadt, Potsdam and other towns. The main street and the main square stayed important but were not as large as during the first period (1950–1955) (Andrä 1996, p. 144). The city center of East Berlin, designed in 1958/1959, was seen as the model for other cities.

Generally, existing historic buildings, squares and housing quarters were undervalued (Topfstedt 1988, pp. 50–54). It was seen as being more socialistic (progressive) to build new instead of restoring old buildings. This resulted in area-wide demolitions of houses often in town centers. But at the beginning of the 1970s, it became clear that the 'socialist' reconstruction of all the town centers was impossible and revised plans for improvements were proposed.

Increasingly, the neglect of the housing stock built before and around 1900 had become an issue because large parts of historic urban areas, especially in the city centers, were simply unlivable. The reader may recall that the housing stock built before 1945 was very high. Hence a move toward restoration and renovation became a necessity.

The real orientation toward restoration and improvement of the 19th-century housing stock started at the beginning of the 1970s. Stimmann (1988) related these activities to the 750th anniversary of the City of Berlin, which took place in 1987 (pp. 5–7). In the 1970s, the city center of Berlin was boring, containing mostly pre-fabricated housing blocks, massive green spaces, the 19th-century town hall and a very high television tower (ironically known in West Berlin as 'the revenge of the Pope' because the glass top showed a cross when the sun was shining), but not very much else. Many historic buildings were still in ruins and others, such as the Royal Palace in Berlin, had simply been demolished as a symbol of capitalism and suppression.

From the middle of the 1970s, when the GDR became increasingly recognized as an independent state, the GDR acknowledged its own history – the Prussian Kingdom. This has always puzzled me as most Prussian kings had been aggressive expansionists and were extremely good at ruthlessly conquering neighboring countries. One would have thought that Prussia was not the ideal model for a socialist country.

The change to more historic values also included the restoration of historic buildings. The newly discovered love for history culminated in the 200th anniversary of *Karl Friedrich Schinkel*, an architect, city planner and painter with an exhibition in 1981 (www.Karl-Friedrich-Schinkel.com, accessed 20.04.2011).

In 1973 the first large regeneration program focused on East Berlin as the showpiece of German communism. It started at *Arnimplatz* (Prenzlauer Berg) and in the following years about 2,300 flats were restored and modernized; this was unheard of in both the East and the West of Germany[7] (Urban 2010, p. 135). Previously, the ideology of East and West German planners had been very similar. Local authorities demolished as much as they could of the old houses, especially 19th-century housing but even houses from much older periods. Admittedly in the West it was more difficult legally to do so. Most of them were not thought to be worth restoring. Originally, the idea in East Germany was that restoration was only to be used to extend the lifetime of old buildings. It was the popularity of this type of housing that led to the abandonment of urban renewal (ibid, p. 131). After the renovation of Arnimplatz, other projects followed (Andrä 1996, p. 158).

In these improved urban areas, small-scale artisans, cafés and pubs reused many ground floor flats, which had been in a terrible state. Some of the buildings at the back and on the sides of these largely 19th-century housing blocks were pulled down and replaced with green spaces and pedestrian footpaths that would be used for short cuts to other streets. Later this was abandoned (Stimmann 1988, pp. 12–13).[8]

Because of the lack of funding, not enough old housing could be restored but the whole restoration program changed the reputation of the 19th-century housing stock, which in the past had been regarded by the communists as an expression of the worst extremes of capitalism. In 1979, a general ban on demolition for all buildings of reasonable quality (still in livable condition) was put into practice. In reality, there were many exceptions but the area-wide demolitions known from the periods before were no longer possible (Urban 2010, p. 136).

Not everybody within the communist party approved of the move toward historic values and many modern public buildings were still constructed during this time. For instance the *Palace of the Republic*, the seat of the East German parliament, was built between 1973 and 1976 on exactly the same site where the Berlin Palace had once stood. Ironically, the federal government in turn demolished the Palace of the Republic in 2006.

In 1982, new guidelines (on socialist development of urban planning and architecture in the GDR) replaced the Urban Planning Principles of 1950. It rehabilitated the multi-storey 19th-century housing block (ibid, p. 136). Although it still allowed the construction of new housing blocks in the town centers, these had to be in line with the surrounding buildings (Stimmann 1988, p. 10). Despite all these renovations, the reality was different, as was shown in an analysis of 87 towns in East Germany carried out at the end of the 1980s. It concluded that the oldest and worst buildings were in the town centers. In general, the conditions were worse in the center than anywhere else in the city. In more than half of the smaller towns (30,000–60,000 inhabitants), fewer than three buildings per year were restored or modernized in the center between 1960 and 1980 (Hunger et al 1990, p. 119).

Pedestrianization in East German Cities

In previous publications, I made a connection between the revaluation and/or the importance of the historic city and the development and growth of pedestrianization. A very similar but even stronger trend was evident in the GDR. The first pedestrianized streets in East Germany were part of modern shopping malls in the town centers – similar to the new towns in post-war Britain. Typical examples were several squares, such as the *Rosenhof* or the *Posthof*, in *Karl-Marx-Stadt* (today *Chemnitz*), built in 1965 and 1966. Newly developed pedestrian precincts were built in the *Weiße Gasse* am Altmarkt and the shopping center *Webergasse* (1964) in *Dresden* or the *Karl-Marx-Straße*, a wide pedestrian street, in *Magdeburg* in 1965. Even by the end of the 1960s, pedestrianization was mostly connected with the reconstruction of new streets, like the *Prager Straße* in Dresden which was completed in 1969 (Andrä et al 1981, pp. 8–10).

Andrä (1996) pointed out that the initiative in the small town of *Torgau* acted as a predecessor to pedestrianization of a different style. There the town and its historic quarters had slowly been improved over ten years. In 1967, the residents of Torgau called all the citizens of the GDR to improve and beautify their cities and villages under the motto *Let's beautify our cities, towns and villages – join us* (p. 150).

Pedestrianization also meant beautifying the town center and improving the historic housing stock and here was the connection to the Torgau's initiative. At the end of the 1960s, the GDR was a grey place, air pollution was high in many parts, everything was organized from the top, and the residents saw their beautiful historic urban areas disintegrating, waiting to be demolished. As money was increasingly tight, this waiting period was often very long and houses stood empty for many years. Some even had illegal squatters in them (Grashoff 2011). When they were finally pulled down, rather soulless prefabricated new housing blocks replaced them. Luckily many of the old houses survived because of the lack of funds.

Changing existing streets into pedestrianized streets had already been part of the urban plans of many towns during the 1950s but these were not put into practice as the main emphasis had been on building modern flats. However, the situation in some towns during the summer months had become desperate.

There were thousands of tourists because the options for foreign travel were limited, and as living costs and rents were low, people had plenty of money to visit other towns. They mingled together with public transportation vehicles, lorries and cars; this had a terrible impact in terms of pollution and accidents, especially in those historic towns with narrow streets. *Rostock* was the first city to change a heavily trafficked road into a fully pedestrianized street in 1968. The example of Rostock had a domino effect on other towns, and pedestrian streets were opened everywhere relatively quickly (Andrä 1996, p. 150).

Pedestrianization in West Germany was not easy in the early years but at no stage could it have had the political effect it had in East Germany. In East Germany everything was determined by the State, cities had no power; they were simply told what to do by the communist party. But the city governments had become disillusioned with the State because no advice was given on what to do for instance during the crowded summer months. Hence cities simply brought out their old pedestrian plans, without asking any questions higher up, and organized and implemented them. Constructing these new pedestrian schemes often occurred at the expense of repairs to existing housing estates. Special workforces were created including the participation of soldiers, sometimes even Soviet soldiers. A powerful movement had developed outside the Party, and this did not remain unnoticed for long. Between 1979 and 1980 no newspaper or journal reported on pedestrianization (Lehmann 1998, p. 88). It was only when Honecker himself gave an interview on the pedestrianized street in the City of Halle in 1980 that the ban was broken and pedestrianized areas were regarded as a socialist achievement (interview with Rainer Lehmann, Berlin, 1 June 2011).

It was these local initiatives which created hope for a step forward in cities. Their principal aim was to restore the historic urban areas. The pedestrianized streets became the instrument for achieving this in practice (ibid, p. 154). Pedestrianization meant not only changing the street layout but also improving and renovating all the existing buildings located along these streets. The old value of the historic city center was re-established and the fear of changing it into a 'socialist' city center faded away with the introduction of pedestrian areas.

Pedestrianization in Rostock was only possible (as seen by the engineers) because additional road space had been created in the *Lange Straße* and the tram route was taken out of the *Kröpeliner Straße* and put into this parallel street (Saitz 1977, p. 182). A similar model was chosen in Dresden and Halle. The trams did not run in the pedestrianized streets. But there were also towns where the trams were kept within these traffic-free streets, for example *Magdeburg*, *Gera*, *Potsdam* and *Erfurt*. Traffic engineers preferred pedestrianized streets to be without trams (ibid, p. 178). This was very much the same in West Germany, although there the trams were often put underground (as they had far more funds available). A new trend to run trams in pedestrianized streets started in the West during the 1980s (see Chapter 4).

In 1969, *Weimar* and *Gotha* followed Rostock, and Gotha in particular had the longest pedestrianized streets in the GDR. Although Leipzig was regarded as owning the largest pedestrianized street network, this was not quite true but opinions varied on what was included. Leipzig has always been famous for the number of arcades it maintained which allowed a considerable pedestrian network between them (Hunger et al 1990, p. 60).

Most pedestrian streets were built after 1972 and that was the same in West Germany. In 1976, 33 East German cities had pedestrianized areas and about 50 more were planned (Saitz 1977, p. 178). Four years later, 120 towns and cities had pedestrianized streets in their centers (Lehmann 1998, p. 87).

Excluding all cities with less than 10,000 inhabitants (because for cities of this size pedestrianization would be unusual), it is evident that about 60% of all East German towns had pedestrianized streets compared to only 32% in West Germany in 1977 (see Chapter 4). The number of West German cities with pedestrianization had further increased by the middle of the 1980s, but the same would have happened in the GDR.

Scheibel (1977) discussed the impact of pedestrianization in town centers, which included an increase in both the number of pedestrians and the retailing turnover (p. 739). In contrast to other city center streets in East German cities, in pedestrianized streets up to 60–85% of ground floor buildings were used for retailing (Andrä et al 1981, p. 16).

Andrä et al (1981) came to the conclusion that pedestrians were changing their behavior within pedestrianized streets. There was more time for everything. Half seriously, pedestrian lanes were discussed. The author was against pedestrian tunnels and bridges to extend the pedestrianized areas when crossing roads with car traffic (ibid, pp. 43–44), in contrast to Saitz (1977, p. 167) who was in favor of them. A notion that was quite often used was that pedestrianization increased *Wohlbefinden* ('the feeling of well-being') in the population. Andrä et al (1981) wrote that according to their experience pedestrianization had led to a positive social quality (which was not defined) and it improved both the safety and comfort of using cities (p. 44).

Feeling well and comfortable was especially important in the GDR where in most other respects (housing, car availability, supply of food and consumer goods, and many other basic goods) the population was very critical and unhappy.

Pedestrianization was also a way of saving existing historic buildings from demolition. Hence it was often mentioned that historic buildings should be used for cultural events and therefore there was no need for new buildings (ibid, p. 20). We see in the GDR at the end of the 1970s a strong connection between keeping the urban inheritance and taking cars out of town center streets. It should, however, be remembered that although the housing facades and houses in the pedestrianized streets were renovated, the neighboring streets looked as poor as ever and the existing houses deteriorated further.

There were discussions about:

* The location of seating areas and how many seats were needed. The principle was the more the better.
* Street art – an art open to everybody – this was very much promoted in the GDR.
* The role of fountains and their importance for urban life.
* How many flower beds and whether trees should be planted or not.

In short all the same discussions and arguments were held as in West Germany.

Again, as in the West, the East German traffic engineers were more conservative and pro car. They wanted to redirect car traffic and servicing vehicles into parallel streets or to build bypasses (ibid, p. 40; Saitz 1977, p. 173).

According to Andrä et al (1981), pedestrian counts showed that the number of pedestrians doubled after road closure (p. 43). In medium-sized towns, 4,000–6,000 pedestrians per peak hour were normal in pedestrianized streets; in large cities the number increased to 10,000 and more (however the peak hour was not defined) (Table 5.3).

Obviously, car ownership was much lower in East Germany and walking played a much more important role compared to West Germany. A study by Socialdata carried out in 1990 indicates that on average in West Germany 23% of all trips were carried out on foot whereas in East Germany it was 39% (Technische Universität Dresden 1990, pp. 3–4).

Without doubt, pedestrianization in the GDR was a very popular transportation policy and more common than in the West. But in contrast to the West, pedestrianization in the East was a political issue, which questioned the core of the existing State. It was the first time that the cities had determined a way forward and not the State. Andrä (1996) called it 'sowing the seeds' for the uprising of the GDR's people against the political system in the autumn of 1989

Table 5.3 A selected number of cities with pedestrianized streets in the GDR

Cities	Size of city in 1,000	Length of ped. street in meters	Number of pedestrians per peak hour	Start of pedestrian- ization
East Berlin	1,129	*	12,000	1973
Leipzig	564	750	7,000	1973
Dresden	515	1,100	7,250	1969
Karl-Marx-Stadt	314	*	6,000	1965
Magdeburg	283	750	6,000	1965
Halle	233	840	10,000	1975
Rostock	225	740	6,000	1968
Erfurt	209	700	8,500	1977
Potsdam	126	720	6,000	1978
Schwerin	116	580	10,000	1975
Cottbus	108	610	4,250	1972
Weimar	63	630	4,000	1969
Gotha	58	1,270	6,000	1969
Wismar	57	1,120	5,500	1974
Zeitz	44	580	5,500	1974
Suhl	42	400	4,800	1977
Weißenfels	41	*	5,500	1977
Güstrow	37	350	3,000	1974
Naumburg	35	240	3,700	1977
Sömmerda	22	*	1,000	1975

Source: Andrä et al 1981.

* No street length given.

(p. 164). He was not alone in this opinion. Keim and Hain (1995) described the human chains around historic city centers and historic quarters that led to significant protests by residents to protect their historic environment (p. 11). The step from there to more massive demonstrations about the overall political situation was a short one, which finally culminated in the fall of the State.

The Change from East to West

With unification in 1990, anything thought and constructed in East Germany was pushed aside by West German politicians, planners and engineers. Even positive achievements were not really acknowledged. Everything in the East was judged by the standards of the West. There was a huge demand for cars, both second-hand and new. But East Germany had terrible roads and often only two-lane motorways. The East Germans were familiar with their relatively slow cars (largely Trabant and Wartburg) and were not used to the much faster West German super models. The accident rate increased dramatically and the number of severe and fatal accidents shot up. Improving road safety in East Germany became a primary concern. There was a need to build more and safer roads and again heated discussions took place, as previously held during the first periods of traffic calming in West Germany, as to whether or not trees should be cut down along roads in order to improve safety.

Trams were another critical issue. Many East German towns had kept their trams, hence East Germany had tramlines even in towns with fewer than 40,000 inhabitants, for example *Halberstadt*. In 2013, there were still ten East German towns with a population under 100,000 that ran trams (Hass-Klau and Crampton 1998). Despite attempts to close the tram routes in these small towns, so far they have mostly been defended successfully. In other cities some networks have even been enlarged, for example *Jena*, *Erfurt* and *Gera*. All three of them are medium-sized towns with between 100,000 and 200,000 inhabitants. Most public transportation infrastructure, including trams, was improved to a high standard, although old tram vehicles can still be seen.

Cheap traffic calming measures were proposed everywhere, but many local authorities only put up lower speed limit signs. Pedestrianization has scarcely grown any further and quite often the West German tourists see them as their 'invention'.

The positive achievements were the renovation of the historic urban areas after unification, especially the city centers, the improvements of the streets, sidewalks and parks. However, the effects of early planning mistakes, post-unification, are becoming more noticeable. There was very early a rapid growth in out-of-town shopping centers, which are mostly an eyesore.

But even more damaging for the existing (housing and retailing) urban structures are the new shopping arcades built within the city centers. The Western dismay about GDR buildings has resulted in replacements by glass buildings, either as office blocks or shopping centers. Most of them are as standardized as the GDR buildings were and they do look as uninteresting as the East German housing blocks of the 1970s and 1980s.

The population exodus from East to West Germany continued but is slowing down. It had been nearly as bad as during the final years of communism: the young, the active and the well-educated population left. Bundeskanzler *Kohl*,

6

THE BRITISH APPROACH TOWARD ROAD TRANSPORT AND THE PEDESTRIAN IN URBAN AREAS FROM THE 1940S TO THE EARLY 1970S

Ideas about Urban Roads and the First Attempts at Traffic Calming

The 1940s can be regarded as the heyday of urban and regional planning with the formation of the *Ministry of Town and Country Planning* in 1943 (Cherry 1974, p. 122). Many important reports by committees and individuals formed the basis of new planning legislation, which changed Britain's economic and social structure substantially (*Barlow Report* 1940, *Scott Report* 1942, *Uthwatt Report* 1942, *Reith Report* 1946, which led to the *New Towns Act* 1946 and the *Town and Country Planning Act* of 1947 etc.). Between 1946 and 1950, a large number of *new towns* (14) were designated, planned and started (Dupree 1987, p. 18). New planning ideas and concepts were developed, not only for the designated new towns but also for the existing built-up areas. Road transportation was seen as a decisive factor in helping to build a *New* Britain.

One of the issues of road transportation policy was still the question of how to improve road safety, as it had been for the previous two decades (for details see Hass-Klau 1990a, p. 40). It was most relevant in built-up areas and it became particularly important in relationship to the increase in both car ownership and speed of motor traffic after the Second World War, though the number of motor vehicles only regained the 1938 level in 1948. Car ownership had reached over three million in 1954 and more than doubled again by 1962 (MacKay and Cox 1979, p. 165).

A new and comprehensive approach toward road building and traffic management was needed. Many criticized the inadequacies of the existing urban road network; it was obvious that it was not able to cope satisfactorily with existing, not to mention future, traffic demands. A Report of the Departmental Committee set up by the *Ministry of War Transport* reacted to the growing pressure by publishing guidelines about the design and layout of roads in built-up areas in 1946. The guidelines included many recommendations first made by *Alker Tripp* (for more detail see below), such as the construction and widening of radial and ring roads, and the segregation of transportation modes (Ministry of War Transport 1946, pp. 21, 26–30). Apart from traffic segregation, road safety played an important part in the guidelines and suggestions about pedestrianizing shopping streets, the construction of arcades and the implementation of precincts were discussed (ibid, p. 32).

Many cities and towns formulated land use plans taking into account the new guidelines by the Ministry of War Transport. All these plans advocated several ring roads (depending on the size of the city or town) and substantially improved and widened arterial or sub-arterial roads. Generally the innermost ring road would run very close to the city center. The basic idea was still to have fast and uncongested access by car to the city center. MacKay and Cox (1979) make the point that the idea that roads should be built to accommodate motor traffic was firmly established during this period (p. 162). One could argue that planners only reacted to what was generally accepted in professional circles and had been advocated for half a century. In fact, *Abercrombie*[1] had already suggested ring roads in his plan for Sheffield in 1924 and again in his plan for the Bristol and Bath region in 1930 (Abercrombie 1924; Abercrombie and Brueton 1930).

It was only after the war, during which some British cities were badly damaged by enemy action, that these plans appeared to be realistic. The models for the road design were the United States. Little was known about the long-term social damage road building could create in built-up areas or about the fact that increased road capacity would in turn generate more traffic, though Abercrombie and Forshaw were slightly doubtful about the implications and concluded that it was impossible to forecast with certainty the effects that such streets might have (Abercrombie and Forshaw 1943, p. 56).

Some of the experts referred to in this chapter also saw the negative impact of motorization. The design of arterial and partly of sub-arterial roads would eliminate any buildings on each side;[2] instead wide green margins were planned and often roads would have the character of parkways. These parkways were seen as the connecting link between the urban areas and the rural hinterland. The limit on parkway design was the cost (Nicholas 1945, p. 55). The most important justification was that these wide roads would greatly reduce both the number of accidents and the level of traffic congestion, which would in turn bring economic benefits. Most planners believed in the separation of trans-portation modes.

In terms of protecting pedestrians from motor traffic, several ideas were floated. Some were borrowed and had been discussed and used already in other countries. They included:

- pedestrianization of shopping streets
- pedestrian arcades and/or
- pedestrian sidewalks at a higher floor level.

Two of these ideas were in part implemented in Germany during the late 1920s, 1930s and 1940s. Small-scale pedestrianization was an acceptable idea if ring and/or bypass roads were built. The idea of physical separation, by which sidewalks would be built usually one or several floors above the roads used by wheeled traffic, was the favorite approach of several French utopian thinkers including Le Corbusier. It was repeated incessantly in the French planning literature. Similar ideas were expressed in the United States and in Germany, largely around the end of the 1920s (Hass-Klau 1990, pp. 18–21).

Pedestrian arcades were not so favorable to the pedestrian environment. They were a compromise between wheeled traffic and pedestrians. The streets had to be widened and the pedestrian sidewalks would be built under the existing buildings. *Thomas Sharp* (1932) suggested pedestrian arcades in city centers to improve access for motor vehicles in his book *Town and Countryside*, first published in 1932 (p. 187).

Another concept, the *Radburn* road layout, which had been developed in the United States (Chapter 1), was strangely enough not well known by British professionals. No article can be found in Britain describing Radburn before the Second World War. This design was acknowledged after Stein's first publications in the British journal *The Town Planning Review* in 1949 and 1950 and with his book *Toward New Towns for America* in 1951.

Yet none of these ideas were put into practice. The most important reason was the powerful role of traffic engineers. For centuries the role of surveyors of highways, who were the predecessors of the traffic engineers, was unchallenged. In and after 1947 with the passing of the *Town and Country Planning Act*, traffic engineers suddenly had as their main rivals county planning officers. The planning profession was largely derived from architecture and ideas about restricting traffic including pedestrianization came from architects and planners – and in the case of Alker Tripp, from a policeman – but only the traffic engineers could put these plans into practice and that was the difficulty, because they had other ideas on what was necessary for the growing car traffic.

London's transportation problems had not changed significantly since the turn of the 20th century. Central London was as always choked with traffic. In 1904, 29,000 vehicles passed through Hyde Park Corner (12 hours) but in 1937, 81,000 vehicles were counted (Tripp 1950, p. 4). At nearly all major junctions and counting points, traffic volumes had more than doubled since 1904. In 1949 traffic had actually fallen by about 10% in Inner London in comparison with 1937, but this was mainly the result of petrol rationing (London County Council 1951, p. 143) and it was not difficult to foresee the future demands for road space.

What had been missing in London was substantial road building, which had already been carried out in other European capitals, mostly in the late 19th century. Major roads had been built mainly during the 1920s and 1930s, but they were wholly restricted to Outer London. Some of them included separate bicycle tracks and independent pedestrian footpaths.

As has already been discussed above, it was not only the volume of motorized traffic but also the number of accidents which worried one profession in partic- ular, the police. One of them, Alker Tripp, had spent his whole professional life (45 years) working for the Metropolitan Police at Scotland Yard. In 1932 he became assistant commissioner and he kept the post until 1947 when he retired. Tripp's main message was stricter traffic control, more road building and a decisive classification of traffic routes in order to protect residential, shopping and working areas from the adverse effects of motor traffic, and pedestrians and cyclists from accidents. His most interesting idea was the demand to create *precincts* renamed later by Colin Buchanan and his team 'environmental areas'.

Tripp's first book appeared in 1938 under the title *Road Traffic and its Control*. A shorter and a slightly changed version of this book was published in 1942, called *Town Planning and Road Traffic*. In his opinion the main weakness of motor traffic was, in contrast to the development of railways, that it was allowed to travel at high speed without providing sufficient safeguards for other road users (Tripp 1950, p. 5).

The problem for him was how to increase safety on roads, which were basically built for horse traffic and not for motor vehicles. He concluded that roads were not yet fit for traffic, thus motorized traffic must be made fit for roads. This implied that traffic participants had to be disciplined by law and regulations until the 'right' (according to his classifications) road network was built, which was based on complete segregation of the different road users (Tripp 1951, pp. 19–24).

Tripp's views on road safety in urban areas were advanced. He wrote that:

> casualties could be reduced very rapidly if vehicle speeds were heavily reduced, and the nearer the speed of cars could be brought to 3 or 4mph the better the results. Obviously, however, so drastic a reduction of speed is not possible; it would destroy the value of modern transportation.
>
> (Tripp 1950, pp. 116–117)

Another interesting quote about pedestrians was published in *The Times*:

> We pedestrians admit that many road accidents are caused by our own carelessness. But we object to the assumption that carelessness should be punishable by death. Even if every accident were directly due to the imbecility of a pedestrian, yet to put to death 100 imbecilities every week is a barbarity which could only be countenanced in an age which frankly prefers machines to men.
>
> (quoted by Tripp 1950, p. 72)

Tripp pointed out that vehicle speeds should be kept low at places where pedestrians and cyclists were numerous but he was in favor of allowing high speeds for motor traffic when they were excluded. When planning new roads, Tripp argued that three types of road should be built. First, arterial roads or motorways. Second, sub-arterial roads that acted as traffic channels, leading from one place to another; here frequency of access was to be reduced to a minimum (no building should be allowed on either side or it should be set back behind a service road). Third, roads for the needs of the local communities; community roads must be designed in such a way that through traffic was kept out for the safety of the people who had access to them (ibid, p. 40). These local roads would give access only to houses, shops and other premises; here pedestrians would have priority (ibid, p. 303).

If these functions were not clearly divided, problems would arise in terms of reduced road safety. He used the example of Oxford Street in London, which combined both functions; it acted as a traffic conduit and as a shopping street, with significant problems for road safety (Tripp 1950, p. 297). This has not really changed in 2014.

His most important contribution was his concept of precincts, which was to become the leading feature of a town plan. Precincts would consist of residential roads that were bordered by sub-arterial (in the later publication he also included arterial) roads. Different types of precincts had to be implemented, such as for shopping, working, residential or for historic buildings. The size of his precincts was to be no more than half a mile at most from arterial and sub-arterial roads (Tripp 1951, p. 77). Gates would be used to control precincts (here we find some of Adshead's ideas) (ibid, p. 80). He wrote that:

> the road layout within the precinct may have to be altered in such a way as to make it deliberately obstructive . . . The broad idea will be to give the traffic a really free run on the sub-arterials and a very slow and awkward passage if it attempts to take short cuts through the precincts.
>
> (Tripp 1950, pp. 332–333)

Tripp enunciated a major part of traffic calming which is advocated today even by conservative traffic engineers. He thought that a major reduction of road accidents could be achieved if sufficient roads of the 'right' kind were built, implying roads that would be segregated as much as possible from buildings and the vulnerable traffic participants. We know how he visualized some of the precincts. They should be like the *Inns of Court* in London.

Unfortunately, he did not propose a wide variety of traffic calming measures, apart from gates and barriers. He did, however, suggest that no treatment of the precincts should be alike and the traffic situation in the neighboring areas had to be taken into account. Tripp's idea of creating precincts in order to protect residents, shoppers and the working population from the adverse effects of motor traffic was most closely followed by Abercrombie. Not surprisingly the idea appealed to him, for he had been brought up in the garden city tradition. All of his wartime and post-war plans included precincts as an important concept of town planning. Other planners also used the idea, largely because it had been included in the manual of the Ministry of War Transport in 1946.

Many of Tripp's ideas were included in the *County of London Plan* of 1943 and in the better-known *Greater London Plan* of 1944, both had been written by Abercrombie. Abercrombie adopted the notion of precincts though it is not clear how he defined them. Despite that, he was concerned about the widespread car invasion of precincts (Abercrombie 1945a, p. 65). A system of arterial and ring roads would allow the planning of precincts for residential, business and industrial areas which should be 'free from the disturbance – noise, dust, danger etc. of the main route traffic' (Abercrombie and Forshaw 1943, p. 51). Abercrombie and Forshaw believed that the planning of precincts would channel traffic away from areas where people lived and worked, and would help greatly to reduce the number of accidents and make London a safer place (ibid, p. 52). Examples of precincts were the Westminster precinct or the university area around Bloomsbury (ibid, pp. 136–137).

The idea of precincts was also used in Watson and Abercrombie's Plan for *Plymouth* in 1943 and in Abercrombie's plan of *Bath* in 1945. In Bath he recommended that:

> between the radials and within the ring, precincts are formed, each of which will be free from the intrusion of buses and traffic which has no business there.
>
> (Abercrombie 1945b, p. 41)

This was also valid for Plymouth (Watson and Abercrombie 1943, pp. 6, 81). As in the London Plan, they wanted to increase pedestrian space by means of an independent pedestrian network and by reducing the carriageways in the precincts and improving the sidewalks (Abercrombie and Forshaw 1943, pp. 50, 53).

Abercrombie's approach to road planning was most sensitive with reference to the urban environment. Some of his ideas, such as the independent pedestrian networks, were reminiscent both of Unwin and of German planning in the 1930s, though the precinct idea was certainly something new. He and Forshaw were very much aware of the destructive effects of motor traffic when they wrote:

> Moreover the motor car was beginning to destroy existing communities within. The danger to life and limb increased from year to year.
>
> (Ibid, p. 112)

Traffic in New Towns and Pedestrianization

In the new towns designated between 1946 and 1955 (from *Stevenage* to *Cumbernauld*), the future level of car ownership was severely underestimated. Even so, transportation planning for the first 15 new towns was based on one principle, which admittedly was achieved to different degrees: the separation of transportation modes in order to improve safety and to a limited extent to reduce the adverse effects of motor traffic. In residential areas this was achieved by having distributor roads surrounding the neighborhoods and service roads for access to housing. In many cases schools and other facilities could be reached without crossing major roads. The typical design in the town centers was the shopping precinct.

It is interesting to note that the street design of the first housing estates had design forms which were common in some countries on the continent during the 1920s and 1930s. Henry Wright, one of the main planners of Radburn, mentioned this when visiting Europe in 1935. He described a housing estate in *Neubühl* in *Zürich* built between 1929 and 1932:

> There are no streets parallel to the rows (of houses) but instead walks (footpaths) run alongside the dwellings, which are entered from the kitchen side. The row arrangement has a distinct advantage over the Sunnyside and Radburn arrangement, since it allows flexibility in block width while the relation of the entrances to the group organization shows distinct gains.
>
> (Wright 1935, p. 57)

He continued to point out that this type of housing block was actually the original housing block of the German architect Ernst May, and many of his buildings had no direct street frontage but were located on footpaths (ibid, p. 87). However, we know that not only Ernst May had used this type of design (see Chapters 2 and 3).

Abercrombie's plan for a neighborhood of 12,000 people in *West Ham* had most houses designed with no direct access to roads, only footways. This type of layout was also used for the New Town *Ongar*, later not designated. Some of the neighborhoods in *Stevenage*, *Glenrothes*, *Corby*, *Harlow* and *Basildon* used a similar design (see maps in Osborn and Whittick 1969). This type of plan became less popular in the later years, and was found, if at all, only in small parts of a neighborhood. *Thomas Sharp* (1940) heavily criticized such layouts:

> The street approach to houses is sometimes deliberately avoided by some modern architects and a terrace or a block of flats being set at right angles to the road and approaches by footpath only. It is argued this is done to avoid traffic noise. To cut off vehicle traffic is a very queer way of planning in a transportation age.
>
> (p. 92)

Many newly built housing estates also attempted to apply design forms similar to the new towns. A well-known example is *Greenhill* in Sheffield (Crompton 1961, p. 210). But, particularly in the early examples of new housing estates and new towns, the road functions for motor traffic were not divided clearly enough and through traffic could easily penetrate the housing areas (Abercrombie 1945a, drawings after p. 170).

The physical separation between vehicles on the one hand and pedestrians and cyclists on the other faded away in the new towns built during the 1960s (Dupree

In one of Buchanan's earliest articles of 1956, 'The Road Traffic Problem in Britain', he already described the positive and negative effects motorization could have in urban areas (p. 221). As in his unpublished book, he showed a great sensitivity toward the accident issue, which he retained all his life and was repeated in nearly all his articles and publications.

His book *Mixed Blessing* was published in 1958. The adverse effects of the car were also unsparingly pointed out, such as accidents, congestion, delay, noise, air pollution, vibration and visual intrusion. Buchanan also talked about atmospheric pollution (ibid, p. 94) and this aspect was later also included in 'Traffic in Towns' (1963) but nobody at the time saw air pollution from cars as a health hazard. Buchanan presented his assumptions to the relevant medical bodies but he received no attention. In a government publication four years later, it was stated that 'no identifiable hazard to health exists' from air pollution by motor vehicles (Ministry of Transport 1967, paragraph 16). This was the official view for many more decades to come.

He foresaw the future of towns with historic and architectural value as places where there would be a 'considerable loss of the door to door value of the motor car and people might even have to walk' (Buchanan 1960, p. 73). In fact, the whole article implies that Buchanan was indeed very critical of cars. This article was not the only one written in a strong anti-car vein. One year later he wrote 'Standards and Values in the Motor Age Towns', which was even stronger in this regard. He pointed out that 'terrible things are coming to pass as a result of the influence of the motor vehicle' (Buchanan 1961, p. 323). He concluded that the pedestrian's environment was of the greatest importance for the motor age and he saw pedestrian segregation as the liberation of the pedestrian. He wrote:

> Pedestrians should have the freedom of the city. They should be free to wander about, to sit around, to look in shop windows, to meet and gossip, to contemplate the scenery and the architecture and the history. They should be treated with dignity and only as a last resort pushed down into tunnels. Discipline is the last thing they need.
>
> (Ibid, p. 325)

His critical views about cars may have softened in later years, very likely under the influence of the other members of the 'Traffic in Towns' team and possibly of Marples himself.

'Traffic in Towns' and its Impact

The team working on 'Traffic in Towns' was truly an interdisciplinary group, which consisted of seven experts, a mixture of architects, planners and engineers. The intention was that the report would be understandable for the man in the street (Buchanan 1965, p. 334). The Steering Group, apart from Crowther, comprised famous politicians and planners like *T. Dan Smith* (Newcastle), *William Holford* and *Henry Weston Wells* (deputy chairman of the Commission for the New Towns). According to Buchanan, Crowther was a big help but the other members were very busy and may not have read all the details. Buchanan (1968) described later that during the early months of 'Traffic in Towns', the Steering Group met during dinners and he alone presented the progress of the work. He wrote about these meetings:

> So there I was trying to put across a new viewpoint about the environment and there were they, well fed, lolling back, cigars going, saying they could see nothing wrong with the environment and what was this chap talking about?
>
> (Ibid, p. 52)

Even so, the Steering Group did not interfere with the contents. The results were, as Colin Buchanan admits himself, certainly not what Marples had expected (Buchanan 1988b).

The report was densely written and unraveled the whole urban road traffic problem and set out the options. These were dependent on the weight applied to each of the following three variables namely:

- Standard of the environment wanted
- Standard of accessibility required
- Availability of financial resources.

One crucial issue was the conflict that was created by cars in urban areas, such as the problem of accessibility, which can be achieved for the motor vehicle but at the same time the damaging effect this has on the urban environment. It was stated that either one restricts the car severely or one accepts massive rebuilding, which had to be carried out on a substantial scale and not as a piecemeal approach (Ministry of Transport 1963, p. 47, paragraph 121). Sentences like the following gave rise to severe misunderstandings:

> If it is indeed desired to have a great deal of traffic in urban areas in decent conditions it is likely to cost a great deal of money to make the necessary alterations.
>
> (Ibid, p. 45, paragraph 116)

There is no doubt when reading the literature of the early 1960s that it was intended to have a great deal of car traffic in urban areas. Thus the conclusion for many was to rebuild Britain's cities in a completely different way, although the report warned about the size of roads and road junctions known from the United States, which would not fit into existing British urban areas. There were some critical questions asked about the need for inner ring roads or the danger of massive road building (ibid, pp. 42–43, paragraph 104–106).

The size and the geography of the city were considered to be important factors governing how much the urban environment had to be changed in order to accommodate full car ownership. It was made clear that in most cities (ibid, pp. 111, 142) three options were possible – for a minimum, medium or large-scale change of the urban environment for the car (ibid, pp. 72–79, 94–96, 111, 130–162).

Car-restricting transportation policies in town centers or residential areas had to a limited extent already been discussed in Britain before 1963 but it was the first time that the different options of restrictions were coupled with the pleasantness, the quietness, the level of air pollution etc. in an urban area in relation to the accessibility by cars.

The most important element of 'Traffic in Towns' was the conclusion that environmental areas had to be designated in residential areas in order to combat motor vehicle traffic. Many elements of Tripp's precincts acted as a model. As Tripp had imagined, the environmental areas would be of different character and the level of traffic would vary according to their function (residential, shopping and industrial).

Overriding consideration was given to road safety (ibid, pp. 44–46, paragraph 113–117). Roads would not only be judged by their capacity for carrying traffic flows but also in terms of environmental capacity, which would be different for residential roads and main distributors. The 'environmental capacity' as a completely new measure for roads would provide both the standards and the limits for the environmental areas. This was truly something nobody had ever heard of before.

It was pointed out that there was some elasticity in the environmental capacity of roads and a metaphor was used to explain it; just as dwellings had some elasticity in the number of people they could house, there is certainly an upper limit otherwise they will become a slum (ibid, p. 45). In terms of protecting the pedestrian, Buchanan and his team favored in some conditions, such as high density of both pedestrians and motor traffic, a complete segregation of one from the other. However, under different conditions, a mixture of pedestrians and vehicles was not seriously harmful *if* vehicles were to reduce their speed and volume (ibid, pp. 49, 51). For shopping areas, pedestrianization was seen as a good concept.

When the report was published it was widely reported in the press, on radio and television. The government accepted Buchanan's conclusions in principle, though later publications made it clear that there were some reservations about them.

About 14 days after the report was published, the British Road Federation organized a conference under the title *People and Cities*. Buchanan made some slightly cynical remarks about the interest the members of the British Road Federation had in people and cities but concluded that they must now be 'passionately concerned' about this issue otherwise they would not have organized the conference (Buchanan 1963, p. 22). The controversy about the report became apparent at this meeting. However, the main question remained unanswered. Was 'Traffic in Towns' a surrender to the car or an attack on it? Marples interpreted the Buchanan Report in his own way, which was the start of its misunderstanding (according to Buchanan he did not fully understand it), when he pointed out:

> It is fundamental to the whole report that it accepts the motor vehicle as a brilliant and beneficial invention. It is in no sense restricting the motor car. All it says is that we must use our motor car to the maximum, and yet be sensible and keep some good environmental areas. We have to face the fact that the way we have built our towns is entirely the wrong way for motor traffic. We want an entirely different type of town.
>
> (Marples 1963, p. 12)

Geoffrey Crowther (1963) commented that people would bitterly resist even the most necessary restrictions of car use. He warned that we may fall into the same trap as the United States where freedom of the car is everything and 'then you have as much environmental standards as there is left over' (p. 25).

Conflicts between *R. J. Smeed*, deputy director of the TRRL, and Buchanan were looming when Smeed argued that there was no need to be so pessimistic about accommodating private cars and he had several suggestions on how to improve road capacity, for example change of vehicle occupancy, staggering of peak hours and smaller cars (Smeed 1963, pp. 28–29). Smeed was at the time already involved in writing a report for the Ministry of Transport on road pricing, researching its economic and technical possibilities, which was published a year later (Ministry of Transport 1964).

In discussing the impacts the Buchanan Report had on Britain, I will concentrate on the ministerial level and on the encouragement to pedestrianize shopping streets and the designation of residential environmental areas.

The main emphasis in the Ministry of Transport did not change even when Labour came into power again in 1964. It moved more and more toward promoting private motor transportation. Buchanan wrote in 1965 that 'the Government is very far from discouraging the motor vehicle' by condoning the construction of motorways, 'fostering the motor industry' and in fact 'setting the seal irrevocably on the motor vehicle as the basic transportation system of this country' (Buchanan 1965, p. 335).

Some achievements were made during this period in terms of road safety, such as the introduction of the 70mph speed limit on motorways, which was part of the Road Safety Act of 1967. (Interestingly enough the present government (at time of writing) is intending to change this to allow an 80mph limit on motorways.) It also included the possibility of prosecuting drivers above a defined level of blood-alcohol, the introduction of compulsory seat belt fittings and annual testing of cars older than four years (Plowden 1971, p. 356).

'Traffic in Towns' encouraged more local authorities to consider pedestrianization of a different kind and a few bold ones actually applied it. It is no accident that *Norwich*, which was one of the case studies in the 'Buchanan' Report, was the second town after Coventry to close a street to car traffic.

The urban planners of Norwich had argued that for the well-being of the city as a regional shopping center, pedestrianization was crucial. It was also seen as the key policy for preserving the city's historic character (Wood 1967, p. 38). Two large pedestrian areas were suggested in the city center, a quite dramatic approach for its time. Alfred Wood, who was the city planning officer, wrote with reference to pedestrianization 'what can be done in Europe should also be possible here' (ibid, p. 40). The truth was that most planners did not dare to go along the Central European road.

Norwich, like many other historic towns, already had several small shopping streets and alleys, which were used by pedestrians only. In 1967 the main shopping street was closed to traffic after the central government had changed the legislation. Before 1967 the conversion of highways was not permitted. It became possible with the Road Traffic Regulation Act of 1967 (Roberts 1981, p. 18). A few other towns followed but pedestrianization was only carried out on a modest scale.

There were plenty of suggestions and plans drawn up which included large pedestrianized areas, for instance the *Manchester Central Redevelopment Plan*. *Liverpool* also had a comprehensive plan for a pedestrian network inside the inner motorway ring (Shankland 1964, pp. 124, 126–127). Other towns and cities, such as *Reading* (1968) and *Leeds* (1970) implemented such schemes relatively early. Leeds, in consultation with the Ministry of Transport and the Ministry of Housing and Local Government, had published an overall concept of planning and transportation, the so-called *Leeds Approach* (Leeds City Council, Ministry of Transport and Ministry of Housing 1969). It included comprehensive pedestrianization in the city center, and about half of the pedestrianized routes were to be upper level walkways (ibid, p. 26). The publication referred to *Essen* (Germany) as the desired example of pedestrianization (ibid, pp. 23, 25). But Essen had never built upper-level walkways.

The number of cities that dared to introduce car-free streets and squares was relatively small. It was later, during the mid-1970s that the number of pedestrianization schemes increased more rapidly (see Chapter 7).

Buchanan believed that the Report 'Traffic in Towns' was more influential abroad than in Britain. 'Traffic in Towns' had some impact in Italy, Norway, the Netherlands, Sweden and Denmark, though the latter three countries were also concerned with improving the environment and had already pedestrianized some shopping streets. In the Netherlands, the *Kalverstraat* in *Amsterdam* had been closed to car traffic before the war (Doubleday 1960, p. 230) and the main shopping street of *Den Haag* was pedestrianized in 1960. *Stockholm* and *Copenhagen* closed some of their main shopping streets in 1962 (GLC 1973, p. 127; Lemberg 1974, p. 96). Sweden had been generating research on how to improve road safety by community planning since 1961 (Swedish National Board of Urban Planning 1968, p. 5).

Buchanan was also of the opinion that the Germans already had quite similar ideas, which in fact is correct. Even so, there is no doubt that the Buchanan Report had some influence on German thinking. It occurred in two phases: first when the Buchanan Report was just published, and second, when traffic calming started to become a topical transportation issue in the second half of the 1970s. A German translation of the Buchanan Report was already available in 1964. Strangely enough it was published by the German equivalent of the British Road Federation (Straßenliga). 'Traffic in Towns' (Stadtverkehr) was required reading for German planners and many engineers.

A Period of Experimentation

As a result of the Buchanan Report in 1963, 'environmental areas' were set up in many British local authorities mostly during the late 1960s. Most schemes were a combination of some form of traffic restraint and housing improvement. According to Appleyard (1981), about 150 such areas were either planned or in existence by 1973. Nearly all were part of the *General Improvement Area Program* (GIA) (p. 154). Between 1969 and 1973 about 900 GIAs had been declared in Britain. Many of them included environmental improvements, such as wider sidewalks, cul-de-sacs, children's play areas, benches, trees and landscaping of the area. The major weakness of the GIA approach was the small size; hence car traffic could easily be displaced into other nearby residential streets (Hass-Klau 1986, p. 14).

The best-known and most successful example of an environmental area in London was *Pimlico* in the City of Westminster. Part of Pimlico was designated as an environmental area between 1965 and 1967. It was an attempt to restrict entry of motor vehicles into the area but to allow free movement once inside (Appleyard 1981, p. 183). Colin Buchanan and Partners (1980) pointed out that the success of the scheme was largely the result of spare capacity on the peripheral roads whereas Appleyard made the point that some of the traffic had actually disappeared. In general, traffic flows in Pimlico were not very high; the highest were up to 250 motor vehicles per hour (Lewes 1988, p. 15).

After the success of Pimlico, *Barnsbury* in the Borough of Islington (London) tried to introduce a similar scheme. The Borough of Islington had published a report about possible environmental improvements in Barnsbury, including not only traffic considerations but also suggestions for housing and businesses. Barnsbury was divided into seven environmental areas, just as Colin Buchanan had advocated. Appleyard gave a detailed account of the political events in Barnsbury (Appleyard 1981, pp. 157–181). Controversy arose between various resident groups in the area. When the first part of the scheme was implemented in 1970, traffic levels rose between 50 and 100% on distributor roads and traffic flows on the internal roads dropped by 25% (Buchanan and Partners 1980, p. 277). But apparently more residents lost out than gained. Appleyard (1981) pointed out that a larger number of people enjoyed lower traffic volumes but people who lived on the distributor roads had more traffic than before the scheme was implemented. Accidents on the residential roads declined by 64% but rose slightly on the peripheral roads (pp. 163–181).

A similar scheme was tried in *Primrose Hill* in Camden Town. The Borough of Camden had suggested an area-wide 'traffic restraining' scheme as it was then called but it was abandoned in 1973, again because of disagreement between different resident associations and political groups (ibid, p. 186).

In *Newcastle upon Tyne* 'environmental areas' were designated (Burns 1967, p. 10) and the *Rye Hill Revitalization Areas* included many interesting car-restraining features, such as a pedestrian spine, the closing of back streets, the construction of playgrounds, and new benches and trees (ibid, pp. 72–73). There were many more towns and cities that had pinpointed environmental areas. The surprising story is how little was published. The idea of environmental areas was not further developed and the real change only came decades later when the discussions about traffic calming and its implementation were shaking long established opinions about car traffic in residential areas.

As a result of the immense publicity of 'Traffic in Towns' but also due to the widespread road construction, many people began to realize what large road programs really meant for the urban environment and protests began. *London* was the center of controversy. The victory of the Labour Party to take over the Greater London Council (GLC) in 1973, and with it the cancellation of the urban motorways, which had originally been proposed decades before by Abercrombie (see above), was the decisive change. Other cities also abandoned their motorway programs, or at least large parts of them (Hall and Hass-Klau 1985, p. 25).

As urban road building became difficult and controversial, the pendulum mostly did not swing in the opposite direction so as to promote public transportation comprehensively, large-scale pedestrianization or any other form of traffic restraint, despite the oil crisis in 1973/74 and the cutbacks in road expenditure by the Labour Party in the mid-1970s. A few local authorities promoted public transportation, for instance *Sheffield*. Funding of new public transportation investment by the central government had been possible under the *1968 Transport Act*, but only the four passenger transport authorities were able to put forward plans for new public transportation modes. Several environmental groups were formed in the early 1970s, such as *Friends of the Earth* (1970) and *Transport 2000* (1972) (Hamer 1987, p. 68). They achieved little to change the car orientation of urban transportation policy according to their objectives but in the longer run they have become much more influential.

Another city that tried relatively early to come to terms with the car was *Nottingham*. The policy introduced in 1972 was known as the *Zone and Collar Scheme*. It was carried out in two stages. The first stage was directed at improving traffic conditions in the city center. The center was divided into four different traffic cells. It was not possible for motor vehicle traffic to move between the cells and car traffic could only enter one cell at a time via a ring road. This policy had been first successfully applied in *Bremen* in 1960 (Hall and Hass-Klau 1985, p. 52). The second stage in Nottingham was to include higher parking charges in the town center, and traffic restraint in residential areas with the introduction of cul-de-sacs and one-way streets. Along the main roads bus lanes were created and buses had priority at traffic lights. This was supported by large park and ride schemes. The experiment started west of the town center in 1975, including five main roads and part of the inner ring road plus two urban areas, one with 11,000 and the other with 44,000 inhabitants. Unfortunately the scheme was not very successful and was abandoned one year later. It failed not only because the public transportation operator increased the fares quite dramatically, but also because the population did not accept the restrictive policies in the residential areas (BMBau 1978, pp. 51–52).

Another development did not help. In 1972, local government had been reorganized. Responsibilities on transportation issues were not only again divided between transportation engineers and land use planners but also between boroughs/cities and counties. The professions which Colin Buchanan and many others had fought to unite were divided again. What did a society expect if one profession was planning the 'halls and corridors' and the other the 'rooms', a metaphor Colin Buchanan had first used during the 1960s (Wood 1967, p. 1)? The result could only be disagreement and inactivity. This, combined with a lack of funds from the mid-1970s onwards, could help to explain a period of what amounted to political paralysis of decision making in land use and transportation planning.

Notes

1   Patrick Abercrombie (1879–1957) was an architect and town planner. He later became editor of the *Town Planning Review*, professor at the University of Liverpool and later at University College London. He also worked as a consultant. He became most famous in Britain for the design of two London plans in 1943 and 1944.
2   This was agreed in the Charter of Athens in 1933 (see Chapter 3).

7

BRITISH ATTEMPTS TO ACHIEVE BETTER WALKING CONDITIONS FROM THE LATE 1970S TO THE 1990S

The Beginning of Traffic Calming

Traffic calming has taken off nearly everywhere in the world in ways which no one could have predicted. It started in the Netherlands as discussed in Chapter 4 and was copied from there and adopted in Germany, and came via both countries to the UK during the 1980s. It fell on fertile ground because Britain had its own history of traffic calming.

I have always thought that the reason for its success was that it is an easy option. It is relatively cheap, especially if done badly. It involves little change in the road layout. It can be dressed up with words, which all politicians are good at, and it can be perceived as doing something positive and 'environmental'. Seen from this point of view, traffic calming in Britain had to be successful but there was another even more important reason.

Since the 1970s, the conditions for most road users had deteriorated. Car ownership had risen from 4.9 million in 1960 to nearly 10 million in 1970 and had reached 15 million by 1980. Although about 17,000km of roads were built between 1970 and 1980, road building was still not fast enough to cope with the ever-growing car traffic. During this time period, car ownership grew most rapidly.

The situation had worsened, especially for pedestrians, cyclists and public transportation users, not only because of the increase in motorization but also due to the size and the numbers of bigger lorries. The number of very heavy (33 to just under 38 tons) lorries had more than doubled (from 11,000 to 27,000) in only two years between 1983 and 1985 (British Road Federation 1987, p. 4). Furthermore there had been a lack of:

- sufficient protective policies for pedestrians and cyclists
- bypass roads
- investment in both urban public transportation and rail transportation
- implementation of policies to discourage car use in congested urban areas.

Already in 1977, the Department of the Environment and Transport had published the *Design Bulletin 32: Residential Roads and Footpaths: Layout Considerations* containing layout guidelines for cul-de-sacs or short-length access roads in the form of *shared space*. Many of the shared space roads were combined with landscaping.

An *Urban Safety Project* started in 1982. It was carried out by the TRRL (Transport and Road Research Laboratory) in collaboration with University College London and the University of Newcastle. The objectives were to reduce the scattered accidents in residential streets and to discourage through traffic (TRRL 1988, p. 1). It was applied in five British towns (*Bradford, Bristol, Nelson, Reading* and *Sheffield*). Accidents were studied five years 'before' and two years 'after'. Each residential area that received treatment had a nearby control area where nothing was done. The applied measures were similar to those in environmental areas in the 1960s and 1970s.

In 1988, the study was completed and the results showed a reduction in the number of accidents of about 10%, which had been the objective. The highest savings were achieved in Sheffield (30%), as it had the lowest car ownership level, and the lowest in Reading with only 4%. The accident savings in Nelson (7%) and Bradford (6%) were also relatively low. The biggest benefit was for the pedestrians and cyclists, but again the savings were smallest in Nelson and Reading (ibid, pp. 4, 6–7).

The *Traffic Regulation Act of 1984* gave local authorities many options to apply traffic calming measures to reduce the speed of cars. Three years later the Department of Transport published a Traffic Advisory Leaflet in 1987, clumsily called *Measures to Control Traffic for the Benefit of Residents, Pedestrians and Cyclists*. The leaflet already included most of the known traffic calming measures that were beginning to be installed in British local authorities (DoT 1987).

By the end of 1987, the Department commissioned a report to discover what kinds of devices were commonly being used by British local authorities to achieve traffic calming. The report by *Dalby* (1988) revealed that traffic calming, as practiced in West Germany, had only just started in Britain. Some of the early traffic calming attempts looked like straight copies of German examples. This could easily have been the case, since several publications had become available during the 1980s (Hass-Klau 1986; Bowers 1986). But many local authorities neither measured the effects of speed reduction nor the change in traffic flows when they implemented traffic calming. Traffic calming measures in *Bradford (Girlington)* showed both substantial speed and accident reductions (Dalby 1988, p. 34).

Initiatives of Local Authorities and Other Professionals

The lack of knowledge about and interest in traffic calming by local authorities changed very quickly because of the growing dissatisfaction with the transportation policies of the Conservatives at the end of the 1980s. It was primarily the senior officers of enlightened local authorities, such as *Geoff Steeley* of Hertfordshire County Council, who changed attitudes. He was a planner by profession and had made several trips to Europe, especially to the Netherlands, Germany and Denmark and thought that the balance between urban design and how motor traffic was handled was so much better there than in England. He was horrified at how road building had wrecked many British cities during the 1960s.

In 1986, I edited a *Built Environment* issue called *New Ways of Managing Traffic*, and upon reading that, Steeley invited me to Hertford (Hertfordshire) in February 1987. His main concern at the time was not only accidents and fast traffic in residential areas but also the future of town centers, especially smaller town centers. He thought that design improvements and a reduction in through traffic could have an impact on the economic performance of smaller towns.

In 1988, Hertfordshire County Council committed themselves to a five-year *Town Center Enhancement Program*, including nine town centers, but traffic calming was also planned in several residential areas and local shopping streets. One of the first towns in need of improvement was *Buntingford.* The historic *High Street* was ruined by through traffic and improvement for the town center was only possible after the bypass was opened in 1987. Although the bypass reduced through traffic substantially, cars were now driving too fast along the high street because of the straight character of the street and the much lower traffic volumes. Traffic calming measures were proposed by the author and at the beginning of 1989, Buntingford high street was redesigned and rebuilt.

Kent County Council was another of the counties that pushed forward traffic calming. The manager of the Traffic Management Policy section, *Malcolm Bulpitt*, was the main engineer in favor of it. He was also in charge of a booklet called *Traffic Calming – A Code of Practice* (November 1990). It was reprinted and revised in April 1991 and fully revised in March 1992 (Kent County Council 1990, 1992). The most common traffic calming measures, even those that had not yet been implemented in Britain, were described. The 1992 edition also included a guide to where measures were best used, and short chapters on 'Signs and Marking', 'Lighting' and 'Maintenance and Materials' were added.

Devon County Council with the help of *Tim Pharaoh* published the first comprehensive book about traffic calming in 1991. It not only gave technical advice but saw traffic calming as a more general issue, for instance how urban traffic could be handled in future (Devon County Council 1991). Nearly half of the examples were from Germany and most importantly the examples were printed in color, which made them look far more attractive than the somber black and white versions from Kent.

Our book was completed in July 1992 and was called *Civilised Streets – A Guide to Traffic Calming* (Hass-Klau et al 1992). Although we had direct competition with the traffic calming manual from Devon County Council and from Kent County Council, our manual was also a great success. In the first weeks after publication we sold 260 copies to British local authorities. We had 1,300 books printed that sold out relatively quickly (more than 200 went to Canada and the United States in 1996). Obviously, we created our own competition by publishing this book but we took that risk. All the various traffic calming measures we knew about were discussed in detail, but there were also sections on area-wide traffic calming, cost-benefit analysis, and critical issues connected with traffic calming, like cycling and public transportation. It was later translated into Chinese and a new shorter edition was published in China in 2010.

During the late 1980s, only a small group of professionals were interested and involved in traffic calming, such as *Tim Pharaoh*, *Philip Bowers*, *John Roberts* and myself. I had several discussions with *Peter Bottomley*, then minister of roads and traffic, who at this time did not see the point of introducing traffic calming at all because, as he stated, Britain had the best road safety record in the world. However, there were other officials in the Department who had a different opinion (see below).

I had already started to give traffic calming advice to various local authorities. The most important project was in Dorset (completed in autumn 1991). The county surveyor at the time was *David Hutchinson* and the traffic engineer who was in charge of the project was *Paul Martin*. We suggested traffic calming measures in three small towns: *Wareham*, *Bridport* and *Gillingham*. The planned traffic calming measures were all European copies, mostly from Germany and the Netherlands. Few British people had ever seen anything like it; they were sophisticated, relatively expensive and there was a large selection of them. The reception we got in these towns was remarkably different during the consultation periods. Whereas in Gillingham the hall provided (the local magistrates court room) was not big enough to cope with the number of people who attended the final presentation, in Bridport almost nobody came. For some strange reason on the last day of the exhibition, a Saturday, suddenly everybody wanted to see it and we stayed longer than planned. We never found out why the residents finally became so interested.

The standardized traffic calming measures we later developed were largely based on the three small cities in Devon. Some of them would today not be classified as traffic calming measures at all, for example central reservation, carriageway narrowing with trees and side strips.

My consultancy was asked for advice in a number of places, for example London (Clerkenwell), Hastings, Oxford, Swansea and Bristol. We did large-scale traffic calming in *Worthing* and several other places in West Sussex. We designed a walking network for *Edinburgh* and suggested traffic calming measures in its historic Old Town.

In England there were restrictions within the 20mph speed limit zones on what type of traffic calming measures could be used and where (see below). That was not the case in Northern Ireland, and when we were invited to tender for an area-wide traffic calming project by the *Department of the Environment for Northern Ireland* in 1992, we were excited.

The area to be traffic calmed was *Holyland*, located east of Queen's University. It had been one of the few remaining mixed neighborhoods, containing Protestants and Catholics. It was also an area where many students and university employees lived. A major problem was that by 1992 it was both difficult and dangerous to carry out traffic calming or any other street projects in purely Catholic areas of Belfast.[1]

In Belfast we were involved in all stages of a traffic calming project:

- project design
- consultation
- technical design of the traffic calming measures, and finally the construction of the scheme.

Inge Nold who had worked with me for many years did most of the legwork. It was a strange feeling when everything was completed and actually built.

Government Action and Criticism

As discussed above, the Department of Transport was very interested in traffic calming at an early stage although it did not actually use the words in its publications until 1992. It was also early in publishing an official leaflet about the *20mph Speed Limit Zones* in May 1991 (DoT 1991). But it was decided that every speed limit zone required the approval of the Department, a remarkable level of centralization. This was a very slow procedure (about 15 months after the initial consent had been given) and was seen by some local authorities that had already gathered experience in traffic calming as simply patronizing. Professionals were also annoyed because some of the people working in the Department clearly lacked practical experience and had no sense that something new and exciting was being discussed and developed. At least, the Department was flexible enough to allow 20mph speed limit zones in areas where accident prevention was not the main criterion. In January 1991, only three zones had been approved. Eight years later (1999) the number had increased to 450 schemes; this was surprising considering the administrative procedure. The schemes were limited in size and area-wide traffic calming, by then common in Germany and the Netherlands, was not widely discussed or used in Britain. The schemes were mostly boring because only few traffic calming measures were allowed.

In March 1992, the *Traffic Calming Act* went through parliament. The Act gave highway authorities permission to construct traffic calming *work* and work was defined as meaning 'work affecting the movement of vehicles and other traffic for the purpose of promoting safety or preserving or improving the environment through which the highway runs' (British Parliament 1992, Schedule I (2b).

However, it was the secretary of state who formulated the regulations, such as the dimensions and location of traffic calming work, the placing of signs and the imposing of any requirements as to consultation and publicity. Under this Act, local authorities had little freedom to implement traffic calming measures of their own.

In the same year, the Department wanted to commission traffic calming research. The intended research was to be in small towns which were in need of a bypass. After the bypass was built, the existing main road running through the town was to be traffic calmed, to reduce the speed there and prevent a build-up of through traffic. If traffic calming could be used as a justification by the Ministry to build more roads, in this case bypasses, then installing traffic calming would have made some real sense for them. It has to be remembered that in 1992 the Department was still very much in favor of road building, and the first critical voices, such as *Phil Goodwin*, had just started to attract some followers. Also the White Paper *Roads for Prosperity* had been published only three years earlier (DoT 1989).

Six small towns were chosen:

- *Berkhamsted* and *Petersfield* in Hampshire
- *Dalton-in-Furness* in Cumbria
- *Market Harborough* in Leicestershire
- *Wadebridge* in Cornwall and
- *Whitchurch* in Shropshire.

Cairns et al (1998) revealed that despite traffic calming in the old main roads, on average about 60% more traffic was counted (adding together the number of motor vehicles on the trunk road and bypass) in four towns[2] after the new bypass roads had been opened compared to the capacity on the main road before. In Berkhamsted and Wadebridge the bypass created the highest growth of vehicle traffic (80% and 115% respectively).

Without doubt, much less motor traffic was using the old roads. The decline of traffic there was on average 49% compared to the period before the bypasses had opened. Petersfield (69%) and Dalton (71%) had the sharpest reductions. Overall, the evidence showed clearly that traffic calming and building a bypass at the same time does not reduce traffic, on the contrary (ibid, p. 203 and own calculation).

Between 1993 and 2000, the Department was very effective in giving advice on traffic calming and this shows the importance this new policy was given. Seven traffic calming leaflets per year were published in 1993, 1994 and 1996, four in 1997, five in 1998, three in 1999 and again four in 2000. Finally, from June 1999 onwards, the local authorities themselves could decide their own 20mph speed limit zones.

Since the end of 2009, 20mph zones can be installed without any traffic calming measures at all (*Local Transport Today* 2009/2010, pp. 1, 32). This method has been used in Germany for many decades and Hamburg was the first city to implement that on a large scale (see Chapter 4). Such a policy has the advantage that large areas can be 'treated' but the speed reducing effect is minimal in most cases and the situation for pedestrians is really no better than it was before.

Most bus operators and many cycling organizations criticized road humps especially but also other traffic calming devices. The objections of the cyclists disappeared relatively quickly, but the bus operators had more serious concerns about the comfort of their passengers and drivers. Ambulance and fire brigade drivers were worried about whether they could reach their targets fast enough or at all because of these measures. In all these cases compromises had to be worked out, often scheme by scheme.

When traffic calming was introduced from the Continent into Britain, there was plenty of opposition against this new policy. Most of them did not realize or know that traffic calming had its own British tradition. The opposition came largely from the old-style traffic engineers and people in power, hardly ever from the residents; most of them were rather enthusiastic about the schemes proposed. This was very different compared to the 1960s and 1970s but it also showed how severe the 'traffic suffering' for many residents had become.

Yet, the criticism did not only come from this side; some of the more radical professionals also did not 'like' traffic calming. For instance, *John Whitelegg* remarked that traffic calming was like rearranging the deckchairs on the *Titanic*. *Mayer Hillman* thought that traffic calming was a distraction from other more important environmental issues. *John Roberts* was convinced that German-type traffic calming was only a new device to create more car parking spaces (Roberts 1989, pp. 31–32). All three critiques were right in their own way. In my opinion it did not in most cases improve walking, but it certainly did reduce pedestrian accidents, especially serious accidents.

Change of Government in 1997 and the Role of the Pedestrians

In May 1997, a new Labour government was formed with *Tony Blair* as prime minister and *John Prescott* as deputy prime minister. John Prescott was also head of the newly created *Department of Transport, Environment and the Regions* (1997–2001). During opposition, Prescott had pointed out that Britain had lacked a modern transportation system and that it would never be able to build its way out of the crisis of congestion and pollution by increasing spending on new and wider roads. In contrast to many of his predecessors he was extremely well briefed when starting his job as secretary of state. He also had direct access to Prime Minister Tony Blair and to Chancellor *Gordon Brown*. As a very senior figure in the Labour government, he had a weight other transport ministers normally do not have.

The *Labour Election Manifesto* included a brief suggestion that a group of experts should give advice on transportation if Labour came to power. The problem was that when Prescott finally was in power, the names of experts suggested by the civil servants were mostly unknown to him. The only name he recognized was Phil Goodwin, who was invited to John Prescott's office to discuss and chair this committee.[3]

There were several long meetings between November 1997 and March 1998. The contents of the meetings included:

- traffic reduction
- road pricing, whether it would be levied on motorways or within cities and what should have priority – most important to us was what would happen to the revenue from road pricing
- workplace parking levies
- the role of buses and trams/light rail
- what should happen with British Rail
- the integration of land use and transportation planning
- transport and the economy as a whole
- traffic in town centers and residential areas
- hypothecation (i.e. funds raised from transportation should be spent on transportation).

In all of these subjects, a high level of agreement was achieved. This was significant considering the wide spread of interests and backgrounds of the group. The White Paper was about making it more difficult for car drivers and more attractive for other users (cyclists, public transportation passengers and pedestrians).

The White Paper was published on 21 July 1998 (DETR 1998). Advisers and planners were aware that this White Paper was very different to many of its predecessors and we would have been delighted if all the suggestions and intentions published had been put into practice. We were as a matter of fact surprised just how much the civil servants had understood the mood of the time. Prescott mentioned in a radio program that 'there was a consensus for radical change and "no change" was not an option' (*The Derailing of Transport*, Radio 4, 18 January 2010). There was a feeling too that professionals and politicians were seeing for the first time eye to eye. If it had worked, it would have radically changed the future of transportation policy in Britain.

Two years later the *Transport Act 2000* came into force. It did not include any policy advice on walking, pedestrianization or traffic calming but it included the legal basis for *Home Zones*[4] (see Chapter 8). Part III contained all the different legal options and advice for road user charging and workplace parking levy. Both needed the confirmation of the national authority – except in Greater London (British Parliament 2000, pp. 103/104, 113). The Transport Act 2000 became law in the same year as *Transport 2010: The Ten Year Plan* (2000) was published.

'The Ten-Year Plan' could have been the realization of the 1998 White Paper. It started with high expectations and ended with a number of embarrassing retreats by the government. For England, it promised during the next ten years (2000–2010):

- £60 billion to be spent on railways and a 50% increase in passenger journeys (DETR 2000a, p. 33).
- £59 billion to be spent on roads, locally and nationally; this included 80 major road schemes, 100 new bypasses on trunk and local roads and 130 other major road and local road improvements and the completion of 40 road schemes. In addition, 360 miles of widened strategic roads (ibid, p. 5) were to be built.
- £59 billion to be spent on local transportation; this included 25 new light rail/ tram systems and extensive bus priority schemes. It was also promised to double light rail use (measured by the number of passenger journeys).
- The backlog in road maintenance was to be eliminated by 2010.
- An increase in bus travel by 10% was to be achieved over the next ten years.
- £25 billion to be spent in London on transportation infrastructure.
- A 40% reduction in the number of people killed or seriously injured in road accidents. The number of children killed and seriously injured was to be reduced by 50% (see below).
- Cleaner vehicles to reduce air pollution and CO_2 emissions. Greenhouse gas emissions to be reduced by 12.5% (from the 1990 levels) and a move towards a 20% reduction in CO_2 emissions were promised by 2010 (ibid, p. 75).
- Safer cycling and walking routes, more 20mph Zones and Home Zones.
- The setting up a *Strategic Rail Authority* (SRA) and a *Rail Regulator* to control train operators and Railtrack (responsible for the network). The SRA was set up in 2001; by 2004, *Alistair Darling* (transport minister) had announced the intention to abolish it and it finally ceased to exist in 2006. Railtrack was replaced in 2002 by *Network Rail* which was officially a private company but all its funding came from central government (Department for Transport and Transport for Scotland). It is very similar in this respect to the Deutsche Bahn AG in Germany.

When reading through the Ten Year Plan more than 14 years later, one can only wonder if anybody took this plan seriously at all. It was like a Christmas wish list. But this generous spending plan was largely based on the assumption of successful public–private partnerships and here was the crux of the problem. Although it appeared that for the first time since the Second World War more funds were to be made available for railways, most of it was to come from the private sector.

So what did the Ten Year Plan do for walking? Very little; first, there was no chapter on walking. There was something called 'for people in towns and cities' and half a sentence which said 'safer environments for walking and cycling, leading to substantial increase in both activities' (DETR 2000a, p. 54). Under targets one could find the following:

> The number of people killed or seriously injured in Great Britain in road accidents to be reduced by 40% by 2010 and the number of children killed or seriously injured by 50% compared with the average for 1994–1998.
>
> (Ibid, p. 75)

This was in fact achieved.

There was also a Traffic Advisory Leaflet entitled *Framework for a Local Walking Strategy*, which was published in the same year (DETR 2000b). It gave advice to local authorities to include local walking strategies in their *Local Transport Plans*. It told them where to find funding and to define performance indicators and most importantly to monitor and review the success of walking.

Six years later a new *White Paper 2004: The Future of Transport* was published, revising and replacing the White Paper of 1998. Chapter 6 was on walking and cycling; it consisted of three pages. They include all the positive statements about improving walking and cycling. The aim was to increase cycling and walking (no figure is given by how much) over the next 20–30 years, a statement which by then had been declared many times before. It mentions that 50 Home Zones will get direct funding from the central government in England. In addition, three towns (*Worcester, Darlington and Peterborough*) would participate in new walking and cycle projects with a total expenditure of about £10 million. The number of towns was increased to six but the emphasis was on cycling and not on walking (DfT 2004a).

When reading this chapter, I had the nagging thought that it was 'too little too late' and one is left wondering why so little active promotion in walking had taken place, considering that the Labour Party had by then been in power for seven years. One can safely assume that sufficient funds for promoting walking could have been made available during a time when the British economy was doing relatively well.

Apart from the White Paper of 2004, there was an additional publication called *Action Plan on Walking and Cycling* by the Department for Transport published in the same year. It is indeed impressive but it still contains mostly intentions (DfT 2004b). In the next chapter I will study in more detail what Home Zones and the Action Plan meant in reality.

Notes

1   Holyland was bounded by *University Street*, *Ormeau Street* (which was used by the Orange Parade – hence we were not allowed to use any design that included small paving stones), *Stranmillis Embankment* and *Rugby Road*. The neighborhood consisted mainly of terraced housing with a few shops and a significant number of offices in University Street. There was too much through traffic during the evening and morning peak hours.
2   No full data set was available from Market Harborough and Petersfield.
3   In October 1997 nine experts were appointed. They were:

- Phil Goodwin (chairman), professor at University College London (UCL)
- David Begg – the new star of the Labour Party having been a city councillor in Edinburgh and professor at Robert Gordon University
- Stephen Joseph, executive director of Transport 2000 (the name was changed in 2007 to *Campaign for Better Transport* (CBT))
- Dr Susan Owens, lecturer in geography, University of Cambridge
- Joyce Mamode, Transport and General Workers Union
- Charles Rice, managing director, P&O Transeuropean Holdings Ltd
- Michael Roberts, head of CBI's Industrial Policy Group
- Bill Tyson, head of Greater Manchester Passenger Transport Executive
- Carmen Hass-Klau, professor at the University of Wuppertal.

4   A kind of Home Zone was already practiced in Britain from the beginning of the 1930s. It was possible to close streets to motor vehicles. According to the *Manchester*

Corporation Act of 1934, non-classified streets could be converted into *play streets* and exclude 'propelled' vehicles (Hansard 1933–1934, Local Acts Ch XCVii, pp. 43–45). Such play streets were also common in other cities during the same time, and *Salford* was especially well known for them (Ministry of War Transport 1946, p. 22). Play streets appeared to have been rather effective, for instance Salford had no fatality among school children during 1936 but it also had very few cars. In addition, Salford had used other methods to improve road safety, for example, erection of barriers at school entrances and teaching children how to cross roads safely (ibid, p. 22). It is strange that no lesson was learned from such results and play streets were only seen as a provisional measure to counteract the lack of playgrounds in inner-city areas. Even so, play streets were known until the 1960s (Hass-Klau 1990a, p. 156).

Part II

PRACTICE

8

WALKING IN GREAT BRITAIN AND THE GREATER LONDON CASE STUDY

Background: The National Trend in Walking

In 1975/6 the modal share of walking accounted for 47% and about the same percentage used cars (46%) in Great Britain. By 2012 the walking share had dropped to 22% compared to 66% for cars[1] (www. gov.uk/government/statistical-data-sets, accessed 24.1.14).[2]

Walking to shops deteriorated even more. In 1991/93, 36% of people still walked to shops and 51% used a car. About 20 years later walking had declined to 22% with a further growth in car use (66%) for such trips (Department for Transport 2012, Table NTSO409). The main reason for the fall in shopping trips on foot has been the growth in out-of-town or edge-of-town shopping centers, which grew at a startling rate during the 1980s and 1990s. The national data show an increase in average shopping trip distance from 3.5 miles (5.6km) in 1993/95[3] to 4.4 miles (7.0km) in 2012 (Department of Transport 1996, p. 12; Department for Transport 2012, Table NTSO405).

In order to counteract car use to shopping centers, some local authorities increased the number and the size of pedestrian schemes in city centers.

Pedestrianization: The last 40 years

As discussed in Chapters 6 and 7, small-scale pedestrianization started during the mid-1950s and continued in the 1960s. A more intensive wave of pedestrianization occurred between 1972 and 1976[4] but a much bigger move to even larger pedestrianization schemes arose during the 1980s and 1990s. This latest policy was supported by a *Local Transport Note* called *Getting the Right Balance*, with guidance on vehicle restriction in pedestrian zones (Department of Transport 1988). It was pointed out that pedestrian areas were generally welcomed but there was also concern about them, especially from disabled people. The rise in the number of such zones was seen as having a direct relationship to the growth in motorization, and it was assumed that in future more streets would be pedestrianized (p. 5).

Although over the last 40 years pedestrianization in most British towns has increased considerably, there have always been reservations about it. The often-repeated criticism is that during the night these streets become ghostlike and are perceived to be occupied only by marginal individuals and outsiders who are seen as potentially dangerous. It is true that many pedestrianized streets are not particularly attractive during the night, especially because British shops often have shutters on the shop windows which makes them unattractive and uninteresting to pedestrians. In general, the real danger in these streets is mostly exaggerated and more thought could be given to improving the urban environment, for instance by adequate street lighting, security cameras, or allowing cyclists to cycle through these streets at times when there are few pedestrians around. It does not help that local authorities are under pressure to save money and are considering cutting expenditure on street lighting.

Research by the *Mail on Sunday* indicated that not all was well on the high street. It concluded that 10,000 charity shops were located in high streets, they had increased by 30% over the last five years and paid minimum business rates (www. thisismoney.co.uk, published 17 August 2013, Neil Craven 'Surge in Charity shops fuels "Clone town" fear'). Conventional retailers complained that they forced out established shops and damaged the perception of the town center. This indicates that certain ingredients for a successful city center are not working, at least not in some British towns. On the one hand, soulless shopping centers at the edge or out of town compete with town center shops. Yet town center shops have no chance because of their location (they normally pay more rent and business rates, have less of a selection of goods and cannot provide free car parking or the amount of car parking wanted by customers). The answer is not to compete in terms of providing as many car parking spaces as possible. Town center car parking can never really compete with out-of-town shopping centers but town centers can acquire what a shopping center will never be able to achieve, 'urban atmosphere'. That means attractive townscapes and facades, an interesting mix of shops (not only chain shops), restaurants, cafes, historic buildings, outdoor seating, art and water features, something for children and grown-ups to do. The streets should have very few cars, if any, but a good walking surface is essential with *Way-finders* and landscaping. In a boring urban environment, to implement pedestrianization may be a waste of money (for more on this issue, see Chapter 15).

Pedestrianization: A Comparison between Germany and the UK (and Other Countries)

In 2014, nearly every British city has pedestrianized streets. They vary substantially in size and design. I compared the length of pedestrianized streets in 27 British with 27 German cities.[5] Pedestrianized streets were measured both from the most recent town plans and from Google Maps, and the results were compared and the highest value was used.[6] There is a difference in street type; only the British plans mark restricted access streets.[7] For this reason I included in Table 8.2 two types of measurements: one column shows pedestrian streets only and another adds to the pedestrian streets (from the ordinance survey maps) the access-only streets. The two different values were compared with the length of the German pedestrianized streets.

Many access-only streets cannot be classified as pedestrian friendly as they are used by large numbers of buses, taxis and service vehicles. However, there are access streets, which are pleasant and peaceful and have hardly any cars (and no buses). They may have an attractive quality of their own if they kept the historic street layout. In fact, they could be more interesting than some of the pedestrianized streets in the city center. Thus access streets can be either very pleasant or very much like a street that contains too much traffic.

I also did not include pedestrianized squares, although car-free squares are a major feature and a great asset of any pedestrianization scheme. British cities are often dominated by covered shopping malls in the city center. Mostly they do not improve the historic urban environment but still add walking meters to a pedestrian scheme. German cities frequently have shopping arcades, which are smaller and neatly tucked away either within small side streets or behind large, often historic house entrances. These lengths have also not been included in Table 8.1 to 8.3. As discussed, the values of the pedestrianized streets presented have a number of caveats but they still give an overall impression of the difference in size (but not in quality) between these two countries.

Most of the chosen cities were major regional cities but a number of smaller and middle-sized towns were also included, plus the two capital cities (Greater London and Berlin). The *median* calculated in terms of population size between the British and the German cities was nearly the same (Germany 267,693 and Britain 276,000). But the *average* population size in Britain without London was 260,000 whereas the average size in Germany even without Berlin was much larger with 425,839 as the administrative structure is different between the two countries; for instance Manchester and Salford would considered one city in Germany. But the variation in pedestrian street size cannot be explained by the difference in population size.

The smallest pedestrianization scheme was found in Southampton with just over 600m and the largest (outside London) in Manchester with 5.7km. A comparison between Southampton and Nottingham is interesting; both cities have a similar population size, but have a completely different length of pedestrianization: 0.6km versus 5.4km. The key difference is in the main public transportation modes (bus versus tram). The pedestrian size in Berlin is nearly the same as in Freiburg, a city of only just over 200,000 inhabitants. One would expect Berlin with 3.5 million inhabitants to have a much larger pedestrian network.

The average length of all pedestrianized streets was 2,753m in the British cities but this measure is distorted because of the 17km in London. Without London this size was only 2,214m. When the access-only streets are included, then the average increases to 3,619m. The average size of the German cities was only slightly more (3,861m) (Table 8.1).

The median is much higher in the German compared to the British cities. Studying the figures more closely, it shows that ten British cities have less than 2,000m, even when the pedestrianized and the access street lengths are combined, whereas in Germany only four cities have such limited size. The research was carried out in 2010 but in the meantime some of the British cities have further enlarged their pedestrianization schemes, for instance my home town of Brighton has closed more streets to car traffic since then. The omission of London makes a big difference to the spread (*standard deviation*) of the English cities whereas Berlin does not make such a great difference for the German cities.

If the pedestrian street length is measured *per population* (meters per 100 population), *York* had a ratio of 3.1 and *Cambridge* had 2.0, but in most of the other UK cities the value was under 1 (in 17 cities). The same indicator showed that out of the 27 German cities only 12 had a ratio under one; *Freiburg* had a ratio of 3.7 and four cities (*Münster, Oldenburg, Osnabrück* and *Regensburg*) had 2 or more.

No real difference between the countries was found in the number of medieval and non-medieval cities. In the UK, 15 cities were already important in medieval

Table 8.1 Comparison between mean, median and standard deviation of German and British pedestrianization

Type of measure	Type of street in meters		
	British ped. streets	British ped. and access streets	German ped. streets
Average	2,753	3,619	3,861
Average without capital city	2,214	3,113	3,694
Median	1,817	2,636	3,600
Median without capital city	1,750	2,629	3,500
Standard deviation	3,103	3,142	2,017
Standard deviation without capital city	1,361	1,726	1,857

Sources: Table 8.2.and 8.3

times and in Germany 17 out of the 27 had the same historical importance. It is generally believed that pedestrianization is easier in cities with a medieval street layout because these streets are normally narrower and more crooked than cities that have a block street network.

The major difference between the British and the German cities is in the type of public transportation and its access to the city centers. Of the 27 German cities, 19 have tram, light rail and/or underground systems. Wuppertal has a monorail (opened in 1901) and an S-Bahn line, which are the main public transportation axes for this urban valley.

A pedestrianized street with trams is more pleasant than a street with a large number of buses, although light rail vehicles are also not ideal because they are rather large and heavy. It is always surprising to watch the behavior of pedestrians in a very crowded pedestrianized street where trams are allowed to operate. One can see all the people walking along the tram tracks and when a tram appears they calmly move to either side, then after the tram is gone, they again occupy the full street space. Such behavior is only possible in pedestrianized streets with a very low number of buses.

From the 1970s onwards, tram or light rail construction was nearly always combined with large-scale pedestrianization in Germany (see Chapter 4). It is no coincidence that Nottingham with its tram network has the second largest British pedestrianized street network outside London. In the last 15 years the French, Norwegian and Italian cities have learnt the lesson from Germany and built even larger pedestrian networks than Germany. For instance:

- Montpellier about 21km (including the roads in the historic city center)
- Strasbourg about 9km
- Rouen about 9km
- Bergen about 9km
- Nantes about 5km
- Como about 6km
- Oslo about 6km
- Vicenza about 6km
- Grenoble about 4km and so on.

Another impressive French example is Paris, with a pedestrianized street network of about 32km. On Sundays many streets are closed to vehicle traffic. I would estimate that the length of walking streets on a Sunday is increased at least by a third.

Unfortunately, there has been hardly any research on British pedestrianization during the last 25 years. There was some research in *Neal Street (London)* on the impact on retailing but with no detailed results (TEST 1987, p. 178). A recent study by the University of the West of England (Sinnett et al 2012) gave some examples, for instance in a newly developed pedestrianization scheme in Exeter, the footfall increased by around 20% (between 2006 and 2008) and as always there was a rise in rent by £5 per sqft in the same time period despite falling prices in the region (pp. 18, 57–58). Similar results have been found all over the world in most shopping streets that have been made car free.

We saw in Chapters 3 and 4 how important public transportation investment was in West Germany to allow large-scale pedestrianization in town centers. What approach did the British cities and the governments have toward public transportation?

Table 8.2 Sample of British cities and their lengths (meters) in pedestrianization

City	Population	Restricted access	Length of ped. street city map	Length of ped. street Google map	Value used	Ped. street and access street	Length of ped. street/ pop x100
Bath	96,100	425	1,002	1,483	1,483	1,427	1.5
Belfast	216,500	1,050	3,260	–	3,260	4,310	1.5
Birmingham	966,000	–	3,200	3,851	3,851	3,851	0.4
Bradford	196,700	1,152	1,288	–	1,288	2,440	0.7
Brighton	139,100	–	1,300	1,197	1,300	1,300	0.9
Bristol	465,500	–	–	1,530	1,530	1,530	0.3
Cambridge	132,800	3,834	1,264	2,617	2,617	5,098	2.0
Cardiff	310,800	–	–	1,964	1,964	1,964	0.6
Edinburg	452,200	5,041	1,034	1,946	1,946	6,075	0.4
Exeter	118,700	819	1,817	318	1,817	2,636	0.3
Glasgow	637,000	2,307	2,414	2,703	2,703	4,721	0.4
Leeds	477,600	1,053	1,962	1,903	1,962	3,015	0.4
Leicester	290,000	3,394	1,682		1,682	5,076	0.6
Liverpool	464,200	–	–	2,621	2,621	2,621	0.6
London	7,619,800	–	12,749	16,769	16,769	16,769	1.5
Manchester	415,000	–	5,738	959	5,738	5,738	1.4
Newcastle	273,000	–	1,000	543	1,000	1,000	0.4
Norwich	194,400	2,603	533	2,685	2,685	3,136	1.6
Nottingham	279,000	–	5,387	2,986	5,387	5,387	1.9
Oxford	165,000	4,762	1,097	423	1,097	5,859	0.7
Peterborough	164,000	–	847	938	938	938	0.6
Reading	236,900	–	–	1,264	1,264	1,264	0.5
Sheffield	458,100	–	–	1,425	1,425	1,425	0.3
Southampton	234,600	1,473	626	408	626	2,099	0.3
Swansea	174,300	–	–	1,661	1,661	1,661	1.0
Worcester	94,000	656	1,064	–	1,064	1,720	1.1
York	148,300	–	3,995	4,642	4,642	4,642	3.1

Table 8.3 Sample of German cities and their lengths (meters) in pedestrianization

City	Population	Length of ped. street city map	Length of ped. street Google map	Used value	Length of ped. street/ pop x100
Aachen*	251,272	2,900	3,204	3,204	1.3
Berlin	3,416,255	–	8,205	8,205	0.2
Bremen*	544,000	5,300	–	5,300	1.0
Cologne*	1,007,000	6,100	–	6,100	0.6
Dresden*	467,000	2,800	–	2,800	0.6
Düsseldorf*	569,000	4,200	–	4,200	0.7
Essen*	605,000	4,100	4,107	4,107	0.7
Freiburg*	224,000	8,000	8,232	8,232	3.7
Hamburg[8]	1,771,000	2,041	–	2,041	0.1
Hannover*	523,000	4,300	–	4,300	0.8
Herne*	173,155	1,200	–	1,200	0.7
Karlsruhe	274,000	4,600		4,600	1.7
Kiel*	230,463	4,300	–	4,300	1.9
Leipzig*	517,000	3,100	–	3,100	0.6
Lübeck*	215,327	1,400	–	1,400	0.7
Mönchengladbach*	267,693	2,000	–	2,000	0.8
Munich	1,353,000	–	6,107	6,107	0.5
Münster*	264,055	5,300	–	5,300	2.0
Nuremberg	506,000	–	7,172	7,172	1.4
Oldenburg*	154,222	3,400	–	3,400	2.2
Osnabrück*	157,035	3,600	–	3,600	2.3
Regensburg*	124,852	2,800	–	2,800	2.2
Saarbrücken*	190,000	2,000	–	2,000	1.1
Schwerin*	95,855	–	1,843	1,843	1.9
Ulm*	115,701	2,000	–	2,000	1.7
Wolfsburg*	122,185	1,200	1,802	1,200	1.0
Wuppertal	350,000	–	3,741	–	1.1

Source: Hass-Klau et al 2002, p. 124 = cities with * and own calculations

Public Transportation

Buses mostly dominate urban public transportation outside London and they have always been regarded by a number of transportation experts as a cheap and cheerful solution to public transportation services. Unfortunately trams have been abandoned, first in London during the 1950s and later in all other cities, except Blackpool. The last trams ran in England in 1961 (Grimsby) and in Scotland in 1962 (Glasgow) (www.lrta.org, accessed 08.01.12).

With the introduction of the Transport Act of 1985, privatization and deregulation of bus services was seen as an important step to solve the public transportation problems of the future. In reality it was a severe misjudgment of what the free market was able to achieve. Privatization, and even more so deregulation of bus services, did very little to improve public transportation. Passenger numbers fell nearly everywhere, especially in the large conurbations apart from London.

The Transport Act of 1995 for London excluded deregulation. More recently bus use has increased in some towns not as a result of privatization and deregulation but because of exclusive bus lanes, more modern vehicles and other quality improvements.

Although trams had been abandoned, several new investments in urban rail services were carried out during the last decades, of which by far the largest were unsurprisingly built in Greater London (see below). Apart from Greater London, a number of urban areas also built new rail public transportation networks, such as the *Tyne and Wear* Metro serving 1.6 million people. It consists of 48 miles (77km). The *Greater Manchester* light rail network serves a conurbation of 2.5 million people. At the beginning of 2014 the network was 48 miles (77km) (www.thalesgroup.com, accessed 9.4.14). Therefore both conurbations have the same length of urban rail service.

The tram system in *Sheffield* serves the conurbation of South Yorkshire with a population of 1.3 million. The problem had been that between planning the lines and operating them, the shift in population was so significant that the areas which were to be served had far fewer residents than originally forecast. In addition, a huge shopping center (*Meadowhall*) was built at one of the end stations, affecting city center retailing in Sheffield negatively. 'Supertram' consists of three lines and has a length of 18 miles (29km).

The *City of Birmingham* is part of West Midlands, a large conurbation of about 2.6 million. It has only built one light rail line 13 miles (20.4km) between Birmingham and *Wolverhampton*. It went into service in 1999 and so far the Department has approved only one extension within Birmingham.

The *City of Nottingham* (307,000 population) has implemented a tram network (*Nottingham Express Transit*). The Greater Nottingham conurbation contains a population of about 676,000. The 9 mile (14km) *Nottingham Express Transit* started operating in 2004. A second line running to the south and southwest (17.8km) will open in late 2014 (www.nottinghamcity.gov.uk, accessed 25.1.14).

Excluding Greater London, the rest of Britain invested in just over 200km of new rail connections, not including the improvements by British Rail. In comparison with other European countries that is quite modest. The lack in public investment has indirectly affected walking as I have explained in other chapters.

Other Policies to Promote Walking

As pointed out in Chapter 7, the Labor government under Tony Blair and John Prescott started to promote a number of policies, which had been common around the rest of Europe for decades and had partly been invented in Britain. One of them was *Home Zones* and the other was *Shared Space*.

Home Zones (Woonerven)

The Transport Act 2000[9] also included the legislation for *Home Zones* – section 268(7) – that came into force in January 2003. Home Zones are one of the strangest, saddest and most interesting transportation policies ever introduced in Britain: strange, because they were officially introduced decades later than in many other European countries. Strange also because the official documents from central government include all the necessary and very positive discussions that would have been essential and useful when introducing traffic calming during the late 1980s in Britain. Sad, because so few Home Zones have been implemented and there is little chance that many more will be built, and interesting because of the published research on house prices.

It is astonishing that Home Zones, which are nothing else than the historic Woonerven,[10] developed by the Dutch in the 1960s in Delft and accepted by the Dutch government in 1976 (Hass-Klau 1990a, pp. 212–213), had taken so long to be introduced into Britain. In fact, Britain had pioneered Home Zones, originally called *play streets* (for more details see Chapter 7).[11]

Approval from the Department for Transport is not required to implement Home Zones (www.homezones.org.uk/public, accessed 5.12.09). The development of the first nine pilot projects took place in England and Wales in 1999 and four were built shortly afterwards in Scotland. Similar to traffic calming, the demand for Home Zones was led by a few local authorities. The Institute of Highway Engineers (IHIE) published design guidelines for Home Zones in 2002.

In 2001, a £30 million *Challenge Fund* was set up to encourage the development of new Home Zones. Sixty-one schemes from 57 English authorities were announced in January 2002, for completion by 2005 (Department for Transport 2005, p. 7). Many of the local authorities identified additional funding for their schemes (ibid, p. 17).

Mostly, the objectives were:

- reduction in vehicle speed
- improvement of the quality of the environment
- growth in play and other social activities
- reduction in real/perceived crime
- improvement in road safety
- promotion of community involvement (ibid, p. 79).

Ironically, these objectives are the same as local authorities had on the Continent for traffic calming about 30 years ago. Only crime reduction is a more recent objective. The roads chosen were residential and already had low traffic volumes and speeds. The type of housing area varied from terrace houses to low density semi-detached houses. The number of households varied from 18 (*London: Haringey*) to 856 (*Derby*) (ibid, p. 10).

The Department for Transport (2005) published the results of these schemes under the grand title *Home Zones: Challenging the Future of our Streets* (2005). It contains practical and useful general advice about the consultation and construction of Home Zones. Most interesting are the research results that were divided into:

- *Traffic impact:* Thirty-nine of the 61 schemes reported that speeds had been reduced to between 10 and 15mph. In some of them even lower speeds were reported but not all the designated Home Zones carried out speed surveys (ibid, p. 80).
- *Wider impacts:* According to the Department, Home Zones create stronger and more integrated communities (though it is not quite clear what this means in practice).

- *Regeneration:* Housing associations and local authority housing departments see Home Zones as adding value to properties and in general properties are often improved because of the new road design (ibid, p. 84). Some local authorities were of the opinion that redevelopment of adjacent derelict areas would occur.

A number of local authorities suggested that house prices in Home Zones increased more than in areas of similar character. Estate agents are using Home Zones as a marketing device. In *Derby*, a 20% price rise in terrace houses in the Home Zone was recorded in one year (2004–2005). In *Morecambe*, a growth of about 11% in house prices in the Home Zone was found relative to the northwest region as a whole. Anecdotal evidence in *Plymouth* indicated a 10–15% increase in house prices in the Home Zone compared to similar properties outside. In *North Shields*, estate agents suggested a jump of 15–20% in the past year (2004) and properties sold faster in the Home Zone (but no comparison was given). Estate agents pointed out that people ask for properties in Home Zones. In *Middlesborough*, a faster increase in property prices for three-bedroom terraced houses (13%) was recorded than for those in adjacent areas (ibid, pp. 88–89).

These results are very much in line with some of our research (Hass-Klau et al 2004; ETP 2007). Improvement of the urban environment does increase house prices. This can be in the form of new attractive public investment, well-designed traffic calmed areas, Home Zones or shared space, another policy that again became popular at the beginning of the 21st century.

Shared Space: Another Old Concept in New Clothes

Shared space was used for a special residential design in the new towns, as discussed in Chapter 6, and was then called *shared access*. The first known examples were built in Runcorn and Washington New Town in 1966, and this kind of design continued well into the 1970s. The Department of Transport recommended in its Design Bulletin 32 (1977) 'shared surface road' for residential cul-de-sacs (www.ice.org.uk, accessed 17.1.10). Admittedly these first shared spaces were relatively short (no more than 40m of unrestrained road).

On the Continent shared space design became fashionable first in the Netherlands, known as Woonerven during the later 1960s and early 1970s. The design spread from there to other European countries (for more details see Chapter 4). Switzerland introduced a similar scheme much later in 2002, called *Begegnungszone* (meeting space) (Gerlach et al 2009, p. 5). All these designs abandoned the division between sidewalks and carriageway and one surface was created on which all road participants mixed and had the same rights. The maximum vehicle speed was restricted to walking pace. The only problem was that although they did work well, they were also rather costly; therefore they were never implemented on a large scale. The road design that is today called 'shared space' is less favorable to walking than the old one as cars do not need to drive at walking pace and children do not have the right to play on the carriageway. Shared space roads are, when well designed, an improvement for the urban surroundings as most of them look pleasant but they are not without difficulties. Many older people and the visually impaired have problems with orientation and feel unsafe.

I cannot see that shared space will ever cover large parts of our street network. It will be a special design in some of the narrow streets and in newly built housing areas and they will be as Tim Pharoah (2009) called them 'vanity projects and photo opportunities for local worthies' (p. 7).

By the early years after the millennium, central government was in favor of more low-key transportation policies. Research into soft measures to change travel behavior was another such initiative.

Smarter Travel Choices but not Smart Enough

The DfT commissioned a research project with the title 'Soft measures: A way of reducing traffic' and the work started in 2002. It included:

- workplace and school travel plans
- personalized travel planning
- travel awareness campaigns
- public transportation information and marketing
- car clubs and car sharing
- teleworking, teleconferences and home shopping.

The report was published in 2004 with the title *Smarter Choices – Changing the Way we Travel*.[12] The overall results were very encouraging. The research team divided the results into two different policy scenarios for the next ten years:

- The *high intensity scenario* needed a significant expansion of activities to a more widespread implementation of all these policies mentioned above. It was also seen as necessary to combine these measures with other car-reducing policies, such as road capacity reduction, more pedestrianization, traffic calming, more cycle facilities, better public transportation etc.
- The *low intensity scenario* was defined as continuing with the present level of local and national activities on soft measures.

It showed for the high intensity scenario a reduction of:

- peak period urban traffic of about 21% (off peak 13%)
- peak period non-urban traffic of about 14% (off peak 7%)
- nationwide of all traffic of about 11% (Department for Transport 2004, p. 362).

Such relatively high reductions would certainly give more space for improving walking facilities. These interesting research results lead to a further study on three cities (*Peterborough, Darlington and Worcester*) between 2004 and 2008. These results were published in 2010 (Sloman at al). The areas of research were enlarged and included:

- workplace travel plans
- school travel planning
- personal travel planning
- public transportation information and marketing
- travel awareness campaigns (see above)
- cycling and walking promotion
- car clubs.

Most of the policies had already been used in the first study. I was particularly interested in the results under 'cycling and walking' and as it turned out it was as it is quite often, mostly the promotion of cycling and not of walking that had taken place. Then again, there were a few exceptions, for instance Darlington pedestrianized its town center during the research period and the whole policy package had some positive impact on walking. The counts in Darlington showed an increase in walking trips per person between 11 and 13% and in distance between 15 and 20%. It was especially the general travel awareness campaigns and personal travel planning that made a difference and trips to the town center increased by 43%. In Peterborough the growth in trips per person was about the same as in Darlington (9–14%) but the spread of the distances walked appeared to be much wider (14–33%). In Worcester the rise in distances walked was largest (25–29%), and the trips per person were about the same as in Peterborough. My own experience was slightly different.

Being interested in the government's initiatives on sustainable travel, I visited one of these three towns. I chose Peterborough as we had carried out research there on cycle safety between 1986 and 1988.[13] When I arrived at Peterborough's main railway station, I would have preferred to wait for the next train back to London, however long it would have taken. I found the exit into the town center extremely uninviting. When leaving the station, there was no signing where the actual town center was so I had to ask. After a 3 minute walk, I arrived at a major ring road (four lanes) but with a wide separate cycle path on one side. Where I stood I could see a pedestrian bridge, which led directly into a modern shopping center. As I did not want to go through a shopping center to reach the town center, I looked for another possible crossing. Finally, I found a pedestrian walk leading me into the town center. This walk had obviously once been part of the independent cycle network (now divided into a cycling and a walking part), which had been built originally for this new town (for more details see Chapter 6). No great progress there. The officers I talked to in the town hall were pleasant and knowledgeable, but as a visitor I did not have the feeling that I was in the heart of a sustainable city despite a fairly large pedestrianized area in the town center, implemented during the late 1970s; an enlargement of this scheme was under construction.

Despite my personal experience, the research results on sustainable travel were impressive. There was an increase in:

- public transportation by 35%
- the number of pedestrians by 14%
- cycling by 12% during the research period.

All the data were backed up by actual counts. It seems that it is possible to change behavior significantly if funding is made available and continued. I am of the opinion that the 'package' approach is a splendid way forward to increase walking, especially if the emphasis on funding is at least shared equally between walking and cycling.

20mph Speed Limits

In recent years, a large number of proposals to reduce car speed in residential streets have been initiated. In Lancashire about 90% of the population is already living or will live in a 20mph zone affecting 1.2 million people (www.lancashire. gov.uk, accessed 4.12.11 and private email 2.12.11). The initiatives by local authorities and the central government on area-wide 20mph speed limit zones have continued. Some cities, such as Brighton and Hove, have introduced such

Table 8.5 Modal split comparison in Greater London: trips to work and all trips in percent

Mode	2001 Trips to work	2001 All trips	2011 Trips to work	2012 All trips
Car, truck and car passengers	36.0	43	27.9	33
Public transportation	42.1	35	48.7	44
Motorcycle	–	–	1.1	–
Bicycle	2.3	1	3.9	2
Walk	8.4	22	8.1	21
Work at home	8.6	–	9.8	–
Other	2.5*	–	0.5	–

Sources: London: UK Census 2001 and 2011 * includes motor bikes; Mayor of London, TfL (2013): Travel in London, Report 6, p. 20

Although the pedestrian fatalities dropped to 148 in New York (City of New York informal information 2012), it was still more than twice as dangerous to walk there as in Greater London (69 pedestrians killed) in 2012 (Mayor of London and TfL 2013b, p. 19).

Congestion Charging (Road Pricing)

In 2000, the then mayor of London, Ken Livingstone, introduced congestion charging in Central London, which started in February 2003 (21sqkm of the total size of Greater London – 1,589sqkm). The area is controlled by cameras (through automatic number plate recognition), which automatically register and store the car numbers at the road entrances of the priced area, so that a central computer can compare them with those that have paid the charge. The objectives were to:

- reduce congestion
- radically improve bus services
- more reliable journey times for car users
- more efficient distribution of goods and services (Mayor of London and TfL 2005, p. 1).

The results have been a reduction in:

- congestion on average of 26% since the introduction of road pricing
- car traffic of 20% (similar results – 20 to 30% of car traffic have been achieved in Stockholm since January 2006 (personal communication: e-mail 16.1.06)
- road accidents (it was estimated that there are 40 to 70 fewer accidents per year)
- exhaust emissions.

There were benefits to bus traffic, with improved reliability and journey times and the condition on the main roads in Inner London stayed stable. It was most important that there was no evidence of detrimental traffic on roads outside the charging zone.

According to the study by the Mayor of London and Transport for London there were no negative impacts on retailing (ibid, pp. 4, 68). The *Overview* of the

Monitoring Report mentioned that the retail sector increased its share of enterprises and employment since 2003 and among businesses 'there were more supporters of the congestion charge than opponents' (Mayor of London and TfL 2006, p. 5).

The time period of enforcement is between 7.00 and 18.00, Monday to Friday and the daily fee was originally £5 (€7), which has been increased several times and in 2014 was £11.50 (€14). Local residents living in the zone enjoy a reduction of 90% of the through traffic charge and have a positive attitude toward the scheme. From February 2007 onward, the area was increased to the west with the new area fully included in the scheme. Boris Johnson reversed this extension in 2011.

Altogether it is not clear what road pricing has done for walking but one can safely assume that there were some positive incentives, such as widening of sidewalks.

Walking

The main walking policy in London has been to develop key walking routes and this approach is rather impressive and very useful for other cities. Key walking routes might link residential streets (areas) with:

- public transportation stations and stops
- schools
- local shopping parades and centers
- health care and community centers
- leisure facilities
- other key destinations.

The way these routes will be improved is by:

- widened and repaved sidewalks and/or footpaths
- new and improved pedestrian crossings
- improved accessibility through step-free access
- removal of obsolete signs, poles, columns and railings
- trees and planting to create green streets
- removal of hiding spaces and blind corners
- signing
- street lighting for pedestrians
- shared space (Mayor of London and TfL 2012a, para. 3.1.1).

A number of examples are provided, some are indeed very good and interesting, for example *Wanstead High Street*, a key walking route. Here the short cut that was available to the tube station has been improved by building a new footpath and made safer by installing street lights. This resulted in an increase in the number of pedestrians during the day by 75% and during the night by 122%.

Other case studies include a shared space design at *Redcross Way* (Southwark). The shared space in this case means only that the carriageway and the sidewalk are physically on the same level, and distinguished by different materials. There were a large number of other examples of shared space throughout London (see below).

Especially impressive is the enhancement of tunnels; this is a crucial aspect to make walking more pleasant; nothing is worse than a dark tunnel crowded with masses of cars. It is important to be able to walk without detours, thus building central reservations (*Piccadilly*, *St. James and Pall Mall*) or removing pedestrian guardrails are steps in the right direction.

Pedestrianization

Pedestrianization has in the past been a difficult subject in London. A few streets had been pedestrianized, for instance in *Soho*, but overall, the schemes were small. The area around *Covent Garden* had several car-free street sections. During the last decade many more car-free streets have been added.

The scheme of partial pedestrianization of *Trafalgar Square* in 2003 was very controversial but works well despite the assumption that the traffic situation would become worse. The north side of the square in front of the National Gallery is pedestrianized. The *South Bank Walk* is the longest pedestrian walk in Central London, which is part of the *Jubilee Walkway*, and there are others, such as the *Capital Ring*, *Green Chain* and the *Jubilee Greenway*.

My View

Writing about walking in London is strange because I have lived close to London since 1977 and I have walked around London thousands of times. My judgment is concentrated on three areas: the City of London, some parts of Camden (the university area) and the City of Westminster. All these three areas belong to Inner London and are therefore in keeping with my walks in other cities.

City of Westminster and Borough of Camden

I started my walk at *Victoria Station* and walked along *Victoria Street* in the direction of *Westminster Abbey*. Victoria Street is an ugly street despite its wide sidewalks (a few parts are uneven and the tiles are slightly cracked). But not all is awful. The square (*Piazza Square*) in front of *Westminster Cathedral* is well designed and another small square has been created at *Wilcox Place*. A further highlight is *Christchurch Gardens*. One side of this small park faces Victoria Street and here a bus stop is located. Quite a lot of people who are waiting for the bus like to sit on the wall of this square; this is a lovely example of informal seating. Some of the pedestrian traffic lights along Victoria Street have countdown periods for waiting but many people are too impatient and walk at red anyhow. The closer one approaches *Westminster Abbey*, the better the sidewalks become but it remains a ghastly street with mostly uninteresting office facades and very few trees.

Around Westminster Abbey and *Parliament Square* there was sufficient green space but a lot of car traffic (two to three lanes in each direction) was circling around Parliament Square and one had to be careful where to cross the streets. The street (*Parliament Street/Whitehall*) going up to *Trafalgar Square* had extremely wide sidewalks (about 11m) on one side. Here one finds the first Way-finder sign that shows what streets or sights one can reach in 5 or 15 minutes. Such signs are extremely useful and one wishes that there would be more of them.

Close to Parliament Street/Whitehall via, for instance, *King Charles Street* one can enter *St. James Park*, and crossing *The Mall* there is *Green Park* and further to the west even *Hyde Park*. All these parks are large and pleasant to walk in. The Mall runs from *Charing Cross* to *Buckingham Palace*; it has wide sidewalks and on Sundays this street is closed to car traffic.

From *Trafalgar Square* one can either walk north along *Charing Cross Road*, which has lots of motor vehicle traffic, to *Leicester Square* or along *St. Martin's Lane* (much less motorized traffic). The sidewalks in St. Martin's Lane were sufficient on one side (about 4 meters) but on the opposite side they were much narrower (about 2m), but plenty of repairs to the sidewalks could be observed. Leicester Square is always full of people, mostly tourists. It is quieter to walk from St. Martin's Lane to *New Row*, which is a narrow 'shared space' street containing only one car lane in the middle. Around this area it is noticeable that there were more zebra crossings and fewer traffic lights, which makes walking so much easier. *King Street* was also a good street to walk along and part of *Floral Street* was again built as 'shared space'. *Long Acre* had well-designed road humps in different materials in the road surface. The whole area around Covent Garden is interesting to walk around although it is a bit touristy, but considering that the whole area was to be demolished in the late 1960s, it has become an asset of Central London.[16] The original GLC (Greater London Council) plan was to build two major roads to relieve the Strand traffic. That would have meant the demolition of large parts of the historic street network and houses. Covent Garden market was to be replaced by a national conference hall and hotels. The southern part of the area was to be linked to Leicester Square and developed as a major shopping area. The whole plan would have destroyed two-thirds of the Covent Garden neighborhood (Borer 1984, pp. 171–178). Local protests started slowly but became more sophisticated as the years went by, and in 1971 a public inquiry was announced. Two years later (1973) the area was saved from demolition. The market hall and its surrounding buildings were restored, and in 1980 the main building was opened again to the public.

Seven Dials (near *Shaftesbury Avenue* and *Mercer Street*) is a mini roundabout where seven streets meet. It is extremely interesting to watch how pedestrians and cars have to negotiate the road space. I will discuss a similar scheme in Cologne.

Kingsway is a very busy road with bus lanes on each side and two car lanes in opposite directions but it had wide sidewalks and trees on both sides. In some sections it was nearly impossible to cross because of a metal fence in the middle of the road. The beginning of *New Oxford Street* coming from *Holborn* (Holborn was very busy with cars and pedestrians) was car traffic free and only buses and cyclists were allowed. It stayed car free up to *Museum Street*, after that car traffic and buses in both directions enter New Oxford Street. Entering *Oxford Street* from the east, the sidewalks were old and uneven and there was too much traffic of all kinds (buses, taxis, lorries, etc.). At Oxford Circus the Barnes Dance (see 'Denver' in Chapter 13) is very much worth watching. The junction is well designed but most pedestrians still cross at the arms and not diagonally (see cover). The area south of Oxford Street, for instance *Soho Street* which leads into *Soho Square*, was quiet and pleasant as this part was more or less closed to car traffic because of building works for *Crossrail* (see below). When walking along *Frith Street* and crossing *Old Compton Street*, I realized how charming the area had become, mostly because car traffic was missing and therefore it did not matter that the sidewalks were not very wide. *Chinatown* is very close and there several streets (e.g. *Gerrard Street*, *Lisle Street*) were pedestrianized and it seemed that everybody was enjoying themselves.

Figure 8.2
Seven Dials in London

I also walked around all the famous squares (*Tavistock Square Gardens*, *Bedford Square*, *Russell Square* and *Bloomsbury Square Gardens*), and apart from the pedestrian times given at the traffic light signals (see below), all of them had wide sidewalks. In some streets surrounding these squares there was still far too much traffic and I felt speeds were too high. The university area was much more pedestrian friendly than I could remember. But the 'shared space' design in *Byng Place*, which was surely expensive, was somewhat shocking. Pedestrians mixed with cyclists but considering the speed cyclists were going it appeared to be a really dangerous place. Most pedestrians may not even be aware that cyclists are using the same space, at least if one is visiting this area for the first time, and it is a popular place for tourists. It was certainly a 'shared space' that I thought did not work at all.

The area around the British Museum which has already been improved, in particular *Great Russell Street*, will be changed either to 'shared space' or pedestrianized.

City of London – the Banking Center of the UK (workforce 350,000)

The City of London is the smallest borough with a size of only one square mile but it is by far the richest. One of the great discoveries in London is walking around in the City of London. This part of London used to be rather boring with few restaurants or bars open in the evening, although some of the important tourist sights are there, such as *St. Paul's Cathedral*, the *Tower of London* and *Tower Bridge*.

A tremendous transformation has gone on during the last 20 years. According to a senior officer from the City of London, most of the workforce either uses public transportation or cycles to work. Private car parking spaces are not provided any more. In the newly constructed buildings, a few spaces for service vehicles are left but instead there are large quantities of parking spaces for bikes with changing rooms and showers. In the opinion of the officer, the future of the City will be to manage pedestrians and cyclists and not cars.

With the 'ring of steel',[17] which was introduced as a counter-terrorism measure in July 1993, car traffic has been severely restricted. The road closures were made permanent in 1994. The volume of cars entering the City of London stabilized and all private car movements have been controlled. Over the years the 'ring of steel' was extended, and in 2013, it covered 90% of the area of the City of London. As a result of taking car traffic out of the City, it was possible to provide a much better pedestrian environment. Although the local authority had ideas about car traffic restrictions before the 'ring of steel' was proposed, the planners and traffic engineers working in the City could be far more radical after the 'ring of steel' was in place. In the decades before, very little was done for pedestrians. At some crossings, there were not even pedestrian green phases, although the City always had plenty of pedestrians.

Since the 'ring of steel' has been introduced, the local authority has been changing the streets dramatically. In the first five to seven years the back streets were improved and transformed mostly to 'shared space' or wider sidewalks were built. Nobody complained or challenged the City. Very little funding was invested at first but with time the city planners had become bolder and more money was provided and spent on street improvements for pedestrians and cyclists.

Everywhere one can find pedestrianized alleyways, wide sidewalks, new trees and benches. Nearly all junctions have raised entry crossings, now called 'courtesy crossings' because a small research project at four junctions indicated that at normal junctions only 50% of vehicles gave way to pedestrians but at raised junctions it was as high as 80%.

At *Cheapside*, a historic thoroughfare, the sidewalks were in most places widened by 3 meters and new trees have been planted. Raised entry crossings were put at all side streets. Cheapside has been changed from a road full of motorized traffic to a 'real' street. Before there were four car lanes and in 2014 only two lanes were left.

All the tourist buses in front of St. Paul's Cathedral disappeared and instead sidewalks have been widened and new walkways created for pedestrians. Contemporary green areas and flowerbeds with seating have enhanced the area around the Cathedral significantly. Especially impressive is the view from

Figure 8.3
View to Millennium
Bridge

St. Paul's Cathedral via the modern pedestrian bridge (*Millennium Bridge*) over the Thames. A remarkable pedestrian axis has been created starting from *Tate Modern* and on to the Cathedral.

Overall, the clutter of signposting has been reduced; traffic signs can now be fixed to house walls. There were useful way-finders to help pedestrians and cyclists to obtain their orientation. Altogether this is one of the best – if not the best – example of an improved pedestrian environment in one of the richest places in the world, and this is also reflected in the quality of the design.

Sidewalks

The number of materials worked with has been limited and mostly York Stone or mastique asphalt has been used.

Pedestrian Crossing Times

The short crossing times pedestrians were given at many junctions horrified me. In many cases I found it was only 7–8 seconds for the green man and then a bit more 'black' time to cross. As the waiting times were very long most people crossed at red, which makes nonsense of the use of traffic lights. Not even an able-bodied person can cross during the green times the TfL is providing, not to mention anyone slower or handicapped. In one case I crossed at a green light and was nearly run over by a lorry. This has never happened to me in all my life. This makes London the worst case in terms of crossing times provided for pedestrians of all the study cities.

That I am not alone with this criticism is shown by the complaints of the *London Assembly*[18] on 15 January 2014. Apparently 568 pedestrian crossing lights are no longer than 6 seconds. This may well have contributed to 69 pedestrians being fatally injured in 2012, a rise of nearly 20% compared to 2010. The number of pedestrians killed and seriously injured increased in the same time period by 25% (http://alternativese4.com/2014/01/15/, accessed 29.1.2014). Some of the roads that have such low pedestrian crossing times were very busy and touristy junctions, such as *Trafalgar Square*, *Oxford Circus* and *Piccadilly* (www.standard. co.uk/news/London/green-man-time-slashed, accessed 29.1.2014).

Traffic Calming

Traffic calming is common in many residential streets in Greater London; mostly cheap asphalt road humps have been built to reduce car speeds. But with the huge number of residential streets in London the quality of the traffic calming measures implemented varies from borough to borough. Since 2013, the *Borough of Islington* introduced a 20mph speed limit in all residential streets (interview with officer from TfL 27.11.2013). In other boroughs new 20mph speed limit areas have been introduced and discussions are taking place in many other boroughs about such speed limit restrictions, even on main roads.

Cycling

Mayor of London Boris Johnson has heavily promoted cycling and many cycle lanes have been created. In addition one-way streets have been converted to two-way use for cyclists. A new initiative of cycle hire started in London in 2010 on a more modest scale compared to Paris or Barcelona.

Public Transportation

The first steam-operated underground railway was running in London in 1863. The first electric tube railway opened 27 years later, in 1890 (Hall 1984, p. 32). The underground network was developed rapidly. Electric trams appeared in London in 1901 (and the last tram ran in 1952) (http://news.bbc.co.uk/onthis day/hi/dates/stories/, accessed 13.11.2006).

After 60 years of non-expansion of the underground, the Victoria Line opened in 1969. The first 36km (22.5 miles) of the Jubilee Line were built ten years later (1979) and this line was lengthened and the extension to *Stratford* opened in 1999.

In total, the underground rail network is 408km (255 miles); it has 12 lines and 275 stops. There are 27km (17 miles) of tram length in Croydon and three neighboring boroughs in the South of London. It consists of three lines and 38 stops. The Docklands Light Railway consists of 32km (20 miles), and has five lines. In addition London has an extensive bus network: 3,730km length, 700 routes and about 17,000 bus stops.

The *London Overground* opened in stages from 2007 to 2012. Nearly all of it contained old railway tracks from the 19th century. The section *Highbury &*

Islington to *West Croydon* ran its first trains in 2010 (it used to be the East London Underground Line and this line closed in 2007). This part includes four new stations and a renovated Thames tunnel (www.tfl.gov.uk, accessed 21.12.11).

Presently a major west–east rail connection is being built (Crossrail: Line 1). Crossrail will run from Reading and Heathrow in the west via *Ealing Broadway* to *Acton*. From Acton it will be operating in tunnel via *Bond Street*, *Farringdon* and *Whitechapel*; after Whitechapel the line will divide, one branch will go east to Stratford and *Shenfield*. The other branch will serve the *Isle of Dogs* and *Abbey Wood* (Mayor of London and TfL 2006, pp. 70–71). Line 2 is supposed to run from the northeast to the southwest. It is a joint venture between TfL and DfT (50:50).

Notes

1   Some 9% were public transportation and 2% cycling (https://www.gov.uk/government/statistical-data-set, accessed 1.12.13).
2   Although car use showed variations during these years walking declined constantly.
3   This was the first year in which a comparison was possible; before trips under a mile were not included.
4   Cashmore (1981) had provided data on 67 examples of pedestrianization schemes: 13 streets had been pedestrianized between 1967 and 1971; 45 streets between 1972 and 1976; and only eight streets between 1977 and 1981.
5   Many of the figures about the size of pedestrianization in Table 8.3 are from 2002. German cities have not expanded their pedestrianized areas very much since 2002.
6   In cases where there was a discrepancy between the two sources, the higher value was taken. Some city maps did not show pedestrianization and in these cases Google maps were used.
7   Germany has restricted access streets but as they are not shown on maps they could not be used here.
8   Hamburg has in addition a pedestrian walk of about 11km along the River Elbe from the *Landungsbrücken* via *Neumühlen* and *Nienstedten*.
9   Scotland has its own Transport Act of 2001.
10 In Norway they are called Gatetuns.
11 It is interesting that at least some of the advocates of Home Zones knew perfectly well that they were re-using a long-established concept, but chose to give it a new name deliberately as a marketing device to get local support.
12 The research was carried out by Sally Cairns, Lynn Sloman, Phil Goodwin, Carey Newson, Jillian Anable and Alistair Kirkbride.
13 ETP studied three British cycle cities (Oxford, York and Peterborough) and three German cities (Münster, Heidelberg, and Ingolstadt).
14 In Britain the figures are from the Census 2011 and in New York it is the average between 2007 and 2011 (ACS data).
15 www.thirteen.org, accessed 20.3.13, and TfL (2011) *Cycle Safety Action Plan* 2011.
16 Details of the horrendous plan of 1968 which included massive road building can be found in Hillmann (1986).
17 The 'ring of steel' consists of 6.5 miles of bollards, police boxes, CCTV cameras and other obstructive devices. Nineteen streets still allow controlled access (www.standard.co.uk/lifestyle/, accessed 2.12.13). The plan was swiftly implemented as it was substantially based on an earlier plan, which had been suggested for many years for traffic reduction, but rejected until the security issues gave it extra urgency (information from the City of London 2013).
18 The London Assembly is the Council of Greater London.

9

WALKING IN GERMANY: IS THERE PROGRESS?

New and Not So New Initiatives

As has been discussed in Chapter 5, German unification in 1990 changed the main emphasis away from pedestrian protection and traffic calming toward road building in East Germany and the reconstruction and renovation of East German cities. The financial efforts undertaken were enormous.

Relatively little has been achieved in the meantime to protect pedestrians from the growing number of cars. Car ownership grew from 36.8 million in 1991 to 42.9 million in 2012 (16.5%).[1] Public transportation has been improved, especially in the large urban areas, but nationally the number of public transportation passengers has only expanded by about 3% (Bundesministerium für Verkehr, Bau und Stadtentwicklung 2000, pp. 143, 218, 2009, p. 218, 2012, pp. 133, 217).

Overall, cycling rose hardly at all (0.3%) between 1994 and 2010 and was 9% of all trips (ibid 2013, pp. 222–223); in some cities, for instance Munich, Freiburg and Münster,[2] cycling has expanded more during the last 15–20 years. Walking nationwide declined from 27% in 1994 to 23.6% in 2010 and was not really replaced by cycling and public transportation trips.

In most cities nothing striking has happened to improve the walking environment. Pedestrianized areas have in some cases been extended but not by very much and there are still no pedestrian networks. Sidewalks are quite often shared with cyclists, and even more annoyingly with parked cars. The 30kph speed limit signs and traffic calming measures do not cover all the residential streets where it would be necessary and appropriate. There is also a lack of pedestrian crossings, especially zebra crossings. In some residential streets trees (or flowerbeds) and children's playgrounds are missing. One reason has been the lack of funds available from local authorities. Another is a strong and powerful German car industry and lobby that has directly and indirectly influenced federal and state governments in favor of not restricting car ownership or use, although every politician and local expert knows that cities cannot cope with the existing car traffic or even worse, with more.

Even so, during recent years there has been something of a spirit of transformation and old initiatives are being revived, for example shared space. Residents everywhere want 30kph speed limits on all residential streets and the demand for 30kph on main streets has become stronger. Residents are annoyed about too much car parking in their streets. In many cities but certainly not all, cycle lanes are becoming standard on roads and there are relatively good public transportation services, but walking is still the stepchild of transportation policies.

Some cities, such as *Berlin*, have presented new transportation plans. The plan in Berlin was agreed in 2011 and it will be even more impressive if what is put on paper is achieved in practice. Walking is supposed to grow from 25.5% (2006) of all trips to 28% in 2025, cycling from about 12% to 15% and public transportation from 27% to 32%. Generally, car ownership is low in Berlin, nearly every second household has no car and the target is that 75% of all trips will be 'green' and in the city center this should increase to 80% by 2025. Berlin had the lowest car ownership in Germany (314 cars per 1,000 inhabitants) in 2006 and it is assumed that this will not grow very much (3.5%) by the year 2025 (325 cars per 1,000 inhabitants) (www. stadtentwicklung.berlin.de, accessed 4.12.13).

A document with good intentions is the *Leipzig Charter*, an informal agreement by European Ministers on 'Sustainable European Cities' in 2007 (http://ec.europa.eu/regional_policy/archive/themes/urban/, accessed 28.1.14). It is a declaration to protect, strengthen and develop cities. The short text has several main headings. Under 'Integrated Urban Development' it is requested that the environment has to be improved and carbon dioxide reduced, among other things. Under the section 'Promotion of Productive and Affordable Urban Transportation' the emphasis is on disadvantaged urban areas, which also suffer from a lack of good and affordable public transportation; it included the demand for connected networks for both pedestrians and cyclists.

A publication by the Federal Ministry of Transport, Construction und Urban Planning debated the different aspects that are important for the well-being of city centers, such as commerce, housing, work, culture, and ethnic integration. Under the caption 'Mobility in City Centers' it mentioned the trend toward more walking and cycling for short distances, especially by young people, and a more intelligent use of the car. One of its conclusions is that the infrastructure for walking and cycling should be further developed, but the text and the conclusions are altogether vague and not really impressive (www.bmvbs, Weißbuch Innenstadt, p. 39).

There is one EU regulation that could have a positive impact on walking: the low emission zones.

Low Emission Zones

Since 2005, there have been agreed European-wide limits for particulate pollution und nitrogen dioxide. In many cities the levels of air pollution are too high. Germany reacted belatedly to this EU regulation and a few cities started to create low emission zones from 2008 onwards. Then again, not all cities have implemented them yet and most of the ones that have, only began in 2013 (www.lowemissionzones.eu, accessed 30.11.12). The technical specification of each car shows the level of pollution in its exhaust. The pollution levels are divided into three groups of which red is the worst, yellow is in the middle and green is the best. These vignettes have to be clearly visible on the windscreen. Group red is normally not allowed to enter a low emission zone. But most cities allow yellow and green.

So far 48 cities have low emission zones (July 2013) but more will introduce them in the coming years (www.umweltbundesamt.de, accessed 30.11.13). Baden-Württemberg, the state with a Green Party prime minister, has 16 designated cities of which all except one only permit cars with green vignettes. North Rhine-Westphalia is the other state where a considerable number of cities (13) have a low emission zone. But here both yellow and green vignettes are still allowed, apart from two cities. The other cities that have low emission zones are spread throughout Germany covering mostly the state capitals and other large cities but the majority of them only permit 'green' cars to enter. In many cities the emission zones are large; all cover the city center, but some also protect most of the built up area. The case study cities (Freiburg, Munich and Cologne) detailed below already have low emission zones. In the next years, the zones will become larger and the regulations more restrictive. The air pollution crisis in Paris and London in spring 2014 will hopefully have some impact on the speed of implementation of emission zones.

Case Studies

In order to understand what is going on with walking in Germany better I focused on three case studies. Starting with the best-known 'green' city, Freiburg, followed by the economically most successful city, Munich, and finally ending with the largest city in the most populous State of North Rhine-Westphalia, Cologne.

Case Study: Freiburg

Population 218,459 in 2013.

Background and Population Growth

Freiburg is located in the southwest of Germany between the *Rhine* valley and the edge of the *Black Forest*. France and Switzerland are close neighbors. The city grew from 1980 to 2011 by 50,070 inhabitants, a population growth of about 29% (Freiburg im Breisgau 2011, p. 3).

Freiburg has a large and well-known university, catering for about 30,000 students (ibid, p. 185). The city has had a high employment growth over several decades, which was higher than its population growth. This is strongly connected with the economic buoyancy of the city as a whole.

Transportation

The wider city center is bordered by a trunk road, the B31, which took years to complete because of environmental protests. This road allows fast car access directly to the *Black Forest*. The plan is to put a section of the B31, which goes close to the center of Freiburg, underground so that this street can also be partly pedestrianized and would give direct access to the attractive riverbank of the *Dreisam*. At present, cars have to drive at 30kph from 22.00 onwards and throughout the night.

Table 9.1 Modal split (all trips) in the City of Freiburg in percent

Mode	1982	1989	1992	1999	2020 Forecast
Walking	35	22	21	23	24
Cycling	15	18	19	27	28
Public transportation	11	16	18	18	20
Car use	39	44	42	32	28

Sources: Freiburg, Tiefbauamt 2003 (not officially published); Socialdata 1998; Freiburg, Stadt 2008

Freiburg proposed its first overall 'green' transportation plan in 1969 and its first cycle plan in 1970. In 1969 it was already decided to keep the trams despite the widespread practice at that time for cities of this size to replace trams with buses (Apel 1992, p. 163).

Modal Split and Reduction of Car Use

The modal split data show a spectacular decline in car use from 1989 to 1999. It is believed that this has continued although no new data is available. During the data collection for the *Noise Action Plan* in all streets with more than 4,500 motor vehicles (24 hours), it was estimated that in 80% of these streets car traffic had declined and cycling increased in 2010 (compared to 1999). The modal split forecast for 2020 does not seem to be very ambitious, but in 2008 the city was still assuming an increase in car ownership by 8% up to 2020 (Freiburg, Stadt 2008, np). The latest forecast gives a much higher value for cycling (35%), slightly more for walking but the share for public transportation will stay the same. A significant 20% decline in car journeys is forecast (www.freiburg.de/radkonzept, accessed 22.11.13).

When studying the travel to work data (the latest are from 1999), the percentage of cycling is already high with 34%, public transportation achieved 15%, car drivers and passengers 37%, and only walking was small with 13%. This was about 15 years ago, I would assume that cycling and public transportation has grown further. Cycling may be as high as 40% and public transportation around 20%. Some 31% of all shopping trips were carried out on foot, 25% by bike, 17% by public transportation and only 28% by car (R+T 2012, p. 27).

The data in Freiburg confirm that it is possible to reduce car use despite a 68% increase in car ownership between 1976 (54,429) and 2006 (91,457)[3] (Landesamt Baden-Württemberg 2002; Freiburg im Breisgau 2011, p. 18). The later figures show a fall in car ownership from 2001 to 2011 from 420 to 375 cars per 1,000 population. One has to be aware that from 2008 onwards the counting method has changed, consequently it cannot be compared with older data. The figure for 2011 would be higher if the old method were used. It is calculated that the difference is about 12% as a nationwide German average. If a 12% adjustment is applied to Freiburg, then there was no change during the last ten years in car ownership, which is plausible (Kraftfahrt Bundesamt, internal information, Flensburg).

The walking data illustrate the decline in the walking share from 35% in 1982 to 22% in 1999 despite a very large and attractive mostly car-free city center and good sidewalks nearly everywhere. The decline in walking represents in part a substitution toward the growth in cycling and even more so by the improvement in public transportation and its fare policies (for more details see below). Thus it is difficult to estimate whether the share in walking would have 'really' declined, stayed stable or even increased, if cycling and public transportation use had not grown so much.

Walking

Pedestrianization

Freiburg had already discussed pedestrianizing the main shopping street (*Kaiser-Joseph Straße*) as early as 1949 but this plan was not accepted (Vedral 1985, pp. 52–53). The planning authority proposed instead to close some side streets in 1954 but because of local protests nothing was done (Monheim 1980, p. 54), and only one short street was closed in 1957 (Monheim 1975, p. 130). Closing the main shopping street was proposed again in 1965 but as before it was not acceptable to local politicians. Still a number of smaller streets were closed. It took until 1973 to devote large areas of the city center to pedestrians. The example of Freiburg has been symptomatic for many other cities. Once the idea of pedestrianization had been proposed, it would crop up again and again, though often in different forms, until it would succeed (unfortunately this is also true for road building proposals). What makes the pedestrianization schemes in Freiburg so special were two factors: first, they were done at a high standard, mostly with local materials, and second, it included a whole network of small streams (*Bächle*) of fresh and clean water which comes directly from the Black Forest. These streams run along the side of most pedestrianized streets, small bridges connect a narrow strip of 'sidewalk' with the main pedestrian street. There are many jokes about what happens when people fall into a stream, which is not unusual as the wine is good and plentiful. The design of the 'Bächle' has been copied throughout Germany, for example, Reichenhall, Ravensburg, but also in cities outside Germany.

According to the official statistics, Freiburg had 8,535m of pedestrianized streets in 2009 (this has not changed in 2013). This does not include squares, such as the large square in front of the cathedral. Plans to pedestrianize a large section of the main inner ring road (the *Rotteckring*) have been discussed for over 30 years. Finally, this major change was carried out in 2013. The function of a ring road has been largely lost although most of the car traffic has been diverted onto *Bismarckallee* (four lanes), a street next to the main railway station. The ring will only contain motorized traffic that needs access to the city center, for example deliveries. Part of the ring road, the area around the *Alte Synagoge* will be changed into a large square. There will also be changes to the tram routes. A new tramline (and other lines as well) will use part of the 'disused' ring road and give some relief to the city center routes.

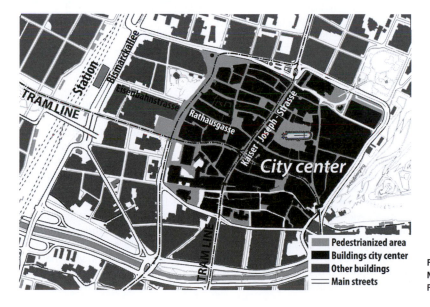

Figure 9.1
Map of central area of
Freiburg

Figure 9.2
New design of an urban ring road in Freiburg; instead of cars a new tram connection and more space for pedestrians

Planning

It was admitted that walking has been neglected over recent years and new funds have now been made available to improve it. All sidewalks will be widened to a minimum of 2.5m. Along the roads with a high level of pedestrian traffic, an additional meter of width will be added and in highly frequented living and business streets a sidewalk width of 5m is desirable (Freiburg, Stadt 2008, np). It is planned to change Freiburg's city center into a barrier-free place (interview with officer of the city of Freiburg, 22.11.13).

My view

When arriving in Freiburg by train one is, as in Odense, confronted with a four-lane road, which has been relatively recently built and is the replacement of one of the sections of the ring road. In addition the two traffic lights in front of the station have a very short crossing phase of only 12 seconds and a long waiting period. The only consolation is that the sidewalks are wide (about 4.5m and in some places wider) and there are cycleways in addition. Having negotiated the first wide car road, the street (*Eisenbahnstrasse*) entering the historic city center is also not outstandingly attractive. The street has a 30kph speed limit and relatively wide sidewalks (4m at the narrowest part). Some parts are asphalt but mostly they are paved. The first street I used within the historic city center (*Rathausgasse*) had grey concrete paving stones, which were commonly used in the 1970s. They now look dated and a few were cracked and new paving material would improve this street. But most parts of the city center and around it had beautiful paving, consisting of flat cobblestones and flat stones from the river

(Rhine pebbles or Iris quartz) put together in attractive patterns. This was all done in the early 1970s and after more than 40 years it still looked extremely skillfully done and distinctive. Everywhere within the pedestrianized streets the street surfaces are in very good condition.

Outside the city center one can often find cars which are fully parked on the sidewalks, a practice very common in most German cities. As most sidewalks are very generous, the sidewalk width left is still between 2.50–3.00m but sometimes it was smaller, especially if there were parked bicycles as well. Wandering around, one finds plenty of shared space areas[4] all built during the 1980s, for example *Tellstrasse*. In general I was aware of how little car traffic there was everywhere, and most streets were indeed traffic calmed with a wide variation of traffic calming measures. An old iron bridge over the railway lines has been dedicated to pedestrians and cyclists only (*Wiwili Brücke*). It runs parallel to a bridge for trams, which also has wide sidewalks to cross the railways.

Even so, there are still plenty of distributor roads with one car lane in each direction and wide cycle lanes (about 2 to 2.50m) on both sides, but there are also distributor roads with more than one car lane. The sidewalks are mostly 2.50m or wider. Yet, it is not uncommon for the sidewalks to be simply divided by a white line, with one side for cyclists and the other for pedestrians. Sometimes the space for pedestrians is too small and two people with shopping would not be able to walk comfortably side by side.

Figure 9.3
Typical surface of pedestrianized street in Freiburg

Pedestrian Crossings

The green phases are good for pedestrians (sometimes even 50 seconds), especially on side roads, but for crossing distributor roads, the phases are very much shorter (often less than 20 seconds) and the waiting times long. Overall, the residents of Freiburg are very patient and waited. In Germany crossing a pedestrian crossing when red is illegal and one can be fined. This is very different to most other countries.

Traffic Calming

Outside the historic city center, all residential streets are traffic calmed with a speed limit of 30kph. Freiburg was the first German city to introduce area-wide traffic calming in 1988/89. The official statistics show that of the 500km of roads inside the City of Freiburg, only 17% (87km) are for through traffic, the rest are for local traffic only and are traffic-calmed (Stadt Freiburg 2014, http://www.freiburg.de, Zahlenspiegel).

Cycling

Freiburg had about 420km of cycleways and cycle lanes[5] and 9,000 parking places for cyclists (within the city center alone 6,000 plus 1,000 bike and ride spaces at tram stops) in 2008 (Freiburg, Stadt 2008, np). There has been no significant change over the last four years. In 2012, some roads carry up to 12,000 cyclists a day and we can safely assume this will further increase.

Sustainable Living

The *Vauban* site, an area of 36 hectares, is located close to the city center. The French army used it previously and after unification this valuable land became available for housing. About 5,000 people live there. As Vauban was planned to become nearly car free, tram access was important. A new short extension serving it opened in 2006. Some 50% of households opted not to have a car and the remainder have car parking spaces that are not close by. The land needed for housing construction was sold, and a large part of the cost of the tramline was covered by the proceeds (Freiburg, Stadt 2003, np). Car ownership in Vauban was only 171 cars per 1,000 population in 2011 (Freiburg im Breisgau 2011, p. 113). Also, the percentage of car sharing was very high: 89% of people without cars were members of the car-sharing club in 2002, compared to only 11% for people with one car.

Public Transportation

In 2012 the total tram network had four lines and was 34km (track length). One has to remember that the tram network is all within the small City of Freiburg. There has been a constant growth of public transportation passengers, from 39.5 million in 1985 to 76 million passengers in 2012 (interview in Freiburg, 22.11.13). The success of the tram is also related to people's access to it. Some 65% of Freiburg's resident population and 70% of all employees can use a tram within less than 300m distance (Freiburg, Stadt: Interview, 2008).

The success of public transportation in Freiburg was also the result of introducing Germany's first '*environmental travel card*' in 1984. This monthly travel card gives unlimited trips on all public transportation modes in the town, and since 1991 also in the transportation region. The card is freely transferable between users

(Hass-Klau et al 2002, p. 38). In 2010, 356,402 of these monthly cards (called *Regiocard*) were sold, which implies that more than half of the population in the region has such a ticket (Regioverbund Freiburg 2011, p. 28). With such a card, extra trips cost nothing, which strengthens the use of public transportation for evening and leisure use.

Case Study: Munich

Population in the city 1.5 million and 1.4 million inhabitants in the rest of the region[6] excluding Munich in 2013.

Background

Munich's major waves of industrialization occurred after the First World War and even more so after the Second World War. The location and growth of firms like BMW and Siemens were of crucial importance for the economic development of the city and its surroundings. In the 21st century it has become the leading high-tech region of Germany (www.acre.soasci.uva.nl, accessed 18.11.13). The City of Munich is the capital of the State of Bavaria, which had 12.5 million inhabitants in 2013 (www.statistik.bayern.de, accessed 18.11.13).

Population Growth

The population in the city grew from 1.1 million in 1961 to about 1.5 million in 2013, about 36% in slightly more than half a century. But the population growth in the rest of the region was much higher, about 122% in the same time period (Landeshauptstadt München Stadtentwicklung 1975, pp. 1–4; www. muenchen.de, accessed 29.1.14). The forecast for the city is a 15% growth over the next ten years (www.muenchen.de/rathaus/stadtverwaltung/stadt enwicklungsamt/grundlagen/bevölkerungsprognose, accessed 16.1.14). Then again the figures between 2002 and 2012 show that the population in the City of Munich increased by slightly more than 12% and in the rest of the region by only 6% whereas the growth of employment was the other way round; Munich expanded by 6% and the region by slightly more than 16% (Planungsverband Äußere Wirtschaftraum München, www.pv-muenchen.de, accessed 30.4.14). The figures show that the trend of increased migration to large cities has already taken place in Munich. Conversely, the growth is not from the suburbs to the City of Munich but the largest element is migration from outside the region (PV 2014, p. 16).

Transportation

The modal split data for the City of Munich show a 7% decline in car use, a 5% increase in cycling and a small decline in public transportation trips over the last 20 years (1992–2012). Most remarkable is the growth in walking of 3%. In total the green modes account for 67% of all movements within the city (Landeshauptstadt München, Referat für Stadtplanung und Bauordnung, interview 6.2.12).

As in many other cities, walking to shops had the highest share with 41%, but still 29% drove, 14% used public transportation and 16% cycled in 2012 (ibid, p. 4).

It is not only car use that declined but also car ownership. The statistics show a reduction in car ownership of about 13% from 1999 (589 per 1,000 pop.) to 2011

Table 9.2 Modal split (all trips) in the City of Munich in percent

Year	1992	2002	2012	2012
Type of trips	All	All	All	Work
Car driver	40	41	33	42
Public transportation	24	21	23	34
Bicycle	12	10	17	14
Walking	24	28	27	10

Sources: Socialdata 1998; Landeshauptstadt München 2013, p. 4

Table 9.3 Cordon counts in 24 hours over time

Year	Crossing the city border	First motorway ring (Mittlerer Ring)	City center ring road
2000	480,000	448,000	84,000
2003	509,000	442,000	52,000
2007/09	483,000	377,000	44,000

Source: Interview in Munich 6.2.12 and information from Dr. Martin Klamt, Stadt München

(512 – taking into account the change in counting system in 2008) (not officially published data from Flensburg 2012). The reduction in the number of cars entering the first motorway ring and city center between 2000 and 2007 is also significant.

The number of cars entering the city itself stayed about the same, but the cars entering the Mittlerer Ring declined by about 16%. But the highest decline was for cars entering the city center ring. This figure nearly halved. According to the city the main reasons for the decline in car use have been:

- car parking management
- promotion of public transportation
- reduction of car lanes by introducing cycle lanes instead.

Walking

Pedestrianiztion

The construction of the first large-scale pedestrian scheme in Munich's city center, designed by the architect *Bernhard Winkler*, combined with the opening of a new public transportation system at the beginning of the 20th Olympic Games in 1972, presented the world with a new German city center image. Munich's public transportation system (see below) channeled not only the workforce but also the shoppers directly into the heart of the city. The newly created vehicle-free urban space was quickly used for entertainment, relaxation and leisure. Discussions on how to design urban space for the purpose of attracting different social groups were part of these early years in Munich.

By the standards of today, Munich's pedestrian scheme is not unusual but at the time it was seen as outstanding. The main city center streets were closed to vehicle traffic (the *Neuhauser* and *Kaufinger Straße*) and included in the scheme were several large squares, such as the *Karlsplatz (Stachus)*, the area around St. Mary's Church and the *Marienplatz*, the historic center of Munich. In total the scheme was about 800–900m in length, not including the squares and a few very short side streets (Hass-Klau 1984, p. 552).

Only a couple of months after the opening, it became clear that the new pedestrian scheme was an utter success. Experts had warned that the existing streets and squares would be far too wide and not suitable for pedestrianization (see also Jacobs 1961, ch. 2). The argument was that not enough pedestrians would fill the existing car-free urban space, and the few who would dare to walk along would simply be intimidated by the width of the streets and squares (Landeshauptstadt München 1983, internal information).

With the introduction of pedestrianization, the number of pedestrians using the area shot up dramatically. Whereas in 1966, 72,000 pedestrians were counted

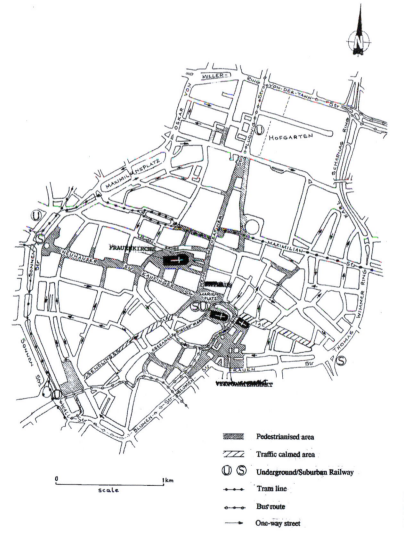

Figure 9.4
Map of city center of Munich

on one day between *Karlsplatz* and *Marienplatz*, in 1972 the number had increased to 120,000 (same hours as in 1966 from 7.00–19.00) (Landeshauptstadt München 1975, p. 3). In 1983, the number had totaled 200,000 pedestrians between the main railway station and the Marienplatz (Landeshauptstadt München 1987, p 23).

Closing the historic streets in the center of the city had another unintended effect. Shopping turnover in the pedestrianized streets increased by about 40% (Landeshauptstadt München 1980, p. 3). The success in Munich changed the opinion of many retailing organizations previously up in arms about pedestrianization; suddenly they became in favor of it.

As a result of the success of the pedestrianization in 1972, the most important food, vegetable and flower market in close proximity to the Marienplatz was opened as a pedestrian area in 1975. With that, the *Viktualien Markt* became one of the most impressive German open markets. In the same year, the *Theatiner Straße*, an upmarket shopping street, was closed to motor traffic. It provided a connecting link between the city center and a large park (*Englischer Garten*) in the northeast of Munich. In 1980/81, the main street from the station to the historic city center was partly closed and several minor streets were pedestrianized. In other city center streets, car traffic was severely restricted. A large section of *Sendlinger Straße*, another important shopping street, was pedestrianized in 2013 (it had been traffic calmed before).

Many other shopping streets (20) in the different districts of Munich are also pedestrianized (Stadt München 2012, internal information). In total the City of Munich has about 6km of pedestrianized streets but there are many car-free squares, which are not included in this calculation.

My View

The pedestrianized area in the historic center of Munich, especially during the summer months, is totally overloaded with people. It is choking on its own success. The number of people is so high that sometimes it is not a pleasure to walk there. Counts in *Kaufinger Straße* between 13.00 and 14.00 estimated 14,130 pedestrians on a Saturday in April 2009. In 2013, 9,300 pedestrians were counted between 11.00 and 12.00 and 17,250 between 16.00 and 17.00 (I assume it was in September but no detail was given). In total 134,314 pedestrians were walking in these streets from 9.00 to 20.00 and in the evening between 19.00 and 20.00 the number was still nearly 12,000 (ibid, p. 4). This really implies that the attractiveness of the car-free area in the city center has stayed the same if not increased.

Although two out of three shops are part of a chain and the shopping environment is not really very interesting, there are still many remarkable historic buildings along the main pedestrian axis (*Stachus* to *Marienplatz*). As the pedestrianized streets are so popular, the shop rents are inevitably extremely high. According to a local newspaper, the highest rent was €340 per sqm and in smaller shops the rent can be as high as €410 per sqm (Thieme 2013, p. 4).

As the main pedestrianized streets were too crowded, I studied a brochure from the Planning Department of the City of Munich with the title 'Across the City Center Back Yards and Passages'. It is a walk that starts at the Viktualien Markt and describes 13 stops. It finishes at another square (*Sankt-Jacobs-Platz*).

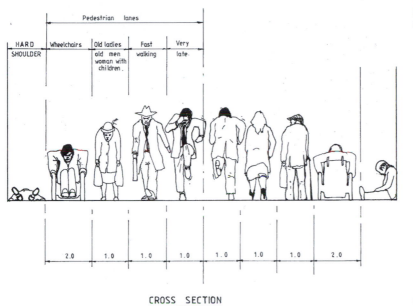

CROSS SECTION

Figure 9.5
Multilane pedestrian
highway

Figure 9.6
Relaxing in the sun,
Odeonsplatz

Altogether it took me three hours to do the round. Quite a bit of time was lost by trying to find the way as there is no real street marking, which is a pity, and the map provided is not really very useful. A number of sites are really nothing more than modern shopping passages, but some of the others are really small and hidden treasures. I would have liked to include fewer shopping passages and more interesting and historic streets, which are not mentioned at all, such as *Hackerstraße*, *Brunnstraße* or *Sebastiansplatz*. More street signs to stress that this is indeed a pedestrian route would have been useful. The street called *Altheimer Eck* was full of delivery traffic and illegally parked delivery vans even at 15.00 so that it was not pleasant to walk along, but it is altogether a great idea from the city since walking in the main pedestrianized streets can be 'painful' at times.

Walking Outside the City Center

A street festival took place in September 2013. For that reason *Ludwigstraße*, normally a wide, busy street full of cars, was closed to car traffic and I walked along this famous street, which starts close to the historic city center (near *Odeonsplatz*) and runs to the *Münchner Freiheit*,[7] which is an interchange station for the underground (U6 and U3) and the tram to *Schwabing Nord* (Number 23). It was a great experience to walk in the middle of a major road and see for the first time the historic facades of mostly early 19th-century buildings and the *Siegestor* (a 19th-century triumphal arch).[8] Even on normal days when traffic is using the carriageway, walking is a pleasure along this street because a line of impressive poplars separates the carriageways from the sidewalks, and these are wide and in good condition. In addition to the trees, a cycleway on each side protects the pedestrians from car traffic.

The side streets right and left from Ludwigstraße were residential with four- and five-storey housing, mostly from the turn of the 20th century. All streets had 30kph speed limits, one row of car parking on each side and good sidewalks. In some streets cars were allowed to park with two wheels on the sidewalk. What I saw in the neighborhood of *Schwabing* was not as bad as what I had noticed in other towns, where mothers with buggies could hardly pass parked cars (on sidewalks).

Greenways

Munich's greenways run along the River *Isar*, a powerful fast-flowing river. On some parts one is allowed to enjoy the river during the summer and surfing is common. The *Isarauen* were originally substantial flood meadows and are now a green area with a large number of fine mature trees. It runs about 2–3km on the right-hand side of the river. On the left-hand side is the famous *Englischer Garten*, one of the first parks in Germany, which was designed in the style of a traditional English park. Unfortunately a main road[9] runs through parts of this park.

Cycling

Cycling has always been important in Munich but in recent years its promotion has been a major policy costing about €4.2 million annually. The latest modal split figure makes clear that Munich has the highest share in cycling (14%) of any German-speaking city of roughly similar population size.

Munich has 1,200km of cycleways and cycle lanes plus 350km of route signing. In recent years a number of major roads have received wide cycle lanes. About 40% of one-way streets allow cyclists to travel in both directions.

Traffic Calming

Some 80% of all the streets in Munich have 30kph speed limits; this implies that cars should drive in all residential streets at this low speed. The safety record of the city is very good (see Chapter 15). Traffic calming measures do exist but they are not particularly popular because of problems with ambulances.

Public Transportation

Munich has the most impressive post-Second World War public transportation system in Germany. Before 1971, the city relied on a large tram and a substantial suburban rail network (from the 1960s onwards called S-Bahn). In 1963, the City of Munich decided to build a new underground system and a suburban rail tunnel (4.2km long) in the city center. It was also agreed to abandon the tram system.

In 1972, the S-Bahn tunnel was completed in time for the Olympic Games and some stretches on the underground lines too (U1, U3). One year earlier, a new public transportation organization, the *Münchner Verkehrsverbund*, had been formed. This allowed passengers to travel with a single ticket within the city and the region. For the first time, there was a unified price structure and one timetable for city and region alike.

Despite the financial losses trams imposed, they were extremely popular with the citizens, and in contrast to the two other large German cities, Hamburg and West Berlin, Munich kept some of its tram network although some lines disappeared. In 1972 Munich still had 111km of tramlines compared to 79km in 2012.

Very recently new tramlines have again been built. The tramline 23 to *Parkstadt Munich*, which opened in December 2009 with a length of 3.1km, or the tramline *St. Emmeram*, which opened two years later (in December 2011) with a length of 4.3km, are good examples. Another new tramline is planned in Munich West (Tram Westtangente, about 9km) (interview in Munich in 2013).

Case Study: Cologne

Population 1,045,000 in the city in 2011.

Background and Population Growth

Cologne was one of the most important Roman settlements north of the Alps. During the medieval period, it was the largest independent city in the German-speaking countries. Cologne, the fourth biggest city in Germany, has an average population density of 2,380 inhabitants per sqkm. It has a strong student culture: over 85,000 students were registered in 2012 (www.stadt-koeln.de/mediaasset/, accessed 26.11.13). The population has grown by nearly 3% since 2000 (1,018,000 inhabitants) (www.stadt-koeln.de, accessed 26.11.13). During the last 30 years, it has become a center for culture, media and art. Cologne is famous for its carnival and street festivals.

Transportation

Cologne has a very good road network and excellent connections to several motorways: the A1, the A3 and the A4. It has also one of the most important railway stations in Germany, though its capacity was limited because most trains had the use of only one railway bridge over the Rhine. This bottleneck has been improved by building an additional intercity station on the eastern side of the Rhine in *Deutz*; the main city center lies on the western side.

The public transportation and cycling share has increased but the share in car trips has not changed significantly in 22 years. If anything, car use has increased and all the green modes taken together declined by 3%. Especially striking is the decline in walking from 39% in 1976 to 26% in 1998, despite many pedestrianized and traffic calmed streets. Then again, the data is now 16 years old and I would expect that the modal share for cars has stayed about the same but cycling and public transportation grew and walking has declined further.

Table 9.4 Modal split (all trips) in the City of Cologne in percent

Mode	1976	1982	1992	1998
Walking	39	32	30	26
Cycling	6	11	11	12
Public transportation	15	15	19	19
Car	38	40	40	42
Others	2	2	-	1

Source: www.socialdata.de/daten/vm_d.php, accessed 19.9.2006

Walking in the City Center

My View

When leaving the main railway station, the sight of the largest cathedral in Germany is overwhelming. One is also confronted with a large car-free square and relatively high steps. It is not immediately obvious how to enter the city center without climbing the steps. If the steps are taken, one reaches a large platform and passes this impressive Gothic edifice and its main entrance. In summer, many young but also older people are socializing around the cathedral. There is mostly music, paintings and skate-boarding. Despite plenty of social activities, this part of the city center is always windy because of the microclimate from the cathedral towers. Not far from the cathedral one reaches the *Hohe Straße*, which was already partly closed to wheeled traffic from 1921 onwards (Hass-Klau 1990a, p. 88). It is a very narrow street crowded with pedestrians most of the day. In the past it had many important shops, which today have mostly been replaced by chain stores. This street is the main axis from the main railway station to the other main shopping streets in the city center, the *Schildergasse*, the *Gürzenichstraße* and the *Breite Straße.*

Schildergasse[10] and Gürzenichstraße have also a variety of shops, again mostly chain stores. As the city center was heavily bombed during the Second World War, it was mostly rebuilt with buildings with large-scale monotonous-looking facades. All these streets are nearly always busy with pedestrians. I noticed that even in November people were sitting outside although the sun was not shining

Figure 9.7
Map of wider city center
of Cologne

and the weather was not particularly pleasant. In summer, the town center is full of tables and chairs. Most of the side streets are either fully or partly pedestrianized and so the whole area is very much car free and easy to walk around.

More interesting than the pedestrianized streets are the streets to the northwest of a large city center square (*Neumarkt*). Although these streets are not pedestrianized, they are partly designed as shared space, for example *Mittelstraße* or part of Breite Straße. Breite Straße has a 10kph speed limit for cars, which is unusual in Germany. In reality cars drive faster than 10kph. Although car traffic is mostly allowed, it is so restricted that it does not distract from the pleasure of walking. In most cases these streets have wide sidewalks, plenty of shops and restaurants and small squares, so that walking around remains a pleasure. Breite Straße becomes a pedestrian street from half-way (from *Auf dem Berlich* onwards). The paving is attractive with black and white stripes and this street is not quite as busy as Gürzenichstraße and Schildergasse. It is a good street because it has a mixture of restaurants, cafes and shops and it is very popular with local people.

In contrast to Freiburg and Munich, Cologne is not a very clean city. There are corners with litter, cigarette ends and other dirt. Unclean streets do not automatically deter walking but it is more pleasant to walk along clean streets.

The historic center (in contrast to the shopping area) is located in immediate proximity to the station and with access to the river *Rhine*. Important squares like the *Alter Markt* and *Heumarkt* are part of the mostly medieval city. Both squares are used for social activities, especially the larger Heumarkt. Nearly half of the Alter Markt is filled in summer with tables and chairs and nearly all of the narrow streets around the squares are without car traffic.

In 1982, the major road along the riverbank was put in a tunnel alongside the city center and the surface of the tunnel was greened, allowing direct pedestrian access to the riverside walks in 1986. It is today mostly a tourist area with hotels, restaurants, cafes, bars and a few shops.

Sidewalks and Trees

The city center sidewalks in the pedestrianized streets have a simple pattern consisting of concrete paving stones and they were mostly in good condition. When studying the sidewalks more carefully one does see small corners that are broken or paving stones that were cracked.

In the historic city center most streets have cobblestones and very much smaller paving stones. The larger cobblestones are not particularly good for walking, especially for women with high heels, as they are rather uneven.

Shared Space

Not far from the city center is an interesting street: *Severinstraße*. It runs from *Mühlenbach* to *Clodwig Platz* (Südstadt) and is 1.2km long (www.koeln.de, accessed 1.12.13). Severinstraße is the central spine of a historic neighborhood (possibly even Roman). It is a very good recently designed shared space street and it works well. The sidewalks were wide (about 5m on one side and about 2m on the other); they were covered with attractive grey paving stones. Bollards prevent cars from parking there but one side allowed parking. Cycling was permitted in both directions. There was only one lane left for car traffic and the cars drove slowly but the traffic flow was continuous. All junctions were slightly raised and there were no traffic lights. Pedestrians crossed wherever they wanted. The further one walks toward Clodwig Platz, the more the street became a mixture of shops of all kinds for locals, and restaurants for both locals and visitors who like this neighborhood. Since the improvements more restaurants have opened.

Walking in an Inner City Area: Sülz

Walking around in one of the popular housing areas in Cologne one is confronted with a large amount of cars parked *on* the sidewalks. The sidewalks were very wide, up to 5m and sometimes even wider. Even with a parked car there was still enough space for two people to walk unhindered, although the aesthetic aspect of the street is impaired. But there were problems in some streets (around the Luxemburger Strasse). Here one finds streets where the sidewalks were reduced to 1.20–1.50m, for example parts of *Petersbergstraße* or *Breiberg Straße*. I saw a mother with two children and asked her whether she found the sidewalks wide enough. She was obviously struggling. She told me: 'I am happy if a car driver is not bumping into me when he/she is trying to park the car'. It is clear that the demand for car parking is extremely high. Most inner cities have high density living and some families own more than one car.

The paving material of the sidewalks is mostly asphalt and sometimes they have been repaired and one can see several layers, again aesthetically not especially impressive. In other locations the asphalt was broken. There were a number of streets which had no trees and they did look depressing. Altogether although it was still an attractive area to live in and had plenty of space to walk around, one wonders what to do with car parking. How it is at present does not seem to be a good solution.

Pedestrian Crossings

Everywhere in the city I saw well-functioning zebra crossings even on distributor roads (with low volumes of cars). I also studied traffic light pedestrian crossings. At some traffic lights at the Luxemburger Strasse it was not possible to cross the street with one green phase; admittedly it is a very wide street. At junctions there were long green walking periods, sometimes 40–50 seconds when crossing the smaller roads, but on major roads the crossing times were not so generous. Nevertheless they were mostly better than in other cities I had visited.

In the city center there were a few crossings where it was not clear who has priority: the pedestrians or the car drivers. As all street users were insecure, they drove and walked very carefully. It is very interesting to watch and I would like other cities to be brave enough to have such 'insecure' crossings as well.

Greenways

Cologne is in the lucky position that as a result of its military history and structure it was able to create two greenways in ring form around the city, including a much smaller one around the historic city (the medieval wall and moat). Stübben already suggested and designed the first green ring in the form of a wide boulevard in 1881 (www.aviewoncities.com, accessed 9.12.13). In Chapter 2, I explained that during the 1920s green axes and parks became an important policy to improve the high density and polluted 19th-century city. This also happened in Cologne. The second greenway was planned by *Fritz Schuhmacher* between 1920 and 1923. In 1929, the final design by *Theodor Nußbaum* was completed and put into practice. It included radial green axes from the city center to the outer ring. Part of this design was a ring road following the model of the US parkways (Kölner Grün Stiftung 2013, pp. 23–24).

Low Emission Zone

The low emission zone in Cologne was introduced in 2008 but was extended from 16sqkm to 88sqkm in April 2012. It now covers most of the city. At present the city still allows cars to enter with a yellow vignette (see above) but this was changed in July 2014 so that only cars with green vignettes can enter.

Traffic Calming

Cologne was a leading city in promoting traffic calming during the 1980s and 1990s. Most of it is done very well. Nearly all residential streets have 30kph speed limits. A street worth a visit is *Palanter Strasse* in Sülz. The street has 3 x 2m large flowerbeds at regular distances which look as if they were planted and looked after by residents.

Cycling

Cologne has a cycle network of 2,000km, of which about 800km are specifically constructed or designed and more than 400km are one-way streets where cyclists can use the street in the opposite direction to car traffic (www.stadt-koeln.de/verkehr/radverkehr/index.html, accessed 11.7.06).

Public Transportation

The city has in total 191.2km of track length of tram and light rail and 49.6km of suburban railways (S-Bahn). The overall public transportation policy of the city has been successful and the number of passengers has grown considerably from 1985 to 2012 (by 66%), and about three-quarters of the passengers travel by light rail or tram (www.kvb-koeln.de/german/unternehmen/leistungsdaten/bahn.html, accessed 20.4.14; Hass-Klau et al 2007, p. 112).[11]

Cologne's public transportation system is integrated into a very large transportation region called *Verkehrsverbund Rhein-Sieg*, which was originally formed in 1987. This allows integrated traveling with one ticket using all modes and provides a unified fare structure.

In 2005, Cologne started to build a new underground tunnel of 4km, which will run southeast from the main railway station (*Breslauer Platz*) with seven underground stops. So far it has not been a great success story. In 2014 the line is still not finished because of serious and unexpected construction problems.

Notes

1   There was a decline in car ownership in 2008 but this coincided with a change in the counting method. Whatever happened statistically in 2008, since 2009 car ownership is rising again.
2   Cycling in Münster grew from 31.7% of all trips in 1994 to 37.6% in 2007 but walking declined from 21.5% in 1994 to 15.7% in 2007, and as car share did not decline very much (about 1%) and public transportation increased little, there has been large substitution from walking to cycling (www.muenster.de, accessed 4.12.13).
3   2006 was the highest number of cars and the highest per 1000 inhabitants.
4   In Germany this area is provided with a paragraph Z325/326SVO or in German Spielstrasse (idiomatic play street).
5   The figure is divided into 170km of cycle paths, cycle lanes, and cycle streets including 2km of the use of a bus lane. 130km were traffic calmed streets and 120km were greenways (information from interview with a representative of the City of Freiburg, 22.11.13).
6   The region is slightly smaller than the transportation region (Verkehrsverbund).
7   It changes its name into Leopoldstraße at Akademiestraße.
8   I am not aware that the Bavarians ever won any battles at this time.
9   It is one major road which is divided into different names: south to north from Widenmayerstraße, Emil-Riedel-Straße continuing as Iffland Straße. There have been a number of proposals to put this street (or parts of it) in a tunnel and that seems to be very likely.
10 *Gasse* means in German a lane or very narrow street.
11 From 165.4 million (123.1 million were rail) in 1985 to 275.1 million in 2012 of which 208.9 million passengers were rail. This is not the passenger number of the Verkehrsverbund, which would be much larger (516.3 million in 2012) covering about 3.3 million population (www.ursinfo.de, accessed 22.4.14).

THE NORDIC APPROACH: DENMARK

Background

The Nordic countries consist of Sweden, Finland, Norway and Denmark. Although I have worked and traveled widely in Sweden and Finland, I selected Denmark and Norway. Denmark because of its long history in promoting sustainable transportation, and Norway because of the way in which it collects funding through road tolls, which also indirectly affects walking. In this chapter I will study in more detail Copenhagen and the third largest city of Denmark: Odense.

Denmark has always been an independent country. In the 21st century, Denmark is the smallest Nordic state in area, containing 5.6 million people in 2012. It is still a kingdom and its population density is low except in Copenhagen.

Transportation

Road Safety Plans

The goal of the *Road Safety Plan* of 1988 was to reduce the number of killed and injured by 40–45% in 2000 compared to the base year of 1986/1987. The first six years were very successful but the campaign soon lost its momentum. A new plan in 1998 had the same goal for 2010 (Laursen 2002, p. 83).

The objective of the *Road Safety Action Plan 2013–2020* has been to reduce all types of casualties in 2010 by 50% (killed, seriously and slightly injured). In 2010, 255 people were killed of whom 17% were pedestrians (43 people) (etsc.eu, accessed 13.11.13). In comparison with 1995, the total number of people killed on Danish roads has declined significantly (582 had been killed), and so has the number of pedestrians killed (118) (Jensen 1998, p. 11).

During the last 15 years, people walked less therefore the decline is not automatically related to safer roads and streets. I assume that a big part of the decline in pedestrians being killed was related to less walking and a change of mode from walking to cycling, especially in Copenhagen.[1]

Planning and Transportation

In contrast to many other European countries, car ownership is relatively low. In 2012 there were 394 cars per 1,000 inhabitants compared to 541 in Germany and 457 in the UK[2] (www.statbank.dk/folk1 and bil707, Statistic Yearbook 2012, www.meinestadt.de, accessed 09.09.13; http://dat.worldbank.org, accessed 20.10.13). This has been partly due to the high taxation of cars but also because cycling has been vigorously promoted in Copenhagen.

Out-of-town shopping centers have been limited because of fear of excessive car travel and they were also acknowledged as a threat to traditional local shopping streets (Laursen 2002, p. 82). Where they exist they damage both city center and neighborhood retailing.

The central government had published a report 'Traffic 2005'. It included the objective that all short trips under 3km should be carried out by bike or on foot. New policies, such as park and ride in the Copenhagen area, were started in the 1990s, as well as carpooling and free bicycles for employees (ibid, p. 85).

Urban Transportation

From 1969 onwards, the Danes adopted the Swedish guidelines, called SCAFT 1968 (Swedish National Board of Urban Planning 1968), which recommended traffic separation and road classifications. The Swedish planners were great believers in Radburn and a number of housing estates were built according to these principles, for example the *Vallingly* Estate in Stockholm (for more on Radburn and similar designs see Chapter 1). The Swedish design – with the footpaths separated from roads – was applied in social housing programs in the 1970s in Denmark (Laursen 2002, p. 81).

According to Langeland (2008), 'Traffic in Towns' by Colin Buchanan and his team (1963) influenced transportation planning in the 1960s and 1970s in Denmark. Other transportation policy ideas, such as the Gothenburg model, were proposed for *Aalborg* but not implemented (ibid, p. 167) (see also Bremen). In the early 1970s traffic calming ideas came first from Sweden and later from the Netherlands. Denmark was one of the leading countries in Europe to promote shared space (also called Gatetuns, Woonerven or Home Zones), and traffic calming measures to reduce speed in residential streets. The Road Traffic Act of 1976 set out regulations for traffic calming in residential roads and speed limits of 30kph and 10kph were introduced (Laursen 2002, pp. 80–81). Possibly as part of traffic calming smaller street signs were introduced in Denmark, which are more attractive than the 'normal' street signs found everywhere else.

Denmark was also one of the first countries to start the 'Walk to school programs' now popular everywhere (Nielsen and Rassen 1986). Pedestrianization was established at about the same time as in Germany; Denmark and the Netherlands have been the leading European countries in the promotion of cycling.

Public Transportation

In 1974 a law came into force resulting in the formation of the first transportation organization of the country in the conurbation of Copenhagen. It was called '*Hovedstadsområdets Trafikselskab*' or HT for short. This organization took over all the public and some private bus operators in the region. HT was responsible for both the planning and the operation of services. In a sense it was similar to a *Verkehrsverbund* (see definition) in Germany. In 1978 a similar law was passed for the rest of the country.

In 1989 the law was changed and competition between bus operators became possible. Private bus operators could compete for various bus routes being offered for tender by the municipalities; the multinational company *Arriva*[3] has been very successful and dominates the market. In 1980 HUR (Hovedstadens Udviklingsråd) became the organization in Copenhagen responsible for the planning and tender procedure for contracts. Since 2001 this has included the rail network of the Copenhagen region. Similar structures could be found from 1995 onwards in the rest of the country (Hass-Klau, Haubitz, and Crampton 2001, pp. 71–76).

Four cities will construct new light rail or tramlines: Aarhus, Odense and Aalborg. Copenhagen will build a line in the western suburbs (interview in Odense, 29.10.13). Copenhagen already has two metro lines and a metro ring is currently being built.

Railways

In 2010 Denmark had an excellent railway network of more than 2,667km[4] (Ministry of Transport 2012, p. 6). Calculated per population Denmark had the highest level of train access of any country I studied (about 0.5km of railway line per 1,000 population). The service is very good and frequent and the trains are comfortable. Most of the lines are electrified.

Research on Walking: The Work of Jan Gehl and his Team

Architect *Jan Gehl* made Copenhagen and the promotion of car-free spaces in urban areas world famous with his first book *Life between Buildings: Using Public Space* (1971).[5] *Lars Gemzøe* has worked with Gehl since the 1970s. Our understanding of pedestrianization and walking would be very different without Jan Gehl and Lars Gemzøe. They have worked widely internationally and have also influenced many cities worldwide.

The first part of their book *New City Spaces* (2000) studies examples of how to win back public spaces in different types of cities. They divide the cities into:

- the invaded city – invaded by cars
- the abandoned city – looking at North American examples
- the reconquered city – conquered back from the car
- new public spaces for new public life.

The main part of the book describes nine cities and nine public space strategies in Copenhagen, Freiburg, Portland, Strasburg, Curitiba, Melbourne, Barcelona, Cordoba and Lyon. It is interesting to note that there is only one German but two Spanish and two French cities, an indication of where the best public spaces are in Europe.

I found the experience in Copenhagen extremely useful because it points out the different social stages when creating public space. First, the authors describe the prejudices in the early 1960s of the public and the local authorities in Copenhagen. It was widely believed that closing roads to traffic and pedestrianizing streets 'will never work in Scandinavia'. The difference in mentality was also used to boycott road closures: 'We are Danes not Italians.' Retailers were convinced 'no cars, no customers and no customers means no business' (Gehl and Gemzøe 2000, p. 54). This is a prejudice that even today is not uncommon among retailers worldwide.

Entertainment

The first pedestrianized street (*Strøget*[6]) in Copenhagen was a great success commercially and very popular with its citizens. The space that was made available was to a very small extent used by musicians but the police did not like them because the first pedestrianized streets were regarded purely as shopping streets and people were supposed to shop and not be entertained. With time the city center changed from a place for shopping, working, living or administrative functions to a place where street entertainment also became an important part and everybody could engage and participate. Research by Gehl and Gemzøe (2000) found that recreational activities had increased more than threefold over more than three decades (1963–1999) in Copenhagen. The authors point out that the size of the car-free areas increased at about the same rate (1968–1999) (3.5 times). 'Every time the city has expanded the pedestrianized area by 14 square metres, another Copenhagener has turned up and set himself down to enjoy what the city has to offer' (ibid, p. 58).

Especially in the UK it has always been argued that pedestrianized areas are dead in the evening. In Copenhagen more and more shops and cafes stay open during the evening, even as late as 23.00 hrs. The number of shops and cafes that are open increased from 287 in 1995 to 409 in 2005 (Gehl et al 2006, p. 45).

Places of Political Expression

Over the years more streets were pedestrianized, including large squares, and the city center became 'the country's largest public forum' (ibid, p. 58). Similar developments can be observed in many other car-free city centers all over Europe.

Outdoor 'Cafe Culture'

In the 1960s, outdoor cafes were practically unknown in Copenhagen but they were also virtually unknown in London and many other cities with similar climates. Since then a 'cafe culture' has developed and in 2000 there were about 5,000 outdoor cafe chairs in Copenhagen, I doubt if anybody has counted these chairs in other cities but the trend has clearly been the same. The figure for 2005 showed a further increase of chairs to 7,020 – in total an increase of 136% since 1986 (2,970 chairs) (ibid, p. 41).

Increase in Time Spent Outside

The last statement both authors made is how long people spent sitting outside. Now chairs are provided for a much longer period than before – from 1 April until 1 November (ibid, p. 59). Again, this can be observed in many other cities with cooler climates, strengthened by the non-smoking policies in most countries.

There are many more informative publications by Gehl and his team, such as *Projects for Public Spaces* in 2009, *Cities for People* in 2010, *How to Study Public Life* (with *B. Svarre*) in 2013. From the middle of the 1990s, many city studies (e.g. London, New York, Perth, Melbourne) have been made available. Anybody who is interested in the subject of walking and city center improvement should have at least one of his books.

Case study: Copenhagen

Population 562,000 in the city[7] and 1.2 million in Greater Copenhagen[8] in 2012.

Background

Copenhagen is the largest city in Denmark and the fourth largest of all the Nordic countries (after Stockholm, Oslo and Helsinki).

Population Decline/Growth

The population in the City of Copenhagen has declined from 700,465 in 1940 to 495,699 in 2000. Since then there was a slight increase in the population to 500,531 inhabitants in 2002 and a much stronger growth (12%) over the last ten years (562,000 population) (ETP 2004). The density in Copenhagen is relatively high at 7,285 per sqkm. In fact among the study cities it was second only to New York (see Table 15.3).

Five Finger Plan

After the First World War, Copenhagen implemented a new regional plan to control growth in Copenhagen and the suburbs. The *Five Finger Plan* was presented in 1947 and became law in 1949. The expansion of the city was to occur along public transportation axes. It was really transit-orientated development (TOD) on a large scale, long before the name was even invented. It created the backbone for a good public transportation system, as car ownership in Copenhagen was very low in the 1950s (there were only 30 cars per 1,000 population). It was a successful scheme and has not been changed significantly since the beginning of the 21st century (http://musemcgill.worldpress.com, accessed 10.9.13; http://www.denstoredanske.dk/Geografi_og_historie/Geografix/Kulturgeografi/Bebyggelsesgeografi/Fingerplanen, accessed 21.9.13).

Transportation

One of the most important elements in the economic development of the Copenhagen region and South Sweden was the *Øresund Bridge*, a fixed rail and car link (15.9km) between the two countries, which opened in 2000. It is the longest combined railway and car bridge in Europe (Ministry of Transport 2012, p. 12). The trip between Denmark and Sweden is quick (25 minutes from Copenhagen by train) and the economic impact on the third-largest Swedish town *Malmö* would be interesting to study. When I visited Malmö recently, I had the feeling that the city had improved significantly compared to my previous visit about ten years before.

Targets for a Greater Copenhagen

It is planned for Greater Copenhagen that by 2025 at least one-third of all trips should be made by bike, one-third by public transportation and no more than one-third by car (walking is not mentioned). The aim is that at least two-thirds of the growth of traffic should be by green modes. As can be seen in Table 10.1, for the city itself this is already the case. But for Greater Copenhagen this implies that the number of public transportation passengers should increase by 20% compared to 2011. The aim is that cycling to work and to school (or university) should make up 50% of all trips by 2015 (City of Copenhagen 2011, p. 25).

Table 10.1 Modal split data Copenhagen and in the whole country in 2011: all and work trips in percent

City/country	Car, truck, van, passengers		Public transportation		Bicycle		Walk		Others	
	All	Work	All	Work	All	Work	All	Work		
Copenhagen	26	25	14	24	32	45	26	5	2	1
Whole country	57	60	6	13	17	20	17	6	3	1

Source: City of Copenhagen 2012a, p. 12

Car Ownership

The City of Copenhagen has by far the lowest car ownership per 1,000 population of all the cities I studied. In 2012 it still had only 237 cars per 1,000 inhabitants compared to 378 in Oslo, 317 in London, or 545 in Munich (www. meinestadt.de, Statistical Yearbook 2012, figure 3, accessed 9.9.13; www. citymayors.com 2013, accessed 2.10.13). In 2000 there were 229 cars per 1,000 inhabitants and the forecast for 2013 was 268 cars (Trafik-og Miljøplan 2003, p. 5). As in many other cities, the forecast was higher than in reality (in Copenhagen about 17% higher).

Figure 10.1
Map of wider central area of Copenhagen within and outside the Metro Ring

Table 10.1 shows that the car share for *all* trips was 26% and car commuting was marginally less in Copenhagen. Some 72% of *all* trips were made by green modes (walking, cycling and public transportation). The 'green' share for work trips in Copenhagen was slightly higher than for all trips but impressively high is the

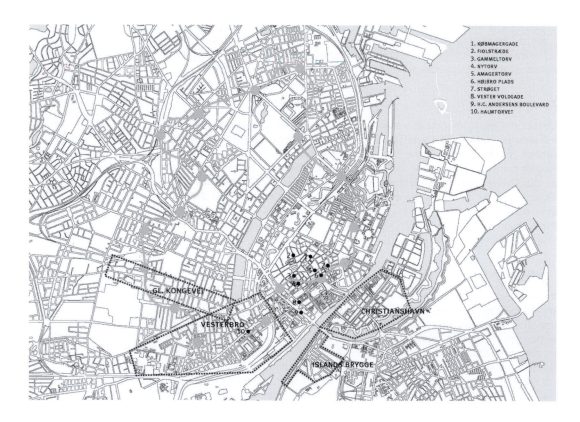

1. KØBMAGERGADE
2. FIOLSTRÆDE
3. GAMMELTORV
4. NYTORV
5. AMAGERTORV
6. HØJBRO PLADS
7. STRØGET
8. VESTER VOLDGADE
9. H.C. ANDERSENS BOULEVARD
10. HALMTORVET

cycle share to work with 45%. The contrast between the data for Copenhagen and the rest of the country demonstrates the marked difference in all modes. In the rest of the country the car is by far the most popular.

City Policies for Car Parking

Public car parking spaces (street parking and other parking spaces) were reduced from 3,100 in 1995 to 2,720 in 2005 (Gehl et al 2006, p. 22). Each year 2–3% of car parking spaces are taken away by the city.

Walking

Development of Pedestrianization

The first street that was pedestrianized was the main shopping corridor (about 10–12m wide) *Strøget* in 1962; its total length is 1.1km. This was quite unusual compared to the rest of Europe; only German planners were similarly courageous but their streets were generally not as long (see Chapter 3). Strøget counted about 25,000 pedestrians on a winter's day between 10.00 and 18.00 and up to 55,000 on a summer's day (Gehl and Gemzøe 1996, pp. 12–13 and see also Chapter 12).

Six years later *Fiolstræde* was made car free. The success of both streets gave the impetus to increase the size of pedestrianization further. In 1973 *Købmagergade* and several other small streets were closed to cars. Købmagergade was also an important pedestrian axis with on average about 24,000–33,000 pedestrians daily (ibid, p. 14). In 1992 *Strædet* became a pedestrian priority street and cars were allowed to drive only at low speed (basically it was a shared space street), the sidewalks disappeared in 1992 (ibid, p. 15).

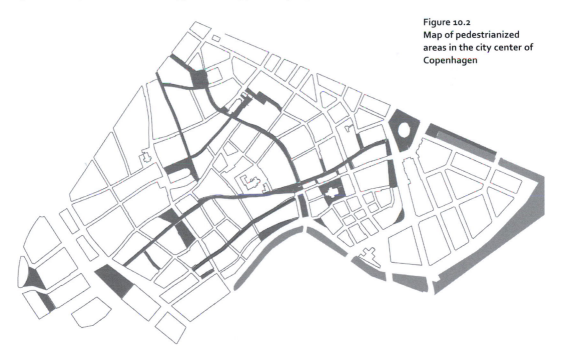

Figure 10.2
Map of pedestrianized areas in the city center of Copenhagen

Figure 10.3
Strøget

The dominance of the car was reduced or taken out in the major squares: *Gammeltorv* and *Nytorv* (1973 and 1992). *Amagertorv* was repaved in 1993 but it had already partly been made car free in 1962 and the car-free area was expanded during the 1980s (ibid, p. 17). By 1990 another six squares had been pedestrianized (ibid, p.19). The last one to be changed was *Højbro Plads* in 1996. This square still has some car traffic but instead of large numbers of parked cars it now has only a taxi stand and some loading and unloading. It has become a market square again (ibid, p. 21). We have very few cities in Europe where the development and growth of pedestrianization is as well documented as in Copenhagen, though Rolf Monheim studied Nuremberg, Bonn and Freiburg in considerable detail.

In the 1980s the waterfront[9] (Nyhavn) was 'discovered' and Copenhagen was one of the first cities in the world to see the walking potential of a waterfront, not only for pedestrians but also for businesses, such as restaurants, cafes and hotels.

I studied the length of the pedestrianized streets in Copenhagen and calculated a total of about 3km. Since the books by Gehl and Gemzøe published in 1996 and 2000, only a small extension of about 700m has been added. Not fully included in this calculation are the squares, but I included the length of the longest side of the square.

The Best Walking Environment

Having a world-famous personality in the midst of Copenhagen and thousands of students, who were taught by Gehl and his associated architects (the consultancy), that had to have some impact on the city's guideline on walking. A list prepared by 'Gehl Architects' for the City of Copenhagen in 2012 summarized the following main features for good walking conditions:[10]

1. A continuous and complete pedestrian network (though I find the word 'complete' difficult to specify).
2. A reliable feeling of safety that means protection from motorized traffic.
3. Security through collective surveillance and activity, especially in darkness.
4. Direct pedestrian routes with sufficient space – wide sidewalks – and no obstacles.
5. Stimulating and detailed facades, services and facilities facing the pedestrian streets.
6. Comfort, such as low noise, good air quality, cleanliness and weather protection.
7. Pedestrian facilities, like clean drinking fountains and toilets.
8. Green spaces, flower beds, trees etc.
9. Seating: formal, informal and commercial seating.
10. Features that invite leisure activities and play.
11. Art that generates identity with the town (and region).

My View

When walking around one is immediately aware that Copenhagen is the ideal city for cyclists but the many pedestrianized streets and squares in the historic city center are also exciting for pedestrians. I saw beautifully designed sidewalks in *Vester Voldgade* (about 7m wide). Two car lanes were converted into sidewalks and only two car lanes were left.

Strøget has always been impressive, in particular the squares. I was not so keen on some of the paving but the citizens of Copenhagen have to like it. I enjoyed the side streets going off Strøget because they had more interesting shops, cafes and restaurants than Strøget itself. Here, the sidewalks were often narrow, about 2m, but it did not really matter, as there was so little car traffic in most streets that it was possible to walk in the carriageway if one wished.

What made Copenhagen so special were three features. The first was that wherever one went and whatever one saw in terms of urban, road and sidewalk design nearly all of the details were right. Whether it was the paved cycleway on a roundabout, or the lack of asphalt when repairs had been made to the surface of pedestrianized streets, Copenhagen was the only city I visited where the pedestrianized street floor was *not* patched up with asphalt.

The second was that something interesting and unexpected in terms of street or urban design could be found all over the city. A striking illustration was the less well-known *Halmtorvet*.

The third feature was not immediately obvious. Wandering around in *Vesterbro*, sometimes one could glimpse the inner yards of the 19th-century housing blocks and appreciate how they had been beautifully designed to cater for both children and residents. There it is possible to enjoy peace and nature but they were also

Figure 10.4
Wide sidewalks at Vester Voldgade

designed for social neighborhood events. They reminded me of the 19th-century yards built in many major cities, such as Berlin but also the yards behind the Karl-Marx-Allee built by the GDR. The opening up of these originally often narrow yards has done wonders for the quality of these housing areas.

In all the streets and squares I saw people enjoying themselves, such as the green areas along *Islands Brygge*. Most streets in *Christianshavn* were delightful. The mixture of new and old houses combined with small open spaces where people were sitting and talking was extremely attractive, especially along the *Christianshavns Kanal*. I wondered whether Copenhagen is not only the ideal city for cyclists but also for pedestrians. Almost, but it was slightly strange that cycleways were extremely wide but parked bicycles often hindered pedestrians on the sidewalks; this was evident everywhere.

Having explored the urban spaces in the city center and some other parts of the inner city areas in Copenhagen, I was intrigued to investigate what was going on in the suburbs. I took the S-Bahn to *Islev* on the C-Line, but it could have been anywhere else. The sidewalks in the residential streets were narrow. In the middle they had a single row of flagstones and it was impossible for two people to walk side by side. Because of the different materials on the sidewalks (flagstones and soil or small paving stones), there was a slight difference in height. The flagstones were sometimes broken. The height difference between the sidewalks and the carriageway was overcome by crude asphalt infills. As there were few cars one could easily walk on the roads.

Figure 10.5
Parked bicycles on sidewalk

On the main road (*Slotsherrensvej*) there were cycleways of more than 3m on each side, separated by a small curb, and next to the cycleway was a parking lane for cars. But getting out of the station in Islev, there were no pedestrian crossings of any kind although there was an ugly pedestrian island (consisting only of asphalt). In short it seems that some of the suburbs in Copenhagen are as bad as anywhere else. In the wealthier suburbs the sidewalks are probably in better condition. Even so, 30kph speed limit signs were visible everywhere.

Pedestrian Crossings

Traffic light times for pedestrians were mostly sufficient, 20 or 30 seconds but with more than 60 seconds of green time for cars. At the junction at Frederiksberg Allé/*Allégade* pedestrians had only ten seconds to cross, impossible for older and other less mobile people to cross safely (this crossing belonged to the City of Frederiksberg). I checked a number of other pedestrian crossings. Some had green crossing times of only 15 seconds but long waiting times of about 60 seconds (*Hammerichsgade*); others had longer crossing times of about 30 seconds (*Vester Farimagsgade*). Especially long was the waiting time at *H. C. Andersens Boulevard*. As the waiting times are too long, many pedestrians cross at red.

Traffic Calming

Most residential streets were traffic calmed by closing the street at one end or complicated one-way street systems, for instance walking along *Gammel*

Figure 10.6
Traffic-calmed street
in Vesterbro –
Skydebanegade

Kongevej. Other streets had simple but well-designed traffic calming measures, especially raised pedestrian crossings at junctions. The streets in Vesterbro were mostly traffic calmed using measures that fit well into this housing area, streets like *Skydebanegade* or *Dannebrogsgade* were especially interesting.

The speed limit varied from 15 to 40kph in residential streets, which was odd as one would have considered 40kph to be too high for car traffic in most residential streets.

Cycling

Copenhagen is world famous for its promotion of cycling. Cycle 'streets', often more than 6m wide, can be found mostly in the central parts of Copenhagen, but 3m is normal on both sides of any carriageway.

Public Transportation

Trams disappeared in 1972 in Copenhagen and were replaced by buses and an extensive suburban rail network of 430km (track length) with seven major suburban railway lines and 80 stations. Nearly all the lines provide a ten-minute service most of the day. Most trains (81%) are operated by the DSB (the Danish State Railway).

The fully automatic underground known as *Metro* has two lines (M1 and M2), 22 stops and is operated along 21km of tracks running at short headways. The Metro opened quickly in three stages between 2002 and 2007. A 15.5km Metro ring line is under construction and will open in 2018, consisting of 17 underground stations (Ministry of Transport 2012, p. 8).

Case Study: Odense

Population 170,000 in the city and 194,000 in the municipality in 2013.

Background

Population Growth

Odense is the third largest city in Denmark. The municipality of Odense had 140,000 inhabitants in 1988 and 193,641 in 2013, an increase of nearly 40% over 25 years. The City of Odense is somewhat smaller and had 170,327 inhabitants in 2013 (www.citypopulation.de, accessed 13.11.13).

Transportation

Major roads were suggested in the early 1960s, including a ring road. During the late 1960s, a north–south road (*Thomas B. Thrigesgade*) was built which cut through the eastern part of the city center and the city. It was opened in 1970 and was one of the most criticized roads built in this period (Odense Municipality 1988, p. 1, available at www.odense.dk). As it was already clear during the early 1970s that the public did not like this kind of road building, they pressured the engineers to introduce alternatives. Finally in 1976 a traffic plan for the *Greater Odense Area* was developed and was implemented in 1988. Part of the plan included:

- a footpath network
- upgrading public transportation
- implementation of traffic-calming measures
- improvement of the existing road network (Nielsen and Rassen 1986, p. 84).

Forty-three years later a new exciting plan for the city intends to close the Thomas B. Thrigesgade completely and change it into a pedestrian boulevard with light rail access instead of cars (interview in Odense, 29.10.13).

City Center

Before 1988 the pedestrian area in Odense was small, only 600m. There was a lack of open space and no facilities for cyclists. Part of the new traffic plan was to increase the pedestrian area to 2.5km including a whole network of pedestrian streets (Odense Municipality 1988, available at www.odense.dk). The pedestrian counts revealed in *Vestergade* 25,000–26,000 pedestrians (10.00–18.00). But a later study by Gehl indicated that the number of pedestrians had declined from 26,435 pedestrians in 1988 to 21,445 in 2008 in Vestergade (Gehl 2008, Urban Realm Strategy, available at www.gehlarchitects.dk, accessed 21.9.13). The main reasons were increased car use and competition from an 'edge of town' large shopping center.[11] In order to improve the city center, Gehl and his team suggested:

- improving the connection between the car parks and the pedestrianized streets
- designing more attractive outdoor spaces
- creating consistency and establish clear crossing points
- upgrading the main square
- improving the links to the pedestrian network
- implementing new green spaces
- finding space for a new square.

Figure 10.7
Map of pedestrianized
streets in the city center of
Odense

Table 10.2 Modal split (all trips) in the municipality of Odense in percent

Year	Car, truck, van, passengers	Public transportation	Bicycle	Walk	Others, including mopeds
2007	44.0	7.3	26.8	16.3	4.6
2012	55.2	4.7	23.8	14.7	1.7

Sources: TEMS: The EPOMM Modal Split Data. Other modal split data were from the City of Odense 2013.

Unfortunately, I do not have modal split figures from the 1980s. The latest figures are rather depressing. During the last six years, the car share has grown by 11% points and all the other modes have declined, even cycling. Although I did not study in detail any other Danish cities, I received the modal split figures for cycling in Aarhus (the second biggest Danish city) and Aalborg (smaller than Odense) for the same time period. In all these cities cycling declined, not as much as in Odense but the decline was larger than 1%; only Copenhagen was the exception. The goal of the municipality is to achieve a share of 36% for cycling in 2020. There was no specific goal for walking.

Walking

My View

Leaving the main railway station, one is confronted with a main road at the front and the back entrance. Both are wide with two car lanes in each direction and at junctions often three. In addition there were wide cycle lanes on both sides but the sidewalks were still wide enough at about 2m. These wide roads reminded me of the layout at Peterborough's (UK) railway station. The roads have the same barrier effect and no signs directing to the town center if one took the wrong exit. I also noticed that cars were driven fast, much faster than in Norway. Luckily, two of the wide roads will disappear, one will be changed to a pedestrian boulevard (Thomas B. Thrigesgade) and the other (*Østre Stationvej*) will lose two car lanes because of a new light rail corridor.

I also observed the pedestrianized streets and saw a number of empty shops. What did strike me was that nearly all the pedestrian streets looked dated; it was like an open-air shopping center with some cafes and restaurants. What was missing were exciting features for children and grown-ups alike. The *Ove Spogøes Plads* and *Jernbanegade* were better designed with benches and hedges, a fountain and art works.

The parking spaces were too close to the pedestrianized streets and there were plenty, which made some of the side streets look unattractive. This also prevents more car restrictions in some of the other city center streets because access to the parking spaces from the pedestrianized streets is necessary. The newly planned light rail line will change the town center completely and will open ways to improve this part of the city center.

Figure 10.8
Ove Spogøes Plads

Sidewalks

Most sidewalks were in good condition and wide enough. I particularly liked that they were paved with very light small bricks. That has the result that any natural unevenness would not automatically break the bricks. Similar small bricks but of different color are used in many town centers in the Netherlands.

Pedestrian Crossings

At many traffic lights pedestrian crossing times were very short. On narrow streets they were often only ten seconds and on wider roads 13–15 seconds. At the junction with *Ejlskovegade* with Thomas B. Thrigesgade, the crossing time was only ten seconds, not really long enough to cross such a wide street.

At the end of one of the pedestrian streets (*Slotsgade)* the crossing times were 15 seconds and the waiting time 32 seconds. I would have thought for a pedestrian axis it should be the other way round. A little further on at *Vindegade* the crossing time was only ten seconds and although it is not a wide street an elderly person would have problems crossing it (I am aware that there is an overlapping period before cars actually move on but not every pedestrian knows that).

Improvements for Pedestrians

A large foot and cycle bridge is planned over the railway lines close to the city's central station. The railway lines were awkward to cross and difficult to understand for a stranger. Apart from a normal railway tunnel, the other option was to go through a shopping center to reach the city center (this was also the main place for buying rail tickets). This 'entrance' to the city center again reminded me of Peterborough in the UK.

Safe Routes to School

Odense invented the 'safe routes to school' program, which is still ongoing. According to the city officer far more children walk to school than in Aalborg. Some 82% of all children above 3rd Grade (about nine years of age) walk or cycle to school (interview in Odense, 29.10.13).

Traffic Calming

All known traffic calming measures today had already been implemented during the 1980s and the regulation covering such measures was that the distance between them should not be more than 100 meters. In the play streets (15kph) they were closer (about 50m distance). These streets already included shared space designs. According to information from the city, 30kph signs are only introduced in residential areas when sufficient traffic-calming measures have been provided. That is the case in about one-third of all residential streets.

I walked around *Vesterbro*, a charming old housing area where former traffic calming measures have been renewed. It was interesting but there was nothing outstanding to observe. The majority of residential streets had a speed limit of 30kph.

Cycling

The policy 'heart' of the city is in cycling. Everywhere I went I saw plenty of wide cycle paths and cycle lanes. In 2013 Odense claimed to have 540km of cycle paths (interview in Odense, 29.10.13).

Public Transportation

Odense has an extensive bus network and a light rail line of 14km is planned.

Notes

1   The official accident statistics (statbank.dk) showed that pedestrian fatalities averaged 1.3 per 100,000 inhabitants in Odense, 1.1 in Aarhus, 0.8 in Copenhagen and 0.8 in Aalborg (using a seven year annual average from 2006 to 2012). All of these figures were higher than the corresponding figures in Norway, although the Norwegian figures were for the county containing the city.
2   As the way of counting cars in the United States is different, it is not possible to compare them with European statistics.
3   Arriva is a subsidiary of Deutsche Bahn.
4   Included in this figure are the 21km of Copenhagen's Metro.
5   Published in English in 1987 – see reference.
6   Strøget is actually not one street but represents a number of streets.
7   Within the City of Copenhagen is another city called *Frederiksberg*, which was the traditional home of the Danish Royal Family. It is located at the west of the city center of Copenhagen between *Nørrebro* to the north and *Vesterbro* to the southeast. In 2013 it had a population of about 100,000.
8   There is also a definition of the Metropolis of Copenhagen, which has 1.6 million (www.norden.org/da/fakta-om-norden/befolkning).
9   Most of it is actually a canal.
10 The 'Gehl Architects' divided the characteristics into necessary and optional features. I found nearly all features necessary and did not distinguish between them (City of Copenhagen 2012b).
11 According to the town planning officer, this shopping center is very large and has increased over time. It does even more harm to other smaller towns than to Odense itself.

11

FURTHER NORTH: NORWAY

Background

Norway was an independent kingdom from 1030 to 1380. Through inheritance it became part of the kingdom of Denmark. That changed in 1814 when it was given to Sweden. It voted for and declared independence in 1905 (www.norway.org.uk, accessed 30.8.13).

Although Norway is in land area one of the largest countries in Europe, it is only sparsely populated; its population was five million in 2012. Just over 4 out of 5 million live in towns and cities. The capital Oslo has about 20% of the total Norwegian population (www.city.pop.de, accessed 10.8.13). Bergen with 264,000 residents is the second biggest city.[1]

Population Growth

There is population migration from the periphery of Norway to the larger cities, especially to Oslo. The major urban areas are growing rapidly and this has been strengthened by migration from abroad. For instance the population in Oslo grew by 21% between 2000 and 2012[2] whereas Norway as a whole grew very little, by about 0.4% in the same time period. According to Langeland (2008) within the city regions there were significant levels of both suburbanization and levels of migration back to the inner cities and city centers (p. 66).

Studying the population density, it is evident that the main cities, except for Oslo, have relatively low densities, comparable to North American cities.

Political Background

Norway is not a member of the European Union in contrast to its neighbors Sweden, Denmark and Finland. It has rich resources in natural gas and petroleum.

Administrative Structure

In the four visited cities, except for Oslo road transportation and public transportation are the responsibility of the counties. Oslo is both a municipality and a county authority (www.oslo.kommune.no, accessed 1.9.13).

Transportation

Road Tolls

Norway was the first country in Europe to introduce road tolls on a large scale not only in cities but also for roads in general. The first city to introduce such

Table 11.1 Population in 1,000 and population densities of the largest cities in Norway in 2013

City	Oslo	Bergen	Stavanger/ Sandnes	Trondheim	Fredricksand/ Scarpsborg	Kristiansand	Tromsø
Population	613	264	201	180	106	82	68
Density/km²	4,484	2,462	2,479	2,622	1,568	2,077	2,501

Sources: www.ssb.no/a/english/, accessed 14.8.13, density figures are for population 1.1.12

charges was Bergen in 1986, followed by Oslo in 1990 and Trondheim in 1991 (Ieromonachou 2006). Other Norwegian cities followed:

- Kristiansand in 1997
- Stavanger in 2001
- Namsos in 2003 (population of only 15,000)
- Tønsberg in 2004 (population of only 50,000) (Fortun and Furuseth 2007).

Toll projects normally last 15 years and can be extended to 20 years. Since 1981 about 30% of total road funding has been financed in this form (ibid). Some cities like Bergen, Stavanger and Kristiansand have opted for a second period.

In *Bergen* the pay stations were located on the access roads to the wider city center. Over 70% of the money was used for road construction, 20% for operating costs and 10% was set aside in a fund. The scheme was extended in 2001 and the priorities were changed. Only 45% of the total income was used for road construction and the rest for city center improvements. Some years later, the rules were modified again and the income could also be used for a new light rail line.

In *Oslo* the toll stations were located about 3–8km outside the city center. The price was also higher at 11 NOK (about €1.3) whereas in Bergen it was originally 5 NOK (about €0.60). The tolls were used for road and public transportation investment but not for operating costs. The main projects were urban road tunnels; the most important was the *Castle Tunnel* below the City Hall Square (see below). Ninety thousand vehicles disappeared below ground and a new tramline opened instead (ibid). By contrast, in the next toll agreement that started in 2002, all the income was used for public transportation investment.

In Trondheim the tolls were used from the start for roads, public transportation investment, pedestrian and cycle facilities, and the price was differentiated by the time of day.

National Transport Plans

Every ten years the Ministry of Transport and Communication (2000, 2013) has to produce a National Transport Plan, which is subject to final approval by the Norwegian parliament. The *National Transport Plan 2006–2015* was replaced by the *National Transport 2014–2023*,[3] which was passed in June 2013. The main objectives of the 2006–2015 Transport Plan that are relevant to the topics in this book included:

- Reduction of fatalities and serious injuries on roads and a continued high level of safety in other transportation modes. The government aims to achieve zero casualties. Although the number of fatal road accidents has been halved since 1970, nevertheless 1,500 people were still killed or seriously injured each year from 1998 to 2002. The government recommends the continuation and increase in funding of targeted road safety measures. The reader will notice later on in Chapter 15 and Table 15.4 that Norway had the best safety record of all the countries I visited.

- This objective has been continued in the White Paper for the Transport Plan 2014–2023 but targets have been included: The number of fatalities and severe injuries should be cut by half by 2023. This implies that the average number of killed and seriously injured, approximately 1,000 a year, should be reduced to 500 by 2023.
- More environmentally sound urban transportation, which will reduce the dependence on private cars and increase the use of public transportation, walking and cycling.[4]

National Trends

Despite its green credentials, road building is still on the government's agenda and in the proposals of the *Transport Plan 2014–2023* the government wants to build a new coastal road between Stavanger and Bergen. In 2014 it was a national highway but many fjords have to be crossed by ferry, which is costly and time consuming. In addition this road runs through many local authorities. This part of Norway has a spectacular coastline, dominated by fjords and it would need a large number of bridges to cover this distance. The environmental damage would be considerable.

Walking Strategy Proposed by the Government

A walking strategy called 'walking for life' was published in 2012. The modal split data included indicated that in 2009:

- 22% of all trips were carried out on foot
- women's walking share was 25%, more than men (19%)
- people living alone walked most (31%) compared to
- families with children (19%)
- family members living in low-income households (under Kr 200.000, about €24,250 annually) made 29% of all trips on foot compared to
- 17% in households with more than one million Kroners (€121,200) per year (Vegdirektoratet 2012, p. 56).

If the national walking figures for Norway are compared with those of Germany, the UK and the United States, then Norway has the same average level of walking as the UK as a proportion of all trips, but more than the US (11%) and less than Germany (24%).

Railways

The railways in Norway are in a poor state considering that Norway is one of the richest countries in Europe. Most of their routes run on single track, for instance Stavanger to Oslo (591km) takes 8 hours and Oslo to Trondheim (542km) nearly 7 hours. The percentage of high-speed track is very low and over 30% of the total km are not electrified. Having said this, the journeys though long are comfortable.

Case Study: Bergen

Population 264,000 in the city and 396,700 in Greater Bergen in 2012.

Background

During the Middle Ages, Bergen was an international trading center and the Hanseatic League – with its headquarters in Lübeck, Germany – had one of its main offices in this city.[5] After Trondheim, Bergen was the capital of Norway until it changed to Oslo in 1299 but it remained the commercial center for most of the subsequent centuries.

In 2013 its main business was in oil, gas and renewable energy as well as maritime industries, media and tourism.[6] Bergen is also an important university town. It had 17,000 students in 2011 (www.uib.no, accessed 1.9.13).

Population Growth

The population increased from 229,496 in 2000 to 267,950 in 2013, a population growth of 17% (City of Bergen 2013).

Transportation

When comparing the modal split data with smaller towns such as Stavanger and Trondheim, Bergen does much better in walking and public transportation but not in cycling. But compared to Oslo, Bergen has far more car and less public transportation use (Table 11.2).

Walking

Infrastructure for Walking

The city is responsible for maintaining 262km of sidewalks of which 19km are cobblestones, and 102km are paths and cycleways. In addition, there are 2,600 speed humps and 9,000 traffic lights. The City of Bergen also has steep unpopulated hills and mountains with 84km of walkways (Greenways) (ibid).

Pedestrian Crossings

Although all traffic lights have pedestrian crossing phases, no pedestrian crossing request buttons were provided, with a few exceptions but as in the UK, pedestrians are legally allowed to cross at red. Crossing times vary according to

Table 11.2 Modal split of Norwegian cities in percent

City	Car and car passengers			Public transportation			Bicycle			Walk			Others		
	All trips		Work	All trips		Work	All trips		Work	All trips		Work	All trips		Work
	2001	2009	2009	2001	2009	2009	2001	2009	2009	2001	2009	2009	2001	2001	2009
Bergen	56	51	59	12	16	22	3	3	4	30	30	13	4	2	0
Oslo	47	35	35	20	25	40	4	5	7	30	34	18	–	–	1
Trondheim	59	56	56	12	9	14	5	8	16	24	26	13	–	–	2
Stavanger	57	61	61	12	11	16	7	5	10	23	23	13	–	–	0

Sources: Norwegian Travel Survey 2009; Liva Vagåne Institute of Transportation Economic 2013, September 2013, correspondence

Figure 11.1
Map of wider central
area of Bergen

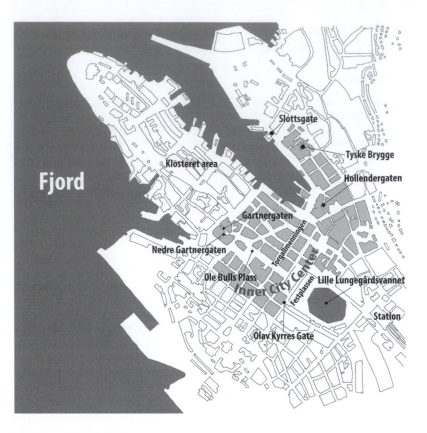

Figure 11.2
Unusual zebra crossing
near the disused cloister

the traffic flows and some had long waiting times and reasonably timed crossing periods (20 seconds) but many junctions have only zebra crossings that
worked well.

Planning

In the early 1970s, the narrow historic *Hollendergaten* became the first pedestrianized street in the city center. After that more and more streets were added,
the last one being *Olav Kyrres Gate* in 2000. I calculated that in total about 9km
of streets are either access-only or totally pedestrianized.

The *Gatetuns*[7] or 'shared space' program was developed and implemented in
the 1980s and plenty of funding was available. The main reason for the generous
government grants was to keep the residents in the historic city. As in the United
States, many houses in the residential areas in the historic centers and inner-
city areas were in urgent need of repair and modernization. As a result of these
improvements to all urban areas in Norway, the population increased in the city
centers and they have become prestigious and expensive places to live.

After the success of the Gatetuns, the politicians decided to do the same for the
commercial part of the city center. In Bergen several areas were improved, for
instance the *Festplassen*, which used to be a car parking lot; it was freed of cars
and redesigned. Most spectacular was the redesign of a long and wide city
center shopping street (*Torgallmenningen*). Part of *Ole Bulls Plass* became
Bergen's central urban square in 1993. It used to be a busy roundabout at the
end of *Torgallmenningen*. The square now connects Torgallmenningen with *Ole
Bulls Plass*, a wide green avenue with trees, which leads to the famous *Den
Nationale Scene* Theatre.

**Figure 11.3 The main
shopping street of
Torgallmenningen**

Figure 11.4
The blue granite stone replaced what used to be a busy roundabout

In 2000 Bergen was selected as the 'European City of Culture' and part of the harbor side, the German wharf and merchant houses, received Unesco World Heritage Status. This also had some impact on car traffic. Consequently the four-lane road (*Slottsgate*) in front of this historic ensemble was reduced to two lanes in 2005. But the Committee of the United Nations is still unhappy with the level of car traffic, so further reductions are needed. Possibly a future tram route through Slottsgate will lower car traffic even more.

My View

Bergen is a rainy and windy city, but when the rain stops or on a sunny day, people pour out onto the streets and squares. It is one of the most beautiful cities in Europe with only a few unsightly large monotonous facades. The combination of the old housing stock with its brightly painted facades and mostly excellent street coverings makes this city a memorable experience for anybody who has a feeling for urban space, history and design.

There are many lovely places in which to enjoy the urban environment, especially around the small lake (*Lille Lungegårdsvannet*). People also like to sit around and on the 'blue granite stone',[8] combined with a water feature at Ole Bulls Plass.

Part of the *Tyske Brygge*, the quay where the Germans used to dock their ships, has been made into a seating, restaurant and cafe area used mostly by tourists. Walking around the *Klosteret* area is also a stimulating experience because nearly all the narrow historic steep streets had no vehicle traffic and were beautifully designed as shared space.

Figure 11.5
Cobblestone design
in Bergen

The excellent quality of the cobblestone design can be observed in Figure 11.5. Some of the streets are very steep and challenging, and one has to be a strong walker to climb up and down. I imagine they are even more difficult in winter when they are icy and snowy.

Then again, not everything was wonderful for pedestrians. Some of the sidewalks were in bad condition, for instance in *Gartnergaten* and *Nedre Gartnergaten* but the cobblestones themselves (allowing car traffic access only) were still in very good order.

Traffic Calming

The old town and nearly all residential areas were traffic calmed either with 30kph speed limit signs or shared space treatment, especially in the historic parts of the town. Some of the design was really very attractive and individual.

In some cities, for instance in Oslo but also in Trondheim, Gatetuns took the form of redesigning courtyards in the large housing blocks (see Copenhagen). In Bergen there were no courtyards, so the streets themselves became the area of redesign. During the last 30 years everything had been done to 'calm down' car traffic in the city and get as many cars as possible out of the residential streets. Yet, the suburban areas around the historic part expanded, and here normally speed limit signs of 30kph were installed in the residential streets.

Cycling

Cycling is not a big issue and Bergen had the lowest cycle share of the cities I visited in Norway. I also did not see many cycle facilities, although large areas outside the historic city are flat.

Public Transportation

The first tramline (10km long) opened in 2010 and it is planned to achieve more transit-orientated development around the tram stops. In June 2013 the line was extended by four more stops and the tramline finishes at a big out-of-town shopping center. When I expressed my doubts that a shopping mall at the end stop of a tramline would tend to take shoppers away from the city center, I was told that the commercial activities had been concentrated too much in the heart of Bergen.[9] The existing tramline will be extended to the airport by 2016.

Figure 11.6
Example of a Gatetun

Case Study: Trondheim

Population 180,000 in the city (2012) and 294,000 residents in the county (Sør-Trøndelag) in 2011.

Background

Trondheim has been an important trading city and in the 18th century German and Dutch traders dominated local politics.

Population Growth

Since the early 1980s, its population has been growing constantly from 134,400 in 1986 to 179,700 in 2013, about 34% (SSB 2013). Some of the growth, especially from 2006 onwards has been in-migration by EU nationals. Trondheim has the second largest university in the country; in 2011 it had 31,000 students. The research sector is strong and the national oil company *Statoil* has its main research department in this town.

Transportation

A new highway bypasses the heart of the city (the 706) and this will give more opportunities for pedestrian improvement. The center is large, a peninsula of about 1.5km x 1.3km, but some of the through traffic still goes through city center streets. With the opening of a new tunnel in 2014, a number of streets can be closed to car traffic.

The modal split indicates a high level of car use and a high level of walking in the city, which increased between 2001 and 2009 but public transportation declined. Cycling is relatively low but grew between 2001 and 2009. According to the official public transportation counts, the number of public transportation

Figure 11.7
Map of wider city center of Trondheim

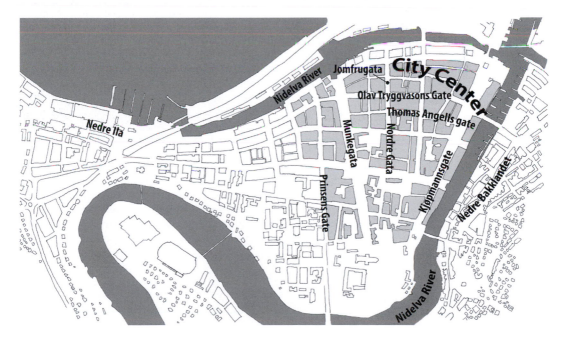

passengers increased by 33% between 2009 and 2012, hence it can be safely assumed that the public transportation modal split also grew. The county (*Sør Trøndelag*) indicates a much higher modal split for car use (74%), lower levels of walking (18%) and less public transportation (4%) and cycling use (4%) compared to the city in 2009 (Table 11.2).

Sustainable Objectives of the City

The objective of the city is to reach a 50% usage of green modes by 2018. In 2009 it was still 8% short of this. It is believed that the target can be achieved with the expansion in cycle facilities and public transportation. According to the city, there has already been a reduction in car use and people seemed quite happy to change to buses instead. The city also wants to reduce trip length and one step in this direction was to move the local government offices from a suburban site to a city center location where no car parking is available. The big issue for the future is to get the university, which has seven different locations within the city and outside, to have its main campus within or close to the city center, although employees resist giving up their car parking spaces.

Walking

Trondheim, although further north than Stavanger and Bergen, is warmer in summer than the more southwesterly cities thanks to the Gulf Stream. Especially in the northern countries people do not want to miss any opportunity to walk or sit outside whenever possible.

My View

When walking around, there was little car traffic in many streets, mostly because barriers have been put at relevant junctions, for instance in *Nedre Bakklandet*, *Kjøpmannsgate*, *Olav Tryggvasons Gate* or at *Nedre Ila*. These barriers cost very little but are very effective in reducing the number of cars. Trondheim is nearly as impressive as Bergen in terms of having been able to preserve many historic parts of the city; some are pedestrian-friendly urban districts, especially in *Bakklandet* and *Mollenberg* but also *Ila*, apart from many interesting and lively streets in the city center itself.[10] As with Bergen, Trondheim still has many historic warehouses and there are attempts to create a walkway next to the river (*Nidelva*) behind these warehouses, although legally it seems to be difficult to achieve a completely separate walkway.

Pedestrianization

In 2013 pedestrianization was rather modest compared to other Nordic cities.[11] Only two streets, *Nordre Gata* (about 500m) and *Jomfrugata* (about 300m), and about half of the main square were free of car traffic. In the near future *Thomas Angells Gate* and *Olav Tryggvasons Gate* will be pedestrianized. The main square will be redesigned and public transportation, which used the square will be redirected to a new bus station at the junction of *Prinsens* and *Kongens Gate*.

Sidewalks

By and large the sidewalks in many areas were not in good condition, whether they were built in asphalt or slabs, but as always there were exceptions, for instance the very wide and good sidewalks (6–7m on each side) in *Munkegata*.

I found it odd that such a rich city cannot afford to provide good sidewalks. When I talked with the city official about this, I was told that pedestrians 'belong to the underclass'. Traffic in Trondheim means 'car' traffic only. This is very apparent in winter. The roads are freed of snow for motor traffic but the snow is then piled onto the sidewalks. Even so, I was also informed that any new sidewalks planned and built have to be between 2.5m and 3m wide.

**Figure 11.8
Barrier in Nedre
Bakklandet**

Greenways

Three greenways or jogging routes can be identified in and close to the city center. One was about 10km, another one was 5km and the last one was 3km; in nearly all of them car traffic is not allowed, for instance along both sides of the River Nidelva.

Traffic Calming

According to the city representative, the Gatetuns (a form of shared space traffic calming) were out of fashion in Trondheim because they were mainly used for additional illegal car parking. Trondheim, in contrast to the historic parts of Bergen, is flat and one can imagine that Gatetuns have been abused for car parking. For me, it seems to be an issue of parking control and not a question of whether a particular transportation policy has failed. I did not see anything like that in Bergen but the geography there (narrow and often very steep streets) did not lend itself to this.

Speed limits in the town center streets were 40kph, although the city wanted 30kph. Finally a compromise between 50kph and 30kph was reached but in many residential areas the speed limit was 30kph.

Figure 11.9
A successful combination of a walkway/cycleway, cycle sharing and good public transportation

Cycling

There were several cycle lanes and even a cycle street (*Nedre Ila*) but many streets were still without any cycle facilities at all.

Public Transportation

Plenty of modern biogas buses can be observed in the town, some routes run at 15-minute, and others at 20- or 30-minute intervals. Clearly, the growth in transit passengers has been a great success. There is also an old-fashioned tramline, which will be modernized, running from the city center to *Lian* outside the city in the hills.

Case Study: Oslo

Population 613,285 in the city and in the wider urban area there were 925,000 inhabitants in 2013.

Background

Oslo became the capital in 1299. The first railway line opened in 1854 and industrialization grew rapidly in the second half of the 19th century (www.oslo.kommune.no, accessed 19.8.13).

Oslo is a hub of foreign trade, banking, industry and shipping. Some of the companies in the maritime sector are among the world's biggest. In addition it is also an important university city and had 28,000 students in 2010 (www.uio.no, accessed 1.9.13). Oslo is one of the world's most expensive cities.[12]

Transportation

Oslo has several semicircular motorways. Ring 1 runs close to the city center but in the central part a tunnel of about 3km was built (see Castle Tunnel). Ring 2 and Ring 3 are 2–4km away from the center. Oslo's road tolls charged 15 NOK (about €2 or $2.50) per car in 2013.

Oslo is doing relatively well in terms of sustainable transportation. Only 35% of all trips were made by car in 2009, and this may well have declined further. Over 2001 to 2009 car use declined by 12% points, which is the highest reduction within a short time period of any city I studied. Public transportation increased by 5% points and walking grew by 4% points, again the highest increase in walking of any city; even cycle use was higher by 1% point (Table 11.2).

Walking

My View

When arriving by train at the well-designed main railway station, the large square in front of the station was the beginning of the main pedestrian axis (*Karl Johans Gate*), which was also one of the most prestigious car-free shopping streets in Norway. This street is 1.3km long and stops short before the Royal Palace (from *Rosenkrantz Gate* limited access by car traffic is allowed). The rectangular large square (*Eidsvollsplass*) between Karl Johans Gate and *Stortings Gate* is bordered on one side by the parliament (*Stortinget*), and on the other by *Frederiks Gate*, a major road that leads to the motorway (Ring 1). It is similar in design and character to the Washington Mall although much smaller. It is surrounded by

Figure 11.10
Map of wider city center of Oslo

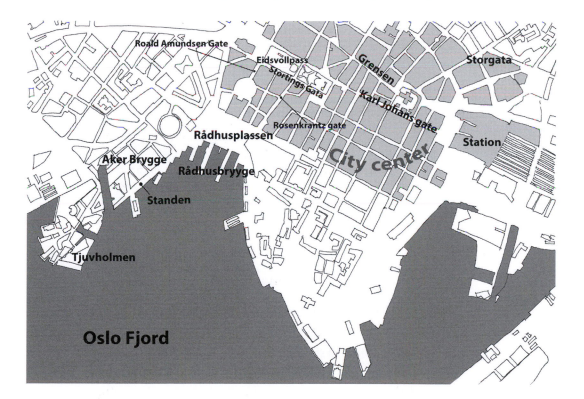

Figure 11.11
Popular square in front of the City Hall

the National Theatre, the historic Grand Hotel and university buildings. It was an impressive area, well designed and full of people. Many facilities were provided for sitting and eating. One side of this square had several rows of trees; one row consisted of lime trees, which have a beautiful fragrance in summer. In the section of Karl Johans Gate (next to the square – Eidsvollsplass), the original historic carriageway was still evident but half of the road space is now occupied by restaurants and cafes. The *Roald Amundsen Gate* allowed a view to the main square in front of a very impressive City Hall (Råthuset).

The parallel street to Karl Johans Gate is *Grensen*, which contained two tram routes. This street had little car traffic and wide and good sidewalks. But the pedestrian crossing lights were too short. *Storegate*, which runs northeast toward *Sophienberg* and the Botanical Gardens, also had two tramlines and again the level of car traffic was low. The area around *Ruth Reesen Plass* was very stimulating with some restaurants and the residential neighborhood was completely traffic calmed (see below).

When walking in the city center it was noticeable how many streets were pedestrianized. I calculated about 6km, which makes the length of these streets not as long as Bergen but still substantial. The large squares were not included in this calculation (and there are three immediately in the city center, not to mention the very large palace garden).

A new housing estate on the harbor front (*Aker Brygge* and *Tjuvholmen*) consisted only of pedestrian streets. It used to be a former industrial site and at the time of my visit it was a mixture of mostly housing and commercial activities. It also included the Museum of Modern Art. It had road access to underground car parks. *Standen*, the main car-free promenade, provided a wonderful view over the islands and harbor and had many modern restaurants. It was very popular with locals and tourists alike. Although this area was designed to represent the ideal pedestrian environment, I did not feel comfortable within the urban space. It was too artificial and more a living enclave for the better-off. Only time will tell whether it will become a 'real' neighborhood.[33] Everything I saw had 'showroom' character and everyday life facilities were missing.

Many streets in the government district (*Hammersborg*) were closed to car traffic because of its reconstruction after the 2012 bombing; that made the whole area pleasant to walk around.

Another large car-free area was the Town Hall Square (*Rådhusplassen*) located between the Rådhusgata, a popular tram route, and *Rådhusbryyge*. Rådhus-bryyge is the local harbor for boats to different locations including *Bygdøy*, where most of the important museums are located. It is indeed a very large square built only very recently but the statues (and the City Hall itself) are designed in the style of the 1930s in order to impress.[34]

Sidewalks

In some streets the sidewalks were not in good condition. In other streets the sidewalks were so narrow that two people could not walk side by side, especially when the original wide sidewalks had been divided into a cycle and pedestrian section, which is an unfortunate and dangerous practice in many cities both for cyclists and even more so for pedestrians. Narrow sidewalks could also be found in many streets in Bygdøy, though fortunately there were not many cars on the carriageways.

Pedestrian Crossings

Again as in Bergen, pedestrian crossings cannot be controlled by pedestrian push buttons and the pedestrian crossing phases were mostly not very long.

Traffic Calming

Most residential streets had 30kph speed limits but the streets were also well protected from through traffic by one-way streets and barriers. Sometimes special gates have been introduced to allow only buses to enter.

Cycling

There were a number of good cycle facilities around the city. In some streets there were wide cycle lanes on both sides and only one car lane in the middle of the carriageway.

Public Transportation

The backbone of the public transportation network is a very good and large underground system (T-Bane), which has six lines and a very extensive suburban rail network. The underground gives access to residential areas and small towns up to 10–15km away from the center. There are still six tramlines, some of which operate with 'period' vehicles. They run at short headways, mostly 10 minutes. They were very well used even late at night.

Case Study: Stavanger

Population 126,500, and 201,000 in the urban area in 2011.

Background

Stavanger had, in the second half of the 19th century, the second largest commercial fishing fleet in Norway. But the largest expansion of the town occurred in 1965 with the discovery of oil. The Norwegian state company 'StatOil' has become the largest employer in the town, and Stavanger is the 'oil capital' of Norway (Municipality of Stavanger 2008, pp. 8, 12). Together with *Sandnes*, *Sola* and *Randaberg*, it is the third biggest urban area (population: 201,000). It has its own university, which opened in 2004 and about 9,000 students were registered in 2010 (www.uis.no, accessed 1.9.13).

Traffic

The E39 motorway bypasses Stavanger but it still has an extension, which comes close to the town but not very close to the city center (I suppose the original plan was rather different). Route 509 gives access to the east. Road tolls are paid on several access roads and it was 20 NOK (€2.5 or $3.20 per car) in 2013.

Figure 11.12
Map of wider city center of Stavanger

The modal split shows that car use increased between 2001 and 2009 and public transportation and cycling declined; only walking stayed the same (see Table 11.2).

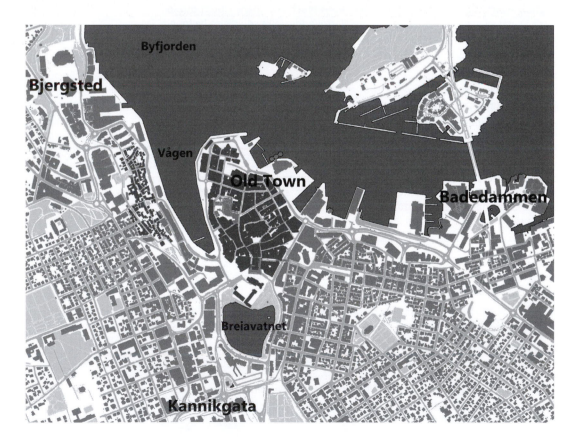

Walking

My View

Figure 11.13
The Old Town

Stavanger has a charming historic town center and an interesting commercial area. Similar to other Norwegian cities, it has plenty of streets without car access, especially in the Old Town and the city center.

Stavanger has an adaptation of the Radburn layout, probably built during the 1970s (for more details see Chapter 1). The Stavanger example is interesting because it is easy to observe what can go wrong with such a design. As the reader may remember, the Radburn design allowed pedestrians to cross busy traffic roads with the help of underpasses. Now here is the crux of the problem because:

- underpasses have to be designed as pedestrian friendly to be helpful
- underpasses have to be implemented at locations where it is useful for pedestrians to cross.

The Radburn underpasses and also the underpasses built in Chicago that connected with the walkways along Lake Michigan are shallow and beautiful building structures; they are easy to use for both pedestrians and cyclists. This is not the case in Stavanger. The underpasses are too steep and uncomfortable to use and as they are applied at a very busy road (*Kannik Gata*), which cuts a residential area in half, they act even more as a barrier than traffic light junctions would. For car drivers the advantage is that they can drive unhindered by traffic lights.

Greenways

There is a 4km urban walk following the waterfront from *Badedammen* to *Bjergsted*. Although the walk was very good around the harbor front itself, other parts of the walk were not so interesting.

Traffic Calming

All residential areas have 30kph speed limits and there were plenty of traffic calming measures but in some streets car traffic can still drive too fast, although evidence suggests that there were few accidents.

Public Transportation

The railway line between Stavanger and Sandnes was improved (a second track was built) in 2009 and trains run every 15 minutes (Müller-Eie 2012). Otherwise public transportation services are not very frequent though most of the buses are modern. Overall the population densities are low, and creating an effective public transportation system is a challenge.

Notes

1 Population figures if not stated otherwise are for 2012.
2 Stavanger/Sandnes grew by about 23% and Kristinansand by 13% in the same time period, 2000–12, smaller cities grew by less: Trondheim by 21% and Bergen by 17%.
3 The election in autumn 2013 changed political control from a red–green coalition to a more right-wing coalition under Erna Solberg (Süddeutsche Zeitung 2013, p. 7).
4 In the proposal it is pointed out that the 'growth of local car travel has to be absorbed by public transportation, walking and cycling' and 'at the same time restrictions must be placed on the use of private cars' (ibid, p. 1).
5 At one time more than 2,000 Germans lived in the city.
6 In summer up to four cruise ships per day dock in the harbour.
7 In the Netherlands that kind of approach was called *Woonerven*.
8 The Blue 'granite stone' actually consists of a concrete block that was coated with Brazilian Sodalite (www.publicspace.org/en/works, accessed 13.8.13).
9 One should remember that Bergen introduced the first toll system in Norway where all car drivers had to pay when entering the city center. It made no difference to the vitality and economics of the city center but I fear access to the new shopping center by tram will.
10 That seems rather to contradict what the representative of the city said about how pedestrians are treated in the city and also what I say below about sidewalks. Nevertheless one has to be aware that Trondheim is also an important tourist location and a high percentage of people do still walk and what would be regarded in a different country, such as the United States, as a wonderful walking city is by Norwegian standards not as good as it could be. I certainly noticed the potholes in sidewalks and uneven coverings.
11 In the section about road tolls above I said that Trondheim had received funding for pedestrian facilities. These appear quite poor compared to other Norwegian cities.
12 In 2009 it was the most expensive city (Boyle 2009) but two years later it was in second place after Tokyo.
13 A 'real' neighborhood is for me a mixture of everything, rich and not so rich housing, all kinds of shops, local restaurants and cafes and local services and activities.
14 It made me aware that what in Germany is referred to as the building style of Hitler or in Italy the building style of Mussolini was indeed a much more general style used in many other nations during the 1930s that were not ruled by a dictator.

12

THE UNITED STATES AND CANADA

An Overview of Walking Research and Policies

Until very recently, urban transportation policies in North America concentrated on accommodating the car and relatively little was done for pedestrians. There has been some public transportation investment in a number of metropolitan areas[1] over the last 30–40 years but it has not been large enough to make a real impact on reducing car trips, except in a small number of large cities.[2] Despite this, impressive research on pedestrian behavior and pedestrian-friendly street design has been published over several decades.

Research in the Use of Urban Space and Pedestrian Behavior

Several US authors have been interested in concepts and use of urban space and pedestrian behavior, for instance, *Lynch*[3] (1960), *J. Jacobs* (1961), *Appleyard* (1981), *Whyte* (1988), *Carr et al*[4] (1992), *A. Jacobs* (1995), *Crowhurst-Lennard and Lennard* (1995). For the reader, many of their demands are self-evident today but when their research was first published, this was mostly not the case. Let us have a look at what some of them were discussing and how relevant these ideas are today.

By far the most important book was *The Death and Life of Great American Cities* by Jane Jacobs (1961). It is a strange read; it comprises ideas that are difficult to follow, with thoughts that even today are relevant and brilliant. Her book has little to do with walking or pedestrian behavior and what she tells us about it is not particularly original any more, but she did discuss some issues concerning pedestrianization and this is partly very stimulating and relevant today (see below).

Donald Appleyard was concerned with how car traffic affected social behavior and social activities in streets. In his book *Livable Streets* (1981) he concluded that people withdrew from streets with high traffic flows. On heavily trafficked streets, families with children had all left. He classified 15 social actions[5] and the lower the level of motorized traffic, the more social activities were carried out. His study also revealed that two-thirds of children were not allowed to play on the street, and one-third were accompanied to school (ibid, p.10). These results were similar to findings in Britain about nine years later by Hillman et al (1990).[6]

He was one of the first researchers who identified that restrictions on the outdoor independence of children will have negative effects on their health. This has become even more of an issue in recent years.

William H. Whyte studied people's behavior on streets and squares (Whyte 1988; LaFarge[7] 1999). Among other things he established that:

- pedestrians usually take the shortest routes
- pedestrian flow itself comes in bunches
- pedestrians like to stay at ground level and will often put up with difficulties at this level, preferring to make detours instead of going up or down
- people like to watch other people
- people eating attract more people
- trees give a feeling of protection to pedestrians
- standing in the middle of a large square is often disliked and corners are preferred
- people like to sit on informal seating facilities, for example steps, walls, sidewalk curbs.

Whyte pointed out elements of attractive streets. He wrote that there are:

> too many pedestrian malls and redone streets are overdesigned. There is too much unified signage, too many award-winning light standards – too much good taste in general, or the pretension of it, and since many designers have the same good taste, the result is a bland conformity.
>
> (Ibid, p. 102)

And one can only agree with this.

In his opinion what is needed are simple benches placed in relation to use and basic amenities, such as clocks, drinking fountains and rubbish bins.

Suzanne Crowhurst-Lennard and *Henry L. Lennard*'s book *Livable Cities Observed* (1995) was based on visits to and observations in several hundred cities. It included the outcome of 16 conferences on this topic and repeated some of the issues described in their earlier research. They pointed out that each city has its own unique character, a statement with which this author fully agrees. But they continued, comparing the life of each city as if it had its own genetic code or DNA structure, something I would question (ibid, p. 7). Crowhurst-Lennard and Lennard argued that those cities which have a unique character are able to provide clear design guidelines.

They went on to describe the principle of designing urban places. They saw the need for urban design to foster a sense of well-being and to encourage contact and connection. In their opinion space, in order to be successful (which means full of people), should have a wide range of social functions.[8]

Allan B. Jacobs influenced urban street design in North American cities with his book *Great Streets* published in 1993.[9] Unfortunately, he did not really mention the European experience of large-scale pedestrianization, traffic calming or any other car-restraining policies. His book is also not really about walking but what he defined as 'great streets'. He acknowledged that the best streets are for people, 'mostly on foot'. He had no problems with cars on a 'great' street as long as they were separated by design from pedestrians (ibid, p. 271). The separation can be done by different means, such as a row of parked cars and/or trees. In his opinion the reason for walking had to do with meeting and experiencing people. He declared that whilst walking one gets involved with the urban environment. He pointed out that 'some numbers may be helpful in gaining a sense of how people walk on various streets' (ibid, p. 273). He did not mention that the number of pedestrians in a street, the so-called 'footfall', is seen in most European countries as a measure of retailing success or failure.

A comparison between the pedestrian flow calculations of Jacobs and other authors is given in Table 12.1. All the pedestrianized streets have a higher pedestrian flow than the streets which allow car access, even taking into account the different years. The street with the highest pedestrian count is the *Kaufinger Straße* in Munich, followed after a long gap by the *Via Condotti* in Rome and *Oxford Street* in London. But the pedestrian density also depends on how large the pedestrian network in the city center is (he does not mention that). The high flow in Munich was not the result of a small network, although the high flow in Dublin (*Grafton Street*) was. The difference in the pedestrian counts in *Strøget* in Copenhagen, which was much lower in 2005 compared to 1990, could possibly be explained by the enlargement of the network.

'Part Three: Street and City Patterns' is fascinating; 60 different street plans of cities around the world are displayed.[10] Some plans show different parts of the same city or are from different time periods. But most intriguing is that they were all drawn on the same scale and this method shows the large variations in street patterns. Jacobs concluded the following:

- The scale of blocks or street pattern became larger over time, especially over the last 150 years and with respect to distance to the center (p. 259).
- The street patterns have become less complicated compared to earlier plans.
- Not all old cities had complex and fine-grained street pattern but that was clearly a tendency in the majority of historic cities.
- Great streets were located in areas where there were more 'things' (p. 260).
- Block size complexity can be defined by the number of intersections per unit area. He used the example of Venice where there were 1,507 intersections compared to New York – Lower Manhattan – with only 218 or Irvine, California – the business complex – with only 15 intersections (p. 262).

In 'Part Four: Making Great Streets', he pointed out the different requirements that make a great street, such as dimensions, spacing of buildings, effects of trees etc. Some were more important to him than others. No evaluation was given about what in his view were the most important characteristics.

Policy-related Research on Walking

In recent years walking has become more policy-orientated and more important in the United States. A number of policy makers, researchers and politicians in urban areas are aware of a paradigm change. *Tuckel* and *Milczarski* (2012) noticed four reasons for this.

1. The baby boom generation – born between 1946 and 1964 – has become a large group and accounted for more than a quarter of the US population in 2010. The 'sporty' part of this generation wants to continue to be active in older age and walking is a good compensation if other sports become too strenuous. This generation also wants to live in places where they can walk to shops or other facilities, that is why there is a strong influx into urban centers.
2. *Generation Y*, born between 1980 and 1999, has different transportation priorities compared to older generations. They are not so interested any

Table 12.1 Pedestrian counts per hour in a number of streets and in different cities

City	Street	Month and year of count	Number of pedestrians	Pedestrianized
Barcelona	Placa de Catalunya	May 1990	4,296	Yes
Barcelona	Ramblas/Theatre Caputxins	May 1990	3,924	No
Rome	Via Cola di Rienzo	May 1986	4,872	No (possibly ped. in 2012)
Rome	South of Via Condotti	May 1986	8,484	Yes
Rome	North of Via Condotti	May 1986	9,960	Some cars (possibly ped. in 2012)
San Francisco[11]	Market Street	Dec 1988	6,600	No
Edinburgh	Princes Street	May 1990	3,720 (4761*)[12]	No
London	Regent St / Great Marlborough St	May 1990	2,280	No
London (G)	Regent Street	2004	3,929	No
London (G)	Oxford Street	2010	9,945	Officially yes, but it has far too many buses, taxis and service vehicles
Copenhagen	Strøget	July 1990	7,836	Yes
Copenhagen (G)	Strøget	2005	5,150	Yes
	Department store	July 1990	9,504	Yes
New York[13]	Between 57th and 58th Streets	1976	4,200	No
New York (G)	Broadway between 31st and 32nd	2007	3,841	No
New York (G)	Times Square	2007	9,814	No
Seattle (G)	Pine Street	2008	2,285	No
Vancouver	Granville Street	2008	2,526	Yes, but buses in street
Tokyo[14]	Harumi-Dori	1976	About 6,000	No
Belfast•	Royal Avenue	1997	7,878	Yes
Birmingham•	New Street	1997	8,799	Yes
Brighton•	Churchill Square	1997	6,261	Yes
Munich•	Kaufinger Straße	1997	15,720	Yes
Dresden•	Prager Straße	1997	5, 490	Yes
Dublin•	Grafton Street	1997	9,516	Yes
Vicenza•	Corso Palladio	1997	6, 684	Yes

Sources: Jacobs 1995, Appendix; LaFarge 1999; and *Hass-Klau[15] et al 1999, p. 114, figure from Vancouver is peak hour, for source see chapter 13; G = Gehl 2010, p. 210 (14-hour counts).

more in driving a car. Between 2001 and 2009, the annual miles driven per capita dropped by 23% and the number of young people who acquire a driver's license has fallen. Research at the *University of Michigan* showed that only two-thirds of those 18 year olds possessed a driving license in 2008, compared to 80% in 1983 (ibid, p. 3, quoted from Ramsey 2012).[16] Generally, there has been a devaluation of the 'drive a car' status. Many young people make a conscious decision not to own a car. Several factors have influenced this decision, most importantly higher petrol prices and the increase in the real cost of owning and insuring a car.

3. Another trend in the same direction is that the young richer households tend to use more alternative modes. Between 2001 and 2009, public transportation trips increased by 100%, cycling by 122% and walking by 37% in the United States (ibid, p. 4, quoted from Frontier Group and US PIRG Education Fund 2012).

4. Increasingly, the suburbs are becoming less attractive. In the past – since the 1920s – the suburbs have grown faster than the urban centers. In the last census period (2000–2010), already three urban metropolitan areas showed a higher growth rate in the main central city (Boston, Oklahoma City and Providence Rhode Island).[17] The US Census Bureau estimated a different population growth using 2010–2011 data; it displayed that about half of the largest 50 metropolitan areas had a main central city that was growing faster than the metropolitan area as a whole (own research on Census data). The authors asked the question why this was the case and concluded:

   a) high petrol prices
   b) quality of life issues
   c) change of an awareness of the urban environment.

Most central cities have become more attractive to live in and people like to walk (or cycle) to carry out their daily errands and are fed up sitting in cars on congested roads. Finally, they pointed out that 'real estate in walkable neighborhoods – where people can shop, go to work, or run errands without having to get into a car – have the highest values'. In fact, research shows that the more walkable a neighborhood is, the costlier the value of the real estate (ibid, p. 7, quoted from Leinberger 2012).

The change in the overall trend in the United States (and North America) has led to a previously unknown interest in walking. This has resulted in a number of practical guidebooks, most notably the *Benchmarking Reports* (produced by the Alliance for Walking and Cycling) and other reports of good practice, for example *America Walks* (Schwartz 2012). A large number of transportation or planning departments particularly in the large cities have developed pedestrian plans.

Benchmarking Reports and America Walks

Since 2007, three benchmarking reports have been published and the basis of their research is rather impressive, including all the official statistical data available. The report in 2012 provides slightly more information on cycling than walking but it is still a good source document for walking. In total all 50 states and 51 of the largest US cities are included and walking and cycling is ranked by

Table 12.2   Modal split in US travel to work and all trips in percent (2009)

Mode	Travel to work (nationwide)	Travel to work (major cities)	All trips (nationwide)
Car	91.5	77.0	86.6
Public transportation	5.0	17.2	1.9
Walk	2.9	4.9	10.5
Cycle	0.6	0.9	1.0

Source: Alliance for Walking and Cycling 2012, p. 10, based on the American Community Surveys.

Table 12.3 The highest-ranking cities in walking (travel to work) in the United States

Ranking	Population in million	Share in %	Safety ranking (low ped. fatalities per capita)[20]
1. Boston	0.6	14	1
2. Washington DC	0.6	11	7
3. New York	8.2	10.3	5
4. San Francisco	0.8	10.0	10
5. Seattle	0.6	8.6	6
6. Philadelphia	1.5	8.4	9
7. Honolulu	0.4	8.0	13
8. Baltimore	0.6	6.7	14
9. Minneapolis	0.4	6.4	3
10. New Orleans	0.4	5.8	22
11. Chicago	2.8	5.8	12
12. Portland	0.6	5.2	11

Sources: Alliance for Walking and Cycling 2012, pp. 24, 31, 53, the pedestrian fatality rate was calculated to be the average over three years, between 2007 and 2009.

the percentage of travel to work trips (Census and American Community Surveys).[18] Anybody who has worked within the field of walking will get nervous about such a single statistical indicator because it includes only a fraction of what walking is really about, since walking to shops and recreational walking is not included.[19] Yet in comparison with other walking statistics – if they exist at all – it is probably the most reliable one and it does say something about the walking environment.

The *America Walks* publication (Schwartz 2012) is a comprehensive guide to walking for a broad audience (city officials, engineers, landscape gardeners, pressure groups etc.). These main issues are strengthened by practical examples from the United States, and frequently quoted are San Francisco and New York (see Chapter 13).

Canada

Modal split data about walking (all trips) are available in Canadian cities. The picture is similar to the United States. Walking as a share of all transportation modes was highest in Vancouver (16–17%) in 2004, an increase of 2–3% compared to 1994[21] (City of Vancouver 2005, p. 5). A Census comparison within the City of Vancouver (24-hour counts) indicates that between 2001 and 2011, walking grew from 12.8% to 17% (information from the Census data was provided by the City of Vancouver). But the latest Canadian statistics on other cities are depressing. Nearly everywhere cycling and especially walking declined further and public transportation did not really increase (www12.statcan.gc.ca/nhs-enm, accessed 12.8.13).

How much people walk depends on a wide range of factors (for more details, see Chapter 15). One of them is the scale of car-free urban streets and the level of public transportation. Let us first study what happened to pedestrianization in the United States.

Pedestrianization

In the European chapters, we have seen the tremendous economic success of pedestrianization and its popularity with citizens and tourists alike. This was in some countries combined with large new – mostly – rail investment in public transportation. So what happened in the United States?

In contrast to Europe, population migration developed differently in North America. In particular, there was a growing spatial division between poorer African Americans and the other lower income families, who stayed or moved into the inner-city areas, and the white population (mostly higher income), who chose to live in the suburbs. This did not happen in such an extreme form in the European cities.[22] The North American migration had a strong effect on city center retailing and housing. Large suburban shopping malls had already reduced the retailing turnover in the city centers during the late 1950s and even more so in the 1960s and 1970s. In an attempt to revitalize the city centers, large new shopping malls were built in some cities and a few city center streets were even pedestrianized. *Kalamazoo Mall (Michigan)*[23] was the first large outdoor shopping mall in the United States (1959); it was basically a central European pedestrianization scheme, designed and implemented by *Victor Gruen*, who was Austrian by origin and had studied in *Vienna*. Gruen provided several plans of other large-scale pedestrianization projects in the United States, e.g. the *Fort Worth Plan* in Dallas. He was aware of the car dependency in the United States when he pointed out that the more space is provided for cars in cities, the greater becomes the need to use them, so that even more space for cars is needed (Jacobs 1961, p. 351).

Gruen's ideas about pedestrianization schemes and how to manage them have not been fully implemented. When reading the details of Fort Worth, one can understand why. It was far too elaborate. In fact, he wanted to change US city centers into a European version with so much additional investment (construction above and below ground) that it would not have been commercial (for more details see Owen 1959, pp. 66–68).

Most local officers I talked to declared that pedestrianized schemes would not work in the United States (though no real reasons were given for it). The lack of enthusiasm about pedestrianzation has already been expressed by Jane Jacobs (1961) with reference to the *Fort Worth Plan* of 1955. There she was right but she was not correct about how pedestrians use car-free streets. She wrote pedestrians 'stay to the sides' even when the car traffic is removed. She did also believe that this may change when sidewalk curbs disappear, but she was still doubtful and concluded that it would need a lot of pedestrians to fill wide streets (ibid, p. 347). Strangely enough her argument was used in Munich against pedestrianizing the city center shopping streets before 1972. It was said that there was too much road space for pedestrians and they would feel lost (Chapter 9).

Very readable is her description of the road closure of *5th Avenue* running through *Washington Square* in New York which was proposed by *Shirley Hayes* and *Edith Lyons* with no widening of the perimeter roads in 1958 (Chapter 1). As always, city officials and Robert Moses thought that if the perimeter roads were not widened they would be in a state of 'frantic and frenetic congestion' (ibid, p. 361) and motor vehicle traffic would increase on other roads.[24]

None of the predictions of increased traffic around the park were borne out.
(Ibid, p. 362).

Jacobs went on to ask 'Where did the traffic go?' and it seems that none of the
streets east and west of 5th Avenue and parallel to it received any extra load –
'these cars or some cars disappeared into thin air' (ibid, p. 362). It is strange,
that despite this great success in reducing car traffic and creating a better
environment for pedestrians, no other schemes were implemented.

Whyte (1977) wrote that a 15-block stretch of *Madison Avenue* in New York was
made traffic-free for two weeks in 1972.[25] During this period, Whyte found that
the number of pedestrians more than doubled from about 9,000 to 19,000.
Similar results were found in Munich with the introduction of pedestrianization,
the number of pedestrians using the area shot up dramatically (see Chapters 4
and 9).

Whyte remarked that the increase in pedestrian numbers was not at the expense
of other streets (quoted from LaFarge 1999, p. 238). Unfortunately, the
objections of the merchants and the taxi drivers' union were too strong and the
scheme was abandoned. How regrettable for New York because most examples
in Europe have shown that they would have gained most from pedestrianization
(Chapter 4).

Figure 12.1
Lincoln Road Mall, Miami
Beach

Having traveled widely through the United States, I saw a number of successful
pedestrianized streets. Rather impressive is *Lincoln Road*, which used to be a

Figure 12.2
16th Street Mall, Denver

100ft wide four-lane avenue in *Miami Beach*. It was pedestrianized in 1960 with the slogan 'a car never bought anything'. It had some hard times during the 1980s and early 1990s but it was redesigned in the mid-1990s and opened again in 1997 (Shulman et al 2010, pp. 278–279).

Downtown Denver has a pedestrianized street, the *16th Street Mall*, which is about 1.2 miles (1.9km) long. Some of this pedestrianized street is designed like a French boulevard with a central reservation for walking (from *Arapahoe Street* to *Tremont Plaza*) and wide sidewalks on each side. This street has always been the main thoroughfare for shopping, theaters and movies. It went through some rough times and many of the historic buildings have been pulled down, but some survived. Despite the decline, the street was pedestrianized in 1976 and was apparently modeled on the pedestrianized street (*Pearl Street*) in *Boulder* (Barnhouse 2010, p. 119). The historic buildings along 16th Street were replaced by high-rise ones, which do nothing to the urban space but may have done something to the economy of the area.

Boulder is another city with a well-designed and wide pedestrianized street (*Pearl Street*), which has been in operation, since 1976 and was inaugurated in 1977 (Pettem 2006, p. 9; www.boulderdowntown.com, accessed 30.7.13). It has kept many historic buildings that have all about the same height. It is four blocks long (440m) and was well visited.

Figure 12.3
Pearl Street, Boulder

The pedestrian streets in the French quarter in New Orleans were closed to traffic at about the same time as the redesign of Lincoln Road took place. *Royal Street* and *Bourbon Street* were closed in 1995 (information from the City Planning Department in New Orleans, April 2013). There are a number of small traffic-free alleys around St. Louis Cathedral.

There are other examples, such as the *Arcades* in Santa Barbara, the *Paseo de St Antonio Walk* in San Jose, the *Nicollet Mall* in Minneapolis. With sufficient time I would find many more well-designed pedestrianized streets and I am just wondering whether the assertion that pedestrianization does not work is a myth invented by somebody official a long time ago. It may well be that it has to be reinvented with a different name to be successful. Maybe 'Green Streets' sounds better and that is exactly what Portland is doing in its new proposal for the *Conway Area* (Chapter 13).

In spite of this, I was also confronted with pedestrian streets with design or other problems, for instance *Winter Street* in Boston or *Alabama Street* in Atlanta. Alabama Street was in a sad condition although it would be very easy to make it a real success. The section from *Peachtree Street* to *Pryor Street* is like a big rectangular square; the height of the buildings is very good as they are uniform and not too high. It simply needs some restaurants and cafes and a few planters. Seating facilities are crucial in the United States to make pedestrian streets a success. If one had chairs and tables in this part of the pedestrianized street one would have a great view of the skyline and the large public water feature. Alabama Street fits well into the whole area, which has lots of pedestrian-friendly corners, sidewalks and squares. With more outdoor facilities more interesting shops would come back.

The second part of Alabama Street is more difficult to redesign as the view is not very enticing since one sees a large car parking facility, but a good water feature there and seating would make this part of the street a success as well (and the car parking could be removed).

Although large-scale pedestrianization has so far not been a success in North American cities, many small-scale traffic-free areas do exist, apart from parks. Examples of this are also the traditional markets, such as in Seattle. One of the most exciting markets I saw was the fish market at *Redondo Beach*, near Los Angeles; it was nearly as good as the fish market in *Hong Kong*. Studying the short history of Quincy Market in Boston provides food for thought. It was an 'old' market manicured into a kind of 'modern' shopping center. This was a great success for a time but had to fail because anything that is manicured has to be repeatedly redone to remain successful and how often can one do that? Quincy Market lost its traditional genuine power and has been replaced by an over-gentrified version of its old identity. It is also not really part of an existing neighborhood. It is a tourist honeypot, nothing more.

Figure 12.4
Fish market, Seattle

Pedestrianization is not a big topic in the Canadian cities either, although many of their pedestrian streets are attractive, but the long winters in most Canadian cities do not encourage outside living. The capital of British Columbia (Victoria) has no pedestrianized street but car traffic is restricted in *Government Street* and *Fort Street*, the main shopping streets in Victoria. Both streets have very wide sidewalks and trees. They are enjoyable streets to walk in and the few cars do not detract from this pleasure. The pedestrian street (part of the 8th Avenue) in Calgary is well designed and has become even more spectacular with its recent new design features.

In the attractive historic parts of Quebec some streets are closed to car traffic and Montreal has some picturesque squares and one pedestrianized street so far (part of *De la Gauchetière*) although there are discussions on doing more. In other Canadian cities in the east, pedestrian streets are established (often including large amounts of buses) but nothing spectacular is known to the author. The most common features are very large shopping malls in the center.

Public Transportation

For some readers the relationship between walking and public transportation may not be evident but if one thinks about it, the connection is relatively easy; how does one get to an urban public transportation stop? According to German research 95% of people walk – only 3% cycle – to a public transportation stop (Brög 2014, p. 14). This percentage is different when one considers railway stations because a relatively high number of people either park and ride or are dropped off ('kiss and ride').

Table 12.4 Modal split for public transportation: comparison of North American and European major cities in percent

North American city	Pop. in million	All trips	Work trips	European city	Pop. in million	All trips	Work trips
New York	8.2	23	55	Greater London[26]	8.2	27	50
Manhattan			59	City center	–	–	90
Washington DC	0.6	–	38	Ile-de-France	12	–	21
Montreal[27]	3.8	–	35	Paris and the inner suburbs	6.5	62	–
				Stockholm	1.3	43	–
Toronto	5.6	24	34	Berlin	3.4	26	–
San Francisco	0.8		34	Madrid	3.1	34[28]	–
Boston	0.6		33	Oslo	0.6	25	40
Vancouver	0.6	17–18	30	Paris[29]	2.1	62	–
Philadelphia	1.5	–	27	Vienna	1.6	37	–
Chicago	2.8	16	27	Rome	10.6	20	–
Ottawa	1.2	–	22	Birmingham	1.1	12	22
Seattle	0.6	–	18	Munich	1.4	23	34
Pittsburgh	0.3	–	18	Copenhagen	0.6	14	24

Sources: www.nachhaltigkeit.wienerstadtwerke.at/daseinsvorsorge, accessed 27.2.13; TfL 2011, p. 39; City of Vancouver 2005, p. 5 (to and within Vancouver); http://forum.skyscraperpage.com, accessed 28.2.2013; http://forum.skyscrapercity.com accessed 28.2.2013; Modal split data for Stockholm; http://ltaacademy.gov.sg, accessed 08.03.13; www.ons.gov.uk, accessed 22.01.14; Census 2011 (for people living in Greater London)

As can be seen from the Benchmarking Report (2012) above, public transport-ation plays only an insignificant role nationwide, except in some major cities. Table 12.4 gives the modal share of public transportation trips in those cities with the highest use. People who use public transportation normally walk to public transportation stops and this may generally encourage walking, therefore substitution between going to work by public transportation (say if it rains) and walking to work is not uncommon (when the sun is shining and the trip length is short). My conclusion is that when public transportation gets better in the United States, walking will also improve.[30]

A comparison with some of the large European cities shows that the ten North American cities with the highest modal split share for public transportation are in the same league as their equivalents in Europe, although a comparison is difficult because the European data indicate *all* public transportation trips whereas the North American data cover work trips; they normally have a higher public transportation share than the classification 'all' trips.

The Canadian Urban Public Transportation Systems

Canadian cities have been quite successful in both developing established and constructing new public transportation systems. Even cities which only rely on buses are doing rather well, for instance Quebec, Edmonton and Victoria which had modal split data for travel to work of about 13% for public transportation (Canadian Census data of 2011).

Traffic Calming

There is not very much to write yet about traffic calming in North America but plenty of discussions have been going on about speed reduction in residential streets, and a number of cities were experimenting with various traffic calming measures (for more see 'New York' in Chapter 13). Apart from this, some traffic calming schemes were already in place; the ones I saw were not very imaginative but I have not seen all of them. Unfortunately, area-wide traffic calming was basically still unknown but that can change very quickly. *Road dieting*, which means reducing the width of carriageway lanes and sometimes even taking out car lanes and putting in cycle lanes and/or wider sidewalks, is being widely discussed and partly implemented. Large-scale traffic calming combined with improved sidewalk design can have a positive effect on walking, as discussed in earlier chapters.

Notes

1 Urban rail public transportation investment had already been implemented in the early 20th century, such as in New York, Chicago or Philadelphia.
2 See Table 12.4.
3 It is not clear whether the people interviewed were pedestrians or car drivers but his concept of asking individuals what their mental picture is of the exterior physical world examined in three US cities would be fascinating to use for pedestrians and compare it to the 'world' of car drivers.
4 Although I have not referred to it in this chapter I will in Chapter 13, but he should be mentioned here.
5 Here are the 15 actions he mentioned: walking pets, people talking, gardening, car washing, playing with toys, house painting, sitting outside, car repairing, parents supervising children, roller skating, ball games, frisbee, jogging, garage sales, building things.

6   They found that about 80% of 7- and 8-year-old schoolchildren were allowed to go on their own in 1970 but in 1990 this had declined to 9% (Hillman et al 1990, p. 106). There was an additional study in 2010 which showed an even more drastic reduction in children's freedom to go to school.

7   The publication by LaFarge is a collection of Whyte's articles and a summary of some of his books.

8   • Safe and easy access for everybody in the community
    • Frequent and regular use by the local residents
    • Help people feel significant and support their self-esteem
    • Reinforce the sense of belonging
    • Increase awareness and enjoyment of the present moment
    • Encourage curiosity and interest in the urban environment
    • Frame meaningful and memorable experiences
    • Orient people and facilitate differentiated activities
    • Make it possible for a variety of people to feel at home in the space
    • Amplify channels for direct interpersonal communication (ibid, p. 28).

9   Paperback version 1995 – page numbers are with reference to the paperback version.

10 Nearly half of them are European but there are also, apart from US cities, others like African, Asian and South American cities.

11 There are more counts in San Francisco but all of them are much lower.

12 Hass-Klau et al (1999) figures for off peak, during peak hours (lunchtime) figures are higher, 5,256. Especially in Scotland there is a large difference between people being around on sunny days or on cold, windy or rainy days, thus the figure by Jacobs may have been on such a day.

13 LaFarge (1999), pp. 234–235, no year is given about the count but the article was written in 1977 and the time period of the count was between 8.00 and 18.00.

14 LaFarge (1999), p. 236, close to a subway entrance.

15 All counts were carried out during the summer months and not on a rainy day.

16 Similar percentage figures are known from Europe.

17 In the 18 cities I studied in more detail, only the City of Boston grew slightly more than the suburbs. Charlotte had a suburban growth rate of over 80%, Savannah 35%, Atlanta 28% and Charleston 25% (although the City of Charleston grew by 24%) between 2000 and 2010. Only five metropolitan areas had a suburban growth rate of less than 10% (New York, Boston, Philadelphia, San Francisco and Los Angeles) (Census data 2000 and 2010).

18 Statistical Variability in the United States: In the United States, the data of the modal split in 2000 is from the Census 'travel to work' but the 2010 Census did not have this question any more, hence I had to work instead with an average of five years 2007–2011 from the American Community Survey. Hence, strictly speaking, the data is not comparable and the results may be slightly misleading but I did not have anything better.

19 Linked trips are also not included, for instance when one walks to and from a public transit stop.

20 We used an average of six or seven years.

21 Walking to and within the city, cycling increased from 1% in 1994 to 3% in 2004.

22 There were several reasons for this: first, the percentage of non-white people was lower in Europe, and second, in some countries, such as France, especially in Paris, immigrants lived in suburbs, mostly to the east or the north of the city. There has also been a different attitude in Europe to city centers, which have always been the historic heart of a city and have been much loved by the citizens.

23 In 1998, some of the streets were opened to cars again.

24 This is a very popular opinion, which is still used rather too often today – see evidence of that in Cairns et al (1998).

25 The year 1972 is interesting because it was the year when in Munich the large-scale pedestrianization scheme opened, this had a signal function for many German cities – see Chapters 4 and 8.

26 UK Census 2011.

27 In Canada the population size is from 2011 and based on the metropolitan areas, Statistics Canada www 12.statcan.gc.ca/census-recensement/2011, accessed 9.3.13 and www.metromontreal, accessed 25.1.14.

28 This is for the region of six million in 2006 (Communidad de Madrid and Concorcio Transportes Madrid 2008, pp. 2–3).

29 Between Paris and the central agglomeration public transportation use was 73% in 2010 (Enquete Global Transportation, p. 12, available at www.stif.info).

30 This does not automatically mean for walking to work but for walking in general.

13

WALKING IN NORTH AMERICA: A EUROPEAN VIEW

The Leaders

What it is like to walk in North American cities? I wanted to know, hence I visited 23 cities[1] in the United States and Canada in 2012 and 2013, of which nine belonged to the largest metropolitan areas. Eight cities are included in this chapter and another eight in the next one. In all cities discussions with local officers and/or academics took place. Books, articles or discussions with academics and city officials determined the choice of cities.

I analyzed two cities in more detail: New York because of its unique character and Charlotte (Chapter 14) because its transportation policies are typical of a number of North American cities that are trying to come to grips with the promotion of sustainable policies in a car-dependent society.

New York City

Population 8.3 million in 2012 and 20 million in the metropolitan area in 2013.

Background

New York has always been the gateway from and to Europe. In many respects new transportation ideas and policies are only small facets of this much wider exchange. But is New York a trendsetter in urban living and urban transportation, or an outsider? Having traveled widely in the United States, my guess is that New York is more an outsider, although the representatives of the City of New York think that it is a trendsetter; maybe it is both.

Population Growth

A comparison between 2000 and 2010 reveals an annual increase of about 0.2% in the City of New York but 2010–2012 indicate an annual growth of nearly 1%, partially due to an undercount in 2010. A lack of available housing will place the biggest limit on population growth (informal information New York City).

Major Characteristics of the Boroughs

New York City consists of five boroughs, which are really like five different cities living in close proximity.

The commercial, economic and cultural center is the island of *Manhattan* but it also has many housing areas of widely differing qualities, most of which could be classified as housing for the highest income groups. Midtown is the retailing CBD and southern Manhattan is the financial district of global importance.

Brooklyn has its own CBD and a population that would make it the country's fourth largest city if it were not a borough. It encompasses strikingly different neighborhoods from the wealthy areas that compete with Manhattan prices to *Brownsville*'s poorer areas.

Queens also has a diverse ethnic character with Greek and Indian enclaves as well as more suburban neighborhoods. Some housing blocks in Queens have recently been built in rezoned industrial areas, such as *Hunter's Point* and *Long Island City*. There are a few very rich neighborhoods within Queens, for example *Forest Hills Gardens* (see Chapter 1), *Douglaston* and *Bayside* as well as very poor neighborhoods.

The *Bronx* has both the poorest and richest neighborhoods in the city. The notorious South Bronx ghetto had suffered rapid population loss, abandonment and many cases of arson until recently in-fill housing developments have created both new low-income housing and working-class owner-occupied one- and two-family homes. At the other extreme, *Riverdale* has mansions overlooking the Hudson River and exclusive private schools.

Finally *Staten Island*, which is the most suburban borough, is easier to reach by road from New Jersey, although the *Verrazano Bridge* connects it to Brooklyn and the popular and free Staten Island Ferry sails back and forth to the southern tip of Manhattan.

City Politics

During the last ten years, New York has been influenced by the politics and policies of Mayor *Michael Bloomberg*, who was in office from 2002 to 2013. The previous mayor, *Rudolf Giuliani*, had successfully brought down the crime rate. The rundown public transportation system of the 1970s had been improved by the 1990s and then with the introduction of the *Metrocard* (1993), integrating the bus and subway systems, the ridership increased rapidly.

The design of city streets and open spaces had been neglected for decades.[2] The mayor wanted a city where more outdoor living and less car traffic was possible. One of his ideas was to create more parks and other new spaces for pedestrians. The opening of *Ferry Point Park*, *Governors Island*, *the High Line*, *Brooklyn Bridge Park* were some of his achievements. The Brooklyn and Manhattan waterfronts have long-term plans for continuous public access as part of a Greenway Network. A ferry connects a few completed segments that are very attractive for walking, full of all kinds of activities and with wonderful views across the river to the Manhattan skyline.

In 2014 a new mayor, *Bill de Blasio*, has pledged radical changes in the inequality of the city, but in terms of transportation no major changes are expected.

Transportation

The main north–south coastal Interstate 95 passes through the Bronx and bypasses Manhattan to the north then crosses the *Hudson River* and continues south on the New Jersey side. The I-95 has a branch, the I-495, that comes toward mid-Manhattan from the west, crosses the Hudson by the *Lincoln Tunnel* toll road, but its traffic then exits into Manhattan. It resumes to the east (and passes the Robert Moses playground), leaves Manhattan via the *Queens Midtown*

Tunnel, and goes off through Queens into Long Island. There are no Interstates that run right across Manhattan.

The modal split figures show a very low car use for travel to work in 2000, which fell even further between 2000 and 2007/2011. New York had the lowest percentage car use of any North American city, followed by San Francisco and Boston. Nevertheless, when walking around, especially during the rush hours, one still has the feeling that there are far too many cars in the streets. Between 2000 and 2007/2011 there was some increase in public transportation use and a very slight growth in cycling.[3]

Walking

One of the main changes in New York has been the creation of new squares (plazas). Interestingly enough, the one US city which had a large number of squares as part of its original street layout is Savannah. What could be more enjoyable than walking from square to square, even in very hot weather? Possibly without knowing it and certainly in different forms and shapes, New York is copying a street layout of US history.

The change toward creating more pedestrian-friendly areas not only took place in Manhattan, but also other boroughs. Brooklyn got nearly as many new plazas as Manhattan but Queens and the Bronx are still lagging behind (www.nyc.gov/plaza-program, accessed 17.03.13). When one studies the 'before and after' photographs, the contrast between the car-dominated roads 'before' and the new pedestrian-friendly oases 'after' is breathtaking. By 2013, 26 new plazas had been built and the city is planning to build at least three additional squares each year. Here are some examples:

- *Willoughby Street Pedestrian Plaza* (Brooklyn), which used to be a side street; this was changed into a small square in 2006 with temporary materials with permanent construction completed in 2013.
- Half of the road space on 9th Avenue at W. 14th Street (Manhattan) was converted into a plaza in 2007.
- In 2008, next to *Madison Square Park* three large plazas were 'instantly' created out of road space by widening sidewalks, expanding a park triangle and absorbing two skinny median islands into the largest plaza. This added about 37,000 sqft of new public space.
- *Pearl Street Plaza* (Brooklyn) the new space, which was previously used for car parking, was created in 2007; this plaza gives a jolly feel to the area.
- *Gansevoort Plaza* (Manhattan) located at 9th Avenue and Gansevoort Street, opened in 2008. The whole area is very walkable and is close to the *High Line*, an old upper level railway line that was converted to a linear park in 2002. It is similar to the upper level railway line in Paris,[4] the *Promenade Plantée* that was converted to a Greenway in 1993.
- *Times Square* (Manhattan) is the most spectacular project in New York. Five blocks of *Broadway* were closed to motor vehicle traffic in 2009 and this was made permanent in 2010. As part of this project, two blocks of Broadway at Herald Square were also pedestrianized.
- *Dutch Kills Green* (Queens), close to the *Queens Plaza* underground station (Lines E, M, R), is another square that had been a parking lot and was finished in 2012. It was like a peaceful green island – litter-free, remembering that another world exists in the midst of too much car traffic, noisy overhead railway lines, neglected historic buildings and office blocks.

Figure 13.1
Madison Square
before

Figure 13.2
Madison Square after

**Figure 13.3
Upper level walkway
in Paris**

**Figure 13.4 Upper level
walkway in New York**

Figure 13.5
Times Square
before

Figure 13.6
Times Square
after

Figure 13.7
Dutch Kills Green

But building plazas is not the only new way to improve urban life, the changes along Broadway are exciting too. Half of Broadway is now an area for walking, sitting and cycling. It is surprising that the change occurred at all because, as in all US cities, a substantial traffic change of this order needs the approval of the State, which is by and large dominated by a rather more conservative engineering staff.

An evaluation report (NYCDOT 2010a, 2010b) presents the results of the changes, which occurred in Midtown.[5] Pedestrian volumes increased overall by 11% at a sampling of 20 locations on an average peak hour between 2008 and 2009.[6] One of the reasons for pedestrian improvements along Broadway and Times Square was the high number of pedestrian accidents, about 137% higher than on other avenues in the area. After one year of implementation the pedestrian accidents were compared six months 'after' to an average of the same six months 'before' over a time period of three years. The pedestrian injuries declined by 35% and injuries to motor vehicle occupants by 63% in the researched area (ibid, p. 28). Included in the report were a number of other interesting results, such as 84% more people were relaxing (reading, eating, taking photographs) in Times and Herald Squares than before the improvements (ibid, p. 32).

My View

Not everything along Broadway I liked. I was especially surprised that some of the crossroads were not closed, especially 46th Street at Times Square but also

43th and 44th, which would have had very little effect, if any, on the overall traffic flows.

Figure 13.8
The new Broadway

Having a strong sense of historic street layouts, I would object to having more streets converted in the same style as carried out on Broadway. When reaching *University Street*, I was relieved that I could walk along a wide sidewalk, although cycle lanes along the carriageway and more pedestrian crossings are needed (as one walks toward south Manhattan, traffic eases a bit). It was a gruesome thought, when walking through *Greenwich Village*, what this area would look like today if the protest, which began against road widening and motorways during the 1950s, had not been successful (for more details see Chapter 1). When reaching *Washington Square*, the past-proposed destruction becomes even more preposterous. What a wonderful and atmospheric square it still is.[7] Some other US cities were not as lucky.

Pedestrian Crossings

The information I received from New York City was that at a normal street with a width of 60ft (18m) for arterial and collector roads, pedestrians have 24 seconds to cross of which 17 seconds are flashing lights. That assumes an average walking speed of 3.5 feet per second. In my opinion that is surely not enough for older people. In fairness it has to be said that in 'Senior Areas' the assumed speed is reduced to 3 feet per second; this is not slow enough for some seniors, handicapped people and parents with toddlers. Of course most senior people do not live in senior areas anyhow, therefore there is a wide distribution of walking speeds everywhere and *all* pedestrian crossing lights should consider the walking speed of older people.

Greenways

The New City Greenway Plan was accepted in 1993 (Olson 2012, pp. 73–74). It was planned to create 350 miles (563km) of landscaped bicycle and pedestrian paths that would serve the five boroughs of the City. By 2013 only 59 miles (95km) had been built and 106 miles (171km) were in need of substantial improvements (www.nyc.gov.html/dcp/htnl/bike/gprea, accessed 23.7.13).

Traffic Calming

The New York City Department of Transportation launched in 2012 the first 13 slow zones in New York City (http://walksteps.org/case-studies, accessed 14.3.13). It featured traffic calming and gateway signage. Communities are invited to apply and they have been very popular. Prior to this program, traffic calming techniques were used as part of safety work to improve high pedestrian injury locations, problem areas near schools and in neighborhoods to increase safety for seniors.

Cycling

There are plenty of cycling facilities and some of them are state of the art, but there are still cyclists missing, and when talking to young people they simply found New York too dangerous to cycle. It may well be that this will change with the introduction of a bike share system: *Citibikes*, which was introduced in May 2013 and has exceeded expectations. The casual bikers drawn to Citibikes will no doubt clamor for more protected bike lanes and this along with increased user numbers will have a positive impact on safety.

Public Transportation

The modal split figures show the great success of public transportation in New York. How did this come about? Let us have a quick look at its history. The first underground line of 9.1 miles (14.6km) opened in 1904, two years later than the first underground line in Berlin but 14 years later than the first underground line in London (1890) (Daniels and Warnes 1980, p. 10).

The line was quickly extended to Brooklyn in 1908 and Queens in 1915. Motorbus services started in 1907 in Manhattan. In 1953 the *New York City Transit Authority* was created, now called *MTA New York City Transit*. In 2003, an 8.1 mile (13km) rail line to JFK Airport started its service. In 2004, Manhattan Bridge reopened after serious renovation and subway services could continue again. In 2009, the annual subway ridership reached 1.62 billion, the highest annual figure since 1950 (www.mta.info/nyct/facts Mta.info, accessed 9.3.13). In 2009, the MTA was serving an area of 14.5 million people. The Metro service is open 24 hours and the total length of the network is 211 miles (337km, route length). The network has 24 lines and about 5.3 million daily passengers. The New York Metro system is smaller than the equivalent system in Greater London but much bigger than in Paris (Ile-de-France region) or Berlin. In term of passengers carried – daily and annually – it is by far the largest.[8] According to the MTA it is the sixth busiest in the world.

There is also a large bus network with about 2.7 million passengers daily but the buses are slow. BRT (bus rapid transit) lanes are planned (www.mta.info-select bus service, accessed 9.3.13).

In addition there are several commuter rail services, especially the *Long Island Rail Road* with a total length of 700 miles (1,263km) and the much smaller *Staten Island Railway* line, which has a length of 13.7 miles (22km). But the Long Island Rail Road is very slow and the service from New York to the East End of Long Island offers limited and unreliable service.

Boston

Population 636,500 and 4.6 million in the metropolitan area in 2013.

Background and Population Growth

Boston was one of the earliest settlements in the United States (1630). It played a prominent role in the start of the American Revolution against the British. The city (with Cambridge, Mass.) is best known for its universities. Connected to this higher education strength, the high-tech concentration is particularly known for its specialism in biotech and life sciences. In terms of demographic change, Boston was the only study city whose population grew faster than its suburbs over 2000–2010.

Transportation

Boston is a sad example of what happened to cities when interstate highways went right through the cities, as Moses (see Chapter 1) envisaged as the only way to solve the traffic problems of the future. The Massachusetts Turnpike went close to the city center and the first section opened in 1957. It became the I-90 two years later and 125 miles (201km) were completed in 1965. A tunnel extension to *Logan Airport* was started in 1991 and finally completed in 2003. The wide streets leading to the I-90 are not really pedestrian friendly.

A second motorway, the Interstate 93, called the *Central Artery*, was originally built as an elevated motorway (Highway in the Sky) and opened in 1959. As a result of this construction, 10,000 residents were displaced and about 1,000 buildings destroyed. During the 1990s, the I-93 was put into tunnel and the surface area was changed into a linear park or a wide Greenway (Rose Kennedy Greenway), which opened to the public in 2008 (www.rosekennedygreenway.org/history, accessed 20.7.13).

The modal split shows a relatively high use of public transportation in 2007–2011, which had increased slightly compared to 2000. Car use was low and declined in the second time period by about 4% points and walking increased by 2% points, the highest in all the North American cities.[9]

Walking

My View

Although Boston is number one in walking according to the Benchmarking Reports, I have not been impressed by it, except for the *Public Garden*, which is a delight, and *Boston Common*. It has many opportunities to become a very

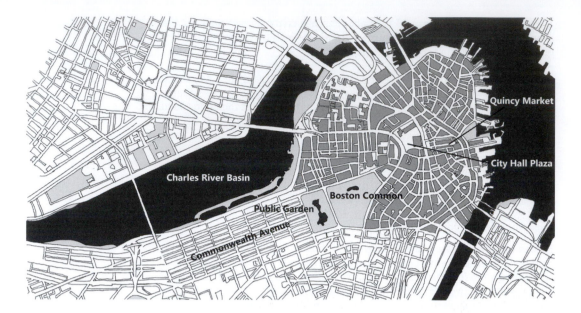

Figure 13.9
Wider city center map

walkable city, which have not yet been fully taken up. *Commonwealth Avenue* – one of the best boulevards in the United States – is a European-style boulevard that needs secured 'straight' crossings at crossroads (high visibility crossings), like the example in Santa Cruz, Tenerife or Portland, Oregon.

Parts of *Winter Street*, *Summer Street* and *Washington Street* (called *Downtown Crossing*) were car-free but they lacked quality street coverings and seating facilities. The litter on the streets did not help to improve their appearance. Equally disappointing is *City Hall Plaza*, a huge square with very few people on it. Carr et al (1992) called it 'Boston's most monumental and least used open space . . . The great barren plaza seems to speak instead of the government's inaccessibility and of the insignificance of the individual citizens' (pp. 88–89). It is a square where one can learn how not to design a square. The City Hall Plaza and the Downtown Crossing[10] are seen by the city as problem areas and are in the process of being improved.

The *Harbor Walk* is a modern walkway along the various wharfs, which had few interesting sites but beautiful views over the water. Beautiful and imaginative was *Dewey Demonstration Gardens* near *South Station*.

When I visited Quincy Market in 2012, I found very little of this market attractive; it was overrun by tourists and crowded with chain shops (for more about Quincy Market see Chapter 12). A far more interesting (shopping) area was *Beacon Hill*.[11]

Cycling

Cycle lanes have been marked but not many cyclists were using them.

Public Transportation

The *West End Street Railway* Company electrified all routes in 1889. Massa-chusetts had more street railway lines per square mile than any other state.

Figure 13.10
Commonwealth
Avenue, Boston

Figure 13.11
Zebra crossings at
junctions with
Boulevard, Santa
Cruz, Tenerife, Spain

Figure 13.12
Dewey Demonstration
Gardens

In 1897 the first subway in the United States opened in Boston and in 1922 the first motorbus route was established. In 1964 the *Massachusetts Bay Transportation Authority* (MBTA) was formed. The service, which had previously covered 14 cities, expanded to 78 municipalities. The MBTA is the nation's fifth largest mass transit system serving a population of 4.8 million (2010). It actually operates in 176 cities and towns. The average weekday ridership was about 1.24 million passenger trips in 2010 (MBTA.com, accessed 24.6.13). In 2012 the light rail vehicles[12] were old and traveling was slow but the T is being upgraded and it is planned to implement high capacity trains on the *Red Line* and the *Orange Line*. In total the urban rail network consists of 64 miles (102km) (www.urban rail.net, accessed 26.1.14).

Washington DC (District of Columbia)

Population 642,000 and 6 million in the metropolitan area in 2013.

Background

Washington DC is the capital of the United States. Its early development and its street layout have already been described in Chapter 1. The first sight of Washington from a place like the *Pentagon* makes one aware that the city does not have any skyscrapers. The highest structure is the memorial to George Washington, an obelisk.

Population Growth

The population of Washington increased by over 5% but the suburbs grew by nearly 20% between 2000 and 2010 whereas the city population had still declined by nearly 6% ten years earlier. The highest drop, about 16%, had been between 1970 and 1980, which was typical for most US cities (District of Columbia 2013, p. 46).

Transportation

Planning

A Pedestrian Master Plan was published in 2009 and since then greater priority has been given to pedestrians. In 2013, the city adopted a new *Sustainability DC Plan*. It has a number of objectives with reference to walking, public transportation and cycling. Not very much has been suggested for pedestrians, except that adequate crossing time at traffic lights will be provided[13] (ibid, p. 84). The objective for 2032 is to increase cycling and walking to 25% of all commuter trips and public transportation to 50%. This is by far the most ambitious objective of all the North American study cities.

Washington has several interstates that cross the city. Despite this, the modal split reveals a low level of car use, the second lowest after New York, and a high demand for public transportation services, again the second highest after New York. Car trips declined by more than 7%, and public transportation journeys to work increased by about 4% and even cycling grew by more than 1% point in the second time period (2007–2011).[14] The high use of public transportation is also connected with the fact that 37% of all households had no car compared to 10% in the United States as a whole (ibid, p. 81).

Walking

My View

The high density living in many areas is very European in style although many historic houses have disappeared. The longest pedestrian walk in the center is the *Mall*. The Mall is so large that one can walk for hours and only at crossings does one have to worry about cars. It is an interesting walk because many museums and memorials are located there.

Visiting the neighborhood of *Columbia Heights* gave a different impression of the city. It used to be a very depressed area after the unrest during the 1960s (following the death of Martin Luther King) as many shops were destroyed and burned out. The 14th Street NW has become a transit corridor with a new metro station that opened in 2003. This certainly has helped to improve the area. Shops and businesses have come back. In addition, the sidewalks have been widened and several built-outs have reduced the carriageway width and helped pedestrians to cross more easily and safely.

Sidewalks

When walking around, one notices that the sidewalks were very wide and in extremely good condition and in some places the design looked like a copy from a design book for architects. Unfortunately, there were also very wide roads with plenty of motor vehicle traffic.

Office of Planning ~ April 22, 2014

Government of the District of Columbia

This map was created for planning purposes from a variety of sources. It is neither a survey nor a legal document. Information provided by other agencies should be verified with them where appropriate.

Columbia Heights & National Mall

★   Points of Interest

Ⓜ   Metro Stations

Figure 13.13
Map of central area of
Washington DC

Pedestrian Crossings

The very long pedestrian crossing times at junctions were an unexpected surprise, sometimes more than 60 seconds. Pedestrian crossing times in the National Mall were mostly shorter (about 30 seconds).

Cycling

Although Washington is a relatively flat city, which would make cycling an enjoyable experience, there were few cyclists despite many cycle facilities. Washington had the first large-scale public cycle sharing scheme in the country and by the end of 2013 the city already had 200 stations (ibid, p. 84).

Public Transportation

The construction of an excellent Metro system started in 1969 and the first part of the Metrorail opened in 1976. It has 106 miles of track (171km) and runs on five lines. A new line, the *Silver Line*, will link Washington DC with the *Dulles International Airport*. This line is under construction and will be 23 miles long (37km). Metro rail and metro bus serve about five million inhabitants and in 2012 about 344 million people traveled on the system, of whom 212 million used the Metro, which makes it one of the largest underground systems in the United States (www.wmata.com/about_metro/, accessed 31.7.13). I found that the underground system was functioning well, easy to understand and full of passengers.

According to the Metro Strategic Plan for 2025, more carriages are required and at some stations longer platforms are needed. Ticketing is still not very advanced; coming from Arlington County one has to pay twice, in the bus and again in the metro. Unified ticketing for the transportation region is only available for monthly cards.

In Washington DC a new streetcar line opened in 2014. It is about 3 miles (5km) long and runs along *H Street Northeast*. Altogether 37 miles (60km) of new streetcar lines are planned.

Portland, Oregon

Population 603,106 and 2.3 million in the metropolitan area in 2012.

Background and Population Growth

Portland has a strikingly diverse economy, ranging from major leisure industries, such as *Nike*, to well over a thousand technology companies. Like Seattle and San Francisco, it has a strong coffee culture, complemented by many micro-breweries. The City of Portland grew by 10% between 2000 and 2010 and the suburbs of the metropolitan area by 15%.

Transportation

Portland has a reputation of being one of the leading US cities trying to achieve sustainable transportation. Like many other US cities, Portland also had a small motorway revolt in the 1960s but despite that plenty of motorway miles have been built.[15]

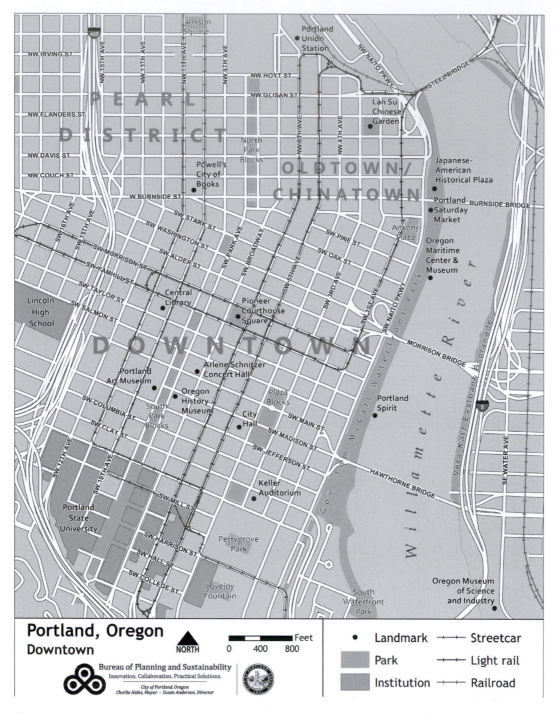

Figure 13.14
Map of central area of
Portland, Oregon

Portland introduced one of the first new light rail lines in the United States in 1986 and by 2013 had a substantial light rail network. Light rail (and streetcars) can have the advantage that car lanes can be replaced by public transportation (if that is politically feasible; although it is general practice in Europe, but even there the issue is often heavily disputed). Portland has managed to do that, especially in the central parts of the city.

The modal split figures (2000 and 2007/2011) show a significant decline in car use of about 6%. Cycling increased to a considerable level (nearly 6%) but public transportation use and walking declined slightly.[16]

Pedestrian Planning

The city published its first pedestrian plan in 1998 and it was the second plan of this kind in the United States, which was adopted. It included guidelines for pedestrian design in a further publication.[17]

The new plans for a mixed-use redevelopment of the Con-Way area, a 20 acre site (to the northwest of the city center) is planned to become a pedestrian district. The main emphasis will be on walking, cycling and public transportation access (by streetcar). *Pettygrove* will be a 'green' street and vehicular access will not be permitted (Kittelson & Associates 2012, p. 9).

There were many interesting planning aspects in Portland, such as the reduction of parking spaces or no car parking spaces at all for some residential housing

Figure 13.15
High visibility crossings at junctions of North Park

Figure 13.16
NW Irving Street in the
Pearl District

areas. Altogether Portland is a city that is way ahead of other North American cities in terms of having adopted many car-restraining policies and such policies mostly help pedestrians.

Walking

According to Jane Jacobs, one precondition for lively streets are short street blocks. Portland has apparently the smallest blocks in the United States (200ft x 200ft = 61m x 61m), and the streets including sidewalks are either 60ft (18m) or 80ft (24m) wide. Most streets are 60ft wide but a few are wider, for example *Burnside Street*. There is no large diversity in street width.

My View

When walking around one does notice that the pedestrian crossing times at junctions are generous. I was particularly impressed that at *North Park* high-visibility crossings had been installed at each block. Altogether the central parts of Portland are pedestrian friendly.

The *Pearl District* has become a delight (I still remember it from when I first visited Portland in 1995); especially pleasing are the private parts of *NW Irving Street* (which are open to the public). They reminded me strongly of a modern version of the courtyard design of Chatham Village or Sunnyside.

A copy of the Paris version of closing a number of streets to car traffic and opening them only for pedestrians, cyclists and similar modes has been introduced in Portland. It takes place on specially defined Sundays in five neighborhoods during the year. It appears that the politicians are still not brave enough to allow it every Sunday (www.portlandoregon.gov/transportation/58929, accessed 20.7.13).

Greenways

Plenty of Greenways have already been built and more are being introduced. I counted four Greenways (24 miles).[18] Portland also has what is called 'neighborhood' Greenways but in Europe we would call them 'cycle-friendly' roads with both low traffic speeds (20mph) and low volumes of motor vehicles.

Traffic Calming

Plenty of traffic calming measures can be observed in residential streets. But most streets still had a 25mph speed limit and only in a few streets was the speed limit reduced to 20mph.

Public Transportation

There were four light rail lines totaling about 84km in 2013 and two streetcar lines of about 12km length. In addition, a commuter rail line (Westside Express Service – WES) runs from *Wilsonville* to *Beaverton* (the end stop of the Blue light rail line) and was nearly 24km long (http://Trimet.org, accessed 6.6.13).

San Francisco

Population 825,000 in the city and 4.5 million in the metropolitan area in 2013.

Background

Spanish settlers founded San Francisco in the late 18th century and its growth took off through the California gold rush in the middle of the 19th century. The earthquake and the fire of 1906 destroyed most of the city; this was followed by a rapid reconstruction phase. The symbol of the city is the *Golden Gate Bridge*, which opened in 1937.

Very early on, its unique geography and culture made San Francisco one of the most sought after big city tourist destinations. *Silicon Valley* is based just to the south toward *San Jose*, and the 'dot.com' and social networking boom was centered there. It has a very strong financial and university sector (Stanford University was one of the drivers of Silicon Valley) and a famously liberal and relaxed culture of personal freedom.

Transportation

San Francisco became well known for its powerful anti-motorway movement (see Chapter 1), which was helped by some earthquakes. Even so, there were still too many wide streets in 2012 (six lanes and more). The city has to cope with high traffic flows to and from the towns, especially from those parts of Silicon Valley that were only connected by CALTRAIN and not by the Bay Area Rapid Transit (BART) lines. An extension from *Fremont* to *Warm Springs/South*

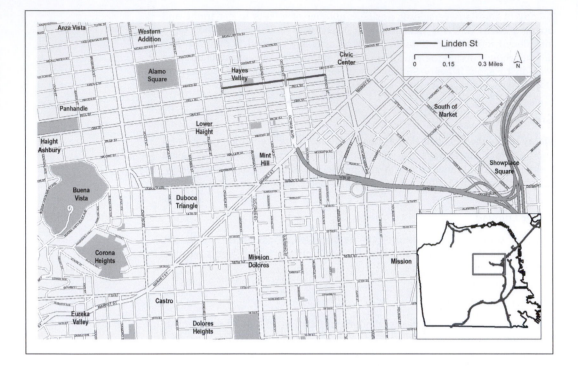

Figure 13.17
Map of central area of
San Francisco

Fremont (1.25 miles; 2km) will open in 2015. There are proposals to extend the line further south into the northern part of San Jose by 2018 (Benedetti 2012, p. B6). All these construction projects will hopefully bring some congestion relief for San Francisco.

The modal split figures indicate a marked decline in car use between 2000 and 2007/11, similar to Portland (although the initial level of car use in Portland was much higher), and an increase in public transportation, cycling and even a slight increase in walking. It has after New York the third lowest car use for trips to work in the North American cities.[19]

Walking

My View

The first walk around the central parts of San Francisco was a bit of a disappointment, as it had nothing of the bold and exciting walking schemes of New York. But if one studies the streets in more detail, it becomes apparent that there is far less car traffic in most streets, not only in the residential but also in the main streets than in other US cities of similar size. In the city center public transportation has its own lanes and these lanes exclude car traffic.

The numerous *parklets* are interesting features of the city. Communities and adjacent property owners initiated these. In order to build them, three to four on-street car parking spaces have been taken away; even in European cities this would not be easy to achieve. When talking with city officials, their overall attitude is environmentally conscious. This 'mood' is also expressed in many 'green' events throughout the year, such as:

Figure 13.18
Typical parklet

- the *PARK(ing) Day* (once a year) where picnics are held in the spaces which are normally used for parked cars (also known in Seattle)
- Healthy Sundays – roads are closed in the Golden Gate Park (every Sunday)
- Sunday streets – several times a year streets are closed in different neighborhoods (as in Portland)
- *Free World Revolution* 'Critical Mass' cycle meeting taking place on the last Friday of each month. It is a large group cycle ride where it is not clear who is leading and where it is going but it is effective in blocking all the car traffic.

Throughout most of the city the sidewalks are in good condition. They are better in the well-to-do areas than in the lower income parts of the city. On some streets the sidewalk widths are very wide. For instance, I measured in *Dolores Street* sidewalks of over 6m on each side. The sidewalks in *Castro Street*, a very trendy and popular street, are also wide but because of the amount of people using this street, they are not wide enough. I was informed that the City Planning Department is working on improving this street. *Market Street*, the most important street in the city center, also has wide sidewalks.

In some streets, house owners are allowed to be creative, develop and pay for their own street design, something that would be near to impossible in most European countries.

Figure 13.19
Street designed by residents in Linden Street

San Francisco has numerous squares and parks and on a sunny day it was crowded with people enjoying themselves. *Union Square* was and still is one of the great squares. Even *Fisherman's Wharf*, which is mostly for tourists, shows that car-free areas are possible, economically successful and enjoyable for everybody.

Figure 13.20 Street life in San Francisco

Cycling

In contrast to many other US cities, which also have an impressive number of cycle facilities but few cyclists, San Francisco has both cycle facilities and cyclists despite the hilly terrain. The bicycle network guides cyclists to avoid the hilly areas.

Public Transportation

There is no unified ticketing in the transportation area of San Francisco, which is a pity. On the *BART* system, a *Clipper Card* has been introduced and works in the same way as the *Oyster Card* in London. In contrast to London, the trips on the Clipper Card are not really cheaper than buying single tickets (which somewhat misses the point of buying the card in the first place). There are no 'Day Tickets' or 'Weekly Tickets', altogether traveling is not as generously priced as in New York where one could get a weekly ticket and have unlimited travel.

One of the best-researched regional rail systems is the BART, which serves the whole San Francisco Bay area. It was first proposed in 1947 and finally funded in 1962 (Starr 2009, p. 123). It was built during the 1970s and the first lines opened in 1972. In 2012 it had a network of 104 miles (167km). It consists of four lines and 44 stations; the system is extremely popular, which can be observed from the overflowing and very cheap 'park and ride' sites near the BART stations. Some of them were already full at 7.00 in the morning.

The City of San Francisco has a wide range of its own public transportation modes, including historic trolley buses, streetcars and six light rail lines. The total light rail network was 34.6 miles (55.7km), too small for such a large city (www.staysf.com, accessed 24.6.13). The maintenance of old vehicles is always costly. They look traditional, maybe even romantic, but they have little to do with an efficient public transportation system, which is necessary to get people out of their cars. In addition there is AC Transit and Golden Gate Transit, SAM trams etc., which serve surrounding counties; they also use the Clipper Card but set their own fares.

Denver

Population 634,300 and 2.5 million in the metropolitan area in 2012.

Background and Population Growth

Denver developed from a mining camp and its first mayor took office in 1859 (Leonard and Noel 1990, p. 480). As early as 1941, the suburban areas grew at a rate nearly five times greater than the city (ibid, p. 269). A relatively high growth in the suburbs (24%) was still continuing between 2000 and 2010, and the city grew by slightly more than 8%.

Transportation

Although Denver used to have one of the largest streetcar networks in the country, they were finally abandoned in 1950 and replaced by buses. A survey from 1931 indicates already a very high level of cars. Nearly two-thirds of all trips entering the city at that time were made by car and only about one-third by streetcar (ibid, p. 265).

The traffic engineer *H. Barnes*, who worked in the city between 1947 and 1953, converted 62 street miles into 'one-way' streets and installed 375 additional traffic lights. He introduced the 'green wave'[20] for car drivers (ibid, pp. 269–271) and announced that

> the time has come to give the pedestrian a 30–70% chance of getting across a street alive.
>
> (Ibid, p. 270)

To make sure that at least some pedestrians crossed busy streets uninjured, he invented the so-called 'Barnes Dance', which meant that at such a junction all traffic lights were red for motor vehicle traffic and at the same time all the lights for pedestrians were green; therefore they could cross all streets, even crosswise.[21]

Denver's first Interstate (I-25) was built along the *South Platte River Valley* and opened in 1958. The I-70 was to run through several poorer neighborhoods, which had to be demolished, a very common practice when building interstates (ibid, pp. 270–273):

> Some wondered, when the I-70 opened in 1966, if it had been urban renewal in disguise.
>
> (Ibid, p. 273)

From 1989 onwards, Governor *R. D. Lamm* refused to fund the southwest section of the I-225 and advocated regulated growth but this was reversed years later and new motorway sections opened again and other infrastructure was built, including a bigger and 'better' airport (ibid, p. 274). In 2013 Denver had several interstates criss-crossing the city and a ring road surrounding the metropolitan area. The I-25 comes close to the city center but it does at least not run through it.

The modal split indicates that the city is still totally dominated by car commuting, although there was a small decline in car use between 2000 and 2007/2011. At the last count, nearly 80% were still using the car, only 4% of people walked and 2% cycled. Public transportation was also low with about 8%. The city is planning to have 15% cycle and walking trips for commuting in 2020, an ambitious aim considering the latest figures.

Figure 13.21
Map of central area of Denver

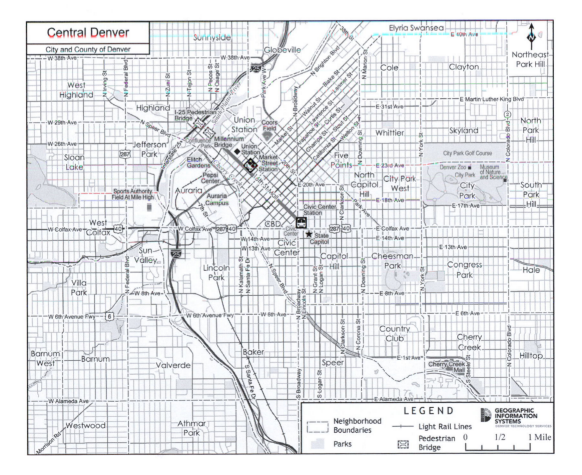

Walking

The pedestrianized street in the city center, 16th Street Mall, has already been described in Chapter 12. It runs from *Union Station (Delgany Street)*, which will become a big public transportation hub when the commuter rail station is finished and more lines are opened, to the *Civic Center (Cheyenne Plaza)*.

My View

Apart from the main pedestrianized axis, walking is also easy in the parallel streets; all of them have very wide and good sidewalks. There is lots of walking and cycling going on along both sides of *Cherry Creek*. Two pedestrian/cycle bridges have been built to cross the creek. One is still open for cars but the wide space provided for cyclists and pedestrians shows where the priority of the city lies. The *Millennium Pedestrian Bridge*, which consists of three sections,[22] gives pedestrian access to *Highlands*, a neighborhood close to Union Station, that offers high-density living. It is in fact a model of a highly desirable TOD. The bridge itself is very impressive with access to new shops and restaurants, mostly at *Central Street*. The wide pedestrian walk in the middle of several housing blocks (between Central Street and *Boulder Street*) reminded me of car-free housing estates in Europe despite its slightly 'Mickey Mouse' look.

The renovation of the historic Union Station building, which was opened in 1881, seems a move in the right direction. In spite of this, the station will be converted into a 112-room boutique hotel, including a large plaza in front of it. At least Amtrak will have an office and a baggage-handling facility on the first floor and

Figure 13.22
Millennium Bridge

there will be Amtrak offices on the ground floor. Even so, it will be a pale shadow of what this railway station used to be (Anon 2013).

Pedestrian Crossings

The pedestrian crossing times at junctions vary between 25 and 50 seconds. It is strange that in many streets in the 'Highlands' neighborhood the traffic lights had disappeared and only high visibility crossings were implemented and they worked well. I was wondering why these were not applied for crossings at the smaller side streets along the 16th Street Mall.

Public Transportation

An extensive light rail network is planned consisting of six lines, one of which had opened in April 2013 (W Line). Two were under construction in 2013, including the East Line, which will access the international airport in 2016. Two are still considered but funding has not been approved. There are also plans for a 18 mile (29km) bus rapid transit lane to be opened in 2015. In total, the public transportation program is very impressive and ambitious. If completed, 122 miles (196km) of new light rail and commuter rail will be built (or modernized), including 57 new transit stations, plus an enhanced bus network (www.rtd-fastracks.com, accessed 2.8.13).

Boulder, Colorado

Population 102,000 and 310,000 in the metropolitan area in 2013.

Background and Population Growth

Boulder was originally a gold mining settlement, which started in 1858 and was incorporated as a town in 1871 (Pettem 2006, pp. 1–2).

It is regarded as the greenest city in the United States and has opted for limited growth and no further road building. It has a well-known university (with about 30,000 students) and several high-tech research bases, like IBM, University Corporation Atmospheric Research (UCAR) or the National Corporation Atmospheric Research (NCAR) (Leonard and Noel 1990, pp. 335–336).

Like Washington, Boulder has no high-rise buildings. There is a three-storey building height restriction, except for the university. The sidewalks are mostly in good condition, although the suburbs had 'Hollywood' sidewalks (narrow sidewalks next to the carriageway without any separation).

According to the Census data, 2000 and 2010, the city grew by about 3% and the suburban areas more than 11% over this ten-year period.

Transportation

Connected with a motorway-like road (Turnpike Road) to Denver, Boulder is less than an hour ride away (by bus). Located closer to the mountains it has plenty of tourists during the summer.

The modal split shows a low level of car commuting, which declined by slightly more than 9 percentage points by 2007–2011, public transportation use was low but increased by the second time period. Walking and cycling was relatively high.[23]

Walking

My View

Within the town center there are plenty of good walking facilities, including a well-designed and wide pedestrianized street (*Pearl Street*), which has been in operation since 1977 (for more see Chapter 12).[24] Like many other high streets, Pearl Street has also suffered from out-of-town shopping centers, such as the *North Broadway Shopping Center*, which opened in 1958, or the *Alpine Community Shopping Center* that took most of the trade away from the city center of Boulder during the 1960s and 1970s (Pettem 2006, p. 135).

The university is separated from the town center but well connected with cycle and walking paths, some of which use underpasses[25] to cross major roads. Close to the pedestrian mall, a number of streets had interesting shops, good cafés and restaurants. Unfortunately, there was still too much car parking close to the center, which really spoiled the urban environment and the townscape. On many streets instead of pedestrian crossing lights high-visibility crossings had been installed, sometimes even without stop lines. Car drivers drove extremely carefully when they saw a pedestrian. Their behavior was similar to what I experienced in most towns in Norway.

Some residential parts of the historic district had cracked sidewalks. Even so, it was still lovely to walk around and few cars were seen. A few traffic calming measures, like some mini roundabouts and some speed humps, could be found but as the driving style was passive there was no real need for such measures. I would predict that 20mph speed limit signs were all that were needed.

The main suburban streets were as bad for pedestrians as everywhere else in the United States. On some of them, pedestrians had to wait for more than 60 seconds to be able to cross, and as these streets are normally very wide and busy, one really prefers to wait. At least the signals did work. It is not uncommon on busy suburban junctions, even when pressing the button, that the walking signal does not appear.

Cycling

Boulder built cycle paths instead of widening roads (Leonard and Noel 1990, p. 341). The high number of cycle facilities (150 miles; 241km) was noticeable. A cycle street had design features that were copied from Vancouver, or Vancouver copied them from Boulder.[26] When I visited, there were not as many cyclists as I had hoped but it was after the end of the semester and many students had left.

Public Transportation

Boulder sponsored its own bus system in addition to supporting the Regional Transportation District (ibid, p. 340).

Canadian City: Vancouver

Population 603,502 and 2.1 million in the urban area in 2011.

Background and Population Growth

Vancouver is the third biggest metropolitan area in Canada and one of the most ethnically diverse Canadian cities. It has a key role as the country's principal west coast city, and as gateway to and from Asia, both for migrants and for trade. The original growth was based on logging and forestry and this has remained its largest industry, followed by tourism.

Between 1996 and 2011, the population increased by 18% and jobs by 16% but in the city center the population and the jobs grew much more rapidly (75% and 26%) (City of Vancouver 2012, p. 10).

Transportation

Vancouver claims to be the most environmentally friendly city in North America. If this is true, then it is depressing because it is also the second most congested city in North America after Los Angeles.[27] Clearly many features and circumstances are not comparable, especially the size of the two urban areas, the road network and the geographical locations. Vancouver has only 75 miles of motorways compared to Los Angeles, which has 1,199 miles (TomTom 2012).[28]

The high level of congestion has generated a trend away from private car use. There was a 5% decline in the number of motor vehicles entering the City of Vancouver and a 20% decline of motor vehicles passing the city center cordon between 1996 and 2011 (City of Vancouver 2012, p. 10). According to the City, the largest shift away from the car has been caused in the past by rapid transit investment. When the *Canada Line* opened in 2009, an increase of over 60% could be observed on the north–south bus route and a drop of 30% in the number of vehicles on *Cambie Bridge*.

According to the latest transportation plan of the city (*Transportation 2040*), the priority in terms of transportation objectives will be given in this order to:

- pedestrians (first)
- cyclists (second)
- public transportation (third)
- taxi/commercial transit/shared vehicles (fourth)
- private cars (last) (ibid, p. 16).

The City of Vancouver is proud of its achievements and is claiming to be near the top of the list of all North American cities in walking and cycling. In the last Canadian Census (2011), the proportion of people who walk to work in Vancouver was 12.5% (in Boston about 15%). The Vancouver percentage of cyclists at 4.4% was high, but the highest was in Portland (6%). The decline in car use was one of the highest in North America and is rivaled again by Portland but the drop was sharper in Boulder (9% points).[29]

The modal split for all trips within the City of Vancouver showed that in 2011 about 46% of all trips were on foot, by bike and by public transportation. The modal split target for 2020 aims to achieve at least 50% by 2020 and 66% by

Table 13.1 Modal split in the City of Vancouver: all trips (24 hours)

Year	Car, truck, van and car passengers	Public transport-ation	Bicycle	Walk	Others
2004	62.5	17.5	3	16.5	0.5
2008	57.9	21.8	2.9	15.4	1.9
2011	54.3	23.3	3.8	17.0	1.5

Sources: Census 2004 and 2011 and City of Vancouver 2006.

2040. The share in public transportation increased by nearly 6% but this is related to the opening of a new line. Walking did not really increase very much and cycling only by less than 1%.

The city also wants to achieve a 20% decline of the average distance driven per resident in 2020, calculated from the 2007 level (City of Vancouver 2012, pp. 11–12). This objective if it is achieved could have a positive impact on both walking and cycling.

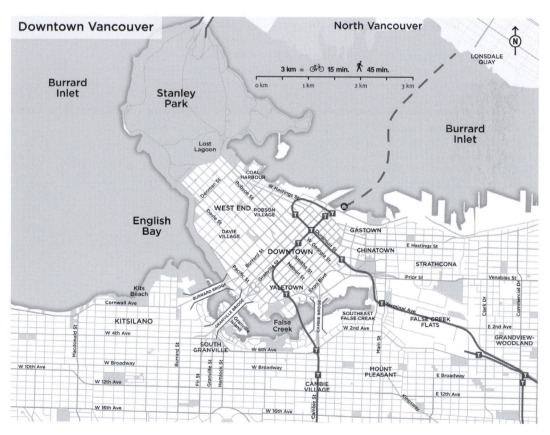

Figure 13.23
Map of wider central area of Vancouver

Walking

Pedestrian Plan

The City of Vancouver was the only North American city I visited that had as their top walking priority 'making streets safer'. The issue of pedestrian road safety is still not as high on the agenda as it should be and some US cities I visited told me that they do not even dare to publish the data (for more details on this topic see Chapter 15).

The statistics in Vancouver on fatalities show that pedestrians are involved in less than 2% of reported accidents but account for 45% of the fatalities. The number of pedestrians killed was 23 in 1994 (the highest) and only nine in 2011 – but it is not a smooth trend and there is a wide fluctuation (NHTSA 2008). The way to improve pedestrian safety is by specified measures, such as:

- providing minimum crossing distances and curb radii at intersections
- implementing raised sidewalks to cross junctions
- reducing car speed through traffic calming measures etc. or a combination of these different measures (City of Vancouver 2012, p. 20).

Another important objective was the demand 'to create public plazas and gathering spaces throughout the city' (ibid, p. 24). A number of pedestrian priority streets (or shared space streets) and pedestrian spaces should be created, for instance by closing 800 block *Robson Street* (*Robson Square*) or sections of Robson and/or *Granville Street*.

A straight copy from San Francisco is the demand to implement 'parklets' and the 'sidewalks to plaza' program is copied from New York.

The publication (*Transportation 2040*) includes a whole range of other measures to make the city more pedestrian friendly, for instance to:

- provide generous, unobstructed sidewalks on all streets (though no specific measures are given)
- make streets and public spaces rain-friendly (especially in winter when there are many rainy days)
- provide accessible public restrooms in high demand locations
- address the gaps in the pedestrian network (ibid, pp. 21–23).

My View

Vancouver has many walkable parts within the city. In the city center, Granville Street was pedestrianized but it remains full of buses; even so, it is a street that functions well and is crowded with pedestrians.[30] *English Bay*, *Coal Harbor*, *False Creek* and some of the residential streets in *South Granville* (but not W. Broadway) are comfortable to walk around, and interesting places in terms of walking design. The high-rise apartment blocks next to the harbor have on the side facing the waterfront only pedestrian access. Robson Square was closed to cars and one could see what a vibrant pedestrian square it would be if it were to be closed permanently. *Granville Island* has too many car parking spaces and too many cars for such a tourist honeypot; walking over *Granville Bridge* is an unpleasant experience, but it is one of the bridges that will be improved according to *Transportation 2040* (see City of Vancouver 2012).

In contrast to many US cities, it is also pleasant to walk around in some of the suburbs of Vancouver.

Pedestrian Crossings

The crossing times for pedestrians at traffic lights on some busy streets are too short, especially for elderly people to cross safely.

Greenways

Four Greenways are mentioned:

- *Central Valley Greenway* (25km; 15 miles) linking Vancouver with *Burnaby* and *New Westminster*. This is already completed.
- The *North Arm Trail* links parks, schools and local shopping areas within Vancouver and Burnaby. The Greenway construction started in 2011 and is already completed; total length 8km (5 miles).
- *Comox-Helmcken* is an east–west connection through the city center, from False Greek to *Stanley Park*. The construction started in January 2013 and the first section was completed in June 2013 (between *Comox* and *Helmcken* Street in the city center).
- From *Point Grey Road* to *Cornwall Avenue*: this Greenway will link the city center to *Kitsilano* and *Point Grey* (at the consultation phase in summer 2013).

Stanley Park is very close to the city center and is relaxing and peaceful to walk around. It is very well used at the weekends and during summer evenings.

Figure 13.24
Mini roundabout

Traffic Calming

The traffic calming measures are not particularly impressive but there are many 30kph signs. Unfortunately, the State of British Columbia has overall control of speed limits, which in urban areas are mostly still 50kph; exceptions of 30kph are only possible in some residential roads.

Cycling

There are plenty of cycle routes within the city and road space has been taken away from the car. In addition selected roads had dedicated bikeways, for example *West 10th Avenue*.

Public Transportation

The *Skytrain* in 2013 had three lines. It is fast, clean, popular and easy to use. The trolley and diesel buses are modern but they have insufficient capacity to cope with the peak hour demand. *Translink* is in charge of regional public transportation planning and providing its service (City of Vancouver 2012, p. 31).

Notes

1 I visited Boston, Philadelphia, New York, Pittsburgh, Vancouver, Victoria, Seattle, Portland, Eureka, San Francisco, Santa Barbara, Los Angeles, Charlotte, Charleston, Savannah, Miami, Miami Beach, New Orleans, Birmingham, Atlanta, Chicago, Denver and Boulder. In most of them I spent two to three days and in New York and Charlotte I spent longer. Some of the cities I had visited before.

2 Mayor Bloomberg created an office to develop a 'Sustainability Plan' that resulted in *PlaNYC 2030*. The plan called for increased mobility options, such as expanded and faster bus service, car-sharing, improved cycling, and enhanced pedestrian access and safety. It addressed congestion through traffic management, not road widening. The 'green' goals included activating the streetscape, creating a network of green corridors, adding parks and public spaces within a 10 minute walk of every resident by capturing under-utilized roadbed or opening school playgrounds with new seating areas during non-school hours, and planting one million trees.

3 For detail data see Tables 15.1 and 15.2.

4 The Parisian upper level park is 3 miles (4.7km) long and starts at the Bastille and runs until the Boulevard Peripherique. Some parts lead through residential streets. It is a greenway in the real sense of the word.

5 The project area covered Broadway from Columbus Circle to 42nd Street and from 35th Street to 26th Street.

6 It showed 20,219 and 22,381 for the peak hour – but it did not make clear when the peak hour was.

7 A major road was approved to bisect the park in the 1950s leading to a community fight led by Shirley Hayes to 'Save the Square'. In 1958 an experiment banned all but buses and in 1959 all traffic was permanently prohibited from entering the park.

8 According to Transport for London annually about 1 billion passengers were carried and daily about 3.5 million in 2012.

9 For more details see Tables 15.1 and 15.2.

10 The Downtown Crossing is managed by a Business Improvement District (a form of local funding mechanism)

11 Beacon Hill is also described in great detail by Lynch (1960, pp. 160–172) as one of the most attractive areas of Boston.

12 The T system is called a metro but only the red line has metro vehicles. The network runs underground in the city center

13 I thought that was a bit thin. There was the action to collect more data to improve understanding of cyclists and pedestrian travel patterns (Action 2.4). The city-wide

multi-modal transportation plan 'MoveDC', which will be completed in 2014, will include a much more robust set of pedestrian objectives.

14   For more details see Tables 15.1 and 15.2.

15   The Interstate 5 runs to the east of the river, the I-405 acts as a city center ring road and the I-205 bypasses the city to the east.

16   For more details see Tables 15.1 and 15.2.

17   Today many US cities have that, at least all the large ones I visited. They normally include a deficiency index that points out missing sidewalks, difficult and dangerous street crossings and the locations where the pedestrian street network is not connected. Mostly the streets with the highest deficiencies are toward the edge of the city (City of Portland, Office of Transportation, Engineering and Development, Pedestrian Transportation Program Pedestrian Master Plan, 1998).

18   Fanno Creek Beaverton Hike, North Portland Willamette Greenway, Portland Maine Scarborough Greenway, South Portland Greenway.

19   For more details see Tables 15.1 and 15.2.

20   'Green waves' meant that if cars are driven at a constant speed, such as 30 or 40 mph, the traffic lights would always be green. 'Green waves' were also introduced in Germany very early on.

21   The introduction of a X-crossing at Oxford Circus in London in 2009 is nothing else than a 'Barnes Dance' introduced in many US cities (first in Denver) during the 1950s and 1960s. It was celebrated in London as a great innovation although it was also used in Britain quite frequently during the 1970s and still in the late 1980s in Edinburgh.

22   One section is crossing the light rail line, another the river and the last one crosses the I-25.

23   For more details see Tables 15.1 and 15.2.

24   From 1908 onward, the Denver and Interurban electrical trains ran through Pearl Street until 1926, when they were replaced by buses (Pettem 2006, p. 9).

25   According to Pettem (2006) underpasses under *Broadway* were built in 1992 (p. 175).

26   The cycle street was separated by flower pots and trees from the main carriageway.

27   According to TomTom (2012) 54% of the morning peak is congested in 2012. Congestion is measured as a comparison of the travel time during non-congested periods with the travel time during congested periods based on GPS measurements, p. 30.

28   It should be mentioned here that when I sent the section on Vancouver to the city, they disputed the way in which TomTom measures congestion. However, when checking the TomTom methodology, I could not agree with the city's argument.

29   For more details see Tables 15.1 and 15.2.

30   The pedestrian counts of 2008 show that 2,526 pedestrians were counted in Granville Street, south of Robson Street, at peak hour (16.00–17.00) and 2,426 pedestrians in the same street south of Georgia also at peak hour (16.00–17.00) in: www.vancouver. ca/files/cov/ pedestrian-study-volume-counts 2008, accessed 22.6.13.

14

WALKING IN THE UNITED STATES: A EUROPEAN VIEW

The Followers

The choice of cities in this chapter was, as in Chapter 13, mostly founded on recommendations. The additional study cities were based on the knowledge that the eight cities discussed in Chapter 13 were not enough to get an overall picture about walking in the US. Most of the cities below have a different basis. They were, for instance, not as lucky to keep their rail-based public transportation system or they still have a high proportion of suburbanization together with a high level of car journeys. Overall the division into the leaders and followers is not strict and should not be seen as such.[1]

Charlotte

Population 775,200 and 1.8 million in the metropolitan area in 2012.

Background

Although the City of Charlotte was incorporated in 1768, it appears today to be a city that has had little time for its own history, very much in contrast to Charleston and Savannah. It has constantly been changing its physical appearance according to the mood and standards of the time. Charlotte's economy was originally based on regional manufacturing and cotton textile production. Its economic impetus was supported by an important railway interchange function. Its heyday was between the 1880s and 1930s (Moore and Ingalls 2010, p. 121). Luckily a number of cotton mills have been saved and converted into housing, shops, entertainment and offices. In recent years its fame has been based on banking. It is the second biggest banking city in the United States after New York, mainly because of successful mergers.[2]

Population Growth

The Census data between 2000 and 2010 shows that the City of Charlotte has had the highest population growth of the 20 US cities I studied (35%), followed by the City of Charleston (24%).[3] The suburban areas grew more than twice as fast as the city (84%). It has still one of the highest suburban growth rates in the United States. This implies that the city's policy to concentrate growth in centers (but also along axes) has not yet been successful.

Transportation

Several motorways dominate the traffic flows in the region and in Charlotte (mostly Interstates 77 and 85). There is also an outer ring, Interstate 485, which is not yet completed. In addition, the city center has a ring motorway, Interstate 277, which makes entering the city center on foot something of a challenge.

The modal split commuting data between 2000 and 2007 /2011 show a decline in the percentage of car use and a very slight increase in public transportation use and walking between 2000 and 2007/11.[4] The data indicate that the City of Charlotte is still dominated by cars although the latest TAP (Transportation Action Plan 2011) gives some hope for pedestrians. It includes ten objectives, of which the following four are important to this book:

- to increase sidewalks
- to concentrate on transit oriented development (TOD)
- to enlarge public transportation service
- to expand the number of traffic calming measures.

Despite its good intentions, a number of conflicting policies are apparent. For instance, at the same time that the first light rail line was being constructed, parts of the outer motorway were also being built, though the costs for the motorway were nearly three times as high as for the public transportation investment (Walters 2010, pp. 222–223). While this is a valid argument, it does not reflect the fact that motorways are mostly funded by the federal government. This is not the case with public transportation investment, consequently the funding is very uneven.

Even so, considering the lack of a really good public transportation service, one would have thought more funding should be spent on public transportation, especially as one of the targets in the TAP is better transit access. It is planned that a minimum of 63.5% of Charlotte's residents will reside within a quarter mile (about 400m) of a transit service (City of Charlotte Department of Transportation, Charlotte-Mecklenburg Planning Department – henceforth CDT and CMPD – 2011, para. 3.3).[5]

Construction of New Sidewalks

As in many other US states, the construction and maintenance of sidewalks are the responsibility of the property owner/developer (this is not the case in neighboring South Carolina). The city also gets involved in the construction and maintenance of sidewalks if they either are not maintained by the property owner or do not exist at all; sidewalks had not been built in Charlotte from the late 1950s till the late 1980s (ibid, para. 4.34). This must be typical for many US cities. The missing sidewalks are now slowly being rebuilt and about $10 million have been spent over the last five years to accomplish that. According to the TAP, there are plans to build 375 miles (about 600km) of new sidewalks by 2035 (ibid, para. 3.16). In 2010, Charlotte had an estimated 1,600 miles (about 2,560km) of sidewalks, of which 55% of the thoroughfares had sidewalks on both sides but 38% of local streets had a sidewalk on only one side (ibid, para. 4.3).

Walking

My View

I personally doubt that this enormous financial effort will seriously increase walking trips. I would not question building some of the missing sidewalks but to rebuild all of them seems a large financial burden, which will bring relatively little result. Why people walk is complex (for more about this subject see Chapter 15). If one has streets with plenty of shops and services but no sidewalks, then

Figure 14.1
Sidewalk plan of Charlotte

Figure 14.2
Close to the New Bern
Stop

they are a must. But in residential streets with low motor vehicle flows, other options are possible. A constant awareness campaign about the benefits of walking and cycling will bring better results than sidewalk building (see Chapter 8). These measures would cost less and are more effective; at least this is the experience in the UK, Germany and Australia; not to mention more and better public transportation services.

Connected with the sidewalk issue is the topic of connectivity. It is differentiated and quantified within the TAP as a connectivity index. As an example, three neighborhoods have been chosen (*Dilworth* being the best, *Cotswold* middling, and *Arboretum* the worst). I would very seriously question the importance of such an index for walking because if one studies the areas carefully, one could argue that in Dilworth everything can be reached by car but in Arboretum there seems to be mostly cul-de-sac roads and a lot of open space. Now, is it not more important to create in future connectivity for pedestrians and cyclists instead of car travel? Hence I would argue that these three different street networks tell us very little about walkability. In fact, it would be much easier to improve Arboretum for pedestrians and cyclists because there is more space for an independent pedestrian and cycle network than in Dilworth. That Arboretum may still fail to be attractive for pedestrians may be for completely different reasons, for instance there are no shops or other facilities within walking distance.

TOD

I found the TODs (transit orientated developments) along the southern light rail corridor impressive. When I saw the first TODs in Portland in 2003, I thought they were a bit of a gimmick and maybe at that time they still were, but when I walked along the existing light rail corridor in Charlotte, especially around the 'New Bern Stop', I could definitely see that TODs are one of the ways to achieve higher population densities (and possibly also higher employment densities). Together with additional investment for shops, restaurants etc. developments like this will not only improve connectivity between centers and along axes but will also get more people to walk and cycle. The level of construction that was still going on was serious. The success of these new housing developments can also be seen in the high sale prices for small flats and town houses when studying real estate agent windows along the line. A market study found that *South End*[6] is one of Charlotte's highest apartment sub-markets (with an average monthly rent of roughly $1,350 in 2012). The city council has also an adopted policy to ensure that developments in these areas include a proportion of affordable housing for lower income residents.

City Center

In Europe the most walkable streets and squares are still found in town centers. How does Charlotte compare, considering it is the second most important banking city in the United States? Smith and Livingstone (2010) tell the story of a former bank executive who complained that they were bringing in people from London who did not actually know how to drive[7] (ibid, p. 149). Hence the banks themselves have an interest in creating a more livable and walkable city center. In order to judge that, one has to know something of the city center's structure and its past.

The city center consists of four wards, of which the first and the second were nearly completely cleared during the 1960s; especially the second ward was once a prosperous African American neighborhood, called *Brooklyn*, which was erased in part by motorway building and replaced with the city's government district (ibid, p. 147). The reconstruction of the first ward during the late 1990s and early 2000s made this ward rather walkable. It reminded me slightly of the housing blocks in Chatham Village and Sunnyside (Chapter 1). It certainly is a delightful area to walk around and it is intended to improve the access to the other wards.

The third ward used to be the industrial district and was changed in the early 1970s. The fourth ward (located to the northwest of the city center) is the only true opportunity for urban revitalization. From about the 1880s to the 1940s it was Charlotte's premier address, but by the 1950s and 1960s the fourth ward had become badly run down. The North Carolina National Bank was the key institution promoting the revitalization of this ward and from the 1970s onwards, the remaining 19th-century housing stock began to be restored (ibid, p. 148).

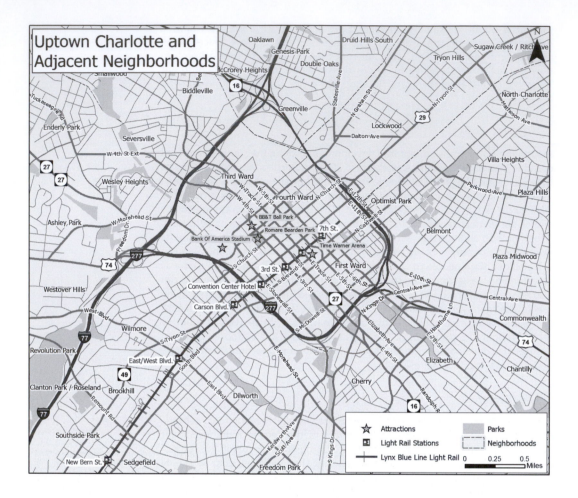

Figure 14.3
Map of central area
of Charlotte

The actual city center, called *Uptown*, which includes the historic junction of *Trade Street* and *Tryon Street*, is a banking neighborhood. Such localities are normally not known for being lively and interesting for shopping or walking or other social activities although a number of restaurants were present.

Traffic Calming

Despite its car-orientation, some schemes have not only given the city a more 'human' face but are of excellent quality. They promote walking and/or improve pedestrian safety. The traffic calming measures and pedestrian crossing facilities along *East Boulevard* (includes also cycle lanes) are worth seeing and copying. There are road humps in a number of streets combined with a 20mph speed limit, for example *Sterling Road* and *Princeton Avenue*.

Road safety is certainly an issue as a relatively high number of pedestrians have been killed in 2011 and 2012.[8] This indicates that cars are still traveling too fast and there may also be a number of other reasons; a more intensive analysis is promised in the TAP.

Greenways

Greenways running through cities are important to promote walking and cycling. As in many other states, the Greenways in Charlotte are the responsibility of the county (County of Mecklenburg). About 7 miles (11.3km) have been built and far more are planned. The *Little Sugar Creek* Greenway is one of these schemes. It starts at *Brandywine Road* and 7th Street and runs along Little Sugar Creek. The new part, which opened in 2011, begins after the creek passes *East Morehead Street*. This part of the creek used to be capped; it was reopened, cleaned and redesigned. It was an expensive scheme but it is beautifully designed, combined with new building constructions such as the *Metropolitan*. The Metropolitan replaced a large-scale shopping center (Charlottetown Mall, which had opened in 1959). The slightly over-the-top name is simply a mixture of buildings containing shops, restaurants, housing and offices. It was not yet a breathtakingly vibrant area but it was certainly better than what was there before. Altogether the walk was varied and gives children in particular many options to play on and in the creek, as the water is normally shallow. At the weekends this Greenway was well used.

Cycling

Many main streets have cycle lanes, which reduced the original carriageway widths, but cycling seems to be mainly a leisure activity carried out at weekends. Throughout the city there are 20 bike hire stations with 200 bikes altogether, which came into operation in 2012. On a sunny day, they were well used.

Figure 14.4
East Boulevard

Public Transportation

The city and the County of Mecklenburg decided in 2006 to go ahead with the *2030 Transit Corridor Plan.* This consists of four rapid transit lines which will create growth for the center, the corridors and the wedge. In fact, it reminded me of the successful *Five Finger Plan* of *Copenhagen* adopted in 1948 (see Chapter 10). The first light rail line opened in 2007 and runs from the city center south along *South Boulevard;* it is 9.6 miles (15.5km) long. Some of the stations outside the city center are elevated, which made it an expensive scheme, but it works well. The light rail has priority over motor traffic even when running at street level, which is something many light rail systems in the United States do not have. It was projected that the line would carry 9,100 passengers on a weekday but the ridership had already increased to 16,000 in 2009 (CDT and CMPD 2011, para. 4.3). I would predict from using the service that the ridership has continued to grow.

There are plans for an extension to the northeast (Blue Line Extension). Work on this line has already started and is to be completed in late 2016. The *North Corridor* will be a commuter rail line and may open in 2019 if private funding can be found (ibid, para. 4.7). A tramline is planned for the *West Corridor*. There is also a bus route[9] along *Elizabeth Avenue*, which will be replaced by modern streetcars.

The TAP suggested headways of half an hour for shuttle bus routes in peak hours and an hourly headway off peak (ibid, para 3.10). Though most routes have a more frequent service in peak hours, an hourly service will not get car users out of their cars. Much shorter headways and dedicated bus lanes or corridors would be needed in order to achieve that.

Charleston

Population 125,583 and 665,000 in the metropolitan area in 2012.

Background

Charleston was founded in 1670 and in the 18th century was the fourth biggest city in the United States; even at the beginning of the 19th century its population was about the same as New Orleans (Rosen 1997, p. 81).

By most people's standards, Charleston is one of the most beautiful cities in the United States because of its architectural heritage. The conservation efforts include not only the historic city center but also other areas, such as *Ansonborough, Wraggsborough* and *Radcliffborough* (ibid, p. 163). The preservation of the historic buildings had already started in the early 1930s (Bland 1999, pp. 82–83). But a number of builders and developers were still successfully destroying older houses and whole areas far into the 1970s. For instance in 1973, a large area (4.5 acres) around *East Bay Street* was to be demolished and replaced by a high-rise development; this would have destroyed large parts of the historic center; it was prevented by the '*Historic Charleston Foundation*' (www.historic charleston.org, accessed 10.6.13).

Rosen (1997) mentioned that 'Life in the late 19th and early 20th century passed Charleston by' (p. 152). A number of European cities also had decades where they went through 'backwater' periods. Often such cities surprise us with rather intact urban structures, especially in the city centers and inner-city areas, and that can generally support a more pedestrian-friendly environment.

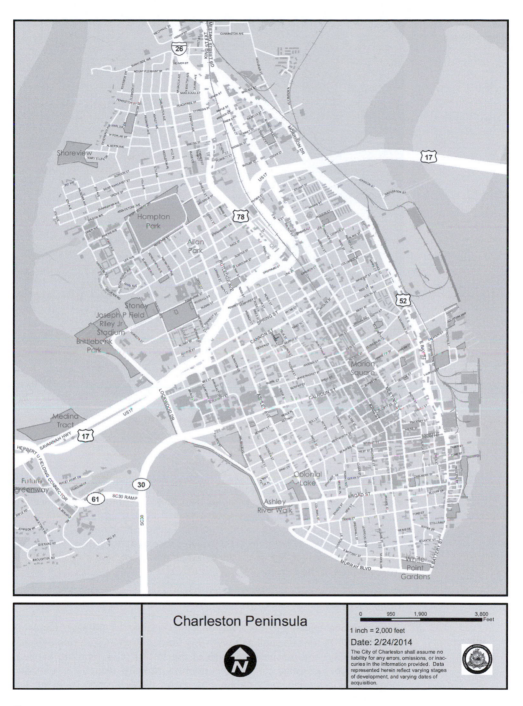

Figure 14.5
Map of historic part of Charleston

Figure 14.6
Rap dancing in Marion
Square

Population Growth

During 2000 to 2010, the population of the city grew rapidly and increased by 24%. The growth was to a large extent caused by second homeowners and college students, which are counted in the Census (interview with the City, 2.4.13). The number of residents in the suburbs rose by about 25%, which implies both a greater desirability of the inner urban areas but also a decline of the attractiveness of the suburbs.

Transportation

Without strong opposition, motorway building certainly did not pass Charleston by. Interstate 26 runs through a modern and faceless *North Charleston* (which is a separate city) and reaches the north of the historic city. As often happens when a motorway ends, car traffic is pouring into the available streets and congestion is inevitable. In the case of Charleston, it was *Meeting Street* but also *East Bay Street*, *King Street* and *Calhoun Street* that were badly congested.

The modal split illustrates a very high level of car use in 2000, which more or less stayed the same in 2007/11 (about 85%). Public transportation use was low and fell but not by very much and cycling was just about 1%; it grew but again only by a small margin. The low values of walking were disappointing and it dropped further between 2007 and 2011.[10] It appears that the 'green' efforts many other North American cities pursued have not yet reached Charleston.

Walking

My View

The contrast[11] between Charlotte and Charleston could not be sharper. Whereas Charlotte denied its own history, the citizens of Charleston preserved its historic past as much as they could. It was a revelation to wander around and experience a real city center consisting of historic houses, streets and alleys and not only a couple of older buildings left in the middle of a soulless core. However, most city center streets still have car parking on both sides, three- and four-car traffic lanes and the sidewalks along some of these streets, especially in King Street, are too narrow to cope with the high number of pedestrians. When bicycles are parked on the sidewalks, then walking becomes even more awkward. According to the NHTSA (National Highway Traffic Safety Administration), Charleston had a serious pedestrian accident problem.[12] There were simply too many pedestrians in a still car-dominated urban environment and the numerous pedestrian crossing lights cannot solve this. It would be easy to take out at least one traffic lane and/or car parking lane in order to widen the sidewalks.

The area 'south of Broad' (Broad Street) had less car traffic but it also did not have many pedestrians, although historically it is one of the most fascinating areas of the city. Here the sidewalks were wide, for instance in Meeting Street, and this street had cycle lanes and only one car traffic lane in each direction. Most streets in this area were very narrow and easy to cross. A few streets still have the original cobblestones, which were not easy to walk on, for example

Figure 14.7
Fountain Park

Adgers Wharf. Similar types of paving could also be discovered in a few alleyways, for example *Stoll Alley* or *Longitude Lane.*

The squares, such as *Marion Square*, were well used, especially on Sundays. The historic *Court Square* had a thoughtful design that led to an old burial ground and the original Court building. Very pleasing and idyllic was a rather small square in the middle of *Elizabeth Street* with a rare 20mph speed limit sign.

Road Closures

Every second Sunday, King Street is closed to cars but residents and shop owners were of the opinion that this cannot be made permanent. The very wide *Market Street* (there was still a market next to it) has been discussed as a candidate for permanent road closure. On normal days this 'double' street (North and South Market Street) between Meeting Street and Bay Street is full of people, mostly tourists.

Greenways

The West Ashley Greenway is 8 miles (13km) long and is a disused railway line. There are plans to extend it and other Greenways are planned.

Cycling

Plenty of cyclists can be seen but they have few facilities. Unusual for the United States was cycle parking in the carriageway, called a 'cycle corral'.

Public Transportation

Since 2011, the use of the local (historic) trolley buses has been free of charge. Public transportation is organized by CARTA (Charleston Area Regional Transportation Authority), which was formed in 1997. There are still discussions about a commuter rail line from *Summerville* to Charleston and an Amtrak connection to Florida, which would stop in Charleston (information from the City).

Savannah

Population 142,000 and 366,000 in the metropolitan area in 2013.

Background

Savannah was founded in 1733 (Wilson 2012, pp. 101–102). This city has probably the most exciting street layout in North America; it has the ideal urban configuration for walking.[13] The most prominent features of historic Savannah are the squares. The original six squares were expanded to 24, and in 2013, 22 squares can still be admired.[14] The first part of the city was laid out between the 18th and mid-19th centuries. However, in the second half of the 19th century, the city expanded to the south and southwest and the traditional street layout was discontinued (ibid, p. 141).

During the 1960s, Savannah's historic center was extremely lucky to escape 'redevelopment' but it did fall into neglect and business was moving away from the main shopping streets as happened everywhere else. Many older houses were destroyed and replaced by roads, parking garages and gas stations (Lane

1994, p. 214). Three squares vanished in the 1930s to make space for highways, or for planned highways that were never built. In 1950, the old city market on *Ellis Square* was demolished and replaced by a parking garage (ibid, p. 214) but was later rebuilt and the cars disappeared underground. Restoration of the historic area started in the mid-1950s (Berendt 1999, p. 5) and in 1966 the city center was designated as a *National Historic District*, the largest of these districts in the United States (Lane 1994, p. 214).

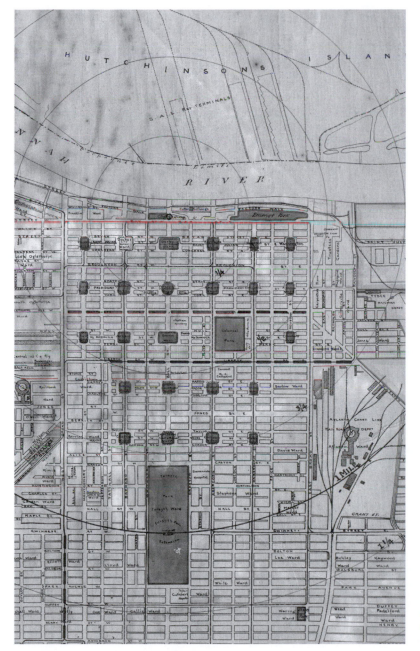

Figure 14.8
Map of historic city
of Savannah

Population Growth

Between 2000 and 2010 the city population increased by only 3%, whereas suburban population grew by 35%. In contrast to Charleston, in Savannah one can still observe a more traditional distribution of high population growth in the suburbs and no or hardly any growth in the main city.

Transportation

Interstate 16 comes relatively close to the historic district and the city center but there are no other motorways nearby. Savannah did not have motorways slicing up the center as in other cities because it 'was not on the way to somewhere else' (ibid, p. 145).

In the course of constructing the Interstate 16 in the early 1960s, the main railway station was demolished.[15] From there, three motorway spurs lead into the city.[16] A new plan from 2012 indicates that the city wants to demolish these spurs and re-establish the original street layout.

East–west traffic (25,000–27,000 motor vehicles per day) is a large problem along *Bay Street* as this street is part of the historic district and close to the popular river frontage. Many pedestrians try to cross the street at the corner of *Bull Street* (on average about 214 pedestrians per hour). But during the night, especially at weekends, the number of pedestrians is also high. At the junction of *Jefferson*/Bay Street, the number of pedestrians totaled 122 per hour between 12 midnight and 2.00 on a Saturday because of the popularity of several restaurants and nightclubs. Even more pedestrians were counted (exceeding 700 people per hour) at *City Market*. A similar problem can be observed in *Liberty Street* (15,000 motor vehicles per day) and *Oglethorpe Avenu*e (12,000 vehicles

Figure 14.9
Historic square as a speed reducing measure

per day), which are also part of the historic district but the pedestrian counts were lower there.

The modal split figures present an even higher level of car use (88% in 2007/11) than Charleston, although it was not as high as in Charlotte; public transportation use was low (4%), so was walking (3%) and cycling was only 1%.[17] So despite having a wonderfully walkable historic city and city center, the rest of the city is by no means walk-friendly.

Figure 14.10
Enjoying the River Promenade

Walking

My View

Walking in the historic parts of Savannah is a delight. It is by far the best walking environment I have experienced in North America. The squares act as speed-reducing measures but give pedestrians straight walking routes. The crossings to the squares were mostly secured either by high-visibility crossings (similar to zebra crossings) or by normal crosswalks (two stop lines).[18] As the street layout is a grid, the squares act as a kind of green axis – interrupted by housing blocks – within the city and it is a pleasure walking from square to square, all being in sight of each other.

City Market, which used to be part of *Saint Julian Street*, was closed to car traffic and included restaurants, shops and other tourist attractions. There are also plans to take cars out of *River Street*. This street still has its original cobblestone paving;[19] it has plenty of restaurants and other shops but also too many cars and tourist buses that mingled with numerous pedestrians, which is a dangerous mix. At weekends (festivals and special events) vehicle traffic is restricted. River Street runs parallel to a wide river promenade, which is well designed, and especially in the evening when the weather is fine, it is crowded with people enjoying themselves.

Public Transportation

As in Charleston, historic streetcars travel around the town and are also free of charge. Otherwise the public transportation system was not very well developed. CAT (Chatham Area Transit) was the public transportation organization of the area. A local company operated the bus service and there were 19 bus routes. Some of the bus services run at half hourly intervals (Route 2 for instance) but others are less frequent.

Miami

Population 413,900 and 5.6 million in the metropolitan area in 2012.

Background

In the early 1980s, Miami was number one on the FBI list of the most crime-ridden cities in America (Diaz 2013, p. 7). The city of crime has changed into a respectable place over the last 30 years (ibid, p. 85). Manny Diaz, who became mayor of Miami in 2001 at the same time as Michael Bloomberg took office in New York, wanted to improve the quality of city life. He also aspired to bring back the middle classes and with them new investment for the city. Another of his targets was better public transportation (ibid, p. 88).

In 2014 Miami had a highly diverse economy with over 170 multinational companies. Its main sectors were in services, real estate, finance, construction, biosciences, technology and tourism (www.city-data.com, accessed 1.8.13).

Population Growth

That the city has been changing can be observed from the Census. Miami's population grew by about 10% and its suburbs rose by only 12% over 2000 to 2010. The wider city center (about 3.8 sq. miles) enlarged its population from 33,413 in 2000 to 66,000 in 2010, a change of nearly 100% in ten years, an increase, which is more than in Vancouver (Goodkin-Focus (2011) DWNTWN (Downtown Miami), estate advisers, www.miamidda.com, accessed 31.7.13).

Transportation

Planning

Before Diaz, the City of Miami had no transportation department because this area was the responsibility of the County. Diaz wanted his own transportation section and he and his team developed a transportation downtown master plan. The plan included proposals to convert one-way streets back into two-way, as it became obvious that one-way streets were not very good for business as cars are driven too fast and it is nearly impossible for the drivers to be able to see

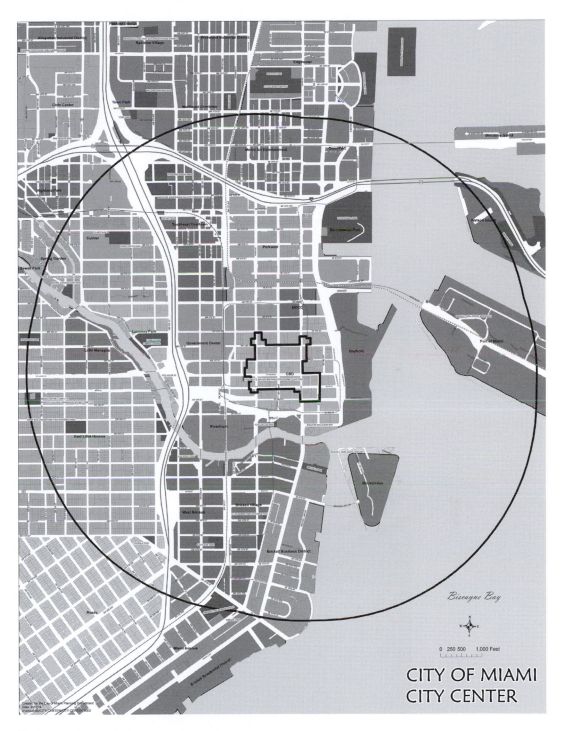

Figure 14.11
Map of the wider central area of Miami

shops or restaurants. His other main aspiration was the removal of the I-395 and I-95 or the tunneling of both interstates, as Diaz was aware of the destruction of a once thriving community, *Overtown* (Diaz 2013, pp. 153–154, 181). Unfortunately, the mayor did not achieve the tunneling of the interstates but he did succeed in implementing other big projects (Miami Art Museum and Miami Science Museum), including a road tunnel to the main port (ibid, pp. 162–163). Another of his initiatives was *Miami 21*, a strategic master plan for Miami. It was the first ever plan for the city (this is extremely difficult for someone from Europe to understand). Two important aspects of this plan were to:

- create walkable neighborhoods[20]
- achieve environmental and economic sustainability (ibid, pp. 172–174).

Miami was for me the city of great hopes when reading about 'Miami 21' but the city is disappointing.[21] When studying the modal split data for travel to work,

Figure 14.12
Built-out in Flagler Street

it indicates that at least in terms of commuting nothing had really changed. Miami is dominated by cars and for all the efforts in public transportation[22] it had very little to show for it. The percentage share of walking is small (4.4%) and stayed small and cycling was about 2%.[23] It compares well with Atlanta in terms of population size and structure but Atlanta has lower car use, slightly higher public transportation use and walking is also higher although not by much.

Walking

My View

Walking around the city center of Miami along *Flagler Street* is fine. The sidewalks are wide and built-outs with palm trees are sometimes combined with benches, which is a good design feature. Cars park on both sides. Flagler Street has come up again in the world. It used to be the main shopping street of Miami but it had similar problems of decline as most city center shopping streets in the United States during the 1950s and 1960s. Street riots in the 1960s damaged the remaining economic viability.

There were a number of impressive buildings along this street, such as the *Dade County Courts*, a building from 1925. The park and gardens around it were pleasant, well designed and cared for. There were plenty of other green areas in this area, such as *Paul Walker's Urban Space* or further on *Lummus Park*. The green expanses around the public transportation hub (*Government Center Station*) created a lively but safe atmosphere.[24]

The heart of the *Little Havana District* is 8th Street. When Fidel Castro took over Cuba in 1959, half a million Cubans settled in the Miami area. Walking along this street – from the 12th Avenue to the 36th Avenue – was another disappointment. Most of the way the road had four lanes of motor vehicle traffic going one way. Only in the last part before the cemetery does the street change into a two-way street. The sidewalks were good and mostly the pedestrian crossing lights were very long as the whole street is wide. It might be an impressive street during carnival but on a normal weekday it was anything but impressive. Far more interesting than Miami is Miami Beach.

Miami Beach

Population 88,000 in 2013 (population in the metropolitan area see Miami).

Background and Population Development

The history of Miami Beach is very short. *Henry Lum* from the federal government bought the island in 1870. It was sold again and the next owners (*E. Field and E. Osborne*) invested in a coconut plantation without great success.

During the 1920s, Miami Beach grew rapidly and even during the depression many small hotels along lower *Collins Avenue* and *Ocean Drive* were built. Miami Beach expanded from 28,012 inhabitants in 1940 to 96,298 in 1980. It lost population from then on and still has not reached the level of 1980. During the 1980s and 1990s, new investment changed Miami Beach to what it is today (www.miamibeachhistory.org/mbhistory.html, accessed 31.7.13). In 2000, 88,000 people lived in Miami Beach and this figure had not changed in 2010.

Figure 14.13
Walking along Ocean Drive

Transportation

The I-195 gives access via a causeway to Miami Beach.[25] The modal split data indicate much lower car use than in Miami with a relatively high percentage of walking. It is the third highest of the North American study cities, at the same level as Washington, but with a higher walking growth rate between 2000 and 2007/11 than the capital. This is rather an achievement in an area which is so car dependent. However, public transportation has declined and that was not the case in Washington.[26]

Walking (in Miami Beach South)

My View

The Art Deco area of the city is large and it was a great experience to stroll around, as the walking conditions were relatively good. The most prestigious street along South Beach is *Ocean Drive* containing most of the famous Art Deco buildings, which would have been destroyed if *Barbara Capitman* (1988) and her restoration society had not saved them.[27] Ocean Drive had several pedestrian walks. One option was along the sea, which was beautifully landscaped with plenty of plants and palm trees. Another ran also parallel to the sea but was the (sea-facing) sidewalks of Ocean Drive. There was a third option, the sidewalk immediately next to the hotels, bars and restaurants, which was too narrow, especially in the evening. The pedestrians had to squeeze between the outside

Figure 14.14
Difficult walking and
serving in and along a too
narrow sidewalk

tables. The carriageway consisted of two motor vehicle lanes plus one lane on each side for car parking. It would be much better to widen this sidewalk and take at least one car parking lane away. In the longer run the second car parking lane could also be removed. Cars could stay on Ocean Drive but car speeds should be reduced. Cars were mostly not driven at high speeds, because the drivers and passengers also wanted to admire the buildings and street life. But this distraction may be dangerous and one could easily miss crossing pedestrians, bearing in mind that Miami Beach was not brilliant in safety terms (see final chapter). I would question whether one could remove cars altogether. In Europe one could, but in Miami Beach one very likely may never be able to do that.[28]

Collins Avenue had parked cars on each side too and two lanes of motor traffic and palm trees on each side. The sidewalks on the eastern side were in parts too narrow for the activities which were going on, especially in the evening. *Washington Avenue* had four lanes of traffic (plus turning lanes at junctions) but the sidewalk widths were sufficient. It also had a central reservation with palm trees in the middle; therefore the avenue had three rows of palm trees (as barriers to car traffic on each side plus the trees in the central reservation) which made it a very attractive street. Walking toward the south of Miami Beach, the sidewalks were wide and at several junctions the width was extended to miniature plazas including seating facilities. As traffic eased from the 5th Street southwards, it became a very pleasant street. At the tip of the peninsular *(South Point)* high-rise housing developments for the well to do and yuppies have been built with park-like features including a pleasant walk along the sea (it looked like a copy of the high-rise residential tower blocks of Vancouver).

Seeing Ocean Drive on a Sunday, I wondered why it was not closed to car traffic. There were so many cyclists, skate boarders and roller skaters on the carriageway that the only reason why no serious accidents were happening was that the cars were driven very slowly.

There were large residential parts of the city that were still also in Art Deco design and wandering around there was pleasant and stimulating.

Pedestrian Crossings

**Figure 14.15
Wandering among Art Deco
residential buildings**

The main roads along the coast (running north to south) are: Ocean Drive, Collins Avenue and Washington Avenue. These three wide streets were difficult for pedestrians to cross because the red phases were too long, although the

pedestrian crossing times were sufficient (about 30 seconds), thus plenty of people were crossing at red lights. But even on pedestrian traffic lights with longer pedestrian phases people crossed at red anyway. On some of these streets, high-visibility crossings may be a better option (see Chapter 15).

Cycling

There are plenty of cycle lanes and many cyclists, for instance on 5th Street.

Public Transportation

I could not judge how good public transportation was (as I walked everywhere) but the buses were not as modern as in other cities.

Atlanta

Population 443,800 and 5.3 million in the metropolitan area in 2012.

Background and Population Growth

The city became economically important as a railroad interchange during the 1850s but it was completely destroyed in the Civil War (1864). But even buildings constructed in the late 19th and early 20th centuries hardly survived, and in this respect Atlanta is similar to Charlotte, which has constantly renewed itself.

Since the 1970s, the city has become the economic focus of the 'New South'. Its economic strength lies in business headquarters, such as *Coca Cola* and *Delta Airlines*, accountancy, private sector research and development, a strong university sector, medical research and treatment, and computer game design.

Atlanta did not really grow very much (less than 1%) between 2000 and 2010 but the suburbs still grew by about 28%.

Transportation

As with many US cities, the interstates are very dominant in the metropolitan region. I-75 and I-85 run very close to the city center in a north–south direction and I-20 runs just to the south of the city center taking an east–west route. In addition there is an orbital motorway, I-285. About 300,000 cars are crossing the city daily on these highways. There were plans for further motorways but some of them were stopped by local protest, for example the *Freedom Parkway* (*John Howell*, *Jimmy Carter* and others fought against this).

The modal split data reveal a small decline in car commuting but an even larger decline in public transportation, which is the result of service cuts and enforced savings. Not surprisingly walking increased slightly and so did cycling.[29]

Planning

Atlanta was for decades a city for the car comparable to Los Angeles but since 2008, a number of changes have taken place. For instance, *Decatur Street*, a major street, which runs from the city center to the east, used to be a six-lane road; this road was reduced to four lanes and wider sidewalks were added. A new reservation and new sidewalks were also built in *Marietta Street*, which is

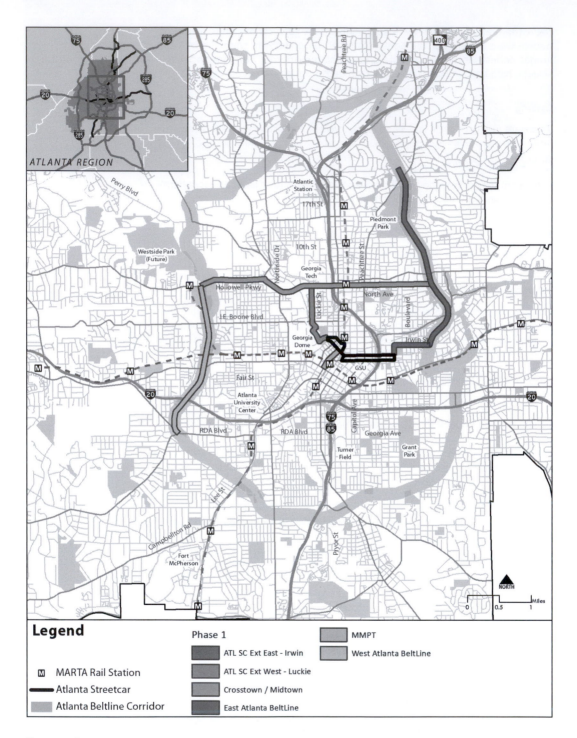

Figure 14.16
Map of Beltline, Atlanta

the continuation of Decatur Street. On 10th Street, new cycle lanes and pedestrian islands were implemented. The total street was rebuilt in autumn 2013. Similar treatments are planned in *Auburn Avenue* and other streets. The *Boulevard* (running north–south of the city center) got wider sidewalks and more pedestrian crossings in 2014. It is intended to reduce the speed of cars by changing one-way into two-way streets.

Atlanta's 'Beltline' will be 23 miles (about 37km) in length, fully within the city limit but at the edge of it. It is a disused railway line and it will connect 45 neighborhoods. It is envisaged to construct high-density housing with their frontage to a wide walking and cycle path (Radburn revisited – see Chapter 1). A streetcar line will run in part along the Beltline with interchange stations to the rapid transit system.

Walking

My View

There are many interesting places to walk but some are more attractive than others. For instance, *Atlantic Station* was a new pedestrian-friendly private development to the northwest of the city but it had a kind of 'Mickey Mouse' feeling to it.[30]

The corner of *Broad Street*, *Luckie Street* and *Peachtree Street* was pedestrian friendly but I would remove the signaled pedestrian crossing at Broad Street as nobody takes any notice of the red light anyway; on Luckie Street and on Broad Street pedestrians should instead have wide crossing facilities. I would also widen the other sidewalk on Broad Street (one side is already widened) and remove the on-street car parking and use it for a two-way cycle lane, allowing access-only to motor traffic.

Pedestrian Crossings

At some traffic lights it is planned to give pedestrians better crossing options, for example near *Woodruff Park*. New types of pedestrian crossing light have been installed (e.g. HAWK: High Intensity Activated Crosswalk Beacon and RRFB: Rectangular Rapid Flashing Beacon) at one road and more are planned.

Sidewalks

In the city center and in *Midtown*[31] the sidewalks are in good condition and some are wide, about 12ft (about 4m) excluding the tree and planting edges.

Public Transportation

'Marta' is the name of the Metropolitan Atlanta Rapid Transit Authority. The original plan for a rail rapid transit system connecting five counties was developed in the early 1960s. It was intended to build 66 miles (105km) with park and ride facilities and feeder bus services. The construction proceeded through the 1970s and 1980s aided by over $800 million in federal grants. The first 'Marta' rail service began in June 1979, and an additional line built to the airport opened in 1990. By 2013, only 48 miles (77km) have been built, too little to make a serious impact on reducing car journeys significantly in a metropolitan area of this size. The system consists of four lines. Marta had 422,400 passengers daily of which only 227,300 were rail passengers in 2012 (www.georgiaencyclopedia. org, accessed 1.8.13).[32] In contrast to other rail-based public transportation systems in the United States, the ridership on Marta has been declining. Since 2001 it lost 15% on trains and 31% on buses according to the AMPTA, consequently its decline in modal split share (www.governing.com/news/local/ mct-marta, accessed 1.8.13). The developments over the last 15 years have focused on transit-oriented development (such as the *Lindbergh* TOD developed in partnership with *BellSouth*), and an expansion of buses using compressed natural gas (www.itsmarta.com, accessed 31.7.13).

In the City of Atlanta, a new streetcar line opened in 2013. The first line has 2.7 miles (4.3km) with 12 stops. It runs from *Centennial Olympic Park* to the *Martin Luther King Natural Historic Site*. Over the next five years, 15 miles (24km) more are planned and will be built.

Seattle

Population 334,500 and 3.4 million in the metropolitan area in 2012.

Background and Population Growth

**Figure 14.17
Westlake Park Square,
Seattle**

White Americans have inhabited Seattle since 1853, and raw material industries like logging were its first economic base. The aircraft manufacturer *Boeing* led its recovery after the Second World War. Its geographical location gave it a

strong economic position as a container port for US–Asia trade. By the end of the 20th century, it was best known as the birthplace of the computer giant *Microsoft* and the leading high street coffee name *Starbucks*.

The City of Seattle grew by 8% between 2000 and 2010 and the suburbs of the metropolitan area by 13%.

Transportation

Seattle is the third most congested city in North America despite a double decker motorway, which runs along the seafront and a highway (Interstate 5[33]), which operates close to the city center. Plans to build a new center tunnel will not help to fulfill the green objectives of the city and will lead to further congestion.

A vast amount of space in the city center and nearby was still provided for ground-level car parking, which is remarkable considering that this space could be used much more economically and productively for housing and service facilities. The restoration of the main railway station (*King Street*), built in 1906, had been neglected for decades and the City bought it in order to refurbish it. It was completed in 2013. The newly renovated railway station is a symbol of the growing importance of rail travel on the west coast. But the existing rail tracks were still not good enough to travel at high speed between Vancouver and Seattle (going on south to Portland).

The modal split shows a decline in car use of about 5%, a slight increase in public transportation, some increase in cycling and a small growth in walking (1.5% points).[34]

Walking

My View

According to the Benchmarking Report 2012, Seattle was ranked as the fourth best walking city in the United States but as a pedestrian one does not have the feeling that it is a very walkable city. It is still very traffic-spoilt, nevertheless there are a number of places with good urban spaces. *Pioneer Square* is one of these, but the area would be even better if all the parked cars, which are presently adjacent to the square, were removed.

As the number of good pedestrian areas is still limited, they are mostly crowded with tourists, but the *Westlake Park Square* is enjoyed largely by locals and worked extremely well, especially because of its irregular shape. I would have liked fewer car lanes (presently four) along the *4th Avenue* next to *Westlake Park* and more pedestrian crossings but surely they will be considered. Lovely walks along the waterfront compensate for the substantial car traffic still present in most streets. A few overpasses help pedestrians to get down to the shoreline. The latest one opened in October 2012 and gave access to a *Sculpture Park*. The walkway from *Pine Street* up to *Freeway Park* is well designed and interesting, although the noise from the motorway does spoil the walk slightly.

Sidewalks

The sidewalks in downtown or in the *Belltown* District are in good condition with dropped curbs in most places. Many streets have trees along them, which offer shade and are more pleasant for walkers than otherwise. Cracked or no sidewalks at all were observed in many suburban areas but this would be typical of most North American cities (for more about this issue see Charlotte).

Pedestrian Crossings

The pedestrian crossing times are generous (mostly 40 seconds and more). In the central areas all junctions have pedestrian crossings with pedestrian traffic lights, but outside the center many junctions still have no pedestrian signals.

Traffic Calming

Speed limits in most residential streets are 25mph. One can observe a limited number of traffic calming measures, such as mini roundabouts at junctions.

Cycling

There are plenty of cycle lanes and cycle priorities, for instance advance stop lines along some of the avenues, for example *3rd Avenue*, but there were not very many cyclists using them. Some sections of the city are hilly, especially the part going down to the waterfront.

Figure 14.18
Bus stop at traffic calming measure in Dexter Avenue

Public Transportation

Over the last two decades, several public transportation investments took place. The first light rail line opened in 2009 and runs from the city center to the airport. A second line is being built to the university and will open in 2016; together the total length will be 17.3 miles (28km) (www.soundtransit.org and www.seattle.gov/, accessed 21.3.13). Rail and all types of buses (trolley and hybrid-electric) use an impressive city center tunnel and the buses had a frequent headway within the city. Efficient rides are helped by bus lanes, either *curb bus lanes*, which were only valid during the morning and evening peak (6.00–9.00 and 15.00–18.00), or by more exclusive bus corridors. Most of 3rd Avenue was used within the central areas of Seattle as a bus corridor and there were others within the city. The traffic calming measure along *Dexter Avenue North* was very cutting edge in terms of modern transportation planning. The bus stop keeps the cars behind the bus when stopping but cyclists have their own lane and are not affected by the stopping bus.

However, the single tramline (it runs in part along *Westlake Avenue*) was not well enough integrated into the public transportation system at *Pacific Place Station*. The tram did not have many passengers during the lunch hour but it may well be packed during peak times. A lack of integration could also be experienced by the short monorail, which only runs from *Space Needle* to the city center (Pine Street).

Los Angeles

Population 3.8 million and 13.1 million population in the metropolitan area in 2013.

Background

Los Angeles was part of Mexico for 30 years before the treaty that led to the formation of the State of California and its incorporation as a city in 1850. It overtook San Francisco as the leading Californian city as a result of the meteoric rise of the film industry in the period between the world wars. Its vast entertainment industry has since diversified into television production, recorded music and computer games. With its neighboring port of *Long Beach*, the southern Californian agglomeration forms the biggest port in America (fifth biggest in the world) and dominates the handling of trade with Asia.

Transportation

The California dream has become a nightmare when traveling on major roads (including motorways) during peak hours in Los Angeles. Easy access to some parts of the city is only possible during the off peak but the peak hours may extend into the evening (up to 20.00). Local people know their way around using residential streets, when traffic arterials are blocked, very much to the annoyance of the people living there. Substantial motorway building and road widening (many boulevards have six lanes for car traffic not including turning lanes) have not helped to cure congestion.

The modal split figures show a high car use, although even Los Angeles experienced a decline of nearly 3% points, between 2000 and 2007/2011; public transportation increased slightly.[35]

Walking

My View

I have concentrated my judgment about the pedestrian friendliness on the city center since in most other parts of the city, except in purely residential areas, the road environment was not only pedestrian unfriendly but in many cases really dangerous, although pedestrian traffic lights quite often provide long crossing intervals to pedestrians (60 seconds are not unusual). One of the main reasons was that car drivers did not expect to have to cope with pedestrians.

In some parts of the city center, sidewalks are wide but quite often bleak without trees, bushes or other plants to separate pedestrians from car traffic, for example *Temple Street*. A number of well-designed squares improve the overall appearance of the city center. Some of them have open markets, for instance the *Bank of America Plaza*. The green area around the Public Library is attractive as is *Pershing Square*. In the *Grand Park* I particularly liked the purple seats and tables, which reminded me of 'Le Plage' in Paris during August. They contrast beautifully with the rest of the square and give it a more informal ambiance. The 'plus one' pedestrian walkway around *Flower*, *Gerry* and *Hope Street* contains stairways, small squares and offer interesting vistas down to street level; it is especially popular with people during lunch hours. It is a similar design as in Seattle without being spoilt by noisy car traffic.

Figure 14.19
Grand Park in Los Angeles

When walking around the city center, I found that the car traffic was not as massive as I had expected and many six-lane streets could easily lose one or two lanes and convert them either into a

Figure 14.20
Upper walkways and squares

- wider sidewalk
- row of trees
- public transportation lane
- cycle lane (or both public transport and cycle lanes).

Very likely many of these streets are congested during peak hours but should the city center streets cater for car demand in peak hours? I think not.

A representative of the city told me that some car lanes have been converted into cycle lanes in *Spring Street* and *Main Street* or in *7th Street* from Downtown to *Koreatown* and along *Colorado Boulevard* in *Eagle Rock*. But looking at the huge street map, there is still a long way to go before Los Angeles will be pedestrian and cycle friendly.

The actual historic town center looked slightly seedy. It needs wider sidewalks in many places and many remarkable buildings would benefit from cleaning of the facades and more renovation.

By far the most impressive transportation experience is the main railway station (*Union Station*). Constructed in 1939 in Mexican style, it was the last big railway

Figure 14.21
Union Station

station built in the United States. It is an Art Deco building, which becomes even more apparent inside. The building is simply beautiful not only in its design but also in terms of its various functions, including two attractive courtyards on each side of the main hall. It contains everything one ever wishes a railway station to have. In contrast to the congestion madness outside on the motorways, it is calm and peaceful, but it feels out of place. Yet the relaxing atmosphere is also related to the limited number of trains that were departing or arriving. What a treasure to have for a 'green' future.

Cycling

Cycle lanes in the center were often short and stopped at critical junctions. There were few cyclists around and they preferred to use the sidewalks instead of the cycle lanes.

Public Transportation

The light rail system, called *Metro Rail*, opened in 1993 with 4.5 miles (7.3km) of undergrounds tracks.[36] It consists of five lines (Blue, Red, Gold, Silver and Expo line) and had a total length of 88 miles (142km) but it is still too small to make any real impact in reducing car traffic. Quite often the LR-lines cross road junctions and were held up by car traffic signals (public transport should always have priority). During off peak, the system was hardly used by middle- and upper-middle-class citizens. It appears that public transportation still has the stigma of being the mode for the low-income population. 'Park and ride' was free and at least on the *Expo Line*, plenty of parking spaces were available at 12.00.

There were a few bus lanes, for example *Figueroa* or the *Metro Orange Line*, but they were only valid from 7.00 to 9.00 and 16.00 to 18.00. Several new busways are being built, for instance the *Wilshire Bus Rapid Transit* lane, which is 12.5 miles (20km) long and opened in 2014. But again it will only run during peak hours and not at weekends.

Notes

1 It had in part simply to do with a division of chapter size.
2 One important factor behind Charlotte's success in the banking world started already in 1927 when a branch of the Federal Reserve Bank chose Charlotte as its location in the south. Second, the construction of an airport in 1941 helped to improve international connections (Goldfield 2010, p. 13). By the end of the 1980s, Charlotte's airport, renamed as *Charlotte-Douglas International Airport*, had direct flights to London and Frankfurt (Lassiter 2010, p. 36). The real breakthrough was the takeover of the *Citizens & South National Bank* from Atlanta by *NCNB* (North Carolina National Bank) located in Charlotte in 1991 (renamed *NationsBank*). The presence of *First Union* (Bank) and NationsBank made Charlotte the third most important headquarters of banking after San Francisco (ibid, p. 35). Another takeover occurred in 1998 when NationsBank merged with the San Francisco based *Bank America Corp.*, and renamed itself slightly *Bank of America*. With this move, Charlotte became the second most important banking center in the United States (ibid, p. 42). Such mergers were only possible since the mid-1980s; previously banks could not expand their business beyond the state's borders (Graves and Kozar 2010, p. 87).
3 Although I studied 20 cities, only 16 are described in the two North American chapters.
4 For more details see Tables 15.1 and 15.2.
5 It does not tell us what kind of encouragement the city is using, either how it calculated the 63.5% or the date when it will be accomplished.
6 South End is located south of Updown Charlotte
7 Funnily enough the same story is told in London about German bankers who demand good public transportation, walking and cycle facilities.
8 There were 17 pedestrians out of 39 fatalities in 2011 and 22 pedestrians out of a total of 44 fatalities in 2012 (for more details see Chapter 15).
9 This was previously a historic streetcar route, which was replaced by a bus route.
10 For detailed modal split results see Tables 15.1 and 15.2.
11 One contrast is also that South Carolina, compared to most other states, is responsible for the condition of sidewalks.
12 The accident data were only available until 2006 and I am sure the city has addressed this problem (for more details see Chapter 15).
13 For the reader who is unaware of the origins, more details are provided in Chapter 1.
14 Many of the late 18th- and 19th-century squares were laid out between 1791 and 1847, the largest square, *Forsyth Park*, was built in 1851 (Dick and Johnson 2001, p. 76). All squares were built before the Civil War (1861–1865).
15 The Amtrak railway station is now a small stop at *Seaboard Coastline Drive*, an industrial section of the city with difficult access.
16 The three spurs are ending up in *MLK Boulevard* and two in *Montgomery Street*; one is an overpass of MLK Boulevard and ends in Montgomery Street.
17 The methods of counting are different between the two time periods hence the results are not strictly comparable.
18 According to state law of Georgia, cars have to give way when pedestrians are on the crossing (this is different in California and Oregon where cars have to stop when pedestrians are standing on the sidewalk similar to most countries in Europe).

19 These cobblestones came from England as ballast on ships, which would be loaded with cotton at the port of Savannah.

20 Both walking and cycling would be encouraged.

21 Similar to New Orleans.

22 The city center of Miami has an automatic monorail called 'Metromover', which was free of charge. There are also two lines of 'Metrorail'; one runs from *Dadeland South* via the city center to the airport. But most of the two lines are in reality only one line, which runs from *Palmetto* to Dadeland South with a spur from *Earlington Height* to the airport (one stop). There are also many bus (Metrobus) routes, which claim to run 365 days for 24 hours (www.miamiwelcome.net/bus/public transportationation.htm, accessed 17.6.13).

23 The methods of counting are different between the two time periods hence the results are not strictly comparable. The modal split figures are in the final chapter.

24 Diaz had created a *Park and Public Spaces Master Plan* with the medium-term goal to have park access within half a mile of every resident and the long-term goal to have park access within a quarter of a mile of every resident (ibid, p. 148). It was published in 2007 (www.miamigov.com/planning/pages/masterplan/parks_public spaces, accessed 31.7.13).

25 There is also the 1A in the south.

26 See Tables 15.1 and 15.2.

27 In 1979, 1,200 buildings in Miami Beach from the first to the 24th Street were identified as historic buildings and the area was registered as one of the National Historic Places (Capitman 1988, p. 17). Most buildings had been built between 1936 and 1939 (ibid, pp. 35–42). Twenty blocks or one square mile are listed on the National Register of Historic Places. The area was bound to the south by *South Point* and is fringed from *5th Street* to *15th Street* by coconut palms that the first settlers planted. To the west the district stops one short of *Alton Road*. But there are many more buildings and apartments outside the designated district, for example *J. J. Astor Estate*, *Pine Tree Drive*, *Flamingo Apartments* at *Flamingo Drive* designed by *L. M. Dixon* in 1940 (ibid, pp. 108–109).

28 Unless something very drastic happens to oil prices or to attitudes.

29 For more details see Table 15.1 and 15.2.

30 Modern relatively cheap design that pretends to copy old street layout.

31 Midtown in Atlanta is defined as being located between the commercial district in the city center and the affluent residential and commercial area of *Buckhead* to the north. It is the second biggest financial district in the city (www.mymidtownmojo.com, accessed 31.7.13).

32 In 2010, 146.2 million passengers used MARTA in a service area of 1.7 million in the Atlanta region. A comparison with Cologne – a city of only one million – shows the difference in public transport use (275.1 million passengers in 2012).

33 Interstate 5 runs in a north–south direction, and to the south of the city center the I-90 runs east–west (and vice versa).

34 For more details see Tables 15.1 and 15.2.

35 For modal split data see Chapter 15.

36 Figures about the length of the system are from *The New York Times*, Saturday 4 May 2013, 'An End to the Free Subway Ride', pp. A11, A14.

15

THE FUTURE OF WALKING

PART I: HISTORY

Synthesis: Pedestrian-friendly Street Designs and the Battle About Livable Streets in the United States, Germany and Britain

Part I tells the story of a complex three-way transmission of ideas and practice between Britain, Germany and North America as all sides tried to manage the relationship between pedestrians and motor traffic in similar ways but with different intensities and success. The idea to build roads for wheeled traffic and to physically separate footpaths – in contrast to constructing roads with sidewalks – was an old European vision from the late 19th and early 20th centuries. Studying the street designs of garden cities and earlier forms of working-class housing in England reveals that separate footpaths had already been included in *Port Sunlight* (1888) and in *New Earswick*[1] (1901/02). At first, economic factors had been the main reasons why footpaths were built, as they were able to replace streets. Yet the physical separation between pedestrians and wheeled traffic did not become a real issue until the number of accidents became a serious problem from about the mid-1920s onward, though later in Germany. The reasons for the high number of accidents were badly maintained and built roads, bad drivers (there was no driving license) and a lack of proper traffic regulations.

Green Belts

In Germany *Bruno Taut* (1919) demanded that the ideal city should include a park or a wide green belt connecting the city center with the countryside. Hence the newly planned German garden suburbs generally included footpaths and green belts (later sometimes replaced by green centers[2]). The concept of green axes was also taken up by planners like *Midge*, *Wagner* and *Jansen*. These wide green bands were not only landscaped but more importantly they contained footpath connections, and sometimes these footpaths were very wide (about 3m). *Hermann Jansen's Plan of Nuremberg* (1923) shows this impressively. His wide green axes of irregular shapes were used as 'connectors' between the planned garden suburbs, and a further green axis with a footpath led to the industrial area.

This idea was picked up in Russia too. The *Schestakow Plan* of Moscow included a green belt and satellite towns beyond this belt. Wide green axes led from the green belt into the inner-city areas. Moscow was planned to become the largest metropolis in the world but also the greenest (Miljutin 1992, p. 9). This plan reminds us of *Ernst May's* city plan of Frankfurt, also put forward in the mid-1920s. A wide green belt had been proposed around London in 1938 (Green Belt [London and Home Counties] Act) and new towns were planned in the same way as in Moscow. The similarity with the *Greater London Plan 1944* by

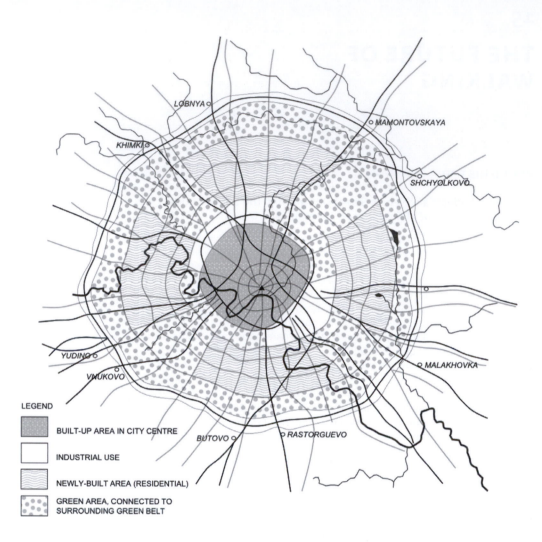

LEGEND

BUILT-UP AREA IN CITY CENTRE

INDUSTRIAL USE

NEWLY-BUILT AREA (RESIDENTIAL)

GREEN AREA, CONNECTED TO
SURROUNDING GREEN BELT

Figure 15.1
Plan of Moscow by
Schestakow 1923

Abercrombie (1945a) is no coincidence. Surprisingly, the green axes were missing in London but instead American-style parkways were to be built.

New Street Layouts and the Need for a Better City

In contrast to Germany and Britain, in most North American cities the street layout was simply designed as blocks. Normally, only sidewalks protected pedestrians from wheeled traffic. The more sophisticated ones were copies of European designs, adapted for US cities. Although the street designs of Fred Olmsted and his son originated from English landscape practice, they acquired their own specific street plans. It could be argued that Fred Olmsted invented the curved street some decades before *Camillo Sitte*[3] preached that curved streets in contrast to the straight ones were the 'ideal' pattern for a city. The architects of the garden cities and garden suburbs were eager to build them in Europe.

By the end of the 19th century, there were efforts to reform tenement housing in the large German cities. This was the beginning of social housing. These newly designed housing blocks allowed generous green spaces, gardens and footpaths within the block but the number of such buildings constructed stayed small. This design was repeated in the 1920s in England and Germany as social housing gained momentum. It is fascinating that the success of Copenhagen today is in part based on having systematically reformed the 19th-century housing blocks by creating children's play areas, gardens and footpaths inside these blocks during the past decades (see Part II).

The United States did not have a strong social housing movement, though the living conditions were also grim, especially in some eastern cities and the mid-west. The Regional Planning Association of America (RPAA), formed in 1923, wanted to change the existing cities into something better. Its ideas were strongly influenced by the already existing European garden cities and garden suburbs. We know that important members, such as *Ackerman*, *Mumford*, *Stein*, *Wright* and *Bauer*[4] toured Britain and Germany to study the newly built settlements there. The best-known construction of the RPAA became Radburn, a suburb in New Jersey (1928/29). It was supposed to become a garden city but most of the important features were missing. However, its road network completely separated pedestrians from car traffic. They built several other small settlements and all included the same form of street division. Although this was 'revolutionary' in the United States, it was nothing special in Germany. Undeniably the heyday of German separate footpath planning and construction was the 1930s and 1940s. They were standard in all new German housing estates, despite the lack of cars. This was also the case in the *Greenbelt Towns* proposed by the US federal government in 1935.[5] Unfortunately, any further expansion was vetoed in 1937. Ironically, the East German communist government later picked up many of the ideas advanced in the Greenbelt Towns. By the 1950s, the US concept that footpaths should be completely separate from motor vehicle streets was 'reimported' into Britain and was partly implemented in the first generation of new towns.

Road Building and Conflicts

Immediately after the Second World War, military tensions with the Soviet Union rapidly developed. It is no coincidence that the federal government took over the responsibility for building motorways and major roads. With the growing danger of a conflict with the Soviet Union, high-quality roads for fast movements of troops and people became an important element of defense and survival. The Federal Aid Highway Act of 1956 (also known as the National Interstate and Defense Highways Act) provided 90% of funding for such roads. Publicly one of the arguments for the rapid expansion of motorways[6] was that the construction would reduce road accidents. Motorways could not be built everywhere but road expansion was often possible only at the cost of abolishing or suppressing pedestrian (and cycle) facilities or/and simply by cutting down trees and reducing front gardens. Hence reducing accidents on motorways was replaced by increasing accidents in urban areas.

In Britain and Germany the issue was slightly different. Although fears of a new war (classified as the Cold War) touched both countries, it was not so easily conveyed to the public or transportation experts; the battle wounds of the Second World War had not healed and massive road building was not yet on the agenda. Britain and Germany had more pressing problems after the destruction of large parts of their cities. In Britain the issue of high road accidents rose up the agenda, promoted through articles and books by the assistant commissioner of the Metropolitan Police, *Alker Tripp*.[7] His ideas and the concepts of *precincts* were the beginning of a long-lasting crusade about pedestrianization, traffic calming and the effective protection of pedestrians, which is still going on.

The uncritical approach in the United States and Canada to road building meant that motorways would run through city centers and/or dense urban areas and destroy everything in their path. It was used as a kind of forced urban renewal with little consideration given to the residents. Without sufficient evidence it was argued that road building was essential for the economic development of the country and specifically for urban areas. No thought was given to the economic destruction of existing neighborhoods, retailing and other businesses in thousands of high streets and neighborhoods. These businesses were only partly replaced by suburban shopping centers where car ownership was essential as public transportation was increasingly dismantled and the distances became too long for walking.

By the end of the 1950s, and even more so at the beginning of the 1960s, a 'battleground' evolved between the supporters of road construction and residents who wanted to keep their well-functioning neighborhoods and communities. This approach was so shocking that it is difficult today to understand the arguments and motives for these road-building programs. But the two examples of New York and San Francisco discussed in Chapter 1 show that this brutality did not go unchallenged, and US citizens led the way in public disobedience; a number of urban motorway proposals were successfully defeated. *Shirley Hayes*, *Jane Jacobs* (New York) and *Sue Bierman* (San Francisco) are only a few of the names to remember. As much as they possibly could, they fought to keep the character of their neighborhoods. It is strange and moving at the same time to walk through these streets and cross the parks today that would have been destroyed. This is not only true for New York or San Francisco but also for all those other urban areas that have been saved from massive road-building programs by courageous citizens (more about that in Part II).

Britain and West Germany Follow only Partly the US Example

During the 1960s, road building started in earnest in West Germany and Britain and car ownership rose at an unpredicted rate. Public transportation was promoted but half-heartedly in West Germany and there was hardly any major new investment in Britain except in London (Victoria Line). As a result of Tripp's work, action against accidents was more effective in Britain than in Germany. The case in favor of a separation of transportation modes in built-up areas was still based on road safety but increasingly the argument that car traffic could flow faster without the proximity of vulnerable road participants was added. Hence the design of independent footpaths still continued. It is thought provoking that West Germany and Britain did not really differ very much. Most residential street layouts in the first generation of British new towns had substantial pedestrian networks (and relatively good bicycle paths) because it was assumed that the majority of workers and residents would walk (or cycle) to work or shops.

In West Germany it is certain that it was a continuation of the standard practice established in the Third Reich. The biggest housing estate with a completely separated footpath (27km/17 miles) and street network was the *Sennestadt* near

Bielefeld; it was planned for 24,000 inhabitants and the first residents moved there in 1958 (it was completed by the mid-1960s). Today it has 21,000 residents and is described as having one of the most advanced street designs. It is not mentioned that the architect who devised the independent footpath network would have been responsible for the planning of the conquered cities in Eastern Europe had there been a German victory.

However, the argument in favor of approving traffic separation for whatever reason did not last very long, and the tradition of differentiated street networks disappeared by the mid-1960s in Britain and Germany. In Switzerland the famous Professor Leibbrand (1964) from the University of Zurich saw independent pedestrian footpaths as 'an exaggeration' and the upkeep as far too expensive (p. 264). Leibbrand's advice was in high demand in West German cities.

More Road Construction and more than a Glimmer of Hope

Gradually in West Germany and Britain the official wisdom was that road building was the answer to the congestion and accident problems in urban areas. Nevertheless, there were critical voices, such as the report 'Traffic in Towns' by Colin Buchanan and his team in the UK (1963) and a similar important publication in West Germany (1965). Buchanan picked up the idea of precincts developed by Alker Tripp and renamed them *environmental areas*. As a result, a first wave of small-scale traffic calming took place in a number of local authorities but by and large the 'successful' policy of road construction continued.

The controversy about road building, which had started first in the United States, moved with some time delay to Britain and West Germany. Protests against urban motorways arose in London and other British cities in the late 1960s and the proposed urban motorways within London were never built. In West Germany the situation was different. General political discontent started in earnest in 1968, initiated by young intellectuals and this was unsettling for the whole country. With a change of government, road building was somewhat reduced, public transportation was more generously promoted and the argument about a separation between pedestrians and cars had not yet died, at least not in the city centers. There was agreement in theory that city center shopping streets should be pedestrianized but putting this into practice was problematic. It took some time to convince shopkeepers in particular that car-free streets were good for business. At the beginning of the 1970s, West German cities were favoring three strategies:

- car use and continuing their investment in road building even within cities
- transit investment in rail transportation
- large-scale pedestrianization.

Britain, torn between a European and a US way of life, encouraged car use further. It also, like the United States, made the mistake of neglecting rail transportation. Later, it moved toward bus privatization and deregulation outside London (in the 1985 Transport Act) and this did not help to make city centers more pedestrian friendly, just the opposite. At the beginning, large numbers of buses of all ages and sizes would block each other in the streets and this was particularly bad when buses were allowed to enter pedestrianized streets, which was the case in many cities. The 1985 Transport Act also had some impact on the scale of pedestrianization. Although pedestrianized streets were discussed and implemented, it proved more difficult than in Germany – one of the reasons being the lack of urban rail transit connections to the central areas of the city.

In West Germany, the pedestrian movement went a step further. By the end of the 1970s a new policy was needed to change residential streets back into more livable streets. It was marketed under the name 'Verkehrsberuhigung', which I translated into 'traffic calming'.[8] This 'new' concept had already been implemented in the Netherlands and was quickly adopted, first in the neighboring German state of North Rhine-Westphalia and somewhat later throughout West Germany. It was another version of the British precincts and Buchanan's concept of environmental areas. Traffic calming was tremendously successful everywhere, possibly because road building had been so brutal with little consideration for the street designs themselves, but more important for the residents living in these streets. It was a policy put forward at the 'right' time and supported by determined and influential professionals. Britain was lagging behind but also later picked up traffic calming with enthusiasm, though it did not provide the funding for the quality and the size of the traffic calmed schemes as experienced in the Netherlands, Denmark, Norway or West Germany.

The Story in East Germany

East Germany, which was under communist rule, included in its first construction phase remarkable examples of pedestrian-friendly designs. It used a typical garden city street layout for its first New Town *Eisenhüttenstadt*. But this phase was short and lasted only until the end of the 1950s. The design of independent footpaths stayed longer and was implemented in other new towns as well. They disappeared in the Le Corbusier-style suburbs built later. The new, mostly half-built city centers all contained car-free streets and squares.

Pedestrianization took place at about the same time as most large-scale pedestrian schemes opened in West Germany. Such streets and squares were even more popular than in the West. It was the first time that city governments decided on their own what to do, and that was clearly a major affront to the communists in power. Pedestrianization helped to protect the historic city centers – or what was left of them – from demolition. Its overwhelming success became a symbol of protest against the communist regime, which had neglected and destroyed the built heritage of the country.

Overall

For me the most disturbing aspect has been that already established separate pedestrian networks on a larger scale simply disappeared virtually everywhere by the mid-1960s when car traffic was rising fast and when they would have been much more needed than in the decades before. It was not because there was a general disapproval of traffic separation in favor of shared space – that came somewhat later.

This first part tells also the story of how important walking is for the structure and well-being of a city. The discussed examples in the United States and in East Germany, illustrate how easy it has been to inflict serious wounds on the fragile configuration of a city with or without capitalism. In the West, road construction was promoted under the banner of progress and freedom, but it was the freedom of the car drivers and not the pedestrians and in the course of that many pleasant and intact communities disappeared. In the East, the communists believed especially that any 19th-century buildings and the housing blocks of this time were an expression of capitalism and had to be destroyed. Instead Corbusier-style city centers and housing estates were built. This also had an impact on walking, and despite fewer cars, distances increased and walking became more of a chore than a pleasurable experience.

In the second part of this book I studied what different countries and cities are doing to promote walking and reduce accidents. The convincing concept of green axes does appear occasionally in some of the study cities as a new invention, as does 'shared space' as an anti-concept to separating pedestrians from motor traffic.

PART II: PRACTICE

Walking: The General Trend

Walking had declined in nearly all the countries I studied during the last 40 to 50 years. In Germany walking trips dropped from 34% (1976) to about 24% (2010) and it has gone down a little more since then. It was not compensated by cycling or public transportation.[9] In Britain the fall was much steeper, from 46% (1975/76) to 22% in 2012.[10] As in Germany, these trips were not offset by growth in other green modes. In Denmark the walking share declined by 5 percentage points between 1975 and 2008 and cycling has not compensated it[11] (Buehler and Pucher 2012, http://policy.rutgers.edu/faculty/pucher, accessed 28.3.14). Norway is the odd one out. Before 1992 there are no reliable data about modal split, but from 1992 onwards, it shows that walking slightly increased by 1 percentage point. But when adding cycling and public transportation together, the green share stayed stable between 1992 and 2009.

In North America the fall in walking started much earlier, from the 1930s onwards. The data available in the United States for walking are normally commuter trips, which are roughly a third of all trips. Between 1960 and 2009 walking to work dropped from 10%[12] to 3%. In Canada walking declined from 7% to 6% in the Census years (2001 and 2011).[13] The decline in walking was offset by a small increase in public transportation (1%). These are national data but surely some of the 'green' cities, especially in Germany or Denmark, must have done better.

In Freiburg, which is by far the greenest German city, walking declined by about the same dimension as the national trend. However, it was more than compensated by a rise in the cycle and transit share. The tendency is similar in Cologne. In London walking has declined from 36% in 1981 to 21% in 2011 (all trips[14]) but again we observe a higher modal split in cycling and public trans-portation (DoT 1997, Mayor of London and TfL 2013a). In the United States, although in Boulder, Colorado car commuting dropped significantly, this did not increase walking, but cycling and working from home grew (Table 15.2). In Washington DC, car use also declined at a substantial rate but walking did not rise. The same story can be told in other cities.

Studying 30 cities, there were only seven where the walking share increased by more than 1% but that does not automatically mean that their walking environment was better than in other cities. It is known that people interchange modes and this can move in both directions as explained in Freiburg (Chapter

9). Walking declined there, also because the public transportation operator had introduced a travel card. Not only was this card widely used because it was cheap but it was also the first German travel card that was transferable between users, thus instead of walking, people use (most of the time or sometimes) public transportation.

Within the seven cities, a drop in the quality of public transportation and/or a fare rise could have caused the small growth in the walking share. In Miami Beach, Pittsburgh and Trondheim[15] the public transportation share dropped about the same amount as walking increased; hence the growth in walking was very likely caused by deficiencies within the public transportation service. It appears that in Boston, Seattle, Munich and Oslo the growth could be related to a better walking environment and/or a more health-conscious population.

The main reason why walking has declined is because our living circumstances have been changing. It is well known that average trip lengths for all purposes have increased to such distances that many destinations cannot easily be walked any more, consequently we have in many cases to take the car or public transportation (if there is efficient public transportation). With that I am not telling the reader anything new. Yet walking is also declining or not growing because relatively little is known about how to promote walking effectively. We have in every large city professionals who are in charge of walking and most of them can write beautifully worded pedestrian plans but what is on the ground is still very limited. This has also to do with the fact that walking is not as glamorous as building new rail infrastructure, and it is far more difficult to improve the pedestrian environment and see results than putting down cycle lanes on carriageways, which are anyhow too wide. But let us first consider what the important ingredients for a good walking environment are.

Important Factors to Promote Walking

Ideally, one would like a change to the whole urban structure if walking were to be promoted seriously. The 'new' city would have short distances from living quarters to shops (no further construction of out-of-town or suburban shopping centers), work, schools, leisure and health facilities but this is an objective, which in reality cannot be achieved in the short or medium term, although it is certainly important. It is notable that the regeneration of many inner cities has been preceded by relatively high-density, new commercial developments, apartment blocks not seen as social housing but as accommodation for wealthier young and middle-aged residents. These often have low parking provision and relatively good public transportation access. Thus it seems possible that in some places commercial pressures have succeeded in doing some of the things that visionary plans have failed. Headicar (2013) suggested for the UK that the previous period of migration from the inner cities to suburbs (1971–2001) had been a process favoring more car use, the more recent migration trends have been in the opposite direction, and therefore led to reduced car dependence.

Population Density

We know from research[16] that walking is related to population density. Normally, the higher the population density, the more people walk because it also means that shops and services are in close proximity. Table 15.3 indicates that ten out of the 30 cities mostly presented in Part II have population densities lower than 2,000 people per sqkm. Interestingly enough five out of these ten low-density cities have done very well in reducing the dominance of the car, for instance Boulder cut car commuting by more than 9 percentage points, Portland by 6% and even the Californian city Santa Barbara by 5% points (between 2000 and 2007/11). Miami with nearly the same density as Oslo lowered car commuting only by half a point whereas Oslo reduced car commuting by 12 percentage points in eight years. Freiburg has reduced car use from 42% in 1992 to 32% in 1999 (the last official figure for *all* trips). When studying another green mode, cycling, the highest growth in cycling also occurred in three low-density cities (Portland, Boulder and Freiburg).

Therefore low population density cities can be as successful in reducing car use as cities with higher densities.[17] When studying population density and the growth in walking among the case study cities, one will find that Boston was in

Table 15.1 Modal split data in North American and European cities: travel to work in percent at various dates

City	Walking	Cycling	Public Transport	Car driver/ passenger	Others/ Work at home	Green modes
North American cities						
Boston	14.9	1.5	33.1	46.1	4.4	50
Vancouver*	12.5	4.4	30.0	51.6	1.6	47
Washington DC	12.0	2.6	37.5	41.9	6.0	52
Miami Beach	12.0	4.5	8.9	63.9	10.7	25
Pittsburgh	11.3	1.3	19	63.7	4.7	32
New York	10.3	0.7	55.4	33.3	5.6	66
San Francisco	9.8	3.1	32.7	45.5	8.9	46
Boulder	9.0	10.1	9.6	59.1	12.3	29
Seattle	8.9	3.0	18.5	62.5	7.1	30
Philadelphia	8.6	1.7	25.9	60.0	3.8	36
Santa Barbara	6.8	4.6	6.1	74.6	7.9	18
Chicago	6.1	1.2	26.9	60.2	5.6	34
Portland	5.1	5.8	12.1	69.3	7.7	23
Charleston	4.9	1.2	2.9	85.3	5.1	9
Atlanta	4.4	0.8	11.5	75.2	8.1	17
Denver	4.3	2.1	7.5	79.3	5.6	14
Miami	3.8	2.1	10.9	80.1	3.1	17
Los Angeles	3.7	2.3	11.0	77.7	5.3	17
Savannah	3.3	1.0	4.1	87.8	4.0	8
Charlotte	2.0	0.2	3.8	88.1	5.9	6
European cities						
Oslo	18	7	40	35	0	65
Bergen	13	4	22	59	2	39
Trondheim	13	16	14	56	1	43
Stavanger	13	10	16	61	0	39
Munich	10	14	34	42	0	58
London	8.1	3.9	48.7	27.9	11.4	61

Sources: US cities: ACS data average of five years 2007–2011; Norwegian cities 2009: Liva Vågane, Institute of Transport Economics 2013; City of Copenhagen 2011; Landeshauptstadt München 2013; City of Vancouver 2012: National Travel Survey 2011; Greater London: Census 2011.

Table 15.2 Decline and increase of commuting in the North American study cities in percentage points between 2000 and 2007/2011

Cities	Decline in car commuting	Increase in public transport	Increase in cycling	Increase in walking	Increase in working from home, other (including motorbikes)
Boulder	9.4	1.3	3.2	0	4.4
Washington DC	7.5	4.3	1.4	0.2	1.0
Portland	6.2	−0.2	4.0	−0.1	2.5
Vancouver	6.0	4.9	0.7	0.3	0.3
San Francisco	5.8	2.0	1.1	0.4	2.2
Seattle	5.2	0.9	1.1	1.5	1.3
Santa Barbara	5.0	1.6	1.2	0.7	0.7
New York	4.9	3.4	0.2	−0.1	1.0
Boston	4.6	0.8	0.5	1.9	1.1
Chicago	4.4	0.8	0.7	0.4	2.5
Miami Beach	3.8	−1.8	1.2	1.3	1.4
Charlotte	3.1	0.6	0.1	0.5	1.8
Los Angeles	2.8	0.8	0.3	0.1	1.2
Denver	2.5	−0.9	1.1	0	1.9
Pittsburgh	2.5	−1.5	1.2	1.5	1.7
Philadelphia	2.0	0.5	0.8	−0.5	0.8
Atlanta	1.2	−3.5	0.5	0.9	3.0
Miami	0.5	−0.4	0.3	0.0	3.2
Charleston	+0.2	−0.7	0.6	−1.7	1.0
Savannah	+1.5	−0.8	−0.1	−1.0	0.3

Source: USA: Census Data 2000 and average of ACS data 2007–2011; and in Vancouver Census 2001 and 2011.

sixth place, Miami Beach seventh, Oslo eighth and Munich ninth and the compactness in the last three cities was lower (Seattle is just higher and Trondheim slightly lower than the median and Pittsburgh was the lowest). Whether cities have high or low density did not seem to be the most important factor. Despite these results, it is still logical and research indicates that high-density cities appear to be generally more successful in promoting walking. What other factors can promote walking?

Climate

William H. Whyte saw sunlight, warmth and lack of wind as important elements of attractive streets. He also mentioned that sunlight becomes less essential during the summer months (Hass-Klau et al 1999, p. 26). These features are particularly crucial in spring and they are vital in countries where sunshine and warmth are not as permanent as in the southern United States or in the south European countries. They are more of an issue when sitting down and not that important when walking. Gehl and his associates have convincingly proved that even with a climate that is not optimal (like the one in Denmark), one can still have town centers full of pedestrians.

Straight or Curved Streets

When studying the engineers and architects at the turn of the 19th century, one can find indicators for a good walking environment. Stübben wrote 'straight streets longer than 1km (0.61 miles) are boring and winding streets are more interesting and should be part of town planning' (Hass-Klau 1990a, p. 30). According to Camillo Sitte[18] (1965) the ideal street was picturesque, curved instead of being straight: 'the winding character of an ancient street keeps sealing off perspective views in them while offering the eye a new aspect at each succeeding turn' (p. 61).

Above we concluded that high density and plenty of sunshine, warmth and lack of wind may be helpful in promoting walking but they are not inevitably necessary. How important are curved streets? We know that boulevards can be straight and much longer than 1km and still be interesting. Nevertheless really attractive boulevards also include plenty of pedestrian space in the middle, with all kinds of street furniture and street art; they are therefore not really comparable with normal straight roads. I would again conclude, as with population density and climate, that curved streets do not necessarily encourage more walking but may account for a more appealing stroll.

Block Size Complexity

Allan Jacobs (1995) mentioned block size complexity, which is very much related to the thoughts of Camillo Sitte. A high number of intersections (junctions) are constantly offering the eye new aspects. Jacobs concluded that most old cities have a complex and fine-grained street pattern and that makes them more interesting, whereas newer cities and newly built areas have fewer intersections per unit area. He used the contrast between Venice (1,507 intersections) and Irvine, California (with only 15 intersections). Here we come for the first time very close to the secret of good walking conditions.

Block Size Complexity and Nature

Block size complexity is also connected to the street layout and this is discussed in the first chapter of this book. I concluded that the historic center of Savannah has the best street layout for walking of all the visited North American cities. Savannah has not only many intersections but also human-scale green spaces and furthermore it has access to an attractive river waterfront. The former was to some extent valid for the street layout in Forest Hills Gardens (New York). In both it is the mixture between the number of street junctions and 'slices' of nature (green spaces and gardens) that is another central element for an enjoyable walking experience.

Table 15.3 Population density per sqkm in 20 North American and 10 European cities

Cities	Population density
New York City	10,427
Copenhagen	7,285
San Francisco	6,631
Vancouver	5,252
Greater London	5,180
Boston	4,928
Miami Beach	4,835
Oslo	4,484
Munich	4,472
Chicago	4,447
Philadelphia	4,394
Miami	4,318
Washington DC	3,786
Los Angeles	3,124
Seattle	2,804
Trondheim	2,622
Stavanger/Sandnes	2,479
Bergen	2,462
Cologne	2,380
Pittsburgh	2,140
Santa Barbara	1,746
Portland	1,690
Boulder	1,518
Denver	1,511
Freiburg	1,424
Atlanta	1,231
Charlotte	948
Odense	560
Savannah	509
Charleston	332

Source: US Census 2010; Canadian Census: Vancouver 2011; Data for European cities are from 2012 or 2013.

Dimension

Several authors put great emphasis on the relationship between the vertical and horizontal dimension of a street. The Renaissance writers Alberti (1966)[19] and Palladio (1965) talked about the relationships between street width and building heights, which were important when designing and constructing an urban street. The reason for this relationship (width versus height) was the need for sunlight, lack of wind and visibility; today one would simply call it the microclimate of an area. This idealized connection also has to do with what a person still can see in detail when standing in a street or square and how 'comfortable' one feels when walking along such a street.[20] Many people find skylines full of skyscrapers wonderful to look at, some of them are really like art, but walking in such streets is a different matter. A lot of them are uncomfortable to walk in. Hence we feel much happier to walk in a city like Paris where the relationship between street width and building height to the cornice line is about two to three.

Trees

This is a sensitive and emotional topic for many people. No doubt trees are wonderful in a street, and walking along a tree-lined sidewalk with interesting buildings, especially when it is hot and sunny, is one of the pleasures in life. There is no question that we need trees in urban areas but they have to be the right size and the correct height (ideally lower than the buildings). This complements the relationship between building height and street width discussed above. The roots should not damage the sidewalks since this can make walking dangerous.

Some trees cause more difficulties than others, for instance poplars and eucalyptus are notorious. The more space trees have on a sidewalk the fewer problems there are with roots. Most trees create problems when they are large and thick (11–20cm diameter at breast height). Most oaks and horse chestnuts can be thicker before roots become an issue. Some research found that the faster trees grow, the more often they interfere with sidewalks. The type of surface material also adds to the conflict. Asphalt is worse than paving stones. Severe crown pruning can reduce root growth. Root barriers, such as deflectors, inhibitors and traps are often not effective enough (Randrup et al 2001).

Wanting to cut mature trees is almost always accompanied by a wave of protest from residents. Sidewalks can be patched up with small cobblestones if roots are a problem. Street trees should be slow growing and modest in size. They should be far enough away from buildings to allow enough sunlight to the lower parts, therefore when trees are planted, then the sidewalks should be especially wide. Trees are not essential for promoting walking if there are small gardens instead or historic and interesting buildings, but they are a must in boring streets (see next point).

Street Facades

Monotonous facades make a street look boring. Sometimes tree planting can mask this but that is not always possible. A town center with only one or two such streets is just bearable but an area, which consists mostly of these streets, is near to unwalkable. Therefore facades where there is something to see and discover seduce people more into walking. Again one will find that buildings in historic city centers have such facades, even in 19th-century city districts. Although the housing facades especially had by then already become 'stand-ardized', they still have many attractive details compared to some modern facades.

Car-Free or Car-Restraint Streets

Another important component is to provide either car-free streets or streets where car traffic and its speed are reduced. In the latter, the width of the sidewalks is important and the type of planting becomes central for the space between the actual carriageway and the walking space. The importance of reducing car traffic is also expressed by the results of a series of surveys carried out in several European cities (Britain, Germany, Italy and Netherlands) and based on a total of 6,600 questionnaires. It was revealed that the three biggest problems that deter walking were *too much traffic*, *traffic too fast* and *crossing the road* in that order. They accounted in the British cities for 71% and in the other European cities for 62% of all walking problems; only 23% in Britain and 28% in the other cities did not experience any walking disturbances[21] (Hass-Klau et al 1997, p. 46).

So far we were able to find some of the most important ingredients for a good walking environment:

- Block size complexity
- Block size complexity with nature
- A good relationship between the width of a street and the height of buildings
- Lack of monotonous facades
- Car-free or car traffic-restraint streets in combination with good and wide sidewalks.

We also concluded that in general terms climate, population density, straight or curved streets and trees were not so crucial but can support walking.

Walking Problems

Above we have discussed important factors that are crucial to encourage walking but we also have issues that discourage walking; some of them are real, others are imagined. I will start with the most important one.

Road Safety

It is a valid argument that parents do not let their children walk to school or other facilities if they fear the roads are not safe. Let us first have an overview of the national accident rates (pedestrians killed) in the studied countries. These were measured as the annual average over six to seven years, per 100,000 population:[22]

- Norway: 0.5 in 2007–2012 (www.ssb.no)
- Germany: 1.0 in 2000–2006 and 0.7 in 2007–2011[23]
- Britain: 1.3 in 2000–2006 and 0.8 in 2007–2012[24]
- Denmark: 0.9 in 2007–2012 (www.statbank.dk)
- Canada: 1.3 in 1995–2001[25]
- United States: 1.7 in 2000–2006[26].

In Germany and Britain the more recent data indicate that the number of pedestrians killed has dropped further. Hence we can also expect that the United States and Canadian figures have improved as well. By far the safest country is Norway but this does not really imply that the walking share is higher in Norway than in other countries. Yet, of all the countries I studied, Germany still has the highest walking share and is also doing well in terms of pedestrian safety.

When studying the 30 cities, a marked difference in the fatality rate between North America and Europe becomes evident. Despite the much lower level of walking, the accident rates per 100,000 population are significantly higher in the North American than in the European cities, even taking into account that the figures are older. The levels in Miami and Charleston are especially disturbing. It is interesting that the three cities (Oslo, Munich and Seattle) which showed a growth in the walking share (that is not caused by substitution from other modes), also had low ratios of pedestrian fatalities. This may be a coincidence

Table 15.4 Pedestrians killed per 100,000 population (annual average of six or seven years)

North American city	Ped. killed per 100,000 population	European city	Ped. killed per 100,000 population
Boulder	0.9	Stavanger/Sandres	0.4
Seattle	1.7	Oslo	0.6
Pittsburgh	1.7	Bergen	0.6
Boston	1.8	Munich	0.6
Portland	1.9	Trondheim	0.7
Vancouver	1.9	Copenhagen	0.8
New York	2.1	Cologne	0.9
Charlotte	2.1	Freiburg	0.9
Philadelphia	2.2	Greater London	1.0
Chicago	2.2	Odense	1.3
Washington	2.4		
LA	2.6		
Savannah	2.7		
Miami Beach	2.8		
San Francisco	2.8		
Atlanta	3.4		
Denver	3.9		
Charleston	5.1		
Miami	6.0		

Sources: Greater London 2007–2012, Polizei Baden-Württemberg, Polizeidirektion Freiburg 2012, average of pedestrians killed over five years in Freiburg 0.89, Polizeipräsidium München 2013, average of pedestrians killed over seven years in Munich 0.55. Polizei Nord-Rhein-Westfalen, Verkehrsunfallentwicklung 2012, Köln, average of pedestrian killed over seven years in Cologne was 0.86. An annual average of six or seven years' pedestrian fatalities per 100,000 population was calculated from 2007 to 2012 in the Norwegian counties. The number of accidents was 0.6 for Oslo, 0.4 for Rogaland (Stavanger/Sandnes), 0.6 for Hordaland (Bergen) and 0.7 for Sør-Trøndelag (Trondheim). The population in the counties was for Oslo 599,230, Rogaland 436,087, Hordaland 484,240 and Sør-Trøndelag 294,066. In Odense the ped./fatality per population was 1.34, Aarhus 1.08, Copenhagen 0.848, Aalborg 0.84 (www.statbank.dk/UHELDK1, accessed 9.11.13) London: Mayor of London and TfL (2013) Surface Transport, Mayor of London and TfL (2012) Surface Transport, Mayor of London and TfL (2011) Surface Transport, Mayor of London and TfL (2010) Surface Transport, Mayor of London and TfL (2009) Surface Transport, Vancouver 2005–2011, population 2011, http://vancouver.ca/police/organization/operations/traffic/pedestrian-safety.html, accessed 21.3.14, (US cities – see also footnotes above at national accident figures).

but it could be similar to cycling, that the more walkers are using the street the safer they become.

Very much related to the issue of pedestrian safety is the right type of pedestrian crossing.

Pedestrian crossings

There seems to be a never-ending debate about what are the safest pedestrian crossings. At a high volume of motor vehicle traffic (above 15,000 motor vehicles), signaled pedestrian crossings are the safest form of crossing (at least when the waiting times are reasonable); between 10,000 and 15,000 motor vehicles, it depends on local circumstances; under 10,000 motor vehicles, other crossings are advisable. However, according to recent research in Germany, zebra crossings[27] (in the United States – high-visibility crossings) are as safe as signaled crossings, independent of how many cars are using the street. It is crucial to have the following criteria for zebra crossings:

- Clear marking with a zebra crossing sign
- Good visibility of the zebra crossing not hindered by parked cars
- The speed restriction has to be adhered to
- Lighting during the night
- Barrier-free access.

In addition, a middle island increases the safety of zebra crossings. If one of these criteria cannot be achieved, one should switch to traffic light crossings (www.udv.de/strasse/planning-und betrieb/wege-fuer-fussgaenger, accessed 19.11.13, see also Brockmann 2013).

Apart from zebra crossings[28] (high-visibility crossings), narrowing the carriage-way to help crossing pedestrians is another good option when the motor vehicle traffic flow is low. One can even combine the narrowed carriageway with a flat-top road hump which is the same height as the sidewalk. I discussed in the city studies some examples (London and Cologne) where it is not clear when crossing who has the right of way, the car driver or the pedestrian. Such facilities work extremely well when they are established.

If one has signaled crossings, it is important that there are signals for pedestrians, they are functioning properly and provide enough time. Pedestrians should be able to cross a street with one green phase even if there is a middle island. Pedestrian crossings often have a long red but a short green phase and that can cause problems. Commonly people get impatient and cross when the pedestrian light is still red, except in Germany where they wait patiently, and there is sometimes a sign suggesting that people wait to set a good example to children.

Noise and Air Pollution

Adverse air quality will have a great impact on the likelihood of walking, although the most dangerous components are the fine particulates (PM2.5) that are normally not seen or felt.[29] The transportation sector is responsible for 58% of all NOx, of which 32% is generated by road transportation. Urban transportation accounts also for 25% of CO_2. The World Health Organization has outdoor air pollution officially classified as carcinogenic (European Environmental Agency 2013, pp. 38, 42). All these pollutants have an effect on the quality of air, which deteriorates at certain times of the year when stable atmospheric conditions mean that pollutants are not dispersed. The latest air quality crisis occurred in Paris in March 2014 and in London in April of the same year; in Paris a temporary measure was introduced with only odd-numbered cars permitted in the city on odd-numbered dates (Lichfield 2014). In London the advice was simply not to jog and keep children inside. It was so bad that sitting in a car appeared healthier than walking. Air pollution is indeed a very serious hindrance to walking.

Another negative impact on walkers is noise.[30] Most people dislike walking along noisy roads, but again as with air pollution few people are aware that it is damaging to their health. The World Health Organization (WHO) has estimated that at least one million healthy lives each year are lost to traffic noise.[31]

Winter Service

In many cities there is no winter service on sidewalks, although such service is available for cars on the main streets. The snow that is moved off the carriageways is then mostly piled onto the sidewalks where it may reach more than 1 meter depth and stay there for months if the weather does not get milder. This is not the worst part in winter; even more lethal, especially for older people, are icy sidewalks. It is appalling that people have to stay at home because of fear of injury. At least streets should be made safe enough that people are able to walk to shops and other important facilities.

Tunnels and Subways

Car drivers normally have no problem driving in tunnels but pedestrians do not like them. It is the enclosure in a tight space, the noise and fumes, which makes walking through tunnels an unpleasant experience. Tunnels can be made more pedestrian friendly with better lighting, colors and/or paintings on the walls and more space for sidewalks even if cars have to wait for each other at the tunnel entrance. In an ideal world pedestrians should not need to walk through tunnels.

Cyclists

Sharing sidewalks with cyclists is a 'yesterday' policy; cyclists belong on the carriageway and should have their own cycle lane. Mixing pedestrians and cyclists on the same sidewalks is rather dangerous for both, because pedestrians are quite often wandering off to the cycle part of the sidewalk and cyclists may use the pedestrian side for various reasons, such as saving time or they have simply forgotten on which side they have to cycle. Another problem with mixed use is that young men in particular often cycle too fast possibly for macho or workout reasons, and pedestrians feel intimidated by such high speeds so close to them.

Street Crime

Street crime is very unpleasant and frightening for anybody who is a victim. Normally the police know where the weak spots are in a city (and quite often even know the petty criminals). In a civilized city this can to some extent be counteracted with sufficient policing. The fear of mugging, assault and other violent crime affects the propensity to walk and this is particularly valid during the hours of darkness. How secure people feel also depends on how many people are on the street even later in the evening, as well as lighting and CCTV coverage.

Rat Running

Rat running is still common in many residential streets. This is the reason why in a number of cities, for instance in Los Angeles, the whole car traffic network has not yet broken down because some through traffic can still use residential streets. A relatively large level of car traffic can be absorbed this way but surely this is not an option for the future. The well-to-do residential areas have been relatively quick in finding ways to stop through traffic; that is not the case in many poorer neighborhoods. As with road building, it is the lower income groups who have to carry most of the burden of excessive car traffic. Car drivers who use residential streets as rat runs tend to drive at higher speeds than the residents who live there, and that is potentially dangerous for anybody walking or children playing on the sidewalks because one false move could be lethal.

Arguments for Doing Not Very Much

In some of the case study cities, I was confronted with a number of excuses for not doing anything or not very much. Often the arguments were that the climate is too hot in summer or the hills are too steep, thus nobody wants to walk (or cycle). That is true with reference to the summer heat in a number of US states or in southern Europe, but the weather in these parts is much more agreeable in winter, spring and autumn than for instance in Portland, Vancouver, Copenhagen or Munich and the level of walking and cycling in these cities is streets ahead. Steep hills can be a problem but if one studies some of the communities in Lisbon, which have to cope with plenty of streets that can only be reached on foot, then some of these excuses are far-fetched.

Another common excuse was that petrol prices are so cheap therefore everybody drives. Most people do not take into account that in reality the total cost of car ownership and use is not cheap, the costs in accidents and deaths are extremely high for society and if one adds the pollution and congestion costs, then each mile driven is expensive. Another serious issue is mode choice. In most US cities there is no option to take the train to go from A to B; there are only roads and cars, and maybe if one is lucky a slow bus.

Really shocking are some of the small Bavarian towns, where the majority of politicians still believe that one has to provide for the car under all circumstances. If one asks politely what about promoting walking by pedestrianizing their main shopping street(s), they will tell you forcefully that it cannot work in their city, and if one answers 'but Munich is very successful with this policy,' they simply laugh and say, 'yes, in Munich it works but not in our small town,' and if one probes a bit longer they may tell you that they tried it and it did not work. When one does not stop enquiring, they will finally admit that they tried it for *two* days and alas – as they knew before – it did not work. If one wants to take out – or reduce – car traffic in a street(s) such a policy needs to be in place for at least six weeks (better still is three months) before one can judge whether it works or not. In any case, one would always introduce it as a provisional measure with the possibility of fine-tuning details of the design, and not as a fully defined *fait accompli*.

Reality: What can be Achieved?

Normally a city consists of a city center, some mostly 19th-century housing areas around or next to it (most of them have their own traditional center), suburban communities and industrial or semi-industrial areas. It is not clear when we talk about a city what is meant exactly; all of it, parts of it, or only the city center? Some cities are very different, for instance Paris consists of 20 districts, which have a lot of similarities. The suburbs are all outside the city because the city is so tightly bounded. One has also to consider that the North American cities are rather different to European cities in their structure, mostly because the standard street layout within a city (the city center and most of the suburban districts) is in blocks. It is no coincidence that the historic European cities are more popular for walkers than cities built in the 20th century, or many North American cities. 'Younger' US cities frequently had little sense of their own history and have repeatedly been redeveloped and renewed. In the book one can find several examples, such as Atlanta, Miami and Charlotte.

If we want to achieve anything in whatever types of cities we live in, we have to start to understand walking and we can only do that by counting pedestrians not only in car-free streets but also in other streets (before and after counts are crucial). We have to understand where people are going to and where they are coming from (origin and destination counts). We should know what the average street length is that people are willing to walk, and we will find that they vary a lot (Hass-Klau et al 1997, pp. 17–21).

Flexible Features that Promote Walking

Some of the factors discussed above are normally fixed in a city; several of the others can be changed. There is relatively little one can do to about block size complexity, existing facades or the dimensions of streets and buildings, but they will affect the pleasure of walking. Yet some features can be changed and we call them here the flexible features, for instance:

- population density (this is not a short term option)
- access to rivers (or lakes)
- new plazas
- car-free streets or a reduction in the number of cars in some streets
- greenways, which run through or close to the city center
- new footways
- footway surface
- pedestrian crossings
- shared space
- traffic calming.

This is a much longer list than the fixed characteristics of a city, which are important and they strongly support our wish to go for a walk (simply consider the example of Paris). The flexible features are most effective if they are combined. Some are more suitable for the town center, for instance car-free streets. Others are better in residential streets,[32] for example traffic calming. Putting up only 30kph (20mph) signs and nothing else will do little for walking. Shared space can be used in both city centers and residential streets. It is brilliant if the space is really shared between all road participants, and if in particular the new space created for pedestrians is wide enough that it can also be used for sitting (benches and informal sitting options) and social space (standing around and talking). Some are equally important, independent of whether we think about the city center or suburbia, for instance pedestrian crossings. I have below only selected a few issues. Some of the others are discussed in detail in other chapters of the book, for example shared space, traffic calming or the importance of plazas. The key issues are how much space does one wish to give pedestrians (and cyclists) and how brave are politicians in reducing car space?

Footway Surface

Pleasurable walking is also connected with a comfortable and non-slippery surface; I do not mean only broken and cracked slabs. There is a wide range of very good-looking surfaces, which are perfect when it is not raining but they are lethal when they are wet, for instance polished granite, wood surfaces or some types of cobblestones. There is also the question of historic street covers. Far too often cobblestones are put down instead of considering the wide range of other 'historic' materials that could be used. Natural stones are always better than artificial ones and local stones are the best but unfortunately they often are the most expensive. It goes without saying that the width of the sidewalks should vary according to the level of pedestrian flows.

Salt and Pepper Features

Street furniture and enhancements, such as new trees, flowerbeds, benches, informal seating, lights, signing, toilets, litter bins, street art, or water features, are as essential as salt and pepper in a meal but again they will be used differently according to the part of the city we want to improve. Another important factor is how well the streets and squares are maintained (this covers the issues of cleanliness and care of flower beds). These are more general points but let us discuss specifically pedestrianization.

Successful Pedestrianized Streets

I will not include in the discussion about car-free streets the considerations of participation with the residents and the different parties affected – that goes without saying. If that is not done early, sufficiently and conscientiously enough, then any project is 'dead in the water'. Whether a pedestrianized street – or any other car traffic-restraining scheme – works or not is not as much dependent on the number of car parking spaces as retailers all over the world want to believe but on many other factors (which we have discussed above). First, access is vital but it does not have to be all by car. Good public transportation is more important than car access because when it works well one can get more people in a shorter time period to the desired destinations. If public transportation is a problem, park and ride could be a good option. Many French cities have both excellent public transportation access and large park and ride sites. Land in city centers is far too valuable to be used for large multi-storey car parking facilities.

Second, there is the land use and retailing mix in a street (or area). Shops that are local to a town or region are far more interesting to visitors and residents than only chain stores. A successful street contains cafes, restaurants with outside seating. But it also needs 'locals' living close by. Different street markets are not only good for the economy but also beneficial in attracting more pedestrians. Well-performed outdoor activities (spontaneous or planned) give an additional special boost to the attractiveness of a community. All these combined with the flexible and fixed factors discussed above and the salt and pepper features make car-free streets and squares a great (social and economic) success even if the dimensions and block size complexity are not perfect.

Side Streets

It is important to inspect side streets and what will happen to them when car traffic is reduced or taken out completely in a parallel street(s). Will they only be full of parked cars or can these streets be improved as well to make them more walkable? Shops and other facilities in these streets are often more interesting because they provide commercial units for lower rents (than in the car-free streets); that in turn will deliver a wider range of different types of shops. It does not help walking if a few streets are car free and the pedestrians are channeled into these streets but the overall number of pedestrians stays the same. That brings me to another topic.

How to Improve Walking in Suburbs

We also have to concentrate more on the suburbs. How can we improve walking to and within these areas? We do not need to build new sidewalks everywhere; taking road space away from the carriageway and using this space for walking is surely a cheaper option. A white line can separate the walking space from the carriageway left for driving and in addition one could use a different surface color for the newly created walking path. I would suggest reducing car speeds to 20mph (30kph) and either make sure that the speed limit is obeyed, or reduce the speed by traffic calming measures (most effective are road humps).

**Figure 15.2
Pedestrian walk on
carriageway, Brighton**

We should also study the smaller traditional shopping streets; they should be made more attractive. Like town centers they also need comfortable seating outside, areas where children can play, small plazas to have some kind of nature to look at and not only a mass of parked cars.

What options are there to walk between the town center and suburbia and between the housing areas and the local shopping street? Can the old dream discussed in Part I of a green pedestrian axis from the urban center to the suburbs become reality?

Walking to and from Public Transportation Stops

What about the distances between public transportation stops and the various housing areas? Do we actually know what routes people are choosing to get there and how can these connections be made more attractive?

Learning from the Case Study Cities

In all the visited cities, the local officers were knowledgeable about the existing literature and were aware of the problems. Allan Jacobs' ideas were the accepted model in the United States although some professionals were not aware of his name. His work includes many issues, which are rather liked by government officers, such as keeping parked cars as a barrier between the sidewalks and the carriageway. However, most of them knew very little about what was going on in Europe and vice versa. Thus learning from comparative experience and ideas is certainly still missing in a number of towns although the ideas and experience tried out in world cities, such as New York, Paris, London and Berlin, are well known and quite often copied.

Most cities have started to develop targets to increase the share of green modes. This is encouraging and some cities are very ambitious, others have already nearly achieved their goals and one wonders what direction these cities can move on to next, for instance Copenhagen. Washington published the most sustainable plan of all the study cities in North America but I had my doubts about how this can be achieved. Atlanta too has ambitious plans to improve cycling and walking but is neglecting its own public transportation system MARTA, which is reducing its credibility to move toward a 'green' city.

The case studies deepened our knowledge about the urban destruction, which occurred when many roads and motorways were constructed. It started in the United States in the late 1940s; it continued far into the 1980s in Europe and is still going on. Nearly every large city can tell a story about the severe damage to parts of the urban fabric. Some of them are more than depressing; not only did whole neighborhoods disappear (mostly the poorer communities) but also the effect had severe social and economic implications for the city centers. One can only understand this period from a historic perspective where everything suburban was 'good' and everything urban was 'bad'. It is important not to go to the other extreme because there have been some very interesting and innovative suburban models, which are working well even today. In Europe the urban renewal of the kind described above may not have been as brutal; even so there has also been demolition of historic neighborhoods. Mostly the historic city centers were not really touched but even that is not strictly true, thinking about Berlin, Stuttgart, Frankfurt not to mention Birmingham and Glasgow. The case studies also tell us stories about successful fights against road building; among the best were Greenwich Village in Manhattan and Covent Garden in London.

In London the 'key walking routes' as defined by Transport for London[33] were impressive. Key walking routes are something similar to a pedestrian network and London has been the only city that seriously worked with this concept. I found the pedestrian improvements in the 'City of London', the financial district of Greater London, very impressive and of high quality. This part of London had to reduce the number of cars significantly because of fear of terrorist attacks. The interesting and important lesson has been that it did not affect the economy of the City negatively; on the contrary it made it a much more livable and attractive place.

Unfortunately, Transport for London also presented the shortest pedestrian crossing times of any visited city, which are not only too short but simply very dangerous. Thus Transport for London is an example of an important organization with internal contradictions. It appears that some sections seriously want to promote walking and others work toward a smooth flow of motor vehicle traffic with insufficient consideration for pedestrians.

Freiburg indicates that it will take a long time to become a really 'green' city. To close one part of the motorway ring was first documented in a land use plan for the city center in 1986. It took until 2002 before it was finally approved by the City Council. It was put into practice in 2012 and the redesign started in 2014.

It also taught me that it is worth spending a bit more on materials when creating pedestrianized streets than doing it cheaply. The expensive street coverings (Rhine pebble) in Freiburg's pedestrianized streets implemented in the early 1970s still look as good as new.

Cologne but also London teaches us that crossings without clear regulations (neither car drivers nor pedestrians have priority) can also be safe. The most impressive mix between cars and pedestrians is at *Seven Dials* in London, near Covent Garden.

In Copenhagen, the variation of design detail is inspiring. It is a city that has managed to reduce car use to an unthinkably low level and despite the fact that it is doing well economically. I found it a very livable place. Very impressive is the city policy for car parking: each year 2–3% of public car parking spaces disappear.

Oslo is another city which is not as much in the limelight as Copenhagen but is moving rapidly toward becoming another Copenhagen. Bergen had excellent street coverings for pedestrian spaces, which are of the same quality and creativity as those one admires in many Portuguese cities.

When studying the North American cities, New York struck me as the most imaginative city in terms of promoting walking. One of the main changes in New York has been the creation of new squares. It taught me that a completely different approach to what is done in Europe could be as exciting and effective. What has been created in New York but also in some of the other US cities has happened in a relatively quick time span, which would be near to impossible in Germany or Britain (though it would be possible in France). I also had the feeling that the residents lead many positive changes, and again this is good way forward.

San Francisco is providing generous road surface for public transportation and cycle lanes and that has reduced car traffic and made walking more pleasurable. This is an important lesson to be learnt for other cities, which are worried about reducing carriageway space for car traffic in order to run public transportation. It should be one of the main policies in every city that public transportation has to have priority over cars. The 'parklet programme', which means taking away on-street car parking spaces, would give some officials in traffic planning departments in many other cities, even in Europe, sleepless nights. But the loss of car parking is counteracted by more commercial activities, including bars, restaurants and other independent businesses.

Pettygrove, a neighborhood in Portland, is one of the first North American cities that is trying to go for car-free living, which appears to be a contradiction in itself in a country where cars still rule the streets.

Santa Barbara made me aware that rich and small cities also have the political power to change their urban environment in a more environmentally friendly direction, if they want to. The same process as in Santa Barbara is happening in a few neighborhoods within a number of visited cities. It is somewhat depressing that in the richer communities all kinds of traffic calming measures were implemented, whereas in numerous poorer streets hardly anything was built to reduce motor vehicle speeds. Speed limits were also often lower in the more affluent areas than in other residential districts.

Boulder was a wonderful example of very careful car driving. Car drivers were constantly aware of cyclists and pedestrians. I have only seen such passive driving in the Norwegian cities.

In Charlotte I saw the most beautifully designed Greenway, which runs very close to the city center. It was an attractive place for children and grown-ups alike; it brought back parts of real nature, something that is urgently needed in our cities. Some of the TOD was also impressive and New Bern Stop was certainly worth a visit.

Cities that were not Included

I did not include Chicago, Pittsburgh[34] and New Orleans,[35] although I visited them, stayed there for several days and even had discussions with professionals. These were cities where there was nothing new to report.

Chicago is without doubt a fantastic city and the endless walks along Lake Michigan were impressive.[36] Trying to find my way around the public transportation system was painful and took a long time. I did not know that there were still railway stations in the United States where you had to flag down a train, for instance at '111th Street' station. When studying the modal split, nothing spectacular can be reported about Chicago (see Tables 15.1 and 15.2). Regrettably I had to leave out cities that also could have offered good lessons in improving walking.

Finally

Walking has continuously declined over the last decades; some proportion of this decline has been the result of substitution toward cycling and transit. Maybe when reading this book one can understand why, because what makes people walk or not is complicated. I discussed above several factors that could intensify the propensity to walk. They clearly do not have equal significance and some were identified as being the most important ones. Unfortunately most of these developed over a longer time period and there is little one can do to change them in the short run. However, in the section 'Reality', there is some hope for those cities, which are not so fortunate to have inherited these five factors.

In total nine topics were presented that discourage walking of which the only really serious ones are:

- fear of accidents
- noise and air pollution
- lack of interest from local and national governments.

All the others can be solved with relatively little effort and manageable resources, given the political will.

I myself doubt that a high number of pedestrians killed or a high accident rate are a deterrent to walking for grown-ups because in most cases it is not known and even when it is recognized, most pedestrians are quite oblivious to the danger of car traffic. Hence only air and noise pollution and a lack of interest from government reduce or stop people walking.

Even when taking into account the complexity of promoting walking seriously, it is strange that walking still has not received sufficient attention, considering its important health implications. It may well be that most politicians are not aware of the general neglect of walking, maybe because it is automatically connected with cycling and cycling is certainly promoted (although still not sufficiently in most cities). This is a disturbing thought but maybe pointing one's finger at the problem is a first step toward remedying it.

Apart from changing our own behavior, we have to concentrate on the younger generation. We need to convince parents not to drive their kids to school, but to walk with them, and after a time to let them go on their own but for this we need safer streets, at least safer than they are at present. But we do not need more guard rails or more pedestrian traffic lights that are in many cases ignored anyway.

It is clear from this book that 'more' walking has to commence in the cities and as the keen reader may have noticed, in some it is already starting. The creation of a walking culture, something many south European cities have still retained, will be important. Some experts such as Gehl and his team have led us in the right direction but more specialists like them are needed as well as more practical knowledge about what works and what does not, in order to encourage more walking.

There are four issues to conclude with:

1. Walking and cycling policies are not the same; in reality these have little in common, apart from the fact that cycling is also good for the environment and for health.
2. It is a complicated and challenging business to promote walking but with some thought and financial resources it should be possible.
3. Some safety projects for pedestrians are not implemented because the costs are too high. This is not only narrow minded but thoughtless and cruel considering the pain and the cost to society that are caused by fatalities or serious injuries.

4. Increasingly research indicates that a good walking environment also benefits the local and wider economy. Thus promoting and financing walking infrastructure is not just an altruistic objective but also a sensible and practical future direction for urban life.

There is statistical evidence that the future will be even more urban than it is today. That will automatically also mean higher population densities and that is in principle good news for pedestrians. But whether people walk more or less depends on different factors discussed above. Some cities see the Vancouver approach with high-rise residential buildings as the model for the future. I myself think the renaissance principles and dimensions did us good service in the past centuries and may also do well for the future.

Notes

1 New Earswick was designed by Unwin and Parker.
2 These were not small parks but quite often a large 'natural' green area with trees and footpaths.
3 Camillo Sitte's book (*City Planning According to Artistic Principles*) was first published in 1889 but Riverside Illinois was already planned in 1869 (Hass-Klau 1990, p. 31).
4 Ackerman had been one of the very few foreign participants at the first Garden City Conference in Birmingham and Bournville in 1901. In 1920 Lewis Mumford had visited Raymond Unwin who had built Letchworth and Hampstead Garden Suburb. In 1924 Stein and Wright also visited England to study the first Garden City Letchworth, Hampstead Garden Suburb and the wartime munitions communities (Hass-Klau 1990a, p. 99). Catharine Bauer made a four-day visit to Römerstadt/Frankfurt in 1929, and went again to Frankfurt to participate in a course about 'New Architecture' in 1930 (Henderson 2010, pp. 323, 326).
5 It is known that members of the RPAA were involved in the planning and design of some of the Greenbelt Towns.
6 It was planned to build 41,000 miles (66,000km) by 1972 (Star 2009, p. 248).
7 Alker Tripp's books were first published in 1938 and 1942 but because of the war they did not get the attention they deserved, though this changed with the second editions in 1950 and 1951.
8 The term was first used in Britain in 1985 in a letter I wrote to *The Times*.
9 Bundesministerium für Verkehr, Bau und Stadtentwicklung 2012, pp. 222–223.
10 www.gov.uk/government/statistical-data-sets, accessed 24.1.14.
11 Cycling increased by 1% point. I found no information about public transportation but my guess is it did not increase nationwide, if anything it also declined. It was already low in 2011 with 6% (see Chapter 10).
12 US Census; workers changed from aged 14+ (1960–1970) to age 16+ (from 1980 onwards). This would have had an impact on the percentages between the different census years.
13 Government of Canada, Statistics Canada, Census 2001, National Household Survey 2011, accessed 11.3.14.
14 Walking to work declined from 13% to 8% of the commuting modal split between 1981 and 2011, ONS Census of England and Wales 1981 and 2011.
15 In Trondheim the public transportation service improved considerably since the last Census in 2009, consequently walking may have declined since then, as the walking environment is still not outstandingly good.
16 There is a wide range of research, especially by Peter Newman (1996), Hass-Klau et al 1997 and Siu (2013).
17 I am aware that the density we have is an average number and within cities there are denser and less dense areas. Hence it could well be that a high number of dense areas are decisive for the walking share. Although when studying the cities that had a higher walking share, there seemed to be no area which struck me as having a very high density, but I have to admit I did not research that in detail.

18   Sitte's book was first published in 1889 – for more about the publication and its impact see Hass-Klau 1990a, pp. 31–32.

19   Leon Battista Alberti (1405–1472) wrote in 1450 (published in 1485) about the law of architecture (*De re Aedificatoria*). His ten books about architecture became the standard publication during the Renaissance. He wrote about city streets that is was important that they were paved with cobblestones and clean. The houses had to stand in one line and should have the same height. The streets would be even better if they have arcades (Vercelloni 1994, Tafel 40). Andrea Palladio (1508–1580) lived 100 years later than Alberti and wrote four books about architecture in 1570 (http//architecture.about .com, accessed 25.4.14).

20   Maybe it has to do with a fundamental instinct of being protected and secured by a wall.

21   In total there were ten British cities including Belfast and nine other cities, six from Germany, two from Italy and Utrecht from the Netherlands.

22   I decided to use pedestrians killed per population, other authors use the indicator 'per km walked', which would certainly be a better measure if one would really know how many miles pedestrians walk.

23   Bundesministerium für Verkehr, Bau und Stadtentwicklung 2012, p. 166 (the population used are for the years 2001 and 2010).

24   DfT Stats19; DfT National Road Traffic Survey, DVLA/DfT; Population Census 2001 and Census 2011.

25   Government of Canada, Transport Canada, Road Transportation, Table 2: Pedestrian fatalities and injuries 1992–2001.

26   US Department of Transportation 2010; NHTSA's National Center for Statistics and Analysis Washington DCFARS Data 1997–2006, Table A-1: Pedestrian crash details by crash type and year (US Department of Transportation 2008).

27   The minimum width of a zebra crossing should be 4 meters (Mennicken 2001).

28   The design of zebra crossings varies slightly from country to country.

29   The other main elements of air pollution are carbon monoxide (CO), CO_2, hydrocarbons and the oxides of nitrogen (NOx).

30   Noise is measured in decibels.

31   In 2012, 19% of the population in London, 20% in Copenhagen and 23% in Oslo were still exposed to levels higher than 55dbL (at night outside) caused by road transportation. WHO recommends no more than 40dbL (night outside) (European Environment Agency 2013, p. 21). Although no data could be found about the North American cities I am convinced that the picture is similar.

32   That does not mean traffic calming is not suitable in a city center; I personally think all streets in the city center should be traffic calmed.

33   Transport for London (TfL) is responsible for the management and planning of London's public transportation system, including *North London Railways*, the *East London Line* and the *London Overground*. In addition TfL is in control of main roads, all traffic lights, the regulation of private taxis and minicabs. TfL is also in charge of congestion charging in Greater London (Hass-Klau et al 2007, p. 43).

34   Chicago and Pittsburgh have been included in Tables 15.1–15.3.

35   The 2005 Hurricane Katrina disaster does of course make New Orleans a completely different example.

36   I could also not make an appointment with anyone from the city although I tried very hard.

REFERENCES

Abel, A. (1942) Grundsätzliches im Städtebau an Hand einer Reihe von Planungen, II. Zurückgewinnung der Verkehrsflächen für den Fußgänger, *Monatshefte für Baukunst und Städtebau*, Vol. 26, 10, pp. 221–232

Abel, A. (1950) *Regeneration der Städte*, Zürich, Verlag für Architektur

Abercrombie, P. (1924) *Sheffield: A Civic Survey and Suggestions Towards a Development Plan*, London, University Press of Liverpool

Abercrombie, P. (1945a) *Greater London Plan 1944*, London, HMSO

Abercrombie, P. (1945b) *A Plan for Bath*, Bath, Pitman

Abercrombie, P. and B. F. Brueton (1930) *Bristol and Bath Regional Planning Scheme*, London, University Press of Liverpool

Abercrombie, P. and J. H. Forshaw (1943) *County of London Plan*, London, Macmillan

Adshead, S. D. (1923) *Town Planning and Town Development*, London, Methuen

Adshead, S. D. (1941) *A New England*, London, Muller

Adshead, S. D. (1943) *New Towns for Old*, London, Dent

Adshead, S. D. et al (1948) *York: A Plan for Progress and Preservation*, York

Alberti, L. B. (1966) *Ten Books on Architecture*, trans. C. Bartoli and J. Leoni, New York, Transatlantic Arts

Alliance for Walking and Cycling (2012) *Benchmarking Report 2012*, Washington DC

Andrä, K. (1996) Städtebauliche Entwicklungen 1945 bis 1989 im Osten Deutschlands, *Alte Städte – neue Chancen*, städtebaulicher Denkmalschutz, Berlin, Bundesminister für Raumordnung, Bauwesen und Städtebau und IRS (ed.), pp. 134–171

Andrä, K., Klinker, R. and R. Lehmann (1981) *Fußgängerbereiche in Stadtzentren*, Berlin, VEB Verlag für Bauwesen

Anon (1953) Die grüne Welle im Großstadtverkehr, *Verkehr und Technik*, Vol. 6, pp. 47–48

Anon (2013) Union Station Interior will become Denver's New Living Room, *The Daily Journal*, Vol. 124, 227, Wyoming, Colorado

Apel, D. (1971) *Ein Beitrag zur Bewertung der von Kraftfahrzeugverkehr beeinflussten Umweltqualität von Stadtstraßen*, Dissertation, Aachen, Rheinisch-Westfälische Technische Hochschule Aachen

Apel, D. (1992) *Verkehrskonzepte in europäischen Städten*, Berlin, Difu

Appleyard, D. (1981) *Livable Streets*, Berkeley, London, University of California Press

Arnold, J. L. (1983) Greenbelt, Maryland, 1936–1984, *Built Environment*, Vol. 9, pp. 198–209

Baedeker, K. (1986) *Der Grosse Baedeker Berlin*, Freiburg, Baedeker

Balchin, J. (1980) *First New Town: An Autobiography of the Stevenage Development Corporation 1946–1980*, Stevenage, Stevenage Development Corporation

Bamberg, A. (2011) *Chatham Village, Pittsburgh's Garden City*, Pittsburgh PA, University of Pittsburgh

Barnhouse, M. A. (2010) *Denver's Sixteenth Street*, Charleston SC, Arcadia Publishing

Bayerische Akademie der Schönen Künste (1985, ed.) *Süddeutsche Bautradition im 20. Jahrhundert*, München, Kastner and Callwey

Baynes, N. H. (1972) *The Speeches of Adolf Hitler*, 2 vols, London, New York, Toronto, Oxford University Press

Beberdick, F. (1998) *Images of America Chicago's Historic Pullman District*, Charleston SC, Arcadia Publishing

Beblo, F. (1935) Die straßenbaulichen Maßnahmen der Stadt München im Jahre 1935, *Die Straße*, Vol. 2, pp. 736–737

Benedetti, C. (2012) Light at end of the Bart Tunnel, *San Jose Mercury News*, early Sunday, 28 October, p. B6

Berendt, J. (1999) *Midnight in the Garden of Good and Evil*, New York, Vintage Books

Bernoulli, H. (1954) Die Fußgängerstadt, *Baukunst und Werkform*, Heft 6 und Plan 11, pp. 27–29

BfLR, BASt, UBA (1983) Flächenhafte Verkehrsberuhigung Zwischenbericht, *Informationen zur Raumentwicklung*, Heft 8/9

BfLR, BASt, UBA (1985) *3. Kolloquium, Forschungsvorhaben 'Flächenhafte Verkehrsberuhigung'* Erste Erfahrungen aus der Praxis, 30 September–1 Oktober, Berlin

BfLR, BASt, UBA (1988) *4. Kolloquium, Forschungsvorhaben 'Flächenhafte Verkehrsberuhigung'* Ergebnisse aus drei Modellstädten, 26– 27 Mai, Buxtehude

Bland, S. (1999) *Preserving Charleston's Past, Shaping its Future, the Life and Times of Susan Pringle Frost*, Columbia SC, University of South Carolina Press

BMBau (1973) *Raumordnungsbericht 1972*, Bonn

BMBau (1975) *Städtebaubericht 1974*, Bonn

BMBau (1978) *Ausländische Erfahrungen mit Möglichkeiten der räumlichen und sektoralen Umverteilung des städtischen Verkehrs*, Bonn

BMBau (1979) *Verkehrsberuhigung. Ein Beitrag zur Stadterneuerung*, Bonn

BMBau (1980) *Wohnstraßen der Zukunft*, Bonn

BMBau (1982) *Planungsfibel zur Verkehrsberuhigung*, Bonn

BMBau (1985) *Verkehrsberuhigung und Stadtverkehr*, Bonn

BMBau (1986) *Stadtverkehr im Wandel*, Bonn

BMBau (1988) *Städtebauliche Integration von innerörtlichen Hauptverkehrsstraßen*, *Städteumfrage*, Bonn

Bogner, W. (1965) Raumordnung und Verkehr, Deutscher Gemeindetag (ed.) *Verkehrspolitik, Raumordnung, Gemeinden*, Bonn

Borer, M. C. (1984) *The Story of Covent Garden*, London, Robert Hale

Bowers, P. H. (1986) Environmental Traffic Restraint: German Approaches to Traffic Management by Design, *Built Environment*, Vol. 12, pp. 60–73

Boyle, C. (2009) So you think London is expensive? *The Times*, 20 August

British Parliament (1992) *Traffic Calming Act 1992*, London, HMSO

British Parliament (2000) *Transport Act 2000*, London, HMSO

British Road Federation (1987) *Basic Road Statistics 1987*, London

Brix. E. (1954) Städtebau der Zukunft, *Verkehr und Technik*, Vol. 7, pp. 158–159

Brockmann, S. (2013) *Sicherheit von Zebrastreifen*, Gesamtverband der Deutschen Versicherungswirtschft e.V., Berlin

Brög, W. (2014) Wollen Sie nur von Haltestelle zu Haltestelle oder von der Wohnung zum Einkauf, *Mobilogisch*, Februar, 35. Jgg. Arbeitskreis: Verkehr und Umwelt e. V. Fuss e.V. Fachverband Fußverkehr Deutschland, pp.14–18

Buchanan, C. and Partners (1980) *Transport Planning for Greater London*, Westmead, Farnborough, Saxon House

Buchanan, C. D. (1956) The Road Traffic Problem in Britain, *The Town Planning Review*, Vol. 26, pp. 215–241

Buchanan, C. D. (1958) *Mixed Blessing, The Motor in Britain*, London, Leonard Hill

Buchanan, C. D. (1960) Transport – The Crux of City Planning, *RIBA Journal*, Vol. 68, pp. 69–74

Buchanan, C. D. (1961) Standards and Values in Motor Age Towns, *Journal of the Town Planning Institute*, Vol. 47, pp. 320–329

Buchanan, C. D. (1963) Traffic in Towns, in British Road Federation (ed.), *People and Cities, Report of the 1963 London Conference*, pp. 15–22

Buchanan, C. D. (1965) What I really said, *RIBA Journal*, Vol. 72, pp. 334–335

Buchanan, C. D. (1968) Presentation of the Gold Metal of the Town Planning Institute to Professor C. D. Buchanan, *Journal of the Town Planning Institute*, Vol. 54, pp. 49–55

Buchanan, C. D. (1988a) A Historical Review of the 'Traffic in Towns' Report of 1963, *PTRC Transport and Planning Summer Annual Meeting*, University of Bath, 12–16 September 1988 (unpublished)

Buchanan, C. D. (1988b) Personal interviews and letters to the author in 1988 and 1989

Bundesministerium für Verkehr, Bau und Stadtentwicklung (2000) Verkehr in Zahlen 2000, 29. Jgg. Berlin

Bundesministerium für Verkehr, Bau und Stadtentwicklung (2009) *Verkehr in Zahlen 2009/10*, Berlin

Bundesministerium für Verkehr, Bau und Stadtentwicklung (2012) *Verkehr in Zahlen 2012/2013*, 41. Jgg., DVV Media Group Hamburg

Bundesministerium für Verkehr, Bau und Stadtentwicklung (2013) *Verkehr in Zahlen 2013/14*. Berlin

Bundesverkehrsministerium (1997) *Verkehr in Zahlen 1997*, 26. Jgg., Bonn

Burnham, D. H. (1906) *Report on a Plan for San Francisco* (reprinted 1971) Berkeley, Urban Books

Burns, W. (1967) *Newcastle: A Study in Replanning at Newcastle upon Tyne*, London, Leonard Hill

Cairns, S. et al (1998) *Traffic Impact of Highway Capacity Reductions: Assessment of the Evidence*, London, London Publishing

Canadian Census 2006 (information from City of Vancouver, 12.07.13)

Canadian Census 2011 (information from City of Vancouver, 12.07.13)

Capitman, B. B. (1988) *Deco Delights: Preserving the Beauty and Joy of Miami Beach Architecture*, New York, E. P. Dutton

Carmona, M. (2002) *Haussmann his Life and Times, and the Making of Modern Paris*, Chicago, Ivan R. Dee

Carr, S. et al (1992) *Public Space*, Cambridge MA, New York, Victoria, Cambridge University Press

Cashmore. J. F. (1981) *Towards an Evolution Method for Pedestrianisation Schemes*, final year Dissertation, Diploma in Town and Regional Planning, Leeds Polytechnic

Chase, C. E., Horak, K. E. and Keylon, S. R. (2012) *Garden Apartments of Los Angeles*, Los Angeles, Architectural Resources Group

Cherry, G. E. (1974) *The Evolution of British Town Planning*, Leighton Buzzard, Leonard Hill

Christensen, C. A. (1986) *The American Garden City and the New Town Movement*, Michigan, UMI Research Press

Churchill, H. (1983) Henry Wright: 1878–1936, in Krueckeberg, D. A. (ed.) *The American Planner Biographies and Recollections*, New York, London, Methuen

City of Bergen (2013) *Facts about Bergen 2013*, Bergen, Information Department

City of Charlotte Department of Transportation, Charlotte-Mecklenburg Planning Department Charlotte (2011) TAP (Transport Action Plan Update), Charlotte

City of Copenhagen (2011) *Municipal Plan 2011*, Copenhagen

City of Copenhagen (2012a) *Trafikken I København, Trafiktal 2007–2011*, Copenhagen

City of Copenhagen (2012b) *Gå-Kvalitet, Best Practice Guide, Københavns Fodgænger-strategi*, City of Copenhagen

City of Nuremberg (1980) *Ergebnisse der Fußgängerzählung am Samstag, den 13.12.1980*, Beilage 2.2 (not officially published)

City of Vancouver (2005) *Downtown Transportation Plan*, Vancouver

City of Vancouver (2006) *Transportation Plan, Progress Report*, Vancouver

City of Vancouver (2012) *Transportation 2040*, Vancouver

Collins, C. C. (2009) Camillo Sitte across the Atlantic: Raymond Unwin, John Nolen and Werner Hegemann, in Bohl, C.C. and J-F. Lejeune (eds) *Sitte, Hegemann and the Metropolis, Modern Civic Art and International Exchanges*, New York, Routledge, pp. 175–196

Communidad de Madrid and Concorcio Transportes Madrid (2008) Madrid 2007–2008 Referente Mundial, Madrid, pp. 2–3

Condit, C. W. (1973) *Chicago 1910–1929, Building, Planning and Urban Technology*, Chicago, London, University of Chicago Press

Crompton, D. H. (1961) Layout: The Influence of Planning on the Local Urban Environment, in The Department of Civic Design, University of Liverpool (ed.) *Land Use in an Urban Environment*, Liverpool, University Press, pp. 185–232

Crowhurst-Lennard, S. and H. Lennard (1995) *Livable Cities Observed*, Carmel, Gondolier Press

Crowther, G. (1963) Discussion: 'Traffic in Towns', in British Road Federation (ed.) *People and Cities, Report of the 1963 London Conference*, pp. 23–26

DAfSL (Deutsche Akademie für Stadt- und Landesplanung) (1961) *Deutscher Städtebau nach 1945*, Hannover

Dalby, E. (1988) *Self-Enforcing Systems for Controlling Traffic Speed in Urban Areas – A Survey of British Experience*, Department of Transport (not published)

Daniels, P. W. and Warnes, A. M. (1980) *Movement in Cities, Spatial Perspectives in Urban Transport and Travel*, London, New York, Methuen

Department for Transport (2004) *Smarter Choices – Changing the Way We Travel*, London, under www.dft.gov.uk

Department for Transport (2005) *Home Zones: Challenging the Future of our Streets*, under www.homezones.org.uk

Department for Transport (2006) *Transport Statistics Bulletin, National Travel Survey 2006*, HMSO, London, under www.dft.gov.uk

Department for Transport (2012) *National Travel Survey*, Table NTS0409 and Table NTS0405, www.gov.uk/government/publications/national-travel-survey-2012, accessed 24.1.14

Department of Transport (1988) *Getting the Right Balance*, Local Transport Note, London, HMSO

Department of Transport (1996) *Transport Statistics Report, National Travel Survey 1993/95*, London, HMSO

Der Bundesminister für Verkehr (1974) *Verkehr in Zahlen 1974*, Bonn

Der Bundesminister für Verkehr (1975) *Verkehr in Zahlen 1975*, Bonn

Der Bundesminister für Verkehr (1978) *Verkehr in Zahlen 1978*, Bonn

Der Bundesminister für Verkehr (1980) *Verkehr in Zahlen 1980*, Bonn

Der Bundesminister für Verkehr (1990) *Verkehr in Zahlen 1990*, Bonn

Der Bundesminister für Verkehr (1992) *Verkehr in Zahlen 1992*, Bonn

Der Bundesminister für Verkehr, Allgemeiner Deutscher Automobil Club (ADAC) (1977) *Sicherheit für den Fußgänger II Verkehrsberuhigung, Erfahrungen und Vorschläge in Städten und Gemeinden und Schlussfolgerungen aus dem Städtewettbewerb 1977*, Bonn, München

Der Minister für Wirtschaft, Mittelstand und Verkehr des Landes Nordrhein-Westfalen (1979) *Großversuch 'Verkehrsberuhigung in Wohngebieten'*, Köln, Kirschbaum

Deselaers, R. (1955) Neuverteilung der Rechte von Kraftverkehr, Fußgänger und Straßen- anlieger, *Der Städtetag*, pp. 509–511

DETR (1998) *White Paper: A New Deal for Transport*, London, HMSO

DETR (2000a) *The 10 Year Plan*, London, HMSO

DETR (2000b) *Framework for a Local Walking Strategy*, Traffic Advisory Leaflet, London, HMSO

Deutscher Gemeindetag, ed. (1941) Anpassung der Stadtstraßen und Nebenanlagen an den neuzeitlichen Verkehr, *Kommunales Archiv*, Vol. 59, Berlin

Deutscher Städtetag (1962) *Die Verkehrsprobleme der Städte*, 2. Entwurf, vorgelegt der Sachverständigen Kommission für eine Untersuchung der Verkehrsverhältnisse der Gemeinden, Denkschrift, Köln-Marienburg

Devon County Council (1991) *Traffic Calming Guidelines*, Exeter

DfT (2004a) *White Paper 2004, The Future of Transport*, HMSO

DfT (2004b) *Action Plan on Walking and Cycling*, HMSO

Diaz, M. (2013) *Miami Transformed, Rebuilding America, One Neighborhood One City at a Time*, Philadelphia, University of Pennsylvania Press

Dick, S. E. and Johnson, M. D. (2001) *Savannah 1733 to 2000*, Charleston SC, Arcadia Publishing

District of Columbia (2013) *Sustainability DC Plan*, Washington DC

Dloczik, M., Schüttler, A. and Sternagel, H. (1982) *Der Fischer Informationsatlas Bundesrepublik Deutschland*, Frankfurt am Main, Fischer

DoT (Department of Transport) (1987) *Measures to Control Traffic for the Benefit of Residents, Pedestrians and Cyclists*, Traffic Advisory Unit, London, HMSO

DoT (1989) *White Paper: Roads to Prosperity*, London, HMSO

DoT (1991) *20mph Speed Limit Zones*, Advisory Leaflet 7/91, Traffic Advisory Unit, May, London, HMSO

DoT (1997) *Household Survey, Walking Journeys and Distances Travelled per Person per Year by Population Density: 1985/86 and 1993/95* (unpublished)

Doubleday, E. H. (1960) Traffic in a Changing Environment, *Journal of the Town Planning Institute*, Vol. 46, pp. 226–234

Dupree, H. (1987) *Urban Transport: The New Town Solution*, Aldershot, Gower

Durth, W. (1999) Wohnungsbau in der DDR, in Flagge, I. (ed.) *Geschichte des Wohnens*, Stuttgart, Deutsche Verlagsanstalt, pp. 55–79

Egloffstein, von G. (1935) Einfluss des Kraftverkehrs auf Städtebau und Landesplanung, *Die Straße*, Vol. 2, pp. 134–137

Ehlgötz H. (1925) Der Einfluß des Kraftfahrzeugverkehrs auf Städtebau und Siedlungswesen, *DBZ, Stadt und Siedlung*, Vol. 59, pp. 44–48, 70–72

Eichenauer, M., von Winning, H.-H., and Streichert, E. (1978) *Sicherheit und Verhalten in verkehrsberuhigten Zonen*, Köln, BASt

ETP (2004) EMTA report on added value, Brighton (not officially published)

ETP (2007) *The Possible Economic Effects of West London Tram*, project for TfL, Brighton (not officially published)

European Environment Agency (2013) *A Closer Look at Urban Transport*, EEA Report No. 11, Copenhagen

Fest, J. C. (1974) *Hitler*, London, Weidenfeld and Nicolson

FfH (1978) *Die Bedeutung der Fußgängerzonen für den Strukturwandel im Einzelhandel*, Berlin, Forschungsstelle für den Handel

Fiebig, K.-H. and Horn, B. (1988) *Umweltverbesserung in den Städten*, Heft 5: Stadtverkehr, Berlin, Difu

Fishman, R. (2007) Revolt of the URBS; Robert Moses and his Critics, in Ballon, H. and Jackson, K.T. (eds) *Robert Moses and the Modern City: The Transformation of New York*, London, W.W. Norton, pp. 122–129

Först, W. (1962) *Chaos oder Ordnung auf unseren Straßen*, Köln, Deutscher Städtetag

Fortun, A. and Furuseth, E. (2007) *Road Tolling in Norway – A Brief Introduction*, Oslo, Norwegian Public Roads Administration (NPRA)

Frampton, K. (1987) The Other Le Corbusier: Primitive Forms and the Linear City 1929–52, Art Council of Great Britain (1987), *Le Corbusier, Architect of the Century*, London, Exhibition Catalogue, pp. 29–34

Frank, H. (1934) Besinnliches über Wohnungs- Bau- und Siedlungsfragen, entnommen: *Baupolizeiakte Hamburg*, Eingangsstempel 7.1.36, A2 3/42386 (unpublished)

Freiburg im Breisgau (2011) *Statistisches Jahrbuch 2011*, Freiburg

Freiburg, Stadt (2003) *Amtsblatt, Oktober, No. 369*, Vol.16, Freiburg

Freiburg, Stadt (2008) *Mobil Verkehrsentwicklungsplan Freiburg 2020*, Amtsblatt, Freiburg

Frenz, E. (1986) Verkehrsplanung in Frankfurt, Mit dem Erbe des Dritten Reiches, *Verkehrszeichen*, Nr. 4, pp. 18–25

Frontier Group and US PIRG Education Fund (2012) *Transportation and the New Generation: Why Young People are Driving Less and What it Means for Transportation Policy*, April

Führ, E. (2010) Geschichtlichkeit im Städtebau am Beispiel der 'Sozialistischen Wohnstadt' Schwerdt, in Betker, F. et al (eds) *Paradigmenwechsel und Kontinuitätslinien im DDR-Städtebau, Neue Forschungen zur ostdeutschen Architektur – und Planungsgeschichte*, Region Transfer 8, Erkner, IRS, pp. 61–91

Funken, M. (2008) *Das Jahr der Deutschen*, München, Piper Verlag

Garbrecht, D. (1978; 1977) Fußgängerbereiche – ein Alptraum? *BAG-Nachrichten*, Nr. 8, pp. 3–5

Garbrecht, D. (1981) *Gehen, Plädoyer für das Leben in der Stadt*, Weinheim, Basel, Beltz Verlag

Garvin, A. (2002) *The American City*, New York, McGraw Hill, second edition

Gehl, J. (1971) *Life between Buildings: Using Public Space*, New York, Van Nostrand Reinhold, English translation published 1987

Gehl, J. (2010) *Cities for People*, Washington, Covelo, London, Island Press

Gehl, J. and Gemzøe, L. (1996) *Public Spaces Public Life*, Copenhagen, Danish Architectural Press

Gehl, J. and Gemzøe, L. (2000) *New City Spaces*, Copenhagen, Danish Architectural Press

Gehl, J., Gemzøe, L. Kirnæs, S. and Søndergaard, B. (2006) *New City Life*, Copenhagen, Danish Architectural Press

Gehl, J. and Svarre, B. (2013) *By Livs Studier*, Copenhagen, Bogværket

Gerlach, J. et al (2009) *Shared Space*, Unfallforschung der Versicherer, Berlin, Gesamtverband der Deutschen Versicherungswirtschaft e.V.

GLC (1973) *GLC Study Tour of Europe and America, Pedestrianised Streets*, London

Glotz, M. (1979) Verkehrsberuhigung und soziale Folgen, *Arch+*, Vol. 47, pp. 44–47

Goldfield, D. (2010) A Place to Come to, in Graves, W. and Smith, H. A. (eds) *Charlotte NC the Global Evolution of a New South City*, Athens, London, University of Georgia Press, pp. 10–23

Grashoff, U. (2011) *Leben im Abriss, Schwarzwohnen in Halle an der Saale*, mitteldeutsche kulturhistorische Hefte, in Gerlach, P. and Götze, M. (eds), Nr. 23, Halle/Saale, Hasenverlag

Graves, W. and Kozar, J. (2010) Blending Southern Culture and International Finance: The Construction of a Global Money Centre, in Graves, W. and Smith, H. A. (eds) *Charlotte NC the Global Evolution of a New South City*, Athens, London, University of Georgia Press, pp. 87–101

Gregory, T. (1973) Coventry, in J.C. Holliday (ed.) *City Centre Redevelopment: A Study of British City Centre and Case Studies of Five English City Centres*, London, Charles Knight, pp. 78–134

Gunkel, F. (1965) Verkehrsprobleme in Verdichtungsgebieten aus der Sicht des Landesplaners, *Verkehr und Raumordnung*, Vol. 35, pp. 7–26

Gurlitt, C. (1929) New Yorker Siedlungen, *Stadtbaukunst*, Vol. 10, pp. 27–31

Haeuselmann. J. F. (1916) Fahrstrassen – Fussgängerstrassen, *Der Städtebau*, Vol. 13, pp. 54–59

Hall, P. (1966; 1984) *The World Cities*, New York, St. Martin's Press.

Hall, P. and C. Hass-Klau (1985) *Can Rail save the City?* Aldershot, Gower

Hamer, M. (1987) *Wheels within Wheels – A Study of the Road Lobby*, London, Routledge & Kegan Paul

Hansard 1933–1934, Local Acts Ch XCVii

Hass-Klau, C. (1984) German Urban Public Transport Policy, *Cities*, Vol. 1, pp. 551–6

Hass-Klau, C. (1986) Environmental Traffic Management: Pedestrianisation and Traffic Restraint – A Contribution to Road Safety, PTRC *Transport Policy*, London, pp. 91–104

Hass-Klau, C. (1990a) *The Pedestrian and City Traffic*, London, Belhaven

Hass-Klau, C. (1990b) *The Theory and Practice of Traffic Calming: Can Britain learn from the German Experience?* Discussion Paper 10, Rees Jeffreys Road Fund, Transport and Society, Oxford

Hass-Klau, C. (1993) Impact of pedestrianization and traffic calming on retailing: A review of the evidence from Germany and the UK, in *Transport Policy*, Volume 1, Number 1, pp. 21–31

Hass-Klau, C. and Crampton, G. (1998) *Light Rail and Complementary Measures*, A Report for the Department of Environment, Transport and the Regions, Brighton, ETP

Hass-Klau, C. Haubitz, M. and Crampton, G. (2001) Wettbewerb im ÖPNV Europas, *Der Nahverkehr* 5/2001, pp. 71–76

Hass-Klau, C., Crampton, G., Dowland, C. and Nold, I. (1999) *Streets as Living Space*, London, Landor Publishing

Hass-Klau et al (1992) *Civilised Streets – A Guide to Traffic Calming*, Brighton, Environmental and Transport Planning

Hass-Klau, C. et al (1997) *Accessibility, Walking and Linked Trips*, a Study for the Department of the Environment and the National Retail Planning Forum (not officially published)

Hass-Klau, C. et al (2002) *Future of Urban Transport Learning from Success and Weakness: Light Rail*, Brighton, Environmental and Transport Planning

Hass Klau, C. et al (2004) *Economic Impact of Light Rail*, Brighton, ETP

Hass-Klau, C. et al (2007) *The Effect of Public Transport Investment on Car Ownership*, Brighton, ETP

Headicar, P. (2013) The changing spatial distribution of the population in England: Its nature and significance for 'peak car', *Transport Reviews*, Vol. 33, 3, pp 310–324

Heckscher, A. and Robinson, P. (1977) *Open Spaces the Life of American Cities*, New York, San Francisco, Harper and Row

Hegemann, W. (1925) *Amerikanische Architektur und Stadtbaukunst*, Berlin, Ernst Wasmuth

Henderson, S. R. (2010) Römerstadt: The Modern Garden City, *Planning Perspectives*, Vol. 25, 3, pp. 323–346

Hillebrecht, R. (1957) Verpasste Chance der Städtebauer, *Der Städtetag*, Vol. 10, pp. 69–72

Hillman, M. et al (1990) *One False Move*, London, PSI

Hillmann, J. (1986) *The Rebirth of Covent Garden*, London, Greater London Council

Hilpert, T., ed. (1988) *Le Corbusiers Charta von Athen*, Texte und Dokumente, Kritische Neuausgabe, Braunschweig, Wiesbaden, Friedrich Vieweg & Sohn Verlagsgesellschaft mbH, second edition

Himmler, H. (1942) Richtlinien für die Planung und Gestaltung der Städte in den eingegliederten deutschen Ostgebieten, in A. Teut (1967, ed.) *Architektur im Dritten Reich 1933–1945*, Berlin, Frankfurt/Main, Wien, Ullstein, pp. 347–357

Hines, T. S. (1974) *Burham of Chicago Architect and Planner*, New York, Oxford, Oxford University Press

Hoffmann, R. (1961) *Die Gestaltung des Verkehrswegenetzes*, Hannover, Jänecke

Hollatz, J. W. (1954) Der Verkehr als Faktor der städtebaulichen Gestaltung, *Verkehrswissenschaftliche Veröffentlichungen*, Heft 3, Stadtverkehr heute und morgen, Düsseldorf, Droste Verlag, pp. 45–68

Hollatz, J. W. and Tamms, F., eds (1965) *Die kommunalen Verkehrsprobleme in der Bundesrepublik Deutschland*, Essen, Vulkan

Horadam, M. C. (1983) *Verkehrsordnungen und Verkehrssicherheit – Rückblick auf deutsche Straßenverkehrsordnungen von Beginn bis heute*, Köln, Bundesanstalt für Straßenwesen (BASt)

Houghton-Evans, W. (1975) *Planning Cities: Legacy and Portent*, London, Lawrence and Wishart

Huber, H. and Müller, A. (eds) (1964) *Das Dritte Reich, Vol. 1: Der Aufbau der Macht*, München, Wien, Basel, K. Desch

Hunger, B. et al (1990) *Städtebauprognose, Städtebauliche Grundlagen für die langfristige intensive Entwicklung und Reproduktion der Städte*, Berlin, Arbeitshefte des Instituts für Stadt-und Regionalplanung der Technischen Universität Berlin, Heft 42

Ieromonachou, P. (2006) Norway's urban toll rings: Evolving towards congestion charging, *Transport Policy*, Vol. 13, 5, pp. 29–40

Jackson, F. (1985) *Sir Raymond Unwin, Architect, Planner and Visionary*, London, A. Zwemmer

Jacobs, A. B. (1993; 1995) *Great Streets*, Cambridge MA, London, MIT Press.

Jacobs, J. (1961) *The Death and Life of Great American Cities*, New York, Random House

Jensen, S. U. (1998) *Pedestrian Safety and Safety Measures*, Analysis Report 148, Danish Road Directorate, Copenhagen

Kahmann, H. (1979) Modell für Deutschland? *Arch*, Vol. 47, pp. 33–37

Kautt, D. (1983) *Wolfsburg im Wandel städtebaulicher Leitbilder*, Wolfsburg, Stadt Wolfsburg

Keim, K-D and Hain, S. (1995) *Reise nach Moskau*, H. Nicolaus (ed.), Institut für Regionalentwicklung und Strukturplanung, Berlin, Dokumentenreihe des IRS, Nr. 1

Kent County Council Highways and Transportation (1990; 1992) *Traffic Calming – A Code of Practice*, Maidstone, Kent County Council

Kiper, M. (1983) Vom Unweltschutzprogramm zur Machtfrage: Die Grünen als etablierte Partei?, in G. Michelsen (ed.) *Ökopolitik, aber wie*? Fischer alternativ, Frankfurt, Fischer Taschenbuch

Kittelson and Associates Inc (2012) NW Portland Con-way Redevelopment, Multimodal Impact Analysis

Klement, F. (1978) *Synthese Architektur und Bildende Kunst: Eisenhüttenstadt*, Rat der Stadt, Abteilung Kultur, Eisenhüttenstadt

Knopp, G. et al (2003) *Der Aufstand 17. Juni 1953*, Hamburg, Hoffmann und Campe

Koller, P. (1939) Die Stadt des KDF-Wagens, Sonderdruck aus der Zeitschrift *'Die Kunst im Deutschen Reich'*, München, Franz Eher

Koller, P. (1940) Die Siedlung Steimkerberg im Rahmen der Stadtplanung, *Bauen, Siedeln, Wohnen*, Vol. 20, pp. 656–661

Koller, P. (1987) Letters to the Author (unpublished)

Kölner Grün Stiftung, ed. (2013) *Grüngürtel Impuls Köln Grundlage zur Vollendung einer Vision*, Köln, Greven Verlag Köln

Körte, J. M. (1958) *Grundlagen der Straßenverkehrsplanung in Stadt und Land*, Wiesbaden, Berlin, Bauverlag GmbH

Kosbar, S. (2002) Die Verfassung der Stadt vom frühen 19. Jahrhundert bis zur Gegenwart, in Stadtarchiv Bautzen (ed.) *Von Budissin nach Bautzen*, Bautzen, Lusatia Verlag, Dr. Stübner & Co KG, pp. 84–99

LaFarge, A. (ed.) (1999) *The Essential William H Whyte*, New York, Fordham University Press

Landesamt Baden-Württemberg (2002) *Statistische Informationen der Kfz-Zahlen 1970–2000*, Stuttgart

Landesamt für Denkmalpflege Hessen (ed.) (1984) *Baudenkmale in Hessen, Stadt Kassel I*, Braunschweig, Wiesbaden, Vieweg & Sohn

Landeshauptstadt München (1980) *Fußgängerzonen in der Münchner Altstadt*, Planungsreferat, HAII/3P 16/51 47/Klein, München

Landeshauptstadt München (2013) *Perspektiven München/Konzepte-Nahmobilität in München – Zu Fuß in einer lebendigen Stadt*, Referat für Stadtplanung und Bauordnung HAI-3 Verkehrsplanung, München

Landeshauptstadt München, Referat für Stadtforschung (1946) *Das Neue München, Vorschläge zum Wiederaufbau von Stadtbaurat Karl Meitinger*, München, Münchner Verlag und Graphische Kunstanstalten München

Landeshauptstadt München, Referat für Stadtplanung (1963) *Stadtentwicklungsplan München, Grundzüge des Gesamtverkehrsplanes, A) Innenstadt*, München

Landeshauptstadt München, Referat für Stadtforschung und Stadtentwicklung (1975) *Stadtentwicklungsplan 1975*, München

Landeshauptstadt München, Referat für Stadtplanung und Bauordnung (1987) *Arbeitsberichte zur Stadtentwicklungsplanung, Planungsgrundlagen für die Münchner Innenstadt*, München

Landeshauptstadt München, Referat für Stadtplanung und Bauordnung (2013) *Durch Höfe und Passagen der Innenstadt*, München

Lane, M. (1994) *Savannah Revisited History and Architecture*, Savannah, Beehive Foundation, first edition 1969

Langeland, A. (2008) *The Quest for Environmental Sustainable Transport Development, a Study of Land Use and Transport Planning in 4 Cities and 4 Countries*, Ph.D., University of Aalborg, School of Technology and Science

Lassiter, M. D. (2010) Searching for respect: From the New South to World Class, in Graves, W. and Smith, H. A. (eds) *Charlotte NC the Global Evolution of a New South City*, Athens, London, University of Georgia Press, pp. 24–50

Laursen, J. G. (2002) Policy Making and Implementation in Denmark, *COST, A City for Pedestrians: Policy-making and Implementation*, European Commission, Brussels

Le Corbusier, C-E. (1925) *Urbanisme*, Paris, Edition Crès

Le Corbusier, C-E. (1930) *Précisions sur un état présent de l'architecture et de l'urbanism*, Paris

Lee, Ch. and Stabin-Nesmith, B. (2001) The Continuing Value of a Planned Community: Radburn in the Evolution of Suburban Development, *Journal of Urban Design*, Vol. 6, 2, pp. 151–184

Leeds City Council, Ministry of Transport, Ministry of Housing and Local Government (1969) *Planning and Transport – the Leeds Approach*, London, HMSO

Lehmann, R. (1998) Entwicklung der Fußgängerbereiche in Altstädten der DDR, in Borst, O. (ed.) *Die alte Stadt*, 25. Jgg, 1/98, Stuttgart, Kohlhammer, pp. 80–99

Leibbrand, K. (1957) *Verkehrsingenieurwesen*, Basel, Stuttgart, Birkhäuser Verlag

Leibbrand, K. (1964) *Verkehr und Städtebau*, Basel, Stuttgart, Birkhäuser Verlag

Leinberger, C. B. (2012) Now Coveted: A Walkable Convenient Place, *New York Times*, 25 May

Lemberg, K. (1974) Copenhagen, Denmark, in OECD (ed.) *Streets for People*, Paris, pp. 87–96

Leonard, S. J. and Noel, T. J. (1990) *Denver: Mining Camp to Metropolis*, Niwot, University Press of Colorado

Lewes, S. (1988) Pimlico, Quantitative Dimensions of Neighborhoods for Comparative Research Systems, *Neighborhood Systems*, Vol. 2, pp. 1–46

Lichfield, J. (2014) An odd day in Paris: French capital bans even-numbered vehicles for one day to reduce pollution, *The Independent*, 17 March

Liedke, G.D. (1995) NS-Stadtplanung, in Diefenbacher M. (ed) *Bauen in Nürnberg 1933–1945 Architektur und Bauformen im Nationalsozialismus*, Ausstellung des Stadtarchivs Nürnberg, Nürnberg, Tümmels, pp. 114–130

Lindemann, H.-E. and Schnittger, P. (1976) Zur Entwicklung verkehrsberuhigter Zonen, *Stadtbauwelt*, 49, pp. 353–355

Litman, T. (2006) *London Congestion Pricing*, Victoria, Canada, Victoria Transport Policy Institute

Liva Vågane, Institute of Transport Economics (2013) September 2013, correspondence

Local Transport Today (2009/2010) New speed limit advice backs Portsmouth-style 20mph limits, *Local Transport Today*, LTT535, London

London County Council (1951), *Development Plan 1951*, London

Lubove, R. (1963) *Community Planning in the 1920s: The Contribution of the Regional Planning Association of America*, Pittsburgh, Pittsburgh University Press

Ludmann, H. (1972) *Fußgängerbereiche in Deutschen Städten*, Köln, Deutscher Gemeindeverlag, W. Kohlhammer

Lynch, K. (1960) *The Image of the City*, Cambridge MA, London, MIT Press

MacKay, D. H. and Cox, A. W. (1979) *The Politics of Urban Change*, London, Croom Helm

Mäcke, A. (1977) Stadt, Region, Land, *Schriftenreihe des Instituts für Stadtbauwesen*, Rheinisch-Westfälische Technische Hochschule Aachen, Aachen

Mäcke, P. (1954) Grundlagen und Grundelemente der Verkehrsanlagen für den motorisierten Stadtverkehr, in Ministerium für Wirtschaft und Verkehr des Landes Nordrhein-Westfalen (ed.) *Stadtverkehr Heute und Morgen*, Verkehrswissenschaftliche Veröffentlichungen, Heft 31, Düsseldorf, Droste Verlag, pp. 117–139

Marg, V. and Fleher, G. (1983) *Architektur in Hamburg seit 1900*, Hamburg, Sautter and Lackmann

Marples, E. (1963) Introduction, in British Road Federation (ed.) *People and Cities*, Report of the 1963 London Conference, pp. 11–14

May, E. (1963) Die Verstopfte Stadt, *Bauwelt*, Heft 54, pp. 183–184

May R. (1999) *Planstadt Stalinstadt, Ein Grundriß der frühen DDR – aufgesucht in Eisenhüttenstadt*, Dortmunder Beiträge zur Raumplanung 92, Dortmund, IRPUD

Mayor of London and TfL (2005) *Central London: Congestion Charging, Impact, Monitoring*, Third Annual Report, London

Mayor of London and TfL (2006), *Central London: Congestion Charging, Overview*, London

Mayor of London and TfL (2009) *Surface Transport Casualties in Greater London*, London

Mayor of London and TfL (2010) *Surface Transport Casualties in Greater London*, London

Mayor of London and TfL (2011) *Surface Transport Casualties in Greater London*, London

Mayor of London and TfL (2012a) *Walking Good Practice, Version 4 – April 2012*, London

Mayor of London and TfL (2012b) *Surface Transport Casualties in Greater London*, London

Mayor of London and TfL (2013a) *Travel in London*, Report 6, London

Mayor of London and TfL (2013b) *Surface Transport Casualties in Greater London*, London

Melzer, M. (1983) Wohnungsbau und Wohnungsversorgung bei beiden deutschen Staaten, *DIW Beiträge zur Strukturforschung*, Heft 74, Berlin, Duncker und Humblot

Mennicken, C. (2001) *Sicherheits- und Einsatzkritierien für Fußgängerüberwege im Lichte der R-FGU 200*, Institut für Verkehrswirtschaft und Städtebau, Universität Hannover (not officially published)

Miljutin, N.A. (1930) *Sozgorod*, trans. into German by Kyra Stromberg, from the English edition (1974) in 1992, Die Planung der neuen Stadt 1930, Basel, Berlin, Boston, Birkhäuser Verlag, second edition 2008, Berlin, DOM

Miller, D. L. (1997) *City of the Century: The Epic of Chicago and the Making of America*, New York, Touchstone Books

Ministry of Transport (1963) *Traffic in Towns: A Study of the Long Term Problems of Traffic in Urban Areas*, London, HMSO

Ministry of Transport (1964) *Road Pricing: The Economic and Technical Possibilities*, Chairman: R. Smeed, London, HMSO

Ministry of Transport (1967) *Better Use of Town Roads*, London, HMSO

Ministry of Transport (2012) *The Danish Transport System*, Copenhagen

Ministry of Transport and Communication National (2000) *Transport Plan 2006–2015*, Report Nr. 24, Oslo (this report went to Parliament in 2003–2004)

Ministry of Transport and Communication National (2013) *Transport Plan 2014–2023*, Oslo

Ministry of War Transport (1946) *Design and Layout of Roads in Built Up Areas*, London, HMSO

Minuth, K-H. (1983) Die Regierung Hitlers, Teil 1: 1933/34, Vol. 1+2,in Repgen, K. (ed.) *Akten der Reichskanzlei: Regierung Hitler 1933–1938*, Boppard am Rhein, Harald Boldt

Mitscherlich. A. (1969) *Die Unwirtlichkeit unserer Städte Anstiftung zum Unfrieden*, Frankfurt am Main, Suhrkamp

Monheim, R. (1975) *Fußgängerbereiche*, Köln, Deutscher Städtetag

Monheim, R. (1980) *Fußgängerbereiche und Fußgängerverkehr in Stadtzentren in der Bundesrepublik Deutschland*, Bonn, Dümmlers

Monheim, R. (1986) Pedestrianization in German Towns: A Process of Continual Development, *Built Environment*, Vol. 12, pp. 30–43

Monheim, R. (1987) Entwicklungstendenzen von Fußgängerbereichen und verkehrs-beruhigten Einkaufsstraßen, *Arbeitsmaterialien zur Raumordnung und Raumplanung*, Heft 41

Moore, T. G. and Ingalls, G. L. (2010) A Place for Old Mills in a New Economy: Textile Mills Reuse, in Charlotte, Graves, W. and Smith, H. A. (eds) *Charlotte NC the Global Evolution of a New South City*, Athens, London, University of Georgia Press, pp. 119–140

Morlock, G. (1987) Öffentlichkeitsarbeit zur Zonen- Geschwindigkeits-Beschränkung, *Der Städtetag*, pp. 593–596

Moses, R. (1970) *Public Works: A Dangerous Trade*, New York, McGraw-Hill

Müller, E. D. (1954) Die Straßenverkehrsnot, in Ministerium für Wirtschaft und Verkehr des Landes Nordrhein-Westfalen (ed.) *Stadtverkehr heute und morgen*, Verkehrswissen-schaftliche Veröffentlichungen, Heft 31, Düsseldorf, Droste-Verlag, pp. 69–81

Müller-Eie, D. (2012) *Urban Environmental Performance and Individual Behaviour: A Comparison Between Freiburg and Stavanger*, Ph.D., University of Glasgow

Müller, F. (1935) Städtebau und Verkehrsunfälle, *DBZ, Stadt und Siedlung*, Vol. 69, pp. 403–404

Müller, P. (1979) Stadtentwicklung und Verkehrsberuhigung, *Arch+*, Vol. 47, pp. 13–17

Müller, P. and Topp, H. H. (1986) Verkehrsberuhigung durch Straßenumbau: Eine neue Art der Stadtzerstörung? *Deutscher Städtetag*, pp. 327–330

Mulzer, E. (1972) *Der Wiederaufbau der Altstadt von Nürnberg*, Fränkische Geographische Gesellschaft, Erlangen, Heft 31

Mumford, L. (1964) *The Highway and the City*, London, Secker and Warburg, republished 1981, Westport CN, Praeger

Municipality of Stavanger, Department of Culture and Urban Development 2009 (2008) *Stavanger Past, Present and Future*, Stavanger

Myhra, D. (1983) Rexford Guy Tugwell, Initiator of Americas Greenbelt New Towns, in Krueckeberg, D. A. (ed.) *The American Planner, Biographies and Recollection*, New York, Methuen, pp. 225–249

Napp-Zinn, A. F. (1933) Zur Verkehrspolitik des national- sozialistischen Staates, *Zeitschrift für Verkehrswissenschaften*, Vol. 11, pp. 77–90

Nelson, W. H. (1970) *Small Wonder: The Amazing Story of the Volkswagen*, London, Hutchinson, first edition 1967

Nerdinger, W., ed. (1984) *Aufbauzeit Planen und Bauen München 1945–1950*, Katalog zum Architekturteil der Ausstellung 'Trümmerzeit' im Münchner Stadtmuseum 2.2.–29.4.1984, München, Beck

Newman, P. (1996) *Reducing Automobile Dependency*, Sage (also under www.sage publications.com)

NHTSA (National Highway Traffic Safety Administration) (2008) *National Pedestrian Crash Report*, Washington DC

Nicholas, R. (1945) *City of Manchester Plan*, Norwich and London, Jarrold & Sons

Niederndodeleben, A. H. (1935) Hans Güldenpfennig: Kölner Verkehrsprobleme und Domumbauung, *Die Baugilde*, Vol. 17, pp. 701–709

Nielsen, O. H. and Rassen, J. (1986) Environmental Traffic Management in Odense, Denmark, *Built Environment*, Vol. 12, 1/2, pp. 83–97

NYCDOT (New York City Department of Transportation) (2010a) *Pedestrian Safety Study and Action Plan*, Technical Supplement, August, New York

NYCDOT (2010b) *Green Light for Midtown Evaluation Report*, New York

Olmsted, F. L. (1852) *Walk and Talks of an American Farmer in England*, New York, George P. Putman

Olson, J. (2012) *The Third Mode: Towards a Green Society*, New York

Osborn, F.J. and Whittick, A. (1969) *The New Towns: the Answer to Megalopolis*, London, Leonard Hill

Owen, W. (1959) *Cities in the Motor Age*, New York, Viking Press

Palladio, A (1965) *The Four Books on Architecture*, Mineola NY, Dover Publications

Peters, P. (ed.) (1977) *Fußgängerstadt*, München, Callwey Verlag

Petsch, J. (1976) *Baukunst und Stadtplanung im Dritten Reich*, München, Wien, Hanser

Pettem, S. (2006) *Boulder – Evolution of a City*, Boulder, University Press of Colorado

Pfankuch, P. (1978) *Von der futuristischen zur funktionalen Stadt in Europa: 1913–1933*, Ausstellung der Akademie der Künste, Berlin, Dietrich Reimer Verlag

Pfau, W. (1990) *Stadtentwicklung in der DDR, Zustand, Probleme und Erfordernisse*, Berlin, Bauakademie, Institut für Städtebau und Architektur

Pfundt, K., Meewes, V. and Eckstein, K. (1975) *Verkehrssicherheit neuer Wohngebiete – Unfall- und Strukturanalyse von 10 Neubaugebieten*, Köln, HUK-Verband

Pharoah, T. (2009) Clearing away confusing thinking on shared space, *Transport & the Urban Environment*, Winter, London, Local Transport Today, pp. 5–7

Pirath, C. (1948) *Die Verkehrsplanung: Grundlagen und Gegenwartsprobleme*, Stuttgart, Julius Hoffmann

Plowden, W. (1971) *The Motor Car and Politics 1896–1970*, London, Sydney, Toronto, Bodley Head

Polizei Baden-Württemberg, Polizeidirektion Freiburg (2012) *Presseinformation Verkehrsunfallbilanz 2012*, Freiburg im Breisgau

Polizeipräsidium München (2013) *Verkehrsbericht 2012 Bayern Mobil – sicher ans Ziel*, München

Pook, B. (1982) Franksche Siedlung, Hamburg, Arbeitsgemeinschaft Hamburger Baureferat (unpublished)

PV (Planungsverband Äußerer Wirtschaftsraum München) (2014) *Region München, ausführliche Datengrundlagen*, München

R+T (Topp, Skoupil, Küchler und Partner) (2012) Verkehrsentwicklungsplan Freiburg, Kaiserslautern

Ramsey, M. (2012) Old Mustang is Put Out to Pasture, *Wall Street Journal*, 16 April

Randrup, T. B. et al (2001) A Review of Tree Root Conflicts with Sidewalks, Curbs and Roads, *Urban Ecosystems*, Vol. 5, pp. 209–225

Regioverbund Freiburg (2011) *Verbundbericht 2010*, Freiburg

Reichow, H. B. (1941) Grundsätzliches zum Städtebau im Altreich und im neuen deutschen Osten, in A. Teut (1967, ed.) *Architektur im Dritten Reich 1933–1945*, Berlin, Frankfurt/M., Wien, Ullstein, pp. 332–341

Reichow, H. B. (1959) *Die autogerechte Stadt*, Ravensburg, Otto Maier

Reindl, J. (1961) *Die Stadt ohne Verkehrsprobleme*, München

Reps, J. W. (1965) *The Making of Urban America, A History of City Planning in the United States*, Princeton NJ, Princeton University Press

Riecke, H. (1954) *Mietskasernen im Kapitalismus – Wohnpaläste im Sozialismus*, Berlin

Ritter, P. (1964) *Planning for Man and Motor*, Oxford, London, New York, Pergamon Press

Roberts, J. (1981) *Pedestrian Precincts in Britain*, London, TEST

Roberts, J. (1989) *User-friendly Cities: What Britain can Learn from Mainland Europe*, Discussion Paper 5, Oxford, Rees Jeffreys Road Fund: Transport and Society,

Robinson, C. M. (1916) *City Planning with Special Reference to the Planning of Streets and Lots*, New York, London, Putnam and Sons

Rosen, R. N. (1997) *A Short History of Charleston*, Colombia SC, University of South Carolina Press, first edition 1982, Smith H.A.

Rowohlts Deutsche Enzyklopädie (1957) *Le Corbusier 1957 an die Studenten die Charte d'Athenes*, Hamburg

Runge, R. (1984) Verlangsamung des Verkehrs in Wohngebieten durch Tempo 30, Hamburger Konzept für eine stufenweise Verkehrsberuhigung, *Zeitschrift Verkehrssicherheit*, Vol. 30, pp. 157–164

Sachs, W. (1984) *Die Liebe zum Automobil, ein Rückblick in der Geschichte unserer Wünsche*, Hamburg, Rowohlt

Saitz, H. H. (1977) *Stadt und Verkehr*, Transpress, Berlin, VEB Verlag für Verkehrswesen

Säume, M. (1934) 'Die Deutsche Siedlungsausstellung' und die Ausstellung 'Die Straße', München 1934, *Die Baugilde*, Vol. 16, pp. 549–557

Schaechterle, K. H. (1970) *Verkehrsentwicklung in deutschen Städten*, München, ADAC

Schaffer, D. (1982) *Garden Cities for America*, Philadelphia, Temple University Press

Scheibel, W. (1977) Hauptfunktion und Einrichtungen im Fußgängerbereich, *Architektur der DDR*, 26. Jgg., Nr. 1277, Dezember, Berlin, Bauakademie der DDR und Bund der Architekten, pp. 739–743

Schlesier, K. (1971) *Halle-Neustadt, Plan und Bau der Chemiearbeiterstadt*, Büro für Städtebau und Architektur des Rates des Bezirkes Halle (ed.), Berlin, VEB Verlag für Bauwesen

Schneider, C. (1979) *Stadtgründung im Dritten Reich: Wolfsburg und Salzgitter*, München, Heinz Moos Verlag

Schöller, P. (1986) Städtepolitik, Stadtumbau und Stadterhaltung in der DDR, *Schriftenreihe für Forschung und Praxis*, Heft 81, Wiesbaden, Stuttgart, Franz Steiner Verlag GMBH

Schreck, K. et al (1979) *S-Bahnen in Deutschland, Planung Bau Betrieb*, Düsseldorf, Alba Verlag, 2. Auflage

Schroeder, K. (1998) *Der SED-Staat: Partei, Staat und Gesellschaft 1949–1990*, München, Wien, Carl Hanser Verlag

Schubert, H. (1966) Berücksichtigung des Fußgängers in der Verkehrsplanung, *Der Städtebund*, Vol. 21, pp. 25–29

Schwartz, S. (2012) *America Walks 2012: Steps to a Walkable Community, a Guide for Citizens, Planners and Engineers*, Portland, Sam Schwartz Engineering

Scott, M. (1969) *American City Planning since 1890*, Berkeley, Los Angeles, University of California Press

Shankland, G. (1964) The Central Area of Liverpool, *The Town Planning Review*, Vol. 35, pp. 105–132

Sharp, T. (1932) *Town and Countryside: Some Aspects of Urban and Rural Development*, London, Oxford, Oxford University Press

Sharp, T. (1940) *Town Planning*, Harmondsworth, Penguin

Shulman, A. T. et al (2010) *Miami Architecture, an AIA Guide Featuring Downtown, the Beaches and Coconut Grove*, Miami, University Press of Florida

Sinnett, D. et al (2012) *Making the Case for Investment in the Walking Environment*: *A Review of the Evidence*, Bristol, University of the West of England, Bristol, and Cavill Associates

Sitte, C. (1965) *City Planning According to Artistic Principles*, London, Phaidon, first published in 1889

Siu, V. W. et al (2012) Built Environment and its Influences on Walking among older Women: Use of Standardized Geographic Units to Define Urban Form, *Journal of Environmental and Public Health*, Article ID 203141 or at www.hindawi.com/journals/jeph/, accessed 05.08.13

Sloman, L., Cairns, S., Newson, J., Pridmore, A. and Goodwin, P. (2010) The Effects of Smarter Choice Programmes in the Sustainable Travel Towns: Summary Report (www.nationalarchives.gov.uk, accessed 25.1.14)

Smeed, R. J. (1963) Discussion: Traffic in Towns, in British Road Federation (ed.) *People and Cities Report of the 1963 London Conference*, pp. 27–29

Smith, C. (2006) *The Plan of Chicago, Daniel Burnham and the Remaking of the American City*, Chicago and London, University of Chicago Press

Smith, H. A. and Livingstone, E. (2010) Banking on the Neighborhood: Corporate Citizenship and Revitalization in Updown Charlotte, in Graves, W. and Smith, H. A. (eds) *Charlotte NC the Global Evolution of a New South City*, Athens, London, University of Georgia Press, pp. 141–159

Socialdata (1998) *Dialog- individualisiertes Marketing*, Zweckverband Region-Nahverkehr, Freiburg im Breisgau, München

Speer, A. (1944) *Neue Deutsche Baukunst*, Amsterdam, Berlin, Wien, Volk und Reich Verlag Prag

Speer, A. (1970) *Inside the Third Reich*, London, Weidenfeld and Nicolson

Staatliche Zentralverwaltung für Statistik (1956) *Statistisches Jahrbuch der Deutschen Demokratischen Republik 1955*, erster Jahrgang, Berlin, VEB Deutscher Zentralverlag Berlin

Staatliche Zentralverwaltung für Statistik (1981) *Statistisches Jahrbuch 1981 der Deutschen Demokratischen Republik*, 16. Jahrgang, Berlin, Staatsverlag der Deutschen Demokratischen Republik

Staatliche Zentralverwaltung für Statistik (1989) *Statistisches Jahrbuch 1989 der Deutschen Demokratischen Republik*, 34. Jahrgang, Berlin, Staatsverlag der Deutschen Demokratischen Republik

Stadt Regensburg, Amt für Stadtentwicklung (2008) *Regensburg im Fokus, 70 Jahre Stadtenwicklung aus der Vogelperspektive*, 2. Auflage 2010, Regensburg

Stadtverwaltung Eisenhüttenstadt (1998) Eisenhüttenstadt: Architektur – Skulptur, Stadtbilder, Eisenhüttenstadt

Starr, K. (2009) *Golden Dreams: California in the Age of Abundance 1950–1963*, Oxford, Oxford University Press

Statistisches Bundesamt (1988) *Zahlen, Fakten, Trends*, Vol. 33, Wiesbaden

Stein, C. S. (1951) *Towards New Towns for America*, Liverpool, Liverpool University Press, second edition 1958, first published in Britain in *The Town Planning Review* 1949 and 1950, Vol. 20, 21, pp. 205–399

Steiner, A. H., Guther, M. and Leibbrand, K. (1960) *München, Stellungnahme der Planungsberater zum Wirtschaftsplan vom 30.1. 1958 und zum Generalverkehrsplan vom 2.7. 1958*, München, Zitzmann

Stimmann, H. (1988) *Stadterneuerung in Ost-Berlin: Vom sozialistischen Neuaufbau zur komplexen Rekonstruktion*, Berlin, STERN Behutsame Stadterneuerung Berlin mbH

Süddeutsche Zeitung (2013) *Kurswechsel im Norden*, Nr. 210, 11.09.13

Sussman, C. (1976) Introduction, in Sussman, C. (ed.) *Planning the Fourth Migration*, Cambridge MA, London, MIT Press, pp. 1–45

Swedish National Board of Urban Planning (1968) *The Scaft Guidelines 1968, Principles for Urban Planning with Respect to Road Safety*, Göteborg

Tamms, F. (1961) *Über die Untersuchungen für einen Generalverkehrsplan der Stadt Düsseldorf, Bericht vor dem Rat der Stadt Düsseldorf*, Düsseldorf

Taut, B. (2002) *Stadtkrone*, Berlin, Geb. Mann Verlag (originally published in 1919, Jena, Eugen Diedrichs)

Technische Universität Dresden (1990) *Mobilität in beiden Teilen Deuschlands*, München

TEMS: The EPOMM Modal Split Data are Data from 2012 (only available for local authorities, not officially published)

TEST (1987) *Quality Streets*, London, TEST

Teut, A. (1967) *Architektur im Dritten Reich 1933–1945*, Berlin, Frankfurt/M., Wien, Uhlstein

TfL (2011) *Cycle Safety Action Plan 2011*, London

Thieme, A. (2013) Einkaufs-Mekka, *Tz*, 45. Jgg, Nr. 206/36, p. 4

TomTom (2012) North American Congestion Index, TomTom International BV

Topfstedt, T. (1988) *Städtebau in der GDR 1955–1971*, Leipzig, VEB E. A. Seemann Verlag

Topfstedt, T. (1999) Wohnen und Städtebau in der DDR, in Flagge, I. (ed.) *Geschichte des Wohnens*, Band 5, 1945 bis heute, Aufbau, Neubau, Umbau, Stuttgart, Deutsche Verlags-Anstalt, pp. 419–462

Trafik- og Miljøplan (2003) *Debat indtil 31. December 2002*, Copenhagen

Tripp, A. (1938; 1950) *Road Traffic and its Control*, London, Edward Arnold

Tripp, A. (1942; 1951) *Town Planning and Road Traffic*, London, Edward Arnold

TRRL (1988) *Urban Safety Project, 2., Interim Results for Area-wide Schemes*, Research Report 154, Crowthorne

Tuckel, P. and Milczarski, W. (2012) *Population Shifts and Implications for Walking in the United States*, in Schwartz 2012

Uhlig, K. (1979) *Die fußgängerfreundliche Stadt*, Stuttgart, Gerd Hatje

Unwin, R. (1923) Higher Building in Relation to Town Planning, *Journal of the RIBA*, Vol. 5, pp. 107–114

Urban, F. (2007) *Berlin/DDR – Neo-historisch, Geschichte aus Fertigteilen*, Berlin, Gebrüder Mann Verlag

Urban, F. (2010) Erker im Plattenbau – die DDR entdeckt die historische Stadt, in Betker, F. et al (eds) *Paradigmenwechsel und Kontinuitätslinien im DDR-Städtebau, Neue Forschungen zur ostdeutschen Architektur – und Planungsgeschichte*, Region Transfer 8, Erkner, IRS, pp. 127–145

US Department of Transportation (2008) National Pedestrian Crash Report, Washington DC

US Department of Transportation (2010) Traffic Safety Facts, Washington DC

Van der Broek J. H. and Bakema, J. B. (1956) The Lijnbaan at Rotterdam, *The Town Planning Review*, Vol. 27, pp. 21–26

Vandergrift Centennial Committee and the Victorian Vandergrift Museum and Historical Society (1996) *Vandergrift Pennsylvania, Something Better than the Best*, Vandergrift, Pennsylvania

Vedral, B. (1985) *Altstadtsanierung und Wiederaufbauplanung in Freiburg im Breisgau*, Freiburg, Schillinger Verlag

Vegdirektoratet, Trafikksikkerhet, miljo- og teknologiavdelingen, Transportplanlegging (2012) *Nasjonal gåstrategi*, Oslo

Vercelloni, V. (1994) *Europäische Stadtutopien*, München, Dietrichs

Verkehrstechnik (ed.) (1939) Kraftfahrzeugdichte in den wichtigsten Ländern, *Verkehrstechnik*, Vol. 20, p. 199

Walters, D. (2010) Centers and Edges: The Confusion of Urban and Suburban Paradigms in Charlotte-Mecklenburg's Development Patterns, in Graves, W. and Smith, H. A. (eds) *Charlotte NC the Global Evolution of a New South City*, Athens, London, University of Georgia Press, pp. 220–246

Watson, J.P. and Abercrombie, P. (1943) *A Plan for Plymouth*, Plymouth, Underhill

Wedepohl, E. (1970) Die Wohngebiete 1896–1918, in Architekturverein zu Berlin und Vereinigung Berliner Architekten (ed.) *Berlin und seine Bauten, Teil IV Wohnungsbau*, Berlin, München, Düsseldorf, Wilhelm Ernst + Sohn, pp. 115–124

Werner, F. (1976) *Stadtplanung Berlin: Theorie und Realität, Teil 1: 1900–1960*, Berlin, Kiepert Verlag

Whyte, W. H. (1977; 1988) *City: Rediscovering the Center*, London, New York, Doubleday

Wilson, T. D. (2012) *The Oglethorpe Plan*, Charlottesville and London, University of Virginia Press

Wood, A. A. (1967) *City of Norwich: Draft Urban Plan*, Norwich

Wright, H. (1935) *Rehousing Urban America*, New York, Columbia University Press

INDEX

Numbers in **bold** refer to tables; numbers in *italics* refer to figures.